# Making the Unequal Metropolis

HISTORICAL STUDIES OF URBAN AMERICA

*Edited by Lilia Fernández, Timothy J. Gilfoyle, Becky M. Nicolaides, and Amanda Seligman*
*James R. Grossman, editor emeritus*

*Also in the series:*

MAKING THE MISSION: PLANNING AND ETHNICITY IN SAN FRANCISCO *by Ocean Howell*

CONFEDERATE CITIES: THE URBAN SOUTH DURING THE CIVIL WAR ERA *edited by Andrew L. Slap and Frank Towers*

THE CYCLING CITY: BICYCLES AND URBAN AMERICA IN THE 1890s *by Evan Friss*

A NATION OF NEIGHBORHOODS: IMAGINING CITIES, COMMUNITIES, AND DEMOCRACY IN POSTWAR AMERICA *by Benjamin Looker*

WORLD OF HOMEOWNERS: AMERICAN POWER AND THE POLITICS OF HOUSING AID *by Nancy H. Kwak*

DEMOLITION MEANS PROGRESS: FLINT, MICHIGAN, AND THE FATE OF THE AMERICAN METROPOLIS *by Andrew R. Highsmith*

METROPOLITAN JEWS: POLITICS, RACE, AND RELIGION IN POSTWAR DETROIT *by Lila Corwin Berman*

BLOOD RUNS GREEN: THE MURDER THAT TRANSFIXED GILDED AGE CHICAGO *by Gillian O'Brien*

A CITY FOR CHILDREN: WOMEN, ARCHITECTURE, AND THE CHARITABLE LANDSCAPES OF OAKLAND, 1850–1950 *by Marta Gutman*

A WORLD MORE CONCRETE: REAL ESTATE AND THE REMAKING OF JIM CROW SOUTH FLORIDA *by N. D. B. Connolly*

URBAN APPETITES: FOOD AND CULTURE IN NINETEENTH-CENTURY NEW YORK *by Cindy R. Lobel*

CRUCIBLES OF BLACK EMPOWERMENT: CHICAGO'S NEIGHBORHOOD POLITICS FROM THE NEW DEAL TO HAROLD WASHINGTON *by Jeffrey Helgeson*

THE STREETS OF SAN FRANCISCO: POLICING AND THE CREATION OF A COSMOPOLITAN LIBERAL POLITICS, 1950–1972 *by Christopher Lowen Agee*

HARLEM: THE UNMAKING OF A GHETTO *by Camilo José Vergara*

PLANNING THE HOME FRONT: BUILDING BOMBERS AND COMMUNITIES AT WILLOW RUN *by Sarah Jo Peterson*

PURGING THE POOREST: PUBLIC HOUSING AND THE DESIGN POLITICS OF TWICE-CLEARED COMMUNITIES *by Lawrence J. Vale*

BROWN IN THE WINDY CITY: MEXICANS AND PUERTO RICANS IN POSTWAR CHICAGO *by Lilia Fernández*

BUILDING A MARKET: THE RISE OF THE HOME IMPROVEMENT INDUSTRY, 1914–1960 *by Richard Harris*

SEGREGATION: A GLOBAL HISTORY OF DIVIDED CITIES *by Carl H. Nightingale*

SUNDAYS AT SINAI: A JEWISH CONGREGATION IN CHICAGO *by Tobias Brinkmann*

IN THE WATCHES OF THE NIGHT: LIFE IN THE NOCTURNAL CITY, 1820–1930 *by Peter C. Baldwin*

MISS CUTLER AND THE CASE OF THE RESURRECTED HORSE: SOCIAL WORK AND THE STORY OF POVERTY IN AMERICA, AUSTRALIA, AND BRITAIN *by Mark Peel*

THE TRANSATLANTIC COLLAPSE OF URBAN RENEWAL: POSTWAR URBANISM FROM NEW YORK TO BERLIN *by Christopher Klemek*

I'VE GOT TO MAKE MY LIVIN': BLACK WOMEN'S SEX WORK IN TURN-OF-THE-CENTURY CHICAGO *by Cynthia M. Blair*

*Additional series titles follow the index.*

# Making the Unequal Metropolis

## School Desegregation and Its Limits

ANSLEY T. ERICKSON

The University of Chicago Press
Chicago and London

The University of Chicago Press, Chicago 60637
© 2016 by The University of Chicago
All rights reserved. Published 2016.
Paperback edition 2017
Printed in the United States of America

23 22 21 20 19 18 17    3 4 5 6 7

ISBN-13: 978-0-226-02525-4 (cloth)
ISBN-13: 978-0-226-52891-5 (paper)
ISBN-13: 978-0-226-02539-1 (e-book)
DOI: 10.7208/Chicago/9780226025391.001.0001

Library of Congress Cataloging-in-Publication Data

Erickson, Ansley T., author.
  Making The Unequal Metropolis : School Desegregation and Its Limits /
Ansley T. Erickson
    Pages : Maps ; Cm. — (Historical studies of urban America)
    ISBN 978-0-226-02525-4 (cloth : alk. paper) — ISBN 978-0-226-02539-1
(e-book)   1. School integration—Tennessee—Nashville—History—
20th century.   2. Segregation in Education—Tennessee—Nashville—
History—20th century.   3. Educational equalization—Tennessee—Nashville—
History—20th century.   4. Busing for school integration—Tennessee—
Nashville—History—20th century.   I. Title.   II. Series: Historical studies of
urban America.
  LC214.23.N37E75 2016
  379.2′630976855—dc23
                                                              2015029148

*for Daniel*
*and*
*for our hopes for our daughters*

# CONTENTS

# ILLUSTRATIONS

TABLES

# ACKNOWLEDGMENTS

My debts extend back in time to long before I began to think of Nashville as the place to answer persistent questions, and they stretch well beyond this work of history. I am awed by and deeply grateful for the wisdom and the kindness so many have shared along the way.

At Brown, Ted Sizer and Nancy Sizer helped me see schools as institutions and as human places. They guided my naive enthusiasm and inchoate interest patiently toward the questions that really mattered. Ted's early vote of confidence in me as a student and colleague was the key turning point in my imagining an intellectual life.

I took many lessons from three years of teaching in public schools in Harlem and the South Bronx. Most important by far was how deeply intelligent and capable my students were. Their insistent hope, their ability to navigate and thrive, and their sharp eye to the injustices and hypocrisies of the world around them humbled me and have motivated me since. We have no excuse if we do not make schools that merit them. We have no excuse for denying our collective selves the benefit of their spirits and their minds fully realized.

Before this project became a writing endeavor, it started with interviews for a documentary video project. Markie Hancock's and Kathryn Gregorio's kind mentorship, and a small grant from the Maxine Greene Foundation, helped support that first phase of work and thus made much of what followed possible.

Dozens of Nashville residents took the time to talk with me or to participate in oral history interviews. I have been honored by their insights, by their stories and their deep hopes for their city. Small moments during some of those interviews—a 2004 conversation with a then high school junior who described how it felt to travel each morning from his city neighborhood to his suburban school; a veteran teacher who recalled what it meant to be in bricklaying classes at his school—lodged themselves in my mind and grew into the central themes of this project. These Nashville residents I spoke to were alive to the contradictions, the possibilities, and the frustrations of their schools and their city, and I strive to be so as well.

I also benefited tremendously from the stories and suggestions of long-time participants in this history. John Egerton, a keen observer of his city and its people, never stopped making sense of it and trying to goad it to be better. Hon. Richard Dinkins and Rev. Sonnye Dixon both went out of their way, time and again, to support and help and remember. Hubert Dixon III reflected on his own experience with remarkable insight and eloquence, and graciously connected me to his father and his niece as well. I am immensely grateful to them, and to the many others who participated in oral history interviews or shared stories. I hope I have captured at least pieces of their truths. I appreciate as well the generosity of Claire Smrekar, Ellen Goldring, and Richard Pride in offering their observations at an early stage. And as the endnotes show, I also learned much from the work of Nashville journalists who documented their city's story as it was unfolding.

Librarians and archivists at Columbia and beyond opened many doors and managed countless queries. Jerry Breeze at Columbia first put me on to the *Kelley* papers, without which this project would not exist. Mary Evelyn Tomlin at the National Archives–Southeast Regional Branch patiently helped as I came back, and back, and back again to them. At the Nashville Public Library Special Collections, Andrea Blackman, Kathy Bennett, Linda Barnickle, Beth Odle, Tracy Howerton, and their colleagues all fielded myriad inquiries over years with patience and great knowledge, as did Ken Fieth and Drew Mahan at the Metropolitan Archives of Nashville/Davidson County and Darla Brock and Vince McGrath at the Tennessee State Library and Archives. Teresa Gray, Kathy Smith, and Molly Dohrmann were a great help at the Vanderbilt Special Collections and University Archives, as was Josie Bass at the MPC Library. In their special efforts to make unprocessed materials from the Avon Williams papers available, I am deeply grateful to Fletcher Moon, Murle Kenerson, Sharon Hull Smith, Loretta Divens, and Yldiz Binkley at Tennessee State University Library and Special Collections.

In the Columbia Department of History, Professor Elizabeth Blackmar helped shape my interest in educational inequality and Nashville into a dissertation, and has since been a model of an academic mentor. As her students know well, Betsy finds the perfect balance between generous intellectual enthusiasm and sharp questions, with an abiding decency and sense of reason. Barbara Fields's model of intellectual rigor, care, and persistence, and Eric Foner's visible enjoyment of and deep respect for the work of history both inspire me as well. I am happy that I connected with Ira Katznelson and Samuel Roberts at the dissertation phase, and have benefited from their insights since.

Also at Columbia, the Mellon/ISERP Interdisciplinary Graduate Program under William McAllister's leadership provided an important physical and intellectual home. Jeremiah Trinidad, Eric Glass, and his colleagues at Columbia's Digital Social Sciences group provided countless hours of help as I learned and relearned the very basics of GIS and census research. Mary Marshall Clark helped introduce me to oral history and kindly encouraged my work along the way.

Jonathan Zimmerman sets a standard for intellectual generosity and commitment to scholarly mentorship well beyond the reach of mere mortals. He has always managed to find time among his myriad other responsibilities to provide excellent advice and encouragement. The history of education writing group Jon convenes sustains, encourages, and challenges, and our field (and this work) is the stronger for it. Over the years I have appreciated helpful comments from writing group members Zoe Burkholder, James Fraser, Joan Malczewski, and Harold Wechsler.

I was fortunate to start my faculty life at Syracuse University, where the Cultural Foundations of Education Department proved a warm and rigorous environment. I will always value Sari Biklen's and Doug Biklen's models of collegial care and scholarly engagement.

Teachers College, Columbia University, has been a rich and dynamic place from which to refine and complete this work. The combined forces of the institution's powerful history and the urgency many of its students bring to understanding and bettering the educational landscape are strong motivators. I am grateful for all the varied ways that Tom James, Cally Waite, Ernest Morrell, and Jeff Henig have made it a supportive, generative place to be. Jeff, along with Amy Stuart Wells, kindly took time to read and discuss parts of this work. I thank Ruth Vinz and Bill Gaudelli for their leadership of our department and their support for new faculty members, and Rachel Rizzo for her steady help in our office.

Our students in the Program in History and Education and in my classes remind me of the energy and the hope that accompany new projects. Their questions and interests resonated with this work in progress and clarified what was at stake. Antonia Smith and Lauren Fox helped with key research tasks, and Viola Huang deserves many thanks for navigating the rights-and-permissions thicket. I appreciate and learn from ongoing conversations with Barry Goldenberg and Nick Juravich.

Long conversations with generous colleagues have helped shape this work. Jack Dougherty, Matt Lassiter, and John Rury have listened well and shared good ideas and questions at many stages along the way, and have opened the way for new opportunities. Working with Mike Rose and Michael Katz on a different writing project helped my thinking here. I also appreciate feedback from James Anderson, Barbara Beatty, Kevin Kruse, William Reese, Bruce Schulman, and Tom Sugrue, in responding to pieces of this work presented at various conferences and seminars over the years. I am grateful for Nancy Beadie's early and continued enthusiasm for thinking anew about schools and cities.

I have been lucky to share the early stages of faculty life with a cohort of talented scholars and good friends. Conversations at writing groups, conferences, and more have been both sustaining and immensely valuable in my work. I take joy in talking ideas and challenges with Jonna Perrillo, Russell Rickford, and Bethany Rogers, and while running with Molly Tambor and Julie Crawford. I am glad that Andrew Highsmith and I share questions in common, and it has been a pleasure and a good challenge to try to answer them together. Nathan Connolly, Leah Gordon, Sarah Manekin, Hilary Moss, Natalia Mehlman Petrzela, Michelle Purdy, and Tracy Steffes offered invaluable feedback and new ways of thinking about various drafts in progress.

I thank the Spencer Foundation's Dissertation Fellowship and an NAE/Spencer Postdoctoral Fellowship for creating the spaces in which many of these friendships grew, and for providing crucial time to write and think. I benefited from support from the Richard Hofstadter Fellowship at Columbia and the Eisenhower Institute/Clifford Roberts Dissertation Fellowship, and research funding from the Tennessee Historical Society, the Lyndon Baines Johnson Presidential Library, and Columbia's Buell Center for Architecture and Urbanism. Columbia's Bancroft Dissertation Prize, awarded for this project in 2011, provided a generous supplement for publication.

For the University of Chicago Press, Harvey Kantor and Daniel Perlstein offered tremendous insight and engagement with this manuscript, making it better in too many ways to count. Becky Nicolaides's support and smart editorial guidance helped at several stages. Robert Devens wisely guided the book to contract, and Timothy Mennel, Nora Devlin, and Johanna Rosenbohm were a pleasure to work with in bringing it to print. This university-press and peer-review team definitely made a better result than I could have alone. The errors that remain, despite the wealth of good help and intelligence around me, are mine alone.

The debts I incurred in doing archival research in Nashville from a home base in New York go on forever. I could not have done it without Debbie Davies, who in trip after trip provided food and shelter and good conversation at the end of long, quiet days in the archives. My mother, Brenda Erickson, kindly hosted granddaughter visits week after week, and Lily and Tessa showed flexibility and patience beyond their years in adjusting to new routine after new routine. Carrie Ferguson Weir and I met courtesy of our then-tiny daughters, and her friendship and laughter and intricate knowledge of the local scene have leavened every stage of this project. I appreciate her grace in not pointing out how much longer it took me to write this than it would have taken a creditable journalist. One happy serendipity, also thanks to Carrie, was connecting with Nancy Rhoda, who so generously helped locate and think through the images she took in Nashville schools in the 1970s.

My extended family—Judy Seltz, Mike Seltz and Gillie Campbell, Jennifer Seltz and Niall O'Murchu, and Steven Seltz and Cybele Maylone—have done it just right: valuing history and writing deeply, and treading lightly on questions of deadlines and completion. I wish Keefer Erickson and Seth Erickson and their families were closer to hand, but I watch with pride as they take on their own long-term projects, and I feel a comradeship across the miles. We are all in our own ways builders, as our parents in their own ways always have been.

Part of my motivation in studying education must come from the contradiction between the opportunities that good schooling has made for me and my own firsthand knowledge of schools that continue to deny such opportunities to the students who invest their time, energy, and good faith in them. My mother's fierce insistence that my and my brothers' education would be strong and encouraging and our hard work rewarded has opened even more doors for us than she may have imagined, and for this I am always grateful. I am also grateful for my father Danny Erickson's love of history, and for the hope I find in the sibling-family he has reconstituted. His story ensures I do not mistake the capriciousness of birth for virtue, or for fault.

My daughters are the counterbalance and the touchstone. Lily, who was born in Nashville, is a writer and a thinker of the first order. She has warmed my heart by celebrating each step toward publication on my behalf, and as she does I see her imagining a future in words for herself. I hope she knows that whatever pride she feels for this work, I celebrate tenfold what she creates. Tessa has a wisdom and a steadiness that most adults I know, myself included, can only aspire to. I delight in seeing how her mind works, taking in machines and the natural world voraciously. I learn from her every day, and her laughter often keeps me afloat.

Then there is Daniel. How do you thank someone who has made every-thing possible? I borrow my confidence as a scholar, thinker, and writer from him, a natural at all of these. He took me to Nashville first, but has been happy to be dragged back in research trips and in countless bits of arcana since. I treasure his patience and steady support for a project that has seemed nearly done, but not quite, for so long. We have made a family that has space for both of us and our intellectual lives while holding our children at the center. There is no one else I would want to walk this path with.

New York, New York
February 2015

# ABBREVIATIONS

| | |
|---|---|
| CVEA | Comprehensive Vocational Education Act |
| HEW | US Department of Health, Education, and Welfare |
| IMF | Interdenominational Ministers' Fellowship |
| LDF | Legal Defense Fund |
| MNPS | Metropolitan Nashville Public Schools |
| MPC | Metropolitan Planning Commission |
| NAACP | National Association for the Advancement of Colored People |
| NHA | Nashville Housing Authority |

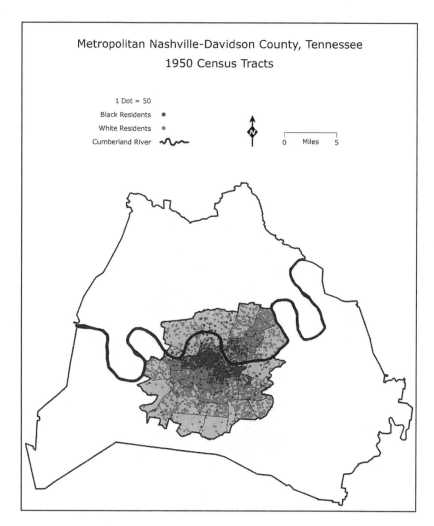

**Metropolitan Nashville-Davidson County, Tennessee**
**1950 Census Tracts**

1 Dot = 50
Black Residents
White Residents
Cumberland River

N

0    Miles    5

This map shows the City of Nashville and Davidson County, which consolidated as Metropolitan Nashville-Davidson County in 1963. Only some portions of the county had been divided into census tracts by 1950. Source: US Census, via Minnesota Population Center. National Historical Geographic Information System: Pre-release Version 0.1. Minneapolis: University of Minnesota, 2004, http://www.nhgis.org. Map by James W. Quinn.

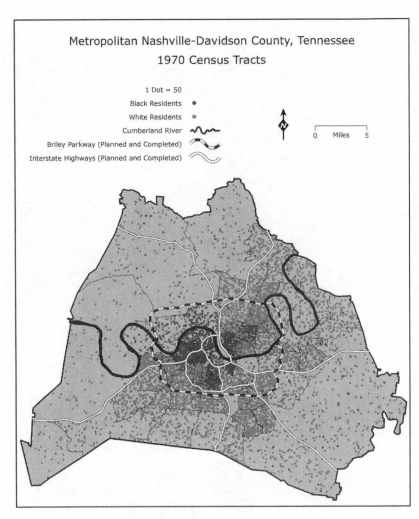

Metropolitan Nashville-Davidson County, Tennessee
1970 Census Tracts

1 Dot = 50
Black Residents
White Residents
Cumberland River
Briley Parkway (Planned and Completed)
Interstate Highways (Planned and Completed)

0    Miles    5

Source: US Census, via Minnesota Population Center. National Historical
Geographic Information System: Pre-release Version 0.1. Minneapolis: University
of Minnesota, 2004, http://www.nhgis.org. Map by James W. Quinn.

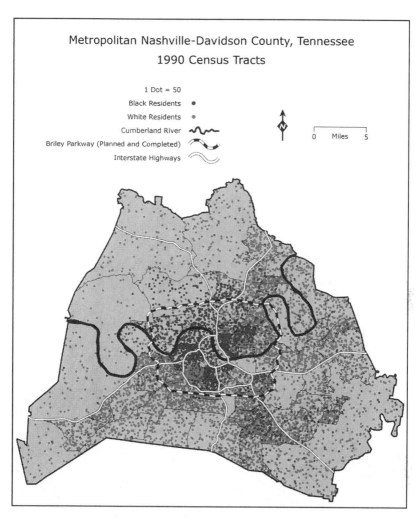

Metropolitan Nashville-Davidson County, Tennessee
1990 Census Tracts

1 Dot = 50
Black Residents
White Residents
Cumberland River
Briley Parkway (Planned and Completed)
Interstate Highways

N

0    Miles    5

Source: US Census, via Minnesota Population Center. National Historical
Geographic Information System: Pre-release Version 0.1. Minneapolis: University
of Minnesota, 2004, http://www.nhgis.org. Map by James W. Quinn.

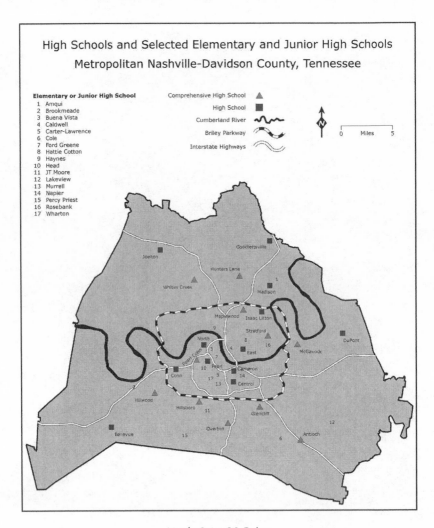

High Schools and Selected Elementary and Junior High Schools
Metropolitan Nashville-Davidson County, Tennessee

Map by James W. Quinn.

# Introduction

## Shifting Inequalities

Hubert Dixon Jr. grew up just outside of Nashville, Tennessee. He began first grade at segregated Haynes Consolidated Negro School in 1939, and graduated from its high school division in 1951. His son, Hubert Dixon III, began kindergarten not far away, at Ford Greene Elementary inside the city boundary, in 1969. Across these two generations, and across the metropolitan landscape, the Dixon family tells the story of segregation, desegregation, and educational inequality.

When the elder Dixon attended school, he faced a muscularly enforced segregation and blunt inequality. Hubert Dixon Jr. recalled the modest wood-frame structure that, in his elementary years, served all grades of black students in Davidson County outside Nashville. He could picture how he watched buses carry fellow black students past white residences and schools on their way to segregated black schools. He remembered as well how he first chose to become a teacher, having found no other avenues for employment where a young black man could deploy the college diploma he had earned.[1]

When the younger Dixon first arrived at Ford Greene, the school remained a segregated institution, like the vast majority of schools in late-1960s America. Nashville schools began to desegregate a dozen years earlier, in 1957, but the school board, administrators, and attorneys who designed the local desegregation plan and won court approval for it ensured only the most meager and gradual change.[2] Starting kindergarten, Hubert Dixon III encountered a solidly constructed brick building where a well-qualified and nearly all-black teaching faculty served exclusively black students. Yet inequality still trailed segregation there, as it did in most American schools. The school board continued to assign Ford Greene fewer resources for its teachers and students, and its community had less political power than Nashville's growing white suburbs to secure more.[3]

Unlike the vast majority of American school districts that reflected the fragmentation of city from suburb, Nashville's school district extended, after 1963, across all of Davidson County's more than five hundred square miles, with its urban, suburban, and even rural stretches. A new federal court order in 1971 moved students across urban and suburban neighborhood lines and radically expanded the reach of desegregation in Nashville. As the younger Dixon started second grade that year, he began riding school buses out of his neighborhood to the first of five more schools before his high school graduation. While Dixon rode the bus across town, on trips of up to ten miles and forty-five minutes along newly completed interstate highways, his school district shuttered schools close to his home and in other majority-black neighborhoods. Dixon recalled, decades after he attended Nashville's schools, that he had thought of himself "as a federal agent whose job it was to desegregate schools throughout Nashville." And in many ways, he was—much more so than his white peers, who often remained in schools close to home for nine or ten of their years in school, rather than the typical black student's two or three.[4] Busing made all of Dixon's schools statistically desegregated, with the number of black and white students in attendance roughly aligned with the district's overall demographic composition.

Nashville was one of desegregation's best-case scenarios. In 1970, almost all Nashville schools had more than 90 percent white students or more than 90 percent black students—one measure used by desegregation scholars to indicate "highly concentrated" black or white student populations. By 1990, after nearly two decades of court-ordered busing, almost none of the district's schools were so highly concentrated, black or white. (The city had very few students of Latino or Asian descent at that time). Nashville's statistical desegregation was a striking achievement against the national backdrop: in 1990, nearly a third of all black students in the US attended schools that had 90 percent or more African American students, while segregation among white students remained high as well. The average white US suburban student's school, as of 1996, included only 6.8 percent African American peers.[5] Through Hubert Dixon's efforts, and hundreds of thousands of Nashville students alongside him, the district became one of the most statistically desegregated school systems in the country over the twenty-seven-year span of busing there.[6]

Busing brought the younger Hubert greater access to educational resources, both material and human. Hubert Dixon III enjoyed previously unavailable social contact with white students, which he felt shaped the course of his life in positive ways. He made lasting friendships in football and debate, where "having a job to do and people . . . counting on you" provided an encouraging context for new relationships. But like many black students attending previously segregated white schools, Hubert also witnessed white teachers applying racist stereotypes, sorting him and other students in their classes based on skin color rather than demonstrated ability. Inequalities in the practice of desegregation took multiple forms, in Nashville as in cities like Chicago, Syracuse, Louisville, Austin, and Milwaukee. There, black students—and particularly black urban-dwelling students—bore disproportionately the burdens of desegregation in travel time, dislocation, and closures of local schools—burdens that gradually eroded support for the idea of desegregation even among many of its historic advocates. Once at school, black students experienced "second-generation segregation," or tracking into lower-opportunity classes or courses of study, remaking unequal opportunity within statistically desegregated schools.[7] "It was always very clear," Dixon remembered, "that you were in the minority. It was never really a sense of being integrated." Recent national studies of students who experienced busing and local studies of cities beyond Nashville underline that Hubert Dixon's story is one example of the experience of millions of students, of the paired benefits and costs of desegregation, of the less tangible but still persistent forces of educational inequality.[8]

Across generations in the Dixon family, inequality had shifted form. Hubert Dixon III drew on strong supports within his own family to finish high school as well as to graduate from college. Yet he saw around him the patterns of uneven educational achievement documented in lower average test scores and graduation rates for black students. Even as Nashville's schools became exceptional for their statistical desegregation, they remained unexceptional in the patterns of unequal educational opportunity they demonstrated. In the desegregation years, Nashville's educational outcomes generally followed national patterns—they both improved, and remained starkly unequal. From the 1960s through the mid-1980s, in the US overall and particularly in the South (which saw the highest levels of statistical desegregation), the gap between black and white students' levels of academic achievement closed significantly.[9] Although the available local data is imperfect, what remains suggests that Nashville saw similar progress in student achievement over the years of desegregation via busing. Test-score gaps shrank by as much as half, but remained significant.

Educational attainment—how many people finished high school, for example—also improved, although a large gap continued. In 1960, only 21 percent of black Nashvillians over the age of 25 had completed high school or beyond; by 1990, 67 percent had. By then, the figure was 80 percent among white residents. Nationally in the same years, levels of attainment for black and white students rose strikingly, particularly before the mid-1970s, when the growth rate slowed. These educational gaps form one crucial part of a broader pattern of lower levels of income, employment, and weaker life chances for African Americans in the late twentieth and early twenty-first century.[10]

The complicated, at times paradoxical, story of school desegregation matters in its own right. But it is also a point of entry from which to understand how, over the late twentieth century, inequality shifted form in American education.[11] The causal roots of educational inequality, in eras of segregation and desegregation, can be found in the interactions between schools and the basic political and economic structures of the city and the metropolis. Segregation and desegregation depended on hundreds of small choices made by local, state, and federal officials, at times in response to legal and other pressures from community advocates. Who would go to school with whom? Which communities would have schools, in what portion of the metropolitan landscape? What would schools teach? Each of these matters became a venue in which schooling interacted with a broad range of municipal policy areas, from city planning practice, housing development, and urban renewal plans to local and state economic development efforts and growth boosterism. In the local roots of inequality and its long branches into the policy, practice, and public discussion of schooling, Nashville is a place like so many others. Inequality has been at once deeply embedded and difficult to fully identify. Making visible its full scope and the broad range of those invested in it is, even today, the first step to challenge it.

## Why Nashville? Desegregation and the Growth Metropolis

Nashville's success at statistical desegregation—like that of other southern metropolitan school districts, including Charlotte and Tampa, Louisville and Raleigh—stemmed in significant part from the scope of its municipal government. Nashville and its surrounding suburbs inside Davidson County became a single, consolidated government and school system in 1963: Metropolitan Nashville–Davidson County. The majority of Nashville's suburbs could be found within the county into the early 1970s.

Therefore, the same jurisdiction encompassed some rural spaces, suburban areas dominated by white families, growing black suburbs, and city neighborhoods with significant black and white populations.[12]

Metropolitan consolidation was not motivated by desegregation; in fact, it may have been enabled by an elite confidence that segregation in schools and housing remained secure even without a city line. Consolidation facilitated desegregation by dampening the impact of white departures from urban areas and public schools. The district did experience losses of white students typical of many urban and desegregating school systems. Private school attendance in Nashville boomed at each point at which desegregation expanded, as in many other districts; white migration to exurban communities beyond the county line also increased markedly. White withdrawal, alongside the falling birthrates of the late-1960s and 1970s, took the school district from over 90,000 students in 1970 to a low of under 56,000 in 1985, when enrollment began to increase again. Enrollment changes altered the experience of schooling and the reality in which school district leaders worked. Yet in Nashville, the phenomenon of white withdrawal was less pronounced when compared to metropolitan areas divided into dozens of separate municipalities and school districts. Nashville's schools served a large majority of white students before desegregation began, and even once it did, the extensive geographic scope of the single metropolitan district made departures to other school districts more onerous than in other settings (although private schooling remained an option for those with financial means). Other desegregating city-only districts quickly became nearly or all black, surrounded by white suburbs, while via the metropolitan structure, Nashville schools continued to serve black and white students both.[13]

Even as it aided statistical desegregation, metropolitan consolidation was no silver bullet for equality in education or other areas of metropolitan policy. Consolidation did allow much of the increasing property tax base created by suburban residential construction and urban and suburban commercial growth to remain within the metropolitan jurisdiction, rather than seeing it flow into separate suburban coffers. But when faced with questions of how to allocate resources—in the form of schools, fire stations, or sanitary sewers—the metropolitan political structure often tilted to the white suburban majority. Dividing lines between city and suburb, familiar across metropolitan areas fragmented by jurisdictional boundaries, emerged without official demarcations as well. Consolidation diluted black voting power when it merged a city population of 38 percent African American residents in 1960 to a county population that was less than

5 percent African American. In the resulting metropolitan government, black citizens made up less than a fifth of the voting population. Marshaling power through the ballot became more difficult than it had been within the separate city. The extensive powers of the mayor's office, elected at-large, and of at-large representatives on the metropolitan council, reinforced the power of the white suburban majority.[14] From the perspective of fragmented metropolises, scholars have often hoped metropolitan governance could offer a solution to segregation and inequality, in education as well as in other arenas.[15] Metropolitan consolidation certainly enabled statistical desegregation, and its benefits, in Nashville. Yet the metropolitan structure alone could not guarantee against inequality in its many modes. Instead, new and powerful lines of division emerged in the metropolis and its schools.

Metropolitan consolidation drew much of its support from local business elites who thought rationalized governance across city and suburb would facilitate the economic growth they saw as the city's greatest need and challenge. Like their counterparts in dynamic Sunbelt metropolises and struggling Rustbelt centers, these local leaders in business and politics wanted to attract new businesses, employ local citizens (and thus increase their purchasing power), expand the tax base (except when offering new businesses generous tax breaks), and spur both downtown and suburban real estate development. Doing so, their rhetoric claimed, promised benefits for citizens across the city. However, such efforts lacked the mechanisms to guarantee a broad distribution of growth's benefits. In fact, boosterish growth rhetoric combined with white racism at times concentrated the burdens of the pursuit of growth in black communities. Municipal leaders shaped urban renewal and highway construction projects to displace black communities and expropriate black property in the name of development that overwhelmingly benefited white businesses and communities.[16]

And Nashville did enjoy significant growth in the second half of the twentieth century. The quiet small city in which Hubert Dixon's father grew up held under 170,000 people in 1940, with a local economy dominated by regional banking and insurance and a mix of light and heavy manufacturing. Some of the seeds the growth-minded elite planted were slow to grow, but by the 1980s many of the city's long-term economic drivers remained present while new ones took off in prime postindustrial sectors like health care and entertainment. Metropolitan Nashville's gradual increase to a population of more than half a million by the end of the century was far from the rocketing growth of Atlanta or Phoenix, but the local effort to use government levers, including school policy, to encourage growth was as firm, energetic, and consequential to ongoing inequality as anywhere in the United States.[17]

As a growing and growth-focused metropolis, Nashville offers a clear contrast to cases—well represented in histories of education in cities—of schooling in the context of urban decline. A growing metropolis provokes new questions: In what ways, and through what policy choices or mechanisms, did growth agendas impact schools? How did they shape segregation and influence desegregation as experienced in general terms, and in the specific lives of students? And what consequences followed when the rhetoric of growth's universal benefits proved hollow—as in years that brought both economic growth and increased poverty?[18]

The particular policy choices that shaped segregation and desegregation in Nashville at times depended on factors as varied as the city's robust embrace of national city planning paradigms or its remarkably broad use of urban renewal. Similarly, the particular expertise and orientation of its civil rights advocates, and the interaction between local and state programs to promote economic growth, all became guiding forces as well. These particularities, however, help illuminate more general patterns of schooling embedded in metropolitan political economy. These patterns are neither Nashville's alone, nor are they specific to Sunbelt metropolises. Understood in its full relationship with the urban and metropolitan political and economic landscape, desegregation emerges as a window into the basic processes of American inequality rooted in myriad uses of state power across different levels of government.

## Educational Inequality and Political Economy

*Making the Unequal Metropolis* examines segregation, desegregation, and educational inequality as problems of political economy. It queries the interactions between schools, economic forces and agendas, and political power. In so doing, it departs from previous views of desegregation in three key ways. It shifts attention from popular white resistance to policy choices that gave desegregation its form; it situates schooling as a force in the making of the city and metropolis rather than as solely a recipient of urban dynamics; and it recasts previous views of government power in educational inequality.

The most familiar images of busing, in both history writing and popular memory, emphasize white protest and withdrawal. White resistance produced violent and visceral responses in Nashville as elsewhere, and helped galvanize a major conservative realignment in the late 1960s—one that ultimately challenged policies like desegregation. Resistance expressed as departures from public schools in general or from specific school districts contributed ultimately to the making of segregation across district lines and the weakening of the school systems most likely to serve black and poor students. Resistance to desegregation had important impact, in schooling and beyond, but within many historical accounts the analysis of reaction has displaced close attention to the policy choices that gave desegregation its form and nature for those who experienced it.[19]

Because of the strength of the resistance narrative, less attention has flowed to other fundamentally important critiques of desegregation. Legal scholar Derrick Bell consistently emphasized the centrality of inequality within desegregation, an inequality not only characteristic of desegregation's outcomes, but of its core design. Bell looked beyond the more frequently recognized inequalities in the first waves of desegregation in the 1950s and 1960s, when many black schools were shuttered and black educators fired or demoted, to note continued inequalities in busing. For Bell and others working in his tradition, these inequalities demonstrate interest convergence, the way policies such as desegregation aided black communities only to the extent that they served white interests. But *how* did desegregation continue to prioritize the felt needs of white communities over black ones? Local and federal desegregation planners achieved statistical desegregation via some policy choices that increased opportunity for students like Hubert and others which undermined opportunity.[20] A focus on the momentary and easily measurable—the ratio of white to black students in a school, especially—took precedence over the deep and long entrenched—as in the consequences of segregationist housing policies or the relationships between schools, communities, and economies—and thus prevented the conversion of statistical desegregation to more broadly constructed equality of educational opportunity.

The emphasis on dramatic white resistance has also shaped the chronological boundaries of many of the leading studies of busing for desegregation. Most accounts examine legal struggles and then court and school board negotiation over the initiation of busing. They offer at times intricate and valuable perspectives on how initial busing plans took shape, but they often stop not long after the first buses roll and loud protests quiet.[21] By stopping at this point, they miss at least two key dynamics. The first is the experience of busing over its longer course—over decades, in places like Nashville. Over time, the various approaches to and meanings of desegregation shifted, as did the metropolitan landscape. Black activists' and legal advocates' perspectives on busing for desegregation evolved not only as a matter of changing ideological currents in the black freedom struggle, but as highly situated responses to local policy choices that had failed to join statistical desegregation with black communities' and individuals' desires for recognition and ownership of educational spaces and processes.

Recent work on black communities' experiences of desegregation, and the only previous book-length treatment of desegregation in Nashville specifically, name white leaders' and citizens' commitments to cultural assimilation as a key cause of desegregation's inequalities. To the extent that desegregation helped black and white students access and share educational resources, that sharing had to happen on white communities' terms, this interpretation holds. School boards shut black schools instead of white ones and focused on mollifying angry white parents. Surely in Nashville as well as in desegregation cases both South and North, powerful white individuals and institutions shared in racist ideology that made them unable to see—much less credit or support—black communities. But their stunted vision was as much material as cultural; their racism a system of power as much as a matter of individual feeling. Basic structures of economic and political power in the metropolis supported, and at times depended upon, disregarding or destroying black communities and institutions, in schooling as in other venues.[22]

Many scholars have examined schooling in American cities, but too few have traced how schools figure in the making of the city.[23] Schools were not simply pawns in a changing and challenging urban and metropolitan context; they helped shape that context. A key example comes in the interactions between schooling and housing that, together, helped construct segregation. Conventional formulations, both in history and in many legal accounts past and present, take school segregation to simply follow residential patterns. In fact, planners and real estate developers identified schools as defining features of neighborhoods, and property markets valued connections between housing and schools. Through their locations, as well as through zoning and student assignment choices, schools helped to segregate the metropolitan landscape. As Nashville shows in years of segregation and desegregation, school policy became an actor in the city, embedded in and contributing to basic structures of metropolitan inequality.

Nashville also sheds light on how government power, at multiple levels, operated in segregation, desegregation, and educational inequality. In cases like the dramatic federal and state confrontation that unfolded in Little Rock, Arkansas, in 1957, federal power can seem to be squarely on the side of desegregation. And indeed, in Nashville, desegregation surely would have proceeded more slowly, and more incompletely, without federal pressure in the form of court orders. Yet desegregation's inequalities in Nashville also had federal court approval—and at times even originated in federally supported ideas. Locating education within the broader land-scape of federal intervention in the metropolis means considering the fed-eral presence in highway construction, urban renewal, and Model Cities alongside desegregation. Federal pressures for desegregation in schools often ran against federal encouragement for segregation through housing construction and neighborhood destruction, for white suburbanization in the form of housing finance, transportation infrastructure, and tax subsi-dies. If some aspects of federal power encouraged desegregation, many oth-ers did the opposite.

A similar complexity is visible in the ideas about government power that various (and sometimes the very same) actors engaged around deseg-regation and other contemporary issues, such as the pursuit of economic growth. Local and state business leaders marshaled multiple government mechanisms to encourage growth—from property seizure and resale to private developers in "slum clearance," or by shaping schooling toward the production of future workers. In the very same years, they joined lo-cal working- and middle-class voices and political officials nationally in declaring busing an overreaching abuse of government power. Whether en-gaged in educational or economic endeavors, Nashville's citizens judged their approach to the power and reach of government intervention depend-ing on the particular issue at hand, a reality that defies any assumption of a coherent small-government conservatism.[24]

Recognizing desegregation and inequality as a problem of political economy means reconsidering how American education and American capitalism have related to one another, the topic of varied yet incomplete historical analysis. In the late 1960s and early 1970s, revisionist historians of education attacked the long-standing progressive consensus that schools were a great engine of American democracy and mobility. Instead, they charged, schooling reproduced class inequality more than challenged it. These provocative assertions emphasized links between school structures and industrial production, or tight connections between the managerial class and those who ran school systems or supported particular school policies. Although these works focused attention on a crucial question, they did not sufficiently examine the basic mechanisms that linked edu-cation and economic growth efforts in the context of post–World War II capitalism. These questions have been partially addressed in case studies of southern desegregation, which show white business elites supporting limited desegregation so as to prevent economically costly civic embarrassment. Elites did the same in Nashville. Yet there, economic growth agendas more substantially shaped the physical and curricular structures of schooling, helping determine which neighborhoods got schools, which schools closed, and what classes schools offered students.[25]

Via myriad choices made by local educators, officials, and advocates, as well as federal officials and the judiciary, Nashville navigated desegregation with relative statistical success while remaining unable or unwilling to value all of the district's students, their communities, and their places in the metropolis. As one of the school systems that came closest to achieving statistical desegregation, Nashville offers a special window into how—and why—inequality has shifted form in the latter half of the twentieth century.

## Making and Remaking Inequality in Three Modes

The story of educational inequality in Nashville unfolded in two periods in time: 1945–1968, when continued segregation and unequal power *made* educational inequality, and 1968–1998, in which desegregation proceeded in ways that *remade* educational inequality in the metropolitan landscape. This division emphasizes both continuities and changes across the latter half of the twentieth century. Educational inequalities built out of the interactions between schooling and metropolitan politics and economics took form in the 1940s and 1950s, and in many cases proved remarkably durable in shaping both the practice and understanding of schooling in local context. Yet even alongside these continuities, changing approaches to desegregation—most significantly busing, which was debated beginning in 1968 before its 1971 initiation—meant Nashville educators and citizens confronted a new context in which, yet again, to make consequential decisions about their schools and their city. Old pressures for inequality, operating in new contexts, produced inequality in new forms.

Educational inequality had deep roots in the era of slavery and the systematic oppression of the post-Reconstruction years. Without denying this long historical lineage, educational inequality continued to be made and remade in the post–World War II years. Persistent and recurring pressures for and reinforcement of segregation and inequality, often through the deployment of government power, continued throughout the twentieth century. They operated before and after *Brown v. Board of Education*, inside and outside of periods of statistical desegregation.

Nashville demonstrates educational inequality made and remade via three modes: in the spatial organization of schooling, the curricular organization of schooling, and the legal and popular narratives that depicted and claimed to explain inequality.

First, the spatial organization of schooling—the product of interactions between schools and markets in land and housing—became a venue for the making and remaking of inequality. Nashville's school board routinely met in front of maps of their city. Large maps stretched floor to ceiling behind crowded meeting tables, the distinctive shape of the serpentine Cumberland River passing by shaded zones and bold marks for school buildings. The visibility of these maps in board business, as well as in court hearings over segregation and desegregation, illustrates how the making of educational inequality, and its subsequent remaking, moved spatially in both practice and ideology. School officials, city planners, and private developers worked to place schools in the metropolitan landscape—by building them or closing them—to serve a mix of political and economic interests. Particular school locations created profit for some while often reinforcing segregation. When local officials closed schools, they undermined community viability. Desegregation meant the movement not only of students and teachers across the landscape, but of schools, land value, and community investment as well. The spatial organization of schooling demonstrates well how schools have interacted with markets in land and housing in the making of the unequal metropolis.[26]

A second mode of making and remaking inequality developed through the curricular organization of schooling: what should schools teach, to whom, and why? At times, these discussions involved educators debating how to think about and design schooling in light of the reality that children's lives had been shaped by the unequal geography of the city. At other times, the conversation centered on the intersection of schooling and labor found in vocational education programs. Talk about curriculum revealed how various communities understood the content and goals of schooling in relationship to the constructed and unequal geographic and economic landscapes. Educational approaches that grew out of these discussions became forces in making and remaking educational inequality for generations of Nashville students.

And Nashville residents engaged a third mode of making and remaking inequality as they told stories about segregation and desegregation. Popular and legal narratives—often containing conceptual simplifications of complex questions, such as how residential segregation developed or why schools were segregated—shaped how Nashville residents understood the segregation they saw around them and what approaches to desegregation they thought were, or were not, possible. As multiple scholars have noted

I.1. Nashville Board of Education hearing on desegregation, March 1956. Courtesy of Nashville Public Library Special Collections.

in studying constructs like black criminality or urban "pathology," such narratives or "public transcripts" carried great power to shape contemporary thinking and limit how people conceived of the available options in addressing social problems.[27] When civil rights attorney Avon N. Williams Jr. litigated for school desegregation, conceptual simplifications like "de facto segregation" became shadow opponents in the courtroom, often harder to best than the defendant school board.[28] Later, these narratives took root as explanatory descriptions in historical accounts as well, proving difficult for historians to engage with critical distance.[29] As individuals in various positions in Nashville narrated segregation and desegregation, they helped make and remake—or, at times, sought to contest—educational inequality.

Part I, Making Educational Inequality, follows these three modes of inequality from the end of World War II through 1968, from the last phases of legally sanctioned school segregation to the initiation of debate over busing for desegregation. Part I begins by examining the reconstruction of Nashville's urban and metropolitan landscape, a multifaceted project motivated by the search for economic growth and profit and enacted through city planning, urban renewal, and government consolidation. Within these processes, schools emerged as key loci in planning practice. The spatial organization of schooling helped construct the postwar metropolis.

While major transformations in the landscape were under way, desegregation via court order began in Nashville's schools in the mid-1950s. Nashville's white elites and educators at once fashioned sophisticated mechanisms of resistance: some spatial (as in gerrymandered school attendance lines that preserved segregation and limited desegregation) and some curricular (as when educators argued that educational principles required classroom "homogeneity" of ability and that, through the distorting lens of their racial ideology, desegregated classrooms would challenge this homogeneity). Meanwhile, some of the same elite figures who helped structure resistance, and their allies, crafted and spread a narrative of moderate, peaceful desegregation, one that contrasted with local working-class white organizing and the concurrent dramatic developments in Little Rock, Arkansas, but veiled the depth and reach of official resistance.

The curricular organization of schooling helped make educational inequality in these years, particularly as it rested upon and cultivated ideas of student "difference" by racial category. At times these ideas of difference emerged from efforts to help black students and increase opportunity. Yet new pedagogical interventions in compensatory education also had the auxiliary effect of presenting black and poor students as fundamentally apart from their white or middle-class peers, an idea that aligned with existing racist ideology and proved an enduring force for inequality.

Vocational education became an area of particular emphasis in the era's discussions of curriculum. For many black Nashville activists and educators, vocational education raised questions long visible in thinking about education for, and in the context of, unequal labor markets. Was education targeted to available jobs a pragmatic path to opportunity? Or was it the reverse, "schooling for second-class citizenship," in James Anderson's words? Could targeted vocational education open routes to fields previously closed to black workers?[30] Approaching the intersection of schooling and labor from a different perspective, Nashville's political and business elite increasingly supported vocational education programs. They did so with less emphasis on possibilities for individual mobility, and more hope for schooling as a lever for economic growth they claimed would be of broad collective benefit. Local business pressure for expanded vocational education was one of the key forces in leading Nashville's school district to adopt, in the late 1960s, a "comprehensive" high school model that would endure through the remainder of the century. Curricular ideas that emerged in the 1960s and asserted the value of dividing students either by ascribed categories of race or predictions about future occupation shaped educational inequality then, and in the decades that followed.

Returning to the spatial organization of schooling, part I closes with an examination of how local officials distributed public goods like schools, and public burdens like urban renewal's displacements and dislocations, in Nashville's metropolitan landscape. In keeping with pro-suburban ideology present in local as well as federal circles at the time, the district embraced a set of plans for school construction that favored suburban spaces and communities over urban spaces and communities. Meanwhile, urban communities faced the brunt of the disruptions and displacements of urban renewal and highway construction. These growth-minded interventions destroyed hubs of black community life. Schools both represented and interacted with the unequal spatial distribution of resources and burdens in the metropolis.

Multiple actors in Nashville and the surrounding county *made* educational inequality in the 1940s, 1950s, and through much of the 1960s, doing so through the spatial and curricular organization of schooling in the district, and through the public narratives that claimed to explain segregation and inequality. Nashville's and Davidson County's schools operated as segregated and unequal institutions for decades after World War II, well after the *Brown* decision. Segregation and inequality in this era resulted from a complex interplay of school policy, housing policy, city planning, and acts of racist exclusion in markets for housing and jobs. These multiple technologies of segregation and inequality gave the lie to the idea that post-*Brown* segregation was the product of individual preference rather than state power. With official investment in segregation still surging through the channels of metropolitan politics and economics, desegregation had made meager statistical progress more than a dozen years after its beginnings. As Nashville courts, legal advocates, educators, and families entered the second decade of debate about desegregation, they lived within a strongly constructed edifice of segregation and inequality. Many of the choices made in these years—and the powerful political and economic forces they reflected—set the context in which Nashville negotiated a more assertive form of desegregation after 1968.

Part II, Remaking Educational Inequality, traces the three modes of inequality in the era of busing for desegregation, from its legal beginnings in 1968 through its negotiated end in 1998. Nominally designed to challenge both segregation and educational inequality, busing for desegregation in fact *remade* educational inequality while securing statistical desegregation. It did so through the spatial and curricular organization of schooling and the public and legal narratives Nashvillians used to explain segregation and inequality. These modes of inequality intertwined across various phases of busing under court order.

In a period of sharp residential segregation, school desegregation was impossible unless students left their own neighborhoods. To achieve more extensive desegregation by busing students across neighborhood lines, legal advocate Avon Williams returned to court in 1968. He secured a court order for busing for desegregation that was implemented in 1971, redesigning the spatial organization of schooling in Nashville. In this effort, as throughout decades of work litigating Nashville's desegregation case, Williams confronted powerful but false narratives that obscured the origins or nature of inequality and segregation in Nashville. The first of these was the concept of "de facto segregation." Juxtaposed against "de jure segregation" formally encoded in law, "de facto segregation" purported to describe segregation as originating from individual rather than state action, custom rather than law. "De facto segregation" became a narrative that obscured the deep roots binding state-sponsored segregation in housing and schooling to one another. Williams tried to attack the popular and legal framework, but it proved enduring even in the legal opinions that expanded desegregation.

"White flight" functioned as a similarly powerful force in thinking about revising desegregation after its first decade. "White flight" appeared, both to those who favored and who opposed desegregation, to be a description of an objective reality: white enrollment in Nashville public schools did fall at striking rates over the 1970s and 1980s as many middle-class families—predominantly white families—moved out of the district and to private schools within it. Yet the idea of "white flight" proved to be another distorting narrative, shrinking the broader and more complex realities of desegregation (including officially encouraged modes of resistance and withdrawal as well as overall population shifts) to the narrow idea that the withdrawal of white students was at once desegregation's chief consequence and the product of individual racism. The white flight narrative reinforced the long-held tendency to think of desegregation in particular, and school policy in general, chiefly in terms of the satisfaction of white middle-class families. It neglected how Nashville's desegregation plans unevenly distributed their burdens, and masked the extent to which various forms of government power enabled and encouraged white withdrawal.[31]

Busing required myriad choices, for school district administrators and federal judges and officials, about the spatial organization of schooling. Where would desegregating schools operate, which residential areas would be tied to which school, which neighborhoods would together be linked through a single school, and which students would ride to which schools via what routes? Within the varied approaches to busing Nashville courts and administrators adopted from 1971 through 1998, the district accomplished significant statistical desegregation via spatial choices that privileged racialized white suburban space over racialized black urban space. In this way, busing sustained long-established patterns of economic as well as social privilege and neglect in the metropolis. Decades of experience with busing on this model informed changing perspectives on desegregation, and on what educational equality might mean, for many black Nashvillians.

The comprehensive high school, the product of decades of building interest and 1970s-era state funding for vocational education, sat at the nexus of the spatial and curricular organization of schooling in Nashville. Over the busing years, Nashville opened or converted eleven large, comprehensive high schools, all but one of them located intentionally in a ring of suburban sites. In Nashville as in many other locales, some educators tracked black students into vocational and lower-skill courses in the desegregation years.[32] Not only the product of racist individual action inside desegregating institutions, this pattern is better understood as an example of the impact of shifting local economic agendas on the curricular organization of schooling. Whether in the hope of opening opportunity for black workers to enter previously unavailable fields or recruiting new business with the promise of a ready workforce, many Nashville residents hoped to put schools to use in interaction with the local labor market. In so doing, they authorized educators to perceive students as future workers, giving schooling much of its specific form for Nashville students in the desegregation years.

Busing was not one monolithic intervention, but took on various forms that emerged from complex negotiations and renegotiations. Designing Nashville's first busing plan meant drawing on abstract principles and examples from elsewhere, but in later decades the local experience of busing informed Nashville residents in their thinking about what busing could, and could not, accomplish. As they redesigned busing beyond its initial 1970s form, including extending busing throughout the county for the first time, educators, parents, and legal advocates revealed how their ideas about equality and inequality, segregation and desegregation, were evolving. Negotiations over the end of court-ordered desegregation, developing gradually over the 1990s, similarly brought to light both long-standing efforts to shape education toward economic growth and new perspectives on the problem of inequality and paths to address it.

Court-ordered busing produced marked statistical desegregation while policy choices that bound together schooling, growth, and metropolitan politics *remade* inequality in Nashville's schools. Previous modes of inequality continued to operate, but took on new forms in the context of the myriad policy choices busing involved. Nashville's experience with busing defies any dichotomous categorization of success or failure; it shows the power, flexibility, and variety of forces that remade inequality.

## Busing Hubert

If the forces that made and remade inequality in Nashville moved at times quietly, through bureaucratic processes often out of view, they nonetheless had direct impact on the lives of individual students and families in the city. All three modes of inequality emphasized in *Making the Unequal Metropolis* are visible in, and shaped, Hubert Dixon III's schooling in Nashville. Dixon, like so many black students in Nashville, traveled away from home to attend school, while the district closed schools near his home in the city. His school district's choices about the spatial organization of schooling led to Hubert's attending high school not at nearby, urban and historically black Pearl High School, but at Glencliff High School, in a suburban white community south of downtown. While Hubert traveled to Glencliff, white students zoned to Pearl, and their families, found the district's transfer provisions (rooted in ideas of curricular choice and the comprehensive high school model) easy to exploit. Pearl saw its enrollments dwindle and struggled to remain open. With their fates entangled, shrinking urban Pearl and crowded suburban Glencliff together became a microcosm of desegregation on metropolitan scale.[33]

Hubert's desegregation experience reflected the ways in which local school and municipal officials alongside federal officials and judges repeatedly made choices about desegregation that privileged suburban, usually white schools and communities and undermined urban, usually black schools and communities. In this way, busing for desegregation in Nashville joined other earlier and concurrent choices in city planning, in highway construction decisions, in urban renewal: they minimized Hubert's and his North Nashville neighbors' claim to a place in the metropolis. And although white suburbanites rarely perceived it this way, these policy choices furthered their already privileged position in the metropolis.

Visions of metropolitan economic growth linking education to labor markets shaped the curriculum and structure of Hubert's schooling as well. Previously a relatively small community high school of roughly 1,000, Glencliff could accommodate students bused in from other neighborhoods in part because it underwent a renovation and expansion in the late 1970s.

The dollars to fund that work came from a new state vocational education initiative that hoped to make school curriculum into a lever for economic growth and claimed that growth meant more opportunity for all. The state and local effort supporting vocational education meant an expanded Glencliff opened in 1978, just before Hubert Dixon arrived as a ninth grader.[34]

For some black students, the confluence of new vocational offerings and racist judgments on the part of educators meant unfair tracking. Some white teachers had treated Hubert this way in his elementary school years. Hubert was able to establish himself as a strong student, though, in part because he was secure in knowing that his parents "had his back." With resources in money and time not available to many of Nashville's black families, Hubert's mother was able to drive to his school even when he had been bused far away, volunteering her time and making herself a visible advocate for her son. Hubert's family, with college-going experiences of their own, could provide the information and familiarity that helped him navigate a large and complex high school in which academic and guidance supports were not always immediately visible or reached black and white students unevenly. Hubert Dixon III graduated from Glencliff in 1982, and continued on successfully to complete college.[35]

When Hubert Dixon credited his own success to family knowledge and support, he highlighted a core reality in the experience of desegregation for many of Nashville's black students. Desegregation taxed black children and families much more than it did white children and families. Therefore— and particularly for those with fewer economic or social resources— desegregation opened up new barriers to educational success. For black students who lacked the family resources Hubert enjoyed, for those students who did not "know to ask about" these supports, high school completion and college-going remained much less likely than for white students.[36] Clear inequalities of both educational opportunity and outcome remained visible in Nashville's schools.[37]

Alongside powerful public narratives about segregation, desegregation, and inequality, Hubert Dixon III crafted his own explanations for his experience in Nashville schools. He identified benefits of desegregation, recalling that being a "federal agent" for desegregation was "worth it" in the ways that it shaped his schooling and his life favorably. He spoke appreciatively even as he noted the visible inequalities in the "methodology" of busing as he saw it. But a wide gap opened between dominant public narratives about desegregation and the experiences Hubert and his peers knew directly. Local narratives about desegregation paid far more attention to white resistance to desegregation—especially, in Dixon's high school years, to concern about "white flight"— than to questions of equality in the experience of desegregation. In the same years Hubert Dixon navigated Glencliff's halls, negotiated new friendships, and bonded with black and white friends at football, public discourse continued to carry demeaning and at times hateful messages about black students. Dominant narratives did little to reckon with the many and powerful roots of educational inequality that had shaped the spatial and curricular organization of Hubert's schooling. Nor did they leave much space to acknowledge the more positive experiences he attributed to desegregation as well, or to take stock of what Dixon and tens of thousands of other Nashville students had accomplished as "federal agents" of desegregation.

An astute observer of the city he called home, Hubert Dixon III saw desegregation's paradoxes, its expansions of opportunity and its persistent restrictions and limits, its inequalities made and remade.

## A Note on Terms

### Busing, Statistical Desegregation, and Inequality of Educational Opportunity

"Busing" is in many ways a misnomer. The use of the term in relationship to desegregation recast a quotidian reality—children rode buses to school—as a novel intervention. School bus transportation for desegregation formed only a portion of what contemporaries gathered under the heading of "busing." As of 1979, more than one-quarter of American schoolchildren attended school in districts under court or federal regulatory pressure for desegregation. Among these, roughly 30 percent were reassigned by their districts from one school to another to increase desegregation. Yet in the peak years of desegregation, because so many children were already riding buses, the number of American schoolchildren who traveled to school via bus within desegregating districts increased by a mere 5 percent. Nashville's 1971 desegregation plan brought a much larger initial increase, but there too the public debates over "busing" turned on much more than the number of students on buses. Here the term "busing" signals not only changes in student transportation, but rezoning, student assignment, and the many related policy choices involved in seeking extensive school desegregation across multiple neighborhood lines.[38]

Broader terms like "desegregation" and "integration" often slide into use without sufficient clarity. The term "desegregation" describes here the broad legal, administrative, and social processes that followed *Brown*, not a specific outcome. "Statistical desegregation" refers to one basic measure—how many white and how many black students attend school with one another? Statistical desegregation became the key measure of desegregation in both legal processes and school administration in Nashville, as in countless desegregating districts, from the late 1960s onward. Exactly how much statistical desegregation was enough remained deeply contested. Whatever the exact target, the measure emphasized what educator Asa Hilliard calls "body-mixing," distinct from other goals—such as an egalitarian ethos in schools, social learning between young people, or full equality of opportunity and outcome across racial categories—often attached to the "integration" Hubert Dixon III spoke of in hopeful tones. The tightly bounded notion of statistical desegregation serves to highlight the space between "body mixing" and these other, broader, and crucial ambitions.[39]

Desegregation in Nashville, as in nearly all school districts, focused on divisions between students by racial category alone. At times statistical desegregation reduced segregation by class, but just as frequently it increased it. Nashville courts, like courts across the country, did in some cases approve as statistically desegregated school populations of poor black and poor white students together. Class markers and class divisions appeared in both public debate about busing and in some cases in policy discussions, but the focus of Nashville's desegregation efforts remained on the categories of black students and white students, in a city that remained biracial more than multiracial into the 1990s.

Speaking of desegregation requires a definition of "segregation" as well. Intentionally to avoid the false dichotomies of de jure versus de facto segregation (which come in for investigation later), "segregation" here applies to any school, neighborhood, or occupation that is all or nearly all white people or all or nearly all black people. This terminology does not ignore the reality that all-black or all-white spaces are at times expressions of voluntary affiliation rather than division. But it acknowledges the impossibility of identifying any twentieth-century US school or community as somehow existing outside of the pressures of historic, if not current, state action to encourage segregation. Further, it avoids the tendency to obscure state-sanctioned segregation under the label of individual or group choice.[40]

*Making the Unequal Metropolis* emphasizes equality and inequality of educational *opportunity*, to keep a firm focus on ways that school policy choices continued to distribute resources—material, human, and social—unequally even within policy interventions ostensibly targeting equality. Without effort to equalize not only the physical and human resources students encountered in schools, but also the quality of their experience in those schools and the extent to which their schooling made them and their communities feel valued, equal educational opportunity remained elusive.[41] Inequalities of opportunity remained strong along racial categories, while inequalities by class grew significantly as desegregation unfolded in Nashville.

Education discourse in the early twenty-first century shifted away from consideration of educational opportunity in favor of educational outcomes, often in the form of talk about a racial "achievement gap" measured by standardized test scores. The achievement gap discourse, while valuable as a call to action, risks bypassing the reality of historical and contemporary inequalities of opportunity. Snapshots of unequal outcomes can become divorced from causal explanations, at worst implying or leaving unchallenged deep-seated notions that such inequalities stem not from policy choices but from purportedly "racial" characteristics. *Making the Unequal Metropolis* seeks to root understanding of contemporary inequalities, of both opportunity and outcomes, in the long history of policy choices that become visible in examining segregation and desegregation.[42]

# PART ONE

# Making Inequality, 1945–1968

# CHAPTER ONE

# Metropolitan Visions
# of Segregation and Growth

In the post–World War II decades, in Nashville as in most American cities, highway construction, urban renewal, and public housing construction reorganized urban space, while the suburban landscape of tract housing spread ever farther outward. Both urban renewal and suburban expansion in Nashville provided venues for planners, developers, and educators to articulate how they understood the relationship between schools, neighborhoods, and segregation.

These years demonstrated clearly how interactions between schools and markets in land and housing made segregation and educational inequality. City planning practice used schools to define neighborhoods; city officials supported real estate developers in their efforts to link their new subdivisions to particular schools, and urban renewal projects joined construction of segregated schools and segregated public housing. Schools became entangled with—in fact, participated in—the making of segregation in land markets. The nexus of school, neighborhood, and segregation within government policy and practice built segregation into the metropolitan landscape in ways that later efforts at desegregation struggled, incompletely, to undo.

These decades also illustrate well the power of the pursuit of economic growth and its impact in shaping the landscape. Growth advocates put urban renewal to use toward growth, hoping to create a commercial downtown, industrial zones, and residential suburbs that could encourage new or relocating businesses to choose Nashville. Segregation was a goal and racism an enabler in growth-focused urban renewal. Segregation helped white elites consolidate the power needed to appropriate land for redevelopment, while portraying particular parts of the metropolitan landscape and their inhabitants less worthy, more appropriate for expropriation and displacement. Although the city's hope for a pro-business facade of moderation helped confront some of racism's manifestations—as when business and municipal leaders pushed to resolve student sit-in protests by desegregating downtown lunch counters—growth agendas more frequently reinforced rather than challenged racism and segregation.[1]

Growth advocates not only remade the physical landscape of their city, but its municipal political landscape as well. The idea of metropolitan consolidation—joining a city and its surrounding county into a single municipal jurisdiction—drew interest and discussion in many American cities in the 1950s, but rarely came to pass. Beginning in the early 1950s, Nashville's elite explored the consolidation of the City of Nashville and surrounding Davidson County into a single metropolitan jurisdiction. After a failed referendum in 1958, consolidation's allies won in 1962, inaugurating in 1963 the "Metropolitan Government of Nashville–Davidson County." Some white and black leaders feared that economic decline and fiscal instability would come with a city core becoming more black, and more poor, as white out-migration continued. But the most powerful voices for consolidation were local growth-minded elites confident in both their own power and the deep foundation of segregation sub-dividing the metropolis. Segregation did not depend on the city line, and, as consolidation's longer trajectory ultimately showed, could remain firm without it.

## Post–World War II Nashville

Historically a trading center rather than an industrial or manufacturing base, at the end of the war Nashville did not depend on one dominant economic sector. By 1950 the industrial landscape included AVCO, building aircraft and components; May Hosiery Mills, producing socks and clothing; and on the eastern shore of the Cumberland River as it curved past downtown, the Nashville Bridge Company, manufacturing steel components, ships and barges.[2] Yet manufacturing never drove Nashville's economy. In 1950 the city and county's 34,400 manufacturing jobs were outmatched by the 75,350 in nonmanufacturing sectors. A fifth of those jobs came from government employment, both in city government and the state offices located around the Capitol. Another fifth were in retail trades, and a fifth in services.[3]

The finance, insurance, and real estate sector reported only 5,700 employees in September 1950, but this sector—particularly its white male leadership—enjoyed outsized influence in local political affairs before and through World War II. Nashville functioned as a trade and finance center for southern agriculture from the nineteenth century.[4] The city's two largest insurance firms, American Life and Casualty and National Life, saw significant growth during the war and just after. Their corporate heads, alongside bank presidents and real estate developers, became increasingly influential in municipal politics, backing successful candidates for mayor and galvanizing reforms that concentrated more municipal power in that office.[5]

At the close of the war, the finance, insurance, and real estate leadership stood generally—if not unanimously—in favor of Nashville's economic expansion and the use of municipal government in this direction. Their views accorded with the editorial stance of the Nashville morning paper, the *Tennessean*; the afternoon *Nashville Banner* remained more skeptical about aligning government power behind growth.[6] Some manufacturers also expressed less enthusiasm about the growth efforts of groups like the chamber of commerce, fearing competition for the area's workers.[7]

If Nashville's white elite left World War II focused on growth, many black Nashville residents—like their counterparts nationwide—exited the war further energized to achieve political equality and representation commensurate with their one-third share of the city population. Although Davidson County ended the local poll tax in 1943 (to combat the influence of political machines that paid voters' poll taxes en masse), the state of Tennessee increased its poll tax in 1945. *The Globe* newspaper, published by the National Baptist Publishing Board's Boyd family and edited by the president of the Nashville NAACP, expressed resentment at the assumption that all black Tennesseans were poor and could be so easily disfranchised. The tax increase energized registration drives and black political organizing.[8] In one majority-black city ward from 1948 to 1952, registered black voters more than doubled. Black political views were not monolithic. The City-County Democratic Civic League drew the majority of black supporters, while attorney Coyness Ennix led a "separatist" Solid Block organization in 1947, criticizing the "traditional" League.[9]

Black Nashvillians did not drive city politics, but they organized themselves into a needed part of the city's governing coalition. A 1949 charter amendment, for which then Vice Mayor Raphael Benjamin (Ben) West claimed credit, made council seats district (rather than larger ward) based. Two districts chose Z. Alexander Looby and Robert E. Lillard as councilmen, the city's first black elected representatives since Reconstruction. Looby and Lillard were strong and respected members of local government, but with only two voices on a twenty-one-member body, their power remained disproportionately limited even if they voted together across their differences. In citywide politics, black voters' power to tip an election yielded a mix of real gains and empty promises. Mayor West, who took office in 1951, appointed Ennix to the city school board, and later in the decade desegregated the city golf course and municipally run restaurants. West was the first mayoral candidate to speak at Fisk University's Race Relations Institute and cultivated a sense of responsiveness to black constituents' interests. But he never delivered on many promises, including desperately needed infrastructure improvements in historically black city neighborhoods.[10]

Emerging from the war years, Nashville had much more political will to use government to make change. But for whom, and to what ends? In city planning practice that bound together neighborhood development, schools, and segregation; in urban renewal projects that relocated or refined segregation; and in the new architecture of a consolidated metropolitan government, Nashville's government went to work in favor of growing a segregated metropolis.

## How Planners Saw Schools in the Metropolis

Although historical studies of education have paid little attention to city planners, both planning thought and planning practice knew the power of schools to mark and shape the landscape, at times in ways that encouraged segregation and inequality.[11] The Planning Commission of Nashville and Davidson County came into its own in the late 1940s and 1950s, and, alongside the Nashville Housing Authority, gained increasing influence as federal housing and urban renewal dollars flowed into the city. Both agencies drew on concepts and traditions circulating in planning practice nationally to shape the local built environment through school construction, highway building, urban renewal, and public housing. In the process, planners reinforced enduring tropes about different constituents in the metropolis: of urban poor people as burdensome and businesses and outlying areas as contributory and productive; of individual fault rather than systemic neglect. When these ideas mixed with planning commitments to homogeneity in population and land use, they cast segregation as both natural and a necessary condition for growth.

As city planning defined itself as a profession in the early decades of the twentieth century, pioneering planners imagined cities tidily sorted into separate and homogenous districts both by land use and types of people. They had a prescriptive vision of the city, one that reflected their progressive-minded "search for order." National planning leaders like John Nolen and Harland Bartholomew went beyond dividing residential from industrial and commercial uses to suggest separate neighborhoods:

one space for blue-collar white workers, another "segregated fine residence section," separate from a "Negro neighborhood." This vision of the subdivided city found support in local zoning codes that, in Nashville as elsewhere, were heavily influenced by real estate developers invested in segregation. Both real estate markets and planning practices operated in line with the "racial theory of property value," equating segregated white spaces with higher property values and black residence as a threat to this value.[12]

Subdividing the city had a long history in social science research that aimed to describe the city, to create an empirical base from which to prescribe social reform. In turn-of-the-century New York's Lower East Side, reformers mapped the concentration of health problems like the incidence of tuberculosis. W. E. B. DuBois conducted a house-by-house survey of physical and social conditions, published in 1899 as *The Philadelphia Negro*. In 1907, the Russell Sage Foundation helped to expand this approach to document an entire city in its *Pittsburgh Survey*.[13]

City planners picked up on this effort to make empirical, even scientific, descriptions of the city and use them to support their own prescriptions. In St. Louis, Bartholomew generated detailed maps showing districts where houses lacked bathrooms. He also created charts comparing city revenue generated from, and expenses needed on behalf of, each city district, which set the groundwork for later judgments about who was deserving of what services.[14] Systematic spatial understandings of urban life became available both for social reform and for growth-minded development.[15]

Nashville's planning community, among the more active nationally, adapted planning practices from elsewhere and helped to further them. In the late 1920s, downtown construction and congestion prompted the Nashville Chamber of Commerce to push for a city charter amendment to create a planning commission, a goal of business progressives in many other cities of the day. The first head of the commission was Gerald Gimre, a University of Illinois–trained planner who dominated Nashville's planning activities from 1931 through the 1960s. Like Gimre, some key planners were recruited to their posts by the chamber. And like Gimre, many came from outside the South, and had studied or worked elsewhere before coming to Nashville. Their work was not uniquely southern, shaped instead by the interaction of national planning trends and local conditions.[16]

Nashville's planners and its social reformers both tried to map and rationalize their understandings of the city. Planner Gimre launched a detailed survey of housing conditions and the distribution of black and white families and individuals. Meanwhile local sociologists led the effort to create census tract boundaries for Nashville, the first city in the South to have these instead of the larger ward boundaries. Vanderbilt sociologist Walter Reckless explained that ward units "did not show the natural distribution of social phenomena of the city since they so frequently cut across local segregations of population."[17] Mapping and census work appealed as well to Charles S. Johnson of Fisk University's Department of Social Sciences and later head of its Race Relations Institute and Department. Like DuBois before him, Johnson made the study of black peoples' lives in Nashville one of the centerpieces of his research program at Fisk and wanted to survey and describe "the city and the Negro areas of the city" for both research and activist purposes.[18] Working in the mid-1930s amid frank Jim Crow segregation, Johnson and Reckless hoped that census tracks more precisely aligned to homogenous population groupings by race would further their ability to see and then remedy the needs of Nashville's black residents.[19] Gimre and other planners approached mapping and the matter of homogeneity differently than did Reckless and Johnson. The social-science and social-reform interest in description became intertwined with later planners' highly prescriptive and at times frankly segregating notions of the city.

The nationally influential planning concept of the "neighborhood unit" stood at the intersection of descriptive efforts to map the city and prescriptive efforts to create a city ordered by distinct and homogenously grouped, meaning segregated, land uses. It guided how Nashville planners thought about land use and residence. In the 1920s, New York–based planner Clarence A. Perry diagrammed an ideal neighborhood in his work on the influential *Regional Plan of New York*. Like other planners—including the British planners Clarence Stein and Ebenezer Howard, who offered their own vision of the unit—Perry made the neighborhood the fundamental building block of the city.[20]

Schools were at the literal and figurative center of Perry's and his colleagues' neighborhood unit. The school, and particularly an elementary school to serve the neighborhood's young children, defined the population and expanse of the neighborhood. For Perry and others, the neighborhood was the area within a half-mile radius around an elementary school, "preferably 160 acres," but "in any case . . . enough people to require one elementary school." Three elementary school–based neighborhoods would join together to support a local high school. And ideally, neighborhood institutions (like schools and churches) would occupy the geographic center of the unit.[21] Sitting at the literal and figurative center of neighborhood community, schools became the binding agent for residence and community in Perry's and his colleagues' neighborhood unit.

Linking school and neighborhood through proximity seems common-

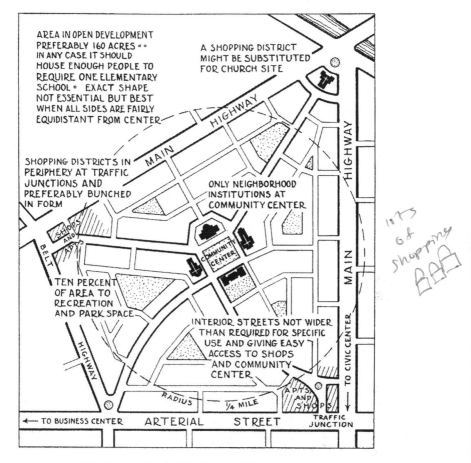

1.1. Clarence Perry's design for a neighborhood unit.

sensical. However, the notion of neighborhood involved presumed homogeneity along a variety of measures. Homogeneity was in fact crucial to many planners' lofty goals for neighborhood units, which by the late 1940s they saw as part of the prescription to counter the ills of postwar life. The neighborhood, with its comfortable community ethos, could counter isolation in a culture that has "created a way of life hostile to neighborliness" which tended "to create mass men in a mass culture—the raw material for a totalitarian society."[22] Perry argued that the neighborhood unit's homogeneity would protect property values and enable positive interactions between people who felt they were part of a community—interactions that he implied could not happen without homogeneity. Mixing his commitments to segregation and the centrality of schools, Perry explained, "The great foe to community life is heterogeneity. The [neighborhood unit] . . . produces homogeneity. Put like people together and give them common facilities to care for and associations among them are bound to spring into existence." Perry was even more blunt elsewhere, identifying "racial and social homogeneity" as necessary for community development. Schools, as a central, defining element of the neighborhood unit, were the ideal "common facilities to care for."[23]

As of 1959 Nashville planners applied neighborhood unit planning to their metropolitan region. They plotted eighty-one "planning units," which they then grouped into sixteen "local communities."[24] Nashville's planning units echoed the ideas of Nolen and Bartholomew and descended directly from Perry's, Stein's, and Howard's neighborhood units. Nashville planner Irving Hand wrote to an audience of planners nationally to extol the benefits of planning with the neighborhood unit in urban and suburban areas. Hand frankly stated support for segregated neighborhoods: "If the families in the area have similar forms of conduct, tradition, customs, and values, then homes, church, school, recreation area, and local shops may help to form and retain a neighborhood unit that provides a satisfactory environment."[25] "Similar ethnic groups" helped define the planning unit, as did "a centrally located elementary school within easy walking distance of every home in the neighborhood."[26]

When Nashville embraced the neighborhood unit, other leaders in the profession indicted the concept for its "casual and unconscionable acceptance of segregation."[27] Like many in the planning profession nationally by the 1950s, Hand acknowledged criticisms of the neighborhood planning unit but defended the concept as useful: "Applying the neighborhood unit idea may result in social and economic homogeneity, for instance," but the concept remained useful because "it permits more effective planning."[28] Hand thought of neighborhood homogeneity as a "natural" result of market forces and individual preferences, not of concern to local government unless "illegal" means were used to exclude an "unwanted" group.[29] Running parallel to the emerging discourse of "de facto segregation," Hand offered a conceptual distinction that conveniently obscured the policy choices of agencies like his own. Nashville planners thus illustrated a local variant of the national pattern in postwar housing policy: powerful government policy in housing intentionally recast in the terms of free-market, private enterprise.[30]

Nashville marshaled its planning units in highway planning, land use, population projections, and urban renewal studies.[31] When Nashville's city planners set about mapping and making long-range projections for school

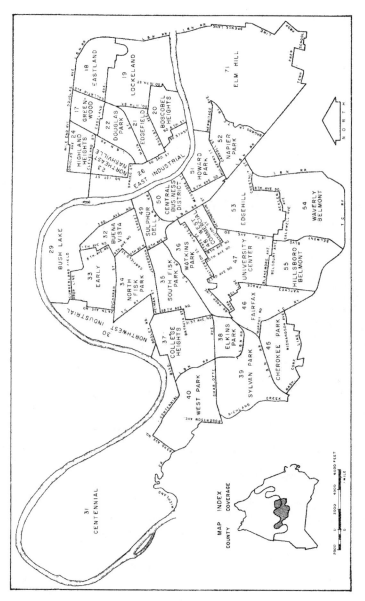

1.2. Planning units in Nashville, Tennessee, 1959. With permission of the Metropolitan Planning Department, Nashville, Tennessee.

facilities in the 1960s, they cited Hand's work and continued the logic of the planning unit to divide the metropolitan region and plan school buildings. Into the 1970s planners referred to the neighborhood unit as a foundational element of their work on school facility planning, and the consequences of earlier decisions lasted decades longer.[32] Following earlier generations of planners, their work bound together neighborhood, segregation, and schooling, and helped create the very homogeneity imagined in the neighborhood unit.

The neighborhood unit concept aligned also with how private housing developers imagined the communities they were creating and marketing in the 1950s and onward. Developers saw profit in linking neighborhood, school, and segregation, and both the Nashville and Davidson County school districts cooperated in their efforts. White developers wanted schools for their new (and segregated) subdivisions, and were willing to help subsidize these schools by transferring land outright, selling it to the school district at reduced price, or building needed road or sewerage infrastructure at their own expense. Moses McKissack, a black Nashville-based developer and pioneer in the construction of black suburbs nationally, also saved land for a school in his College Heights subdivision (near the campus of segregated black Tennessee Agricultural and Industrial College). He sold it to the board of education at a 50 percent discount to facilitate the construction of a new, segregated black school—named after himself and opened in 1954.[33] McKissack built for black home buyers (although he might have sold to white purchasers if they had been interested). Several of his white colleagues took the same approach, as in the construction of the Charlotte Park subdivision and the school its developers lobbied to secure. Ads for the development showed winding suburban streets moving outward from the school at the center.[34]

At times, developers petitioned school administrators not just for a school, but for a specific school to match their development. And they skillfully wove together their interests and what they thought to be the interests of the school system. The right school could help define privileged and more valuable suburban spaces. The developers of West Meade Estates, a 220-lot subdivision in the southwestern quadrant of Davidson County, lobbied county school superintendent J. E. Moss to ensure that their homes be zoned to Hillwood High School and its feeder schools, avoiding the more rural and generally poorer communities found at two other (and still all-white) local schools. As the developers explained, their targeted buyers "have a reluctance and more often, flatly refuse to buy homes placed in" school zones they felt to be less desirable than Hillwood.[35] Builders at

Hillwood Park subdivision also wanted a Hillwood zoning. They explained that it was "inherent in the Democratic capitalistic system" for parents to want to send their children to class-homogenous schools. Making sure that school officials appreciated their own stake in this matter, they reminded the superintendent: "There is considerable [sic] more tax income on a $30,000 house than there is on a $15,000 house."[36] The class- and race-homogenous, school-centered, and supposedly property value–preserving planning unit found allies in both public and private practice in Nashville. Superintendent Moss replied to Hillwood Park developers with a general assurance. "The Board makes an effort to avoid zoning low income groups with high income groups as far as practical," putting into his own words the neighborhood-unit attachment to homogeneity.[37] Hillwood's developers illustrated that schools mattered in defining a suburban belt of privilege, even within a single school district. This belt of privilege measured itself not only from the inside, by distance from black and white poor urban residents in the city core, but from the outside as well, distinguishing itself from the white (and a few black) farmers and tradespeople who made up Nashville's rural fringe.

From their establishment in the 1930s, Nashville's planning commission and housing authority became key venues for imagining a segregated metropolis; the school district's general approach, as well as specific decisions about school construction and zoning, helped realize this vision. Urban renewal and public housing dollars flowed to Nashville from the 1930s onward, and in some cases helped realize planners' imagined relationship between school, housing, and segregation in brick and mortar.

## Urban Renewal: Consolidating Residential and Educational Segregation

Nashville's housing and planning agencies emerged from World War II ready to capitalize on developing federal programs in slum clearance and urban renewal.[38] Nashville received a volume of urban renewal and housing funds disproportionate to its size.[39] From projects that razed large districts, constructed new housing projects, or undertook broad housing renovation, urban renewal funds helped remake the local landscape to suit elite hopes for growth and to deepen segregation. Consistently, the search for economic growth operated to rationalize privileging white Nashville residents over their black counterparts.

An early proposal for a new municipal auditorium captured the tenor of later efforts. The chamber of commerce led the late-1940s effort to select

1.3. Mayor Ben West (center) and Coordinators Committee for Urban Renewal and Redevelopment, 1957. Gerald Gimre is seated to the left of West; Irving Hand stands on the right. Courtesy of Metropolitan Archives of Nashville-Davidson County.

a downtown location, to be razed before construction. The chosen site was the "center of the most important Negro business section in the city of Nashville," as one occupant put it, home to law and professional offices, the city's major theater for black patrons, the black-owned National Baptist Publishing Board, and several small businesses and restaurants.[40] Only one building within the site boundaries could remain: the white-owned Catholic church.[41] From headquarters just outside the site, *The Globe*, a black-owned newspaper, called the plan "drastic, fantastic, and probably approved."[42] The auditorium bond issue failed at first, but the message remained clear: a coalition of downtown, growth-minded businessmen and their allies in local planning agencies would push for major changes to the downtown landscape, to "clean up" Nashville, in the words of one white leader. The segregated nature of the downtown business district made it easier to target black commercial areas for renewal, with the expropriation and displacement leaving most white businesses (if not white landlords) untouched.[43]

Later projects targeted residential as well as commercial areas, and drew associations between long-neglected city areas and the people who lived there to justify clearance and displacement. Tennessee's grand, neoclassical state capitol sat atop the highest point in Nashville's center, commanding a view to the south and east of downtown and the serpentine Cumberland River, and to the far west of rolling green hills and affluent, segregated white residential communities. The landscape just to the north and northwest, on the very slopes of the hill the capitol crowned, provided brutal contrast to the capital city's aspirations of grandeur. On this steep incline and the flat land stretching north to the Louisville and Nashville (L&N) railroad lines, poor African American and some white individuals and families made their homes in conditions of extraordinary privation. In the late 1940s, while local leaders drew plans for the municipal auditorium, leaning wood-frame shacks sat just a few hundred yards from the state capitol door, their residents lived without indoor plumbing. They shared outdoor

1.4. Capitol Hill before redevelopment, including outdoor privies. Courtesy of Metropolitan Archives of Nashville-Davidson County. When printed in a "City Planning" brochure published by the Nashville Housing Authority for an exhibit on urban renewal projects in the downtown area, the caption read, "Above the hill, the state, above the state, the Heavens." (Quotation from "City Planning," Vanderbilt University Special Collections, Molly Todd Papers, box 23).

1.5. Clarke and Rapuano planning model for Capitol Hill
redevelopment, 1952. Copyright Ezra Stoller/Esto.

spigots and outhouses. The city had not paved the streets or provided suf-
ficient drainage, so heavy rains brought "miserable flood conditions."[44]
Once-stately nineteenth-century mansions lined the western edge of the
Capitol Hill area, now carved into boarding houses, described by planner
Gerald Gimre as centers of "nefarious enterprises," "low Negro rackets" in
prostitution, and high rates of petty crime.[45]

Representations of Capitol Hill depicted its physical environment as
inseparable from is occupants' character, and deficits in each seemed to
reinforce the unworthiness of the other. Both journalists and government officials traded in metaphors that linked decrepit spaces with subhuman existence and subhuman inhabitants, and suggested that the only
appropriate remedy to both was the bulldozer. Housing official Charles
Hawkins spoke of urban renewal projects as "turning up the corner of the
rug," while J. M. Miller, who oversaw relocation for the NHA, portrayed
the more than 1,100 people within 351 families and the 279 single residents of the area as feeling at home in the slums and rarely bothering to
pay rent.[46] Louise Davis, a features reporter for the *Tennessean*, said that the

residents, "like human rats," were "not offended by the filth and ugliness that shocks us."[47]

The *Tennessean* identified Capitol Hill as an area in which the city had been "remiss in civic responsibility," but most representations implied that the "outrageous" slum existed without culpability for anyone except its residents.[48] Poverty itself became a justification for government neglect. As consulting urban planner Gilmore Clarke put it in 1960, "People in Nashville, Tennessee, just don't bother much about paving roads in front of Negro houses. I once asked a southerner why they let the roads deteriorate in the Negro district and he replied, 'We don't collect much taxes from that area so I don't see that there is any reason to spend a lot of money there.'"[49] Imagery of filth and blame helped white planners and boosters rationalize renewal and distract Nashville residents from the less easily reconciled aspects of the Capitol Hill story: irrefutable evidence of long-term government neglect, and the displacement of viable businesses in the project area.

Despite the deplorable conditions, Capitol Hill's redevelopment "had less to do with the needs of the people [than] to improve the view from Capitol Hill," as one consulting planner explained the project decades later.[50] Domenico Annese's remarks captured the central fact of urban renewal in Nashville, as in cities like Chicago and Atlanta: the presence of poor, primarily African American families and individuals living in miserable conditions provided a plausible target for urban renewal and made a compelling case for action. But in fact, the abysmal conditions that state and local governments had witnessed but not rectified over decades were a foil to renewal projects' fundamental intent: to remove slums as barriers to growth, increase area property values, and draw new businesses. To the extent that local activists saw opportunity for improved housing or services, their agendas only partly overlapped with this broader growth agenda.[51]

As they continued to do through the 1970s, Nashville planners and their business allies organized speedily to claim available federal redevelopment dollars. The chamber of commerce put banker Walter Diehl at the head of an urban renewal committee.[52] On word of the developing Housing Act of 1949, Diehl, Nashville Housing Authority head Gimre and colleagues quickly mobilized and contracted the New York landscape and planning firm Clarke, Rapuano and Holleran, known for their work on Robert Moses's West Side Highway in Manhattan, to guide the design of a new Capitol Hill.[53] These local allies moved so quickly that when Charles Hawkins delivered Nashville's proposal to Washington, he noted with pleasure that the program director had not had time to purchase a desk chair for himself, or print up official application blanks.[54]

Clarke, Rapuano and Holleran planned to remove all residential and commercial structures from the northern and western sides of the capitol as well as commercial plots to the east. They imagined the northern slope as a mixture of parklike green space and terraces for parking, with a curved four-lane parkway to ring the base of the hill, reserving lots on both sides of this parkway for private office, hotel, or residential development.[55]

Guided by its vision of growth and a cleaner Capitol Hill, the project made meager arrangements for rehousing the areas' residents. As planner Gilmore Clarke, founding partner of Clarke, Rapuano and Holleran, recalled well after the project's completion, creating housing near the capitol would violate the "peculiar local customs" of southern cities.[56] Initial plans for the project included relocation maps, with bold arrows flying off of Capitol Hill to five extant or new public housing projects (all segregated black) around the city. But just as frequently, displaced residents navigated the inhospitable Nashville housing market on their own. Hill residents received little actual assistance in relocating, and only a small portion of residents did in fact move into public housing.[57] As of 1969, the NHA had placed only 20 percent of families from urban renewal project areas into public housing, and an additional 9 percent into private housing. "The rest of the families relocate themselves," a housing administrator explained.[58] Housing displacements, even from poor quality housing, only worsened the preexisting "scarcity of Negro housing accommodations in Nashville" where, as in many other urban renewal sites, new areas of substandard housing developed just outside the boundary of the renewal area. One such area, with wood-frame shacks and no plumbing, took shape only a few blocks to the north of the Capitol Hill project—but just far enough north not to disturb the view from the capitol.[59]

Lack of attention to resettlement was one prompt for Councilman Z. Alexander Looby to vote against the Capitol Hill project, a vote joined by Robert Lillard and three other councilmen serving urban areas. When the plans passed the council over their objection, Looby denounced the body for having "sold the Negroes of Nashville down the river."[60] Looby, Lillard, and other black Nashville residents were most angered by the project's impact on Nashville's black professional office and business district, also on Capitol Hill. The area's 143 "legitimate" businesses did not appear in most representations of the area. Photographers from the *Tennessean*, the *Banner*, and other publications captured the project from the same angle— looking up at the tall stone capitol from the northwest, across the rooftops of low, rickety wood-frame houses and a few businesses. This angle left out evidence of the project's takings to the east, where it claimed many

businesses in fine condition.[61] Although the statutes authorizing urban renewal emphasized its public purposes, redevelopment allowed what the *Tennessean* described as the "condemnation of private, non-slum property for
later re-sale to other private investors."[62] Landowners on the hill—black-led
organizations such as the St. John African Methodist Episcopal Church;
white-owned businesses serving black clientele, such as the Bijou Theatre;
and white-owned businesses such as H. G. Hill Realty—brought legal challenges to the project but were unsuccessful.[63] One court acknowledged that
none of the businesses involved were "unsightly, unsafe, or unsanitary," yet
found the "public purpose" of the project to justify clearance. Landowners
saw the taking of private property for sale "at a profit to private enterprise."
In fact, most sales were for less than the cost of acquisition and clearance.
Thus public funds subsidized new private development in the name of
growth.[64]

Private redevelopment cast as "public purpose" became central to the
chamber of commerce's support for the project.[65] The organization with-
held its crucial support until the project set significant land aside for private development.[66] Capitol Hill's focus on private development concerned
some, even within the pro-growth chamber of commerce, who noted the
expanded use of government funds and power in ways that could threaten
private property rights and fiscal restraint. In 1951 the Nashville Chamber
of Commerce stated opposition to "new federal spending commitments
excepting those directly essential to national defense."[67] A fiscal justification for urban renewal helped smooth these contradictions. Renewal advocates argued that the city would profit via increased property values and
increased tax revenues, and recover all costs within ten years. They promised as well that razing Capitol Hill slums would end supposedly expensive
demands on police, fire, and other municipal services. It was businessmen,
Mayor Ben West explained, who "pay most of the cost of city services," and
that slums thus "cost businessmen money."[68] Rhetorical turns like these
helped the chamber of commerce consolidate a strong position in favor of
the use of federal and local dollars and power toward growth.

Some form of intervention for Capitol Hill was doubtless necessary,
with outhouses, open sewers, and dirt floors long tolerated by Nashville's
municipal and state governments. For those residents who made it into
public housing, urban renewal meant access to improved if imperfect residential facilities. When most residents found themselves still subject to
a segregated and exploitative housing market, the project simply shifted
Nashville's housing crisis a few blocks north. The Capitol Hill Redevelopment Project did, however, have clear accomplishments. It built a stronger

consensus around and leadership cadre for growth than had been in place earlier. The chamber of commerce never represented all of Nashville's business elite, nor was that elite always unified; but the organization had consolidated itself further in the embrace of growth. Justifications for urban renewal that linked a humanitarian veneer with private and public fiscal interest overcame reluctance to embrace sweeping government projects, and particularly those supported with federal dollars.[69] As the Capitol Hill project attracted visiting delegations from Bethlehem, Pennsylvania, and Columbia, South Carolina, as well as speaking invitations in Baton Rouge, Louisiana, and inclusion in a St. Louis urban renewal exposition, Nashville representatives boasted that "a determined city actually can reach down and pull cancerous slums out by the roots."[70]

Nashville's commitment to urban renewal for growth continued into a range of other projects in the city, which added up to fully one quarter of the area of the City of Nashville engaged in renewal at some point. A "University Center" urban renewal project began in 1961 to link Nashville's premiere Vanderbilt University with smaller Belmont College in clearing land for campus expansion.[71] (See figure 4.4.) By 1965, the project emphasized aiding growth in the music industry as well. Clarke and Rapuano planner Domenico Annese recalled that country music industry advocates pushed to shift the boundaries of the University Center project to include the streets on which recording companies and music studios had been operating in converted early-twentieth-century bungalows. Not only would inclusion in the University Center project help businesses connected to country music move to the developing Music Row, but country musicians and industry representatives could profit handsomely as landlords by purchasing land included in the project area still zoned residential, realizing huge increases in value as it was rezoned commercial.[72] As Annese put it, "The musicians knew that they were on to expensive property, and that [renewal] was going to make it more expensive. . . . They were pretty clever, those hillbilly musicians."[73] Having only gradually moved beyond their snobbish reluctance to embrace country music as part of the city's economic landscape, the chamber of commerce in its support of the University Center project identified the goal of helping consolidate Music Row, linked to the new branding of "Music City USA," as part of the mission of the project.[74] From the chamber's perspective, the music industry had economic potential but a troubling down-market image; a newly sleek central business district facilitated by urban renewal could help.[75]

In the late 1950s Mayor Ben West began speaking publicly about another urban renewal project for Nashville that had a more firmly residen-

Music City

1.6. The cover for a 1959 urban renewal exhibition in Nashville: "An adaptation of Blake's creation," by Jack Kershaw. Kershaw was a white supremacist polymath and a leading segregationist organizer during school desegregation in 1957. Courtesy of Vanderbilt University Special Collections.

tial focus. As part of the planning, the Nashville Housing Authority and the Nashville Chamber of Commerce organized a tour of other cities with urban renewal projects underway. Seventeen council members, the head of the Nashville Home Builders Association, and Mayor West—called "argonauts of urban renewal" by a reporter traveling with them—visited Baltimore, Washington, DC, and Philadelphia.[76] In Baltimore, the black members of the delegation were told they could be served only in a private dining room; councilman Z. Alexander Looby immediately left the group, rejoining in Washington, DC. Two others, including councilman Robert Lillard, chose to remain.[77]

The new project targeted East Nashville, and sprawled over more than two thousand acres home to established neighborhoods, as well as industrial and commercial uses. The $24 million project ranked, in both absolute size and in per capita expense, as the largest in the Southeast and one of the largest in the nation.[78] If the Capitol Hill project demonstrated the raw power of city elites to marshal federal dollars in support of a growth ideal despite clear opposition from—and with weak follow-through on the needs of—black Nashville residents, the East Nashville project illustrated how closely federally supported housing construction and schools could connect. Urban renewal projects provided a key venue for expanding segregated housing and schooling in tandem, in the same years in which Nashville's school desegregation efforts began. Urban renewal deepened segregation's foundation in ways that endured through, and beyond, desegregation.

East Nashville was a region of the city more than a single neighborhood, although some identified it as "Nashville's step-child" and "a 'sore-spot' of crime, delinquency, poor housing" and "family degeneracy."[79] Traveling directly across the Cumberland River to the east of downtown in the early 1950s meant crossing a low-lying flood-prone area dominated by light and heavy industrial uses, but interspersed as well with one-story shotgun-style bungalows home to both black and white residents. As the elevation rose, homes and smaller commercial establishments became more substantial, and two low-rise and segregated white public housing projects appeared. As the hill leveled off, the large Victorians of Nashville's first streetcar suburb came into view, but farther to the north and east smaller turn-of-the century and some postwar housing predominated. Although the housing stock was more substantial than that of Capitol Hill, its condition and public services remained inconsistent. Sewer systems were insufficient, some homes remained without indoor plumbing, and many streets were unpaved.[80] The population, scale, and conditions in East Nashville differed greatly from those around the Capitol Hill plan, but the underlying motivation for renewal remained the same. As Mayor Ben West put it, the aim of the program was to "increase the value of every foot of real estate in East Nashville."[81]

The public rhetoric and justifications for the East Nashville project took on strikingly different tone and emphasis than had been the case around Capitol Hill. Even before the initial surveying of East Nashville for project planning, Gerald Gimre reassuringly offered that "such violent disruptions of the landscape [as seen in Capitol Hill] and surroundings need not to be feared by East Nashville families."[82] Not only was Gimre's reassurance missing in the Capitol Hill discourse, but so was his willingness to identify residents of the predominantly white area as families.

Where officials blamed and described Capitol Hill residents in pathological terms, they did not hold East Nashville families responsible for the deterioration of the houses in which they and their neighbors lived. Gimre, West, and other officials noted that deterioration in the area was "due to inherent weaknesses and deficiencies in public services, such as street pattern, utilities, playgrounds, et cetera," and described the project as "doing all the things we should have done 50 years ago."[83] Urban renewal portrayed East Nashville, with a significant constituency of white working- and middle-class residents, in a very different image than it did on predominantly black Capitol Hill. And urban renewal in East Nashville had a different political reception as well, with enthusiastic endorsement from all six of the area's representatives, and a unanimous vote in the council.[84]

When the East Nashville project was in the works, the NHA continued to operate segregated facilities, and had no public housing for black residents in East Nashville. Segregation had long been a core practice of the Nashville Housing Authority, as it was in much public housing nationally. In the 1930s through the early 1950s, the NHA built pairs of projects, one black and one white, and operated them into the early 1960s on a frankly segregated basis.[85]

East Nashville's urban renewal plan went far beyond rehabilitating poor housing and improving infrastructure. The broader project worked to maintain or create two types of sorting in the neighborhood. The first was by land use. Like on Capitol Hill, the East Nashville renewal project sought to consolidate single-use areas, removing remaining residences from commercial and industrial sectors. In East Nashville, new highways marked boundaries between industrial uses on the west, toward the Cumberland River, and residential use on the higher land to the east, with neighborhoods divided by a corridor of commercial space running along Main Street.[86] As highways could divide the landscape into commercial and residential zones, housing construction decisions within urban renewal also firmed up lines of division between black and white residential areas. Planners described East Nashville as "transitional," signaling some concern about the changing boundaries of black residential location. Maintaining firm boundaries that contained low-income and black residents was crucial to the project of "preserving values," particularly for areas of white residence included in the urban renewal zone and the middle-class white areas just adjacent to it.[87]

Housing authority leaders met with community groups to present their plans in East Nashville schools, speaking before all-black audiences at segregated black Meigs School and all-white audiences at nearby segregated white Kirkpatrick School.[88] But schools were more than convenient spaces for presentations. They became central nodes in marking segregated space

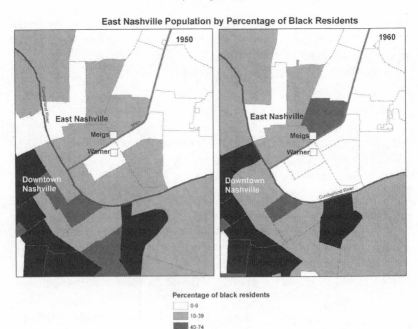

**East Nashville Population by Percentage of Black Residents**

Percentage of black residents
- 0-9
- 10-39
- 40-74
- 75-100

1.7. East Nashville urban renewal area, population by race, and location of Meigs (segregated black) and Warner (segregated white) schools. Population data from 1950 and 1960 US Census, via Minnesota Population Center. National Historical Geographic Information System: Pre-release Version 0.1. Minneapolis: University of Minnesota, 2004, http://www.nhgis.org.

and planning new segregated housing construction.[89] Urban renewal efforts like Capitol Hill related to the neighborhood-unit or planning-unit concept in the most general terms—through their shared interest in both social homogeneity and homogeneous land use. But the East Nashville urban renewal project had a much more direct connection, as the project used segregated schools as anchors and markers for neighborhoods. With a project population more white than black, and with emphasis on residential rehabilitation as much as displacement, the East Nashville project focused on refining boundaries of segregation by further linking housing and schooling.

The East Nashville project area included four schools, one segregated black and the others segregated white. Meigs School had served black students in first through eighth grade, but the board of education expanded it to reach through grade 10 in the summer of 1956. This was a belated attempt to ward off further legal challenges to segregation by moving toward the "separate but equal" standard established by the Supreme Court's 1896 ruling in *Plessy v. Ferguson*.[90] Meigs sat on the north side of the Main Street dividing line; Warner Elementary sat on the south side and was a segregated white school.[91]

Housing officials designated the "Warner School/East Park" area the first demonstration site for the urban renewal project, expanded the school's outdoor facilities, and connected them to adjoining East Park. Warner served children in nearby public housing and single-family homes, some of which were under renovation via urban renewal. Meigs School got a more comprehensive upgrade, with the addition of fourteen classrooms, an auditorium, and a cafeteria (which it had earlier lacked). Previously operating without a playground, its outdoor facilities expanded with a new twenty-acre park behind the school.[92] Just to the north and east of Meigs, in an area it referred to as the "Meigs School/Douglas Park area," the NHA planned its first East Nashville public housing for black residents. The 195-unit complex and its linked and expanded school channeled black residential growth north and west of Main Street, likely in the hopes that it would limit black movement into areas south and east of the Main Street/Gallatin Pike divider.[93] From 1950 to 1970, the East Nashville renewal area's black population grew, but became increasingly concentrated in two census tracts, while the black population in two other tracts decreased through residential clearance.

If black leaders in Nashville were concerned about the increased segregation stemming from the location of new public housing, they were in a poor position to negotiate. The dislocations brought by urban renewal had greatly increased the demand for low-cost housing in the area. The NHA continued to exclude black families from its other projects in East Nashville.[94] A coalition of ministers had formed to press for the inclusion of public housing in the project, especially given shortages exacerbated by urban renewal.[95] Given their frustration about limited attention to housing in the Capitol Hill project, councilmen Looby and Lillard came to support the East Nashville project.

As the East Nashville urban renewal project concentrated black residents north of Main Street, it maintained and even increased the white majority south of Main. The city's largest public housing project, James A. Cayce Homes, with 781 units, and the Edgefield Manor homes with 220 units just across the street, were segregated white facilities.[96] Construction on a segregated low-income development by the Communications Workers of America was under way one block away.[97] The low-income white students in these developments attended either Warner or Kirkpatrick elementary schools, and proceeded to East High School, as would the working- and middle-class white families who lived on the neighboring streets.

Via the East Nashville renewal project, the area became differently segregated than it had been twenty years earlier. Working from notions of neighborhood as defined by homogeneity and by the neighborhood school, the NHA used federal urban renewal dollars to concentrate black residents near newly expanded segregated black schools, as they reinforced nearby segregated white facilities. Urban renewal built upon existing public housing and school construction patterns to deepen residential segregation by both class and color in East Nashville in the late 1950s and early 1960s.

The Meigs and Warner school areas were just a few blocks from one another, as were segregated black and white housing projects. As if to embody the contradictory reality of linked housing and schooling within a geography that could have enabled desegregation had planners or the school board valued it, a municipal photographer climbed up to the rooftop of Meigs School and captured the landscape of public housing units that stretched out before him. The photograph captured the Sam Levy homes, not far away, when its residents were all white.[98] By the late 1960s, the Sam Levy project became all black once the Nashville Housing Authority relaxed the policies that had guarded its all-white projects, and additional and all-black housing had been constructed around Meigs. By then, the view from Meigs's rooftop represented concentrated segregation rather than potential integration. NHA's East Nashville projects, following the city pattern overall, remained as segregated as twenty years earlier: six projects home to 2,281 white residents and five projects home to 2,125 black residents.[99]

By the late 1960s, East Nashville's white families also had multiple incentives to leave the renewal area. Nashville's city and county leadership together eased the relocation process for white residents, and often helped them move outside of the urban renewal zone. Although the East Nashville project respected the City of Nashville boundaries and was administered by the city's Housing Authority, it was interconnected with Tennessee's interstate highway construction program, and that program extended into surrounding Davidson County as well. The county's executive, Judge C. Beverly Briley, in a characteristically entrepreneurial approach to federal programs, applied for urban renewal status for the entire county in 1957. When it was awarded, Davidson County was only the third county nationally to have been so designated. That status made it even easier for residents to choose to locate farther into the suburbs, as they could enjoy a forty-year mortgage with no down payment anywhere in the county.[100] This assistance became meaningful only for those who could find a lender willing to make the loan, much more easily accomplished for white residents than black.

If Briley's effort helped poor and working-class white people move to the suburbs, black buyers remained shut out by discriminatory practices in home finance and real estate sales. However, white families' moves to the suburbs made space for many middle-class black families to move northeast into previously segregated East Nashville neighborhoods like Inglewood. This was the choice made by Alfred Z. Kelley and his family, including young Robert W. Kelley, a few years after Kelley became the lead plaintiff in Nashville's school desegregation case.[101] Over the 1950s and 1960s, the combined effect of increased public housing concentration in East Nashville and the dispersal of middle-class residents to near-in suburban communities intensified the isolation of black and poor families around Meigs. In the long run, urban renewal efforts to renovate houses in concert with expanded schools and parks had been less powerful than programs that facilitated white families' moves to the suburbs. Over the 1970s, black residents moved across the Main Street divider as white residents moved out. The property-value-seeking East Nashville project had largely failed at that goal, but had furthered a landscape of segregation entwining housing and schooling.

Growth-minded urban renewal efforts transformed Nashville's central core. These projects demonstrated the consolidated power of local business elites and their allies in planning and housing offices to make the landscape conform to their vision of growth and segregation. Their efforts added to the ongoing displacements from highway construction and pushed even more Nashville residents with resources—both black and white—to move out of the city and into nearby suburban areas. Their movements, however, did not mean that the city core depopulated. Instead, further public housing construction brought more poor black residents into selected city neighborhoods. The brick-and-mortar construction of segregation remained visible in housing, planning, and school policy, in ways that would continue to shape the urban and metropolitan landscape. Together these policies created the patterns of residential and educational segregation that later necessitated crosstown busing to achieve statistical desegregation.

## United Government in a Divided Landscape

In the same years that Nashville's white business and political leaders marshaled federal dollars for urban renewal projects and transformed the city's physical landscape, they also reworked the basic structure of their government. After more than a decade of planning, discussion, and persuasion, Nashville and Davidson County voters supported a 1962 referendum to consolidate the city and county into a single political unit. In an era of increasing metropolitan fragmentation, many cities discussed the idea, but few built sufficient support for consolidation to make it happen. Where it did, the successful examples were nearly all in the South and West, in cities enamored of growth and business-friendly efficiency on the Sunbelt model.[102]

Metropolitan consolidation and urban renewal were motivated by many of the same concerns, and came about in similar ways. Both aimed at readying Nashville for growth, both originated in exclusive discussions among predominantly white business and political elites before coming before the public, and both reveal the narrowed choices available for black activists. Consolidation removed most jurisdictional lines that in other cities helped reinforce segregation, but Nashville segregation in no way depended on those lines. Finally, consolidation was much less than an equal merger of city and county constituencies. It proceeded largely on suburban terms. The experience of consolidation in Nashville created important opportunities but also left many inequalities untouched by jurisdictional reorganization.

The City of Nashville as of the late 1950s covered just over twenty-three square miles, with boundaries virtually unchanged since 1929, and a population of roughly 140,000. Davidson County's 533 square miles included the residents of the city, its suburbs, and the rural areas that reached to the county line. Tennessee cities lacked home rule, and county legislative delegations used charter revisions to constrain city power. Charter revisions in 1947 and 1949 strengthened the office of the mayor, but also kept county operatives in key and separate agencies. A county judge was the executive who convened the quarterly court of sixteen members. City residents—still more than half of the county's total—had only one seat on the quarterly court, which had not been reapportioned since 1905. The disproportionality mirrored the rural-dominated state legislature that became the Supreme Court's test case for the one-man, one-vote principle of *Baker v. Carr*.[103] For black voters, underrepresentation was a problem in the city—where the 38 percent black population yielded only two African American members of the city council—but access to county governing structures was even more difficult for the surrounding county's 5 percent of black voters.[104]

The city and county competed with one another for resources, and the county and their state legislative allies generally enjoyed the upper hand. City residents enjoyed a larger per-capita tax base, more public services, and their own municipal government, while the county government tilted heavily to the interests of suburban and rural residents but nonetheless drew some funds from the city's property base.[105] This knotty structure meant that city and county authorities were frequently at odds over the allocation of state, county, and city-generated revenue.[106] Residents navigated a "maze" of services provided by public and private sources. City residents benefited from a tax-supported fire department, but county homeowners paid private subscription companies. County residents bought water from local water companies who themselves purchased it wholesale from the city. But the same residents could not hook up to the city sewer system. They relied on often insufficient septic systems, one-tenth of which at any one time the county's sanitary engineer judged to be leeching waste above ground and into the water supply.[107] The overlapping governments offered a tangled yet insufficient web of services, while rapid population growth in new suburban areas made the need even more pressing. The county saw rapid growth as the population outside the city limits increased by 64.1 percent from 1940 to 1950 and was on similar pace for the 1950s. The old city boundaries no longer corresponded to Nashville as an economic community, and residents on both sides of the city line had a "common need" for municipal services.[108]

In the post–World War II years, some Nashville planners and leaders joined those from other cities around the country in considering new political forms that would serve both city and county. In most other contexts the idea produced policy briefs but no more; however, consolidation had powerful allies in Nashville. The chamber of commerce had been speaking since 1951 of expanding city boundaries to better serve joint city and suburban needs; the planning commission was already functioning as a joint city-county entity.[109] Expert voices and civic commissions weighed in for consolidation, and venues for discussion of urban renewal—like a "New Cities for Old" conference sponsored by the chamber in 1956, bringing to town spokespeople for redevelopment projects from Detroit, New York, and New Haven—also helped lay the groundwork for the consolidation idea. If not formal consolidation (which remained impossible under the state constitution), then major annexation for the city and consolidation of school and health services seemed necessary.[110] A local elite consensus developed around the idea that consolidating the city and county governments into a single metropolitan government would increase efficiency and encourage growth. Even those who were reluctant supporters of the idea, including city Mayor Ben West, saw consolidation as a preferred alternative to static city boundaries or to the adversarial relationships established in annexation by ordinance.[111]

A 1955 change to the state constitution authorized cities to annex adjacent land without a referendum of the people residing there, shifting the discussion from theoretical to immediate. Over the summer, the joint city and county planning commissions prepared studies on integrating the city and county governments. Incoming Nashville Chamber of Commerce President Victor Johnson felt it was his job to keep the results of these studies out of public view, reflecting both close cooperation between the commission and the chamber and the extent of elite control over the idea of consolidation.[112]

County Judge Beverly Briley became the local politician most vocally identified with consolidation and its most consistent advocate. Briley, first elected as county executive in 1950, grew up in a densely populated area of East Nashville outside the city limits. He attended Caldwell and Glenn elementary schools and graduated from Davidson County's Central High School. Briley made fast progress through school, aided by the county's insufficient infrastructure: schools were overcrowded, and to make more space for others, administrators promoted students who could do more advanced work. Twice selected for such a promotion, Briley entered Vanderbilt University at sixteen. He then studied at Cumberland Law School, to the east of Nashville, and became the youngest attorney ever admitted to the Tennessee Bar, at eighteen, after successfully challenging restrictions on the practice of law by minors. After a stint in the Navy in World War II, Briley returned to Nashville, established a law practice, and became active in local politics.[113] He entered a political milieu accustomed to long tenures and close identification between the city or county administration and the particular individuals (and their political machines) in office. Ben West was only Nashville's third mayor since 1923, the two previously having served at least twelve years. The county judge who preceded Briley had served thirty-two years.[114] When Briley argued for consolidation, he offered himself for county-wide leadership.

Briley began an extended campaign in favor of consolidation with a July 1955 speech to the Nashville Rotary Club. He recounted the twelve planks in his reelection platform, but closed with a call to action on county-wide consolidation. The speech positioned Briley as the elected official out front on consolidation. He had shifted the conversation from the city's power to annex to how consolidation could serve the county's interests.[115]

Briley's comments cast consolidation as more than a variation upon annexation by the city: it would be its reverse, a shift of power to the county structure. Speaking as the president of the National Association of County Officials, Briley first defended suburbanites from those who would criticize them for having become "refugee[s] from reality" or "tax dodger[s]."[116]

Instead, Briley praised those who had moved to the suburbs as having worked hard for their down payment and having good reason to leave the city. The city offered them only "substandard housing," "poverty," and "the political rule of the city machine made up of a snarling hodgepodge of minorities" who were "united only by the relief check, the bail bond, the traffic ticket fixer and the hand-outs from some ward boss or sub-boss." For Briley, it was only reasonable to say, "I want no more of it."[117] Instead, the suburbs offered the (presumably white) homeowner the opportunity to live "in a more genial atmosphere of people of his own kind that are culturally, racially, religiously, politically, and otherwise of his own group," unlike the city's "babble of voices."[118]

In Briley's view, consolidation promised "a single strong [municipal] voice," and that voice would be the county government's.[119] County residents could secure stronger municipal services without fear. (Additional reassurance came in consolidation's limits. Six previously incorporated areas in Davidson County outside of Nashville, including some very elite neighborhoods, retained control over zoning and policing.) Briley promised that suburban privilege could be maintained within a metropolitan government that would see white suburbanites as its chief constituency.

County population growth put particular pressure on school facilities, which were both overcrowded and of poor quality as compared to those available to white city residents. (Black city residents experienced faulty or lacking infrastructure in some schools as in other areas of city infrastructure, although there were also well-built facilities constructed as part of the depression-era Works Progress Administration or, in the 1950s, in efforts to equalize school facilities.) Even if many county residents shared Beverly Briley's condemnation of the city, they still knew that in education as in other aspects of municipal services, the city remained ahead of the surrounding—and substantially rural—county. Good-government advocates who wanted more developed educational infrastructure, like George Cate, became voices in support of consolidation (and Cate became the first vice mayor of the government known as "Metro" as well).[120]

For city residents, consolidation promised to more broadly distribute the operating expenses of a central business district that served tens of thousands of commuters, using roads, bridges, and other city infrastructure without paying for them. It also promised to increase tax revenues, whose growth was slowed by the transfer of property from taxable to nontaxable uses (such as parks, roads, public housing, and schools), often via urban renewal projects.

Having considered benefits for city and county residents, Beverly Briley and his allies in the chamber of commerce emphasized establishing a growth-friendly environment for business. Cities like Atlanta for years had lured business by extending water and sewer services to aid industrial relocation.[121] Nashville leaders hoped providing such services would be more possible with a consolidated government. Consolidation also could prevent the uncertainties of possible annexation by the city. The state's 1955 provision for annexation by fiat made highly valuable business and industrial facilities in Davidson County outside of the Nashville limits— including those of Victor Johnson's Aladdin, aircraft builder AVCO, and clothing manufacturer General Shoe Corporation (or GENESCO)— tempting targets for annexation by a city in search of a broadened tax base. Consolidation, for county businesses as well as county residents, offered a way to manage city needs on terms more acceptable to suburban residents and businesses.

Not long after the chamber's "New Cities for Old" conference, Davidson County's nine representatives moved a home rule measure through the state legislature, enabling city and county governments to alter or consolidate their municipal governments by referendum. Soon a Charter Commission began its work. With five members appointed by the county's Judge Briley and five by the city's Mayor West, the group met frequently over months, debating myriad details from public service appointments to teacher pay scales, from water rates to school board district boundaries. In the end, they emerged with a new charter keeping the so-called strong mayor model traditional in the city of Nashville, with a twenty-one-member metropolitan council composed of fifteen district representatives and six at-large. Charter commission member Z. Alexander Looby argued successfully against efforts to make half the seats at-large, which would further have diluted the voices of black communities. Generally, the new charter followed the essential outlines of the 1956 planning report Victor Johnson had worked to keep under wraps.[122]

Despite Looby's efforts, consolidation effectively meant vote dilution, producing a county-wide government with half the proportion of black residents compared to the previously separate city. The number of black elected officials did not decline only because there were still disproportionately few in the city into the late 1950s. Under the proposed charter, two of the fifteen district seats clearly were gerrymandered to preserve black representation, but these voices were more than outweighed by the new presence of six at-large, nearly certainly white, representatives.[123] The new demographics of the consolidated metropolis also meant that a Metro mayor likely could build a governing coalition without including black constituents. Z. Alexander Looby expressed initial concerns about consolidation because of vote dilution, but later changed his opinion.[124] Looby may have been convinced by those who linked consolidation to the very survival of Nashville as a viable city. They said Looby had a stark choice: he could support consolidation, or be the first black mayor of the "dying city" of Nashville.[125]

Looby and his allies who supported consolidation diverged from another group of black leaders in Nashville who favored the existing city political machine. Robert E. Lillard, city councilman from a South Nashville district, worked with and within that white-dominated machine structure as an important ally of Mayor West. Lillard "would hit low while a teammate hit high," as the local civil rights organizer Rev. Kelly Miller Smith put it. When Z. Alexander Looby sued to desegregate public golf courses, Lillard argued for a new, but segregated, course.[126] Lillard worried that consolidation would bring vote dilution and weaken the limited but established alliance between Nashville's black voters and the city political machine. Yet when West supported consolidation in 1958, Lillard followed suit.[127]

With the chamber of commerce, Briley and West, organized labor, the League of Women Voters, and myriad other organizations on board, the proposed charter came before the voters in a referendum in the summer of 1958. The elite consensus that had pushed for consolidation as early as 1951 was nearly complete, but just a week before the election, yellow leaflets appeared throughout the county warning of a communistic "One Government," and cautioning suburban and rural residents against the encroaching power of the city. Several observers cited Edward Potter, a local banker known for a small-government orientation, as having funded the campaign. His intervention sharpened county opinion already leaning against. Only one county district voted in favor. County opposition overwhelmed the modest majority in favor in the city, yielding defeat at the ballot box.[128]

The 1958 defeat led to events that ensured consolidation's ultimate passage. In the three years after the failed referendum, Mayor Ben West used his powers of annexation and taxation to shore up the city's fiscal base. As West demonstrated what the city could do without consolidation, many previously reluctant suburbanites came to favor consolidation over the specter of annexation by fiat. West annexed three parcels of land in 1958, all high-value industrial areas, including the Ford Glass plant and Victor Johnson's Aladdin factory just over the old city line to the southeast. These seven square miles contained few residents to be angered by the annexation, but did spur factory owners (including metropolitan consolidation leader Johnson) to sue to block annexation, ultimately unsuccessfully.[129]

Earlier, West promised voters that he would not annex residential areas without a referendum. Thus it was the city council—working with West's tacit support and overriding his symbolic veto—that annexed forty-two suburban square miles home to 80,000 people in 1960. In these neighborhoods and others, the county had not provided many basic services, including street lighting, sewerage, or sufficient school facilities. The failure of the 1958 consolidation measure and the assumption that annexation would be next led the county to cancel planned improvements, only worsening the situation. When he annexed these areas, West had to provide services quickly to prove city capacity. If he failed, he would draw the ire of annexed suburban residents while hardening those in the surrounding county further against city annexation.[130]

Annexation also made schools central exhibits for the potential benefits of consolidation over annexation. The annexed suburban residential land included twenty-one schools and nearly 13,000 students, previously part of the Davidson County schools. What would happen to these schools, and these students, under annexation? Would the city pay the county for their facilities? How would the annexed areas have a voice in school governance? For pro-consolidation leader Victor Johnson, the question of these schools best exemplified the need to move beyond frequent bickering between city and county to a newly streamlined and rationalized structure. The Citizens' Committee for Better Schools picked up the argument as well, linking consolidation to school quality by arguing that public dollars would flow more efficiently into schools under one system rather than two.[131]

In a move less effective in increasing city revenue than in shifting public opinion, Mayor West imposed a wheel tax. County residents who crossed the city limits for more than thirty days per year needed a ten-dollar green sticker. The move annoyed thousands of commuters and yet was ultimately unenforceable with a small city police force.[132] The sticker became yet another symbol of a city government, and a mayor, thought by many suburbanites to be at once overreaching and incompetent.

West also revised his position on consolidation. An ally in 1958, he became an opponent by 1962, trying to hold on to his city power base and mobilizing his allies, including Lillard, against consolidation. Lillard organized his networks against consolidation, including recruiting Boy Scouts to circulate anti-consolidation material as West pressed city firemen and police officers into the same service.[133]

While West switched sides, a second charter commission revisited the 1958 version and negotiated a few changes. New language in the 1962 draft required an appointed rather than elected school board, and had an enlarged city council, expanded from twenty-one to forty-one members. Of these, thirty-five were elected from districts, and five (plus a vice mayor) chosen at-large. Smaller geographic districts helped increase the number of black-majority districts, thereby increasing somewhat the proportional representation of black Nashvillians on the council. Nonetheless, the six at-large seats offset the six districts drawn to yield black councilmen.[134]

While Lillard organized against consolidation alongside Mayor West, Z. Alexander Looby remained an ally. Looby, his law partner Avon N. Williams Jr., and other leaders in the black middle class— many with connections to Tennessee A & I State College (later Tennessee State), Fisk University, and Meharry Medical College—formed the Davidson County Independent Political Council (DCIPC).[135] Looby carried his own district for Metro, and many of his colleagues in the DCIPC contributed time and energy to the metro advocacy organization Citizens' Committee for Better Government. They chose to fight for representation within consolidation over annexation of majority-white suburban areas with no guarantees of representation.[136] When a "Civic-Minded Quartet" of Aladdin's Victor Johnson, Mayor Ben West (before his 1962 defection from the cause), County Judge Beverly Briley, and black banker Alfred Galloway announced their support for Metro in 1961, Galloway assured black voters that the new charter could "guarantee the protection of accrued benefits" and "safeguard the representational rights of Negroes."[137]

Galloway's reference to "accrued benefits" may well have been a reference to the limited but real victories black Nashville residents had won over the Jim Crow order. School desegregation litigation begun in 1955 yielded a token but still consequential desegregation plan in city schools in 1957; direct-action campaigns waged largely by college student activists took down pieces of segregation in downtown eating and shopping beginning in 1960. Surely, to some white city and suburban residents, consolidation appealed as a mode of reducing the growing proportional influence of black city dwellers as they asserted their power. But consolidation was not the only possible means to that end—city annexation of white-majority outlying areas would have had this effect as well.[138] In 1962, when consolidation passed, the white suburbanites who became the swing voters on the issue could still feel assured that segregation remained firm under a consolidated government, with public-accommodations desegregation concentrated in a few contested downtown or city neighborhoods and school desegregation operating within very tight boundaries.

White elite leaders had failed to connect their enthusiasm for consolidation to grassroots support in 1958; they stepped up their efforts to educate and mobilize before a second referendum in June 1962. Charter commission member Victor Johnson urged his hundreds of Aladdin employees to vote for consolidation because it would help industrial recruitment for the city.[139] As Mayor West's administration failed to deliver on promised services to the annexed areas, West's administration pushed suburbanites one step closer to accepting consolidation. George Cate, whose home was included in the 1960 annexation, recalled that in the week leading up to the referendum, the city administration hurriedly delivered piles of street-lighting poles and installed them around the clock, but simply did not get the job done fast enough. Voters in the newly annexed areas became the swing vote for consolidation, polling 72 percent in favor.[140] By contrast, the old city wards followed Mayor West in opposing consolidation.[141]

Unlike the 1958 referendum, which had passed in the city but failed in the county, the 1962 referendum received 56 percent support in the county, with 44 percent turnout. The city, newly enlarged by annexation, was politically divided. The old city went 55 percent against consolidation, but the newly annexed areas were heavily in favor. The city tally came to 57 percent for consolidation. Thus the City of Nashville and Davidson County became Metropolitan Nashville–Davidson County.[142] As historian Don Doyle describes it, and as Beverly Briley had foreseen in his 1959 address, "righteous suburbanites rose up in anger—this time to swallow the city rather than repel it."[143]

Mayor Ben West chose not to compete to be the first metropolitan mayor, and Briley secured the new post. Briley's election represented another important shift away from power for many black Nashvillians. Although West had often angered black residents by failing to deliver on promises, he nonetheless considered black voters important to his governing coalition. By contrast, Briley clearly felt he could govern without the support of black voters. As he put it in an interview near the end of his life, he did not see much need to concern himself with black voters' support, as he estimated them to be 13 to 17 percent of the voting population.[144]

Consolidation brought a fundamental shift in the position of black voters relative to their government. Not only did consolidation reduce black voters' proportional influence, but it placed even more power in the hands of the mayor, elected county-wide. The new Metropolitan Charter gave the mayor appointive power over all administrative boards, including education, planning, and housing.[145] Consolidation with the suburbs and gerrymandering in favor of seats for black representatives also reduced the proportion of majority-white districts with significant minorities of black

1.8. Beverly Briley stood before a banner linking consolidation to growth at his 1963 inauguration as the first mayor of Metropolitan Nashville-Davidson County. Courtesy of Metropolitan Archives of Nashville/Davidson County.

voters—making alliances between white politicians and black voters even more rare.

Black Nashville residents seeking equitable schooling for their children found the terrain on which they worked shifted subtly but significantly through consolidation. Once desegregation began, key decisions fell to the members and professional staffs of local agencies and commissions appointed by the mayor. The planning commission, for example, developed school construction plans in collaboration with school administrators and within the frame of city redevelopment and growth plans.[146] Their world of population projections, expert judgments, and professional standards corresponded to the powerful local growth coalition's interests, but limited access and recourse for black activists. To the extent that analogous processes had been open to democratic participation before consolidation— largely through Mayor West's appreciation of the power of the significant, and voting, black minority in his city—that influence was much reduced through both the demographics of consolidation and the new leaders in charge. Consolidation in the form it took in Nashville significantly reduced

ᶠ black voters to push their interests either as a unified block or
ty agencies that had previously had as their purview only city
ȝave way to consolidated agencies responsible for both city
precincts. Already underserving a still predominantly urban
...ᴜᴏn of black residents, these agencies operating at metropolitan
scale became even less responsive.

## Conclusion

In the post–World War II decades, Nashville's pro-growth elite transformed
their city landscape and its governmental structure. They did so in part by
linking housing and schooling together, demonstrating how segregation
and inequality have been made through the interactions between schools
and markets in land and housing. Whether in the conceptual underpinnings of the "neighborhood unit" or the lobbying efforts of local builders to make schools value-generating aspects of their private developments,
schools became organizing nodes in the metropolitan landscape.

Local urban renewal efforts illustrated the extent of elite and official
power to remake the basic geography of the city, often in the name of economic growth alongside a deep commitment to segregation. In fact, to
many white planners and business leaders enmeshed in the dynamics of
both suburban housing construction and urban public housing development, segregation seemed a necessary condition for growth, a tool in its
pursuit. The rhetoric of growth as both necessary and of universal benefit
provided a potent and hard-to-challenge rationale. Nashville's organized
black political communities navigated within these constraints, as they
would in confronting later phases of metropolitan politics.

And these were the years in which Nashville consolidated its government. Although present-day policy talk frames metropolitan consolidation
as a boon for city governments, Nashville leaders imagined and designed
consolidation on suburban terms. By joining more city-dwelling black residents with more suburban-dwelling whites, consolidation did create a diverse demography that enabled later metropolitan desegregation. But in
the 1950s and 1960s, when consolidation first took hold, the technologies
of city planning, urban renewal, and suburban development continued to
work powerfully across the metropolitan landscape to structure segregation. The multipart, state-sanctioned, and highly durable systems of segregation built in these years proved resilient even as local civil rights attorneys
and activists struggled to apply *Brown v. Board of Education* to Nashville.

# CHAPTER TWO

# Desegregation from Tokenism to Moderation

Grace McKinley walked her daughter Linda and Linda's friend Rita to Fehr School early on September 9, 1957. The girls were among the nineteen black first graders to enter previously segregated white elementary schools and begin to desegregate Nashville's schools. On that morning, their parents readied their youngsters with warm breakfasts, pressed clothes, and whispered hopes. McKinley and her charges stepped by angry white protesters, cars decorated with Klan lettering, and citizens wielding hatefully worded posters. Iridell Groves made a similar walk with her son Erroll, whose new first-day-of-school clothes she had laid out carefully the night before. Forewarned by escalating protests in the week before school started, and multiple accounts of verbal threats against families who had registered their children at previously segregated white schools, Nashville police officers formed an escort for the walk. Police presence might have been some reassurance, but one insufficient to calm a parent's imagination about what their young ones might find as the school day progressed. The first graders at the center of the drama may have sensed the fear, or, as fellow student Lajuanda Street remembered it, they perceived "a parade of people" accompanying their first walk to school. Young Lajuanda recalled that she "was not afraid. I had my big daddy's hand to walk with."[1]

Now decades past, the walks taken by the McKinleys, the Streets, and the Groves carry echoes of the steps Ruby Bridges took to enter her previously segregated elementary school in New Orleans in 1960, or the mob Elizabeth Eckford navigated to return home from Little Rock's Central High School in 1957. They also symbolize how much, and how little, hard-won change came to late-1950s and early-1960s Nashville. For local attorney and city councilman Z. Alexander Looby, their walks marked a key turn in a decades-long struggle against educational inequality and segregation.

2.1. Grace McKinley walks her daughter Linda and Rita Buchanan to school at Fehr Elementary, September 9, 1957. Courtesy of Nashville Public Library Special Collections.

2.2. Iridell Groves and her son Erroll at Buena Vista Elementary School, September 1957. Courtesy of Nashville Public Library Special Collections.

Well before the Supreme Court's 1954 ruling in *Brown v. Board of Education*, Looby had worked with the NAACP's national legal staff on education cases across Tennessee. In Nashville, he challenged and defeated a racist salary schedule that rewarded white teachers more than it did black teachers with the same credentials and experience. "Since education itself has no color line, I don't believe a system built on segregation can be educational," Looby remarked in 1950.[2]

In Nashville and its schools in the decade after *Brown*, all three modes of making segregation and inequality were on display. The spatial organization of still-segregated schooling reflected and perpetuated educational inequality. The "neighborhood unit" idea attached (segregated) schooling to (segregated) housing, but did not guarantee quality facilities to serve all neighborhoods. Black students in Nashville and surrounding Davidson County more frequently attended substandard—even dangerous—buildings with fewer materials to support learning as white-dominated school boards and districts channeled resources to schools unequally. In urban areas, segregated black schools, often serving segregated black neighborhoods, demonstrated neglect and divestment; in rural areas, poor facilities combined with broadly dispersed settlement and segregation's rules to place schools often challengingly far away from home. Once desegregation began, school officials and key members of Nashville's elite collaborated to limit desegregation's reach by manipulating zoning boundaries and tightening segregation.

Nashville schools' curricular offerings and rationales also helped make educational inequality. As was the case in other southern cities, Nashville's segregated black schools, especially at the high school level, had long offered a more limited range of course offerings than segregated white schools at the time. But in the context of mounting legal pressures for desegregation, white educators turned again to curriculum and ideas about pedagogy to argue for the preservation of segregation or the most gradual desegregation. Local educators continued to believe that skin color marked meaningful differences not only in student achievement but ability, and argued against desegregation on the grounds of what they portrayed as good educational practice.

Although Nashville typified Jim Crow educational inequality, including after *Brown*, local narratives cast the city as a standout for its moderate approach to school desegregation. Events in Nashville did seem somewhat more temperate than the extreme confrontation between state and federal power visible in Little Rock, less entrenched than the outright school closures of massive resistance in Prince Edward County, Virginia.[3] Nashville was neither Little Rock nor Prince Edward County, yet the juxtaposition overstates compliance and understates both the local violence and the depth and extent of resistance to desegregation that did exist. Gradualism and parental-choice mechanisms ensured that only a tiny proportion of Nashville's students participated in desegregation in the late 1950s.

Responding to court-ordered desegregation, Nashville's white officials and white communities demonstrated resistance in multiple registers. People differently positioned at the local level adopted various ways of working against desegregation—from quiet but effective elite manipulation of zoning, to loud protest and threats of violence from street-level organizers. Federal court pressure for desegregation was tempered by local bureaucratic manipulation of desegregation. Local narratives of "moderation" obscured the depth of bureaucratic, official, and at times court-sanctioned resistance to desegregation that operated alongside more visible popular protest. Nonetheless, local officials also acted to keep resistance to desegregation within tight bounds, to limit those forms of resistance that were untidy or unseemly or challenged the local elite's carefully fostered image of order and compliance to befit a growing metropolis.

## Jim Crow Schools in Nashville

In May 1954, just days before the Supreme Court issued its ruling in *Brown*, Minnie Couch led a group of parents from Wharton School's parent-teacher association to appeal to the City of Nashville Board of Education to remedy dire conditions at their school. The board secretary captured her description of both hazards to safety and barriers to learning. Couch "pointed out that the steps were worn, banisters needed from the first to the second floor, the lighting was insufficient, the seating was bad, sanitary facilities inadequate, the septic tank stopped up. She stated there was no auditorium, music room, gymnasium, clinic or library." Wharton parents had made similar appeals fully three years earlier.[4] Wharton served a section of historically black North Nashville home to an economically diverse population of African American families, including public housing residents, public school teachers, faculty and staff at nearby Fisk University, Meharry Medical College, and Tennessee A & I, and businesspeople whose offices lined Jefferson Street nearby, or the black professional district less than a mile away downtown. The area's economic diversity came in part from the power of discriminatory real estate and home finance practices, which in the 1950s restricted opportunities for middle-class black families to move to all but a few of Nashville's suburbs. Without the option of mobility, black parents like Minnie Couch joined others in communities around the country working to secure better educational opportunities for their children by improving the schools they had, seeking to realize the promised link, in planning rhetoric, between housing and school facilities.[5]

As the local black newspaper, the *Nashville Globe and Independent*, opined, the school board could force Wharton's community to "occupy a school that merely qualifies as 'good enough for Negroes,'" but they could not "make either the teachers or the pupils endure the discrimination happily."[6] At Wharton and elsewhere, black parents and community members fought to secure reasonable educational facilities for their children. Many schools serving Nashville's black students converted basement spaces into classrooms and still had to consider moving to double shifts (denying students a full instructional day) to accommodate all the children. Classrooms designed to hold no more than thirty contained forty-four students.[7] At Wharton, the board avoided double shifts when a nearby youth center stepped forward to rent two rooms to the school, an arrangement that endured for at least two years.[8] Instead of addressing the Wharton parents' concerns directly, the board responded that they "realized the inadequacy" of the school facilities but thought that relief for overcrowding would come when a new school opened less than a mile away.[9] The school board chair claimed the board was "fully aware of the poor and inadequate facilities," but took no action.[10] Overcrowding and inadequate facilities reached some segregated white schools as well.[11] For white children in white neighborhoods, however, the board more speedily remedied the situation, and at times responded to predictions of overcrowding rather than waiting for it to materialize.[12]

Stories of overcrowding would suggest that the City of Nashville school system simply had too few classrooms. This was not in fact the case. As of fall 1951, Nashville's director of facilities reported that of the 339 classrooms in the city, more than 10 percent sat vacant.[13] Nashville did not lack classrooms, but the district's commitment to segregation manufactured a shortage of classrooms as its population grew and shifted geographically. Insisting on segregated schooling meant that classrooms in segregated white schools sat empty as nearby black schools were bursting at the seams. School board actions guarded segregation inside schools even as communities around these schools experienced periods—even if short ones—of racial diversity.

Elliott School, which sat in a densely populated, mixed-use area just north of Nashville's downtown, remained a segregated white school in

1951. Since World War II, white families had departed the area and black families arrived. The school's zone included 420 black students and 403 white students. Elliott would have been a substantially desegregated school if it had served all the students in its zone. Instead, dividing Elliott's local students into segregated schools produced overcrowding in nearby black schools like Wharton and empty seats at white schools. To address the overcrowding within the boundaries of segregation, white area councilman William P. Doyle joined with black minister Rev. Andrew White in asking the board of education for the "conversion" of Elliott into a "Negro school."[14]

Doyle argued for the conversion while conveying his certainty that complete residential and educational segregation would be preserved. Although the school's zone remained almost 50 percent white, Doyle explained that "the population of Negroes almost completely surrounds Elliott School now and in a few years the entire area will be colored." In Nashville as in so many cities, Doyle's prediction was accurate, realized through the dynamics of residential succession fed by profit-maximizing real estate agents moving black families into areas vacated by white families who enjoyed the federal policy–smoothed road to the suburbs or to new segregated white public housing opening elsewhere. But Doyle's comments reveal the broader importance of ideas about residential succession in shaping the city. Doyle's predictions of residential transition, made when the Elliott school zone held nearly equal proportions of white and black children, led the board to convert Elliott from a segregated white school to a segregated black school. Schools served as important markers of neighborhood identity, and the transition aided the area's shift to an all-black neighborhood. Doyle's predictions not only responded to patterns he saw in his ward, but helped produce them.[15]

The board frequently mentioned plans to create a new black high school—as urged by city councilman Robert E. Lillard and two council allies and the Southeast Nashville Civic League—or build a replacement for Wharton School.[16] Unlike other school districts and states that tried to preempt *Brown* by embarking on school construction binges to claim separate could be equal, Nashville leaders simply stalled. They did not act on community calls for new facilities in the early 1950s (except where, as at McKissack School, they served newly built black subdivisions). Instead, overcrowding at segregated black schools continued, eased by short-term patches like church-basement rentals.[17]

Uneven facilities may have contributed to inequality in educational achievement. In both the city and county schools, black students attended and graduated high school at rates lower than their representation in the school system. While black children made up one-third of Nashville's students, they were only a quarter of its high school graduates. County graduation rates were similarly low and imbalanced.[18]

In the early 1950s, before consolidation, the City of Nashville and Davidson County operated separate school systems. Historically the latter was the smaller system with less developed infrastructure. Baby boom growth and postwar suburbanization helped the county system become more populous than the city's. As of 1954, the City of Nashville served 27,441 students in forty-five segregated schools. Nashville's mayor selected the board of education's nine members, who drew from a range of city neighborhoods. With his election in 1951, Mayor Ben West had appointed the Board's first black member, Coyness Ennix. The county's quarterly court appointed seven school board members who oversaw 32,075 students in seventy-eight smaller and more dispersed schools. In the city, white students comprised just under two-thirds of the student population, while in the county they made up 94 percent. The quarterly court appointed no black county residents to serve on the county school board.[19]

City and county systems confronted differing challenges in the 1950s, but were equally wed to maintaining segregation. Davidson County operated only one high school for black students, creating an extreme travel burden for families widely but thinly dispersed across a twenty-mile span, east to west and north to south. The high school, located north of downtown Nashville, was more than an hour away for many students living in the south of the county. The inconvenience of travel helps explain why the city's Wharton School, extremely overcrowded and patently substandard, nevertheless drew eighty-six students from the county.[20]

For both black and white students, county facilities compared poorly to those in the city. In 1954, Davidson operated twelve "one-teacher schools." Although one of these schools was a segregated white institution serving a rural area, eleven were segregated black schools. At least one-third of the black children in Davidson County schools attended a one-room schoolhouse, where a single instructor tried to meet the needs of children across an age span of at least eight years.[21] Davidson County's rural schools exemplify how segregation compounded inequality. All rural children suffered from schools with fewer offerings and less staff simply because of their size. When the population was split in two along racial categories, this difficulty was magnified, splintering students into even smaller groups and further fragmenting limited resources.

Poor facilities like those at Wharton and overcrowding at schools around Elliot were only the more obvious examples of inequality within the segregated City of Nashville schools. For black administrators (who were assigned to supervisory positions only in segregated black schools), segregation both restricted and created opportunities for advancement.[22] Until 1942, with Looby's successful pay-equity suit (to which the NAACP's Thurgood Marshall contributed), black and white teachers worked on separate and unequal salary schedules that offered white teachers more than 40 percent above what was offered to their black peers. These inequalities were particularly galling given that Nashville's black teachers were more likely to be highly educated and experienced than were white teachers. This was a by-product of discriminatory practices in other fields rather than any intentional effort on the part of the Nashville City Schools to equalize or seek particularly qualified black teachers: exclusionary racist hiring practices in many fields left college- and graduate-school-educated black people fewer professional opportunities than their similarly educated white peers, making teaching a relatively more attractive choice.[23] Board of education attorneys later argued that, given teacher skill, black students in Nashville were receiving equivalent educational opportunity.[24]

Although few black teachers in Nashville felt that the city school system provided equitable facilities and opportunities, many identified positive attributes within segregated education. Not only did segregated black schools provide relatively well-paid municipal employment to black teachers and administrators after pay equalization, but for their students they offered caring and close-knit communities that often generated pride and gave students a sense of high expectations.[25] Pride flowed in part from the strength of Nashville's flagship high school, Pearl, in comparison to most southern schools for black students. The elegant art-deco building, erected in 1939 by the Works Progress Administration, drew faculty members who had come from around the South to Nashville to attend Fisk or Tennessee A & I. Other teachers, Nashville natives, came back to Pearl after studying in the North.[26] Former teachers and students in Nashville schools remembered the physical signs of inequality that confronted them at school each day, some of them even at Pearl—the classrooms so poorly lit that no work could happen on cloudy days; the open coal stoves that spat searing embers; the out-of-date books marked by white students—and the daily indignities, insults, and at times violence that came with walking past nearby segregated white schools to get to their own. But the same students and teachers valued encouraging relationships based in high expectations shared by teachers and the class-diverse communities they served. These relationships aided students in their progress toward their "PhD"—Pearl

2.3. In a Nashville school hallway, c. 1954. Courtesy of
Metropolitan Archives of Davidson County.

High Diploma.[27] Especially for those students whose ambitions aligned
with those of their skilled faculty, Pearl became a powerful base from
which to understand the segregated world and prepare to navigate it. Nashville's segregated schools could be at once distinctly unequal and central to
the communities they served.

One Pearl student—future historian and chair of the US Commission
on Civil Rights Mary Frances Berry—walked into downtown Nashville in
May 1954 to run a few after-school errands with one of her teachers. Berry
noticed headlines announcing the Supreme Court's decision, in *Brown v.
Board of Education*, that school segregation was unconstitutional. She asked
if this meant black and white students would go to school together the
next year. "Not so fast, Mary Frances, not so fast," her teacher replied.[28]

## The Beginnings of School Desegregation

The evening edition of the May 17, 1954, Nashville *Banner* announced the
*Brown* decision in huge type just below the masthead: "SEGREGATION

OUT!" But immediately below, the *Banner* assured its readers that "little would change" locally.[29] While denouncing "demagogic appeals" to protest, the *Banner* stuck to its states' rights dogma and doubted if the decision would reach implementation. The less conservative *Tennessean* took a more positive, yet measured, tone. The paper referred to the decision as the "law of the land," requiring achievable adjustments that would give "new honor to the principle of democracy."[30]

Immediately after the Supreme Court issued its decision in *Brown*, both Z. Alexander Looby and representatives of Nashville's active NAACP chapter approached the city school system to initiate desegregation. The local branch of the organization enjoyed more than 3,500 members, benefiting from the critical mass of black middle-class affiliates of Fisk, Tennessee A & I, and the local black-owned religious publishing and insurance companies.[31] The NAACP wrote to both the city and county boards asking for prompt movement toward desegregation.[32]

After the *Brown* decision, some black leaders found themselves caught between competing imperatives: securing better resources immediately, holding out for the principle if not the practice of desegregation, and protecting black teachers' employment. The Nashville NAACP, Looby, and their allies made desegregation their strategy. In several instances, Councilman Robert E. Lillard instead pushed for better resources and facilities for black Nashvillians without challenging segregation. For black teachers, *Brown* raised the hope of better resources for black children, but potentially threatened their own careers. Segregated black schools had been important and reliable sources of employment for college-educated black men and women. The NAACP asserted that its "fullest resources" would be used to ensure that black teachers were not discriminated against during desegregation, but the concern remained. Other teachers doubted that *Brown*'s mandate for desegregation would be achieved in Nashville.[33]

Was it better to claim immediate improvements to segregated schools, or hold out for desegregation? School board member Coyness Ennix faced this question, one confronted over decades within NAACP legal strategy nationally, at overcrowded and segregated black Wharton School. Ennix knew the great need for new facilities to serve students then crammed into Wharton, but deliberated before deciding to support construction of a new school there. Ennix had considered opposing any new construction that accepted segregation, but reversed his position when he decided that the facility would be needed within a segregated or desegregated system. The *Tennessean* praised his shift, optimistically asserting that "we cannot believe integration is going to cause a mass flight from the city by white families,"

2.4. A. Z. Kelley, right, the Nashville barber and NAACP leader who became the named plaintiff in the city's school desegregation suit, with, from left, Rev. Kelly Miller Smith, Thurgood Marshall of the NAACP Legal Defense Fund, and local civil rights attorney Z. Alexander Looby. Courtesy of Nashville Public Library Special Collections.

implying that a new Wharton would ultimately serve both black and white students.[34] In fact, it did so only after the beginning of busing in 1971.

In some cases, the Looby and Lillard approaches intersected, as in the conversion and expansion of South Nashville's Cameron School into a high school. Black students in the neighborhood had previously been forced to cross town to attend Pearl if they hoped to obtain a high school education. Beginning in 1951, Lillard and community members pushed the council and school board for Cameron's expansion, but their calls were not acted upon until the *Brown* decision provoked a defensive local effort to bring segregated black facilities closer to parity.[35]

*Brown* prompted some efforts at equalizing school facilities, but both the *Banner* and skeptical black teachers predicted correctly: broader change did not come quickly. Neither the city nor county school boards took any substantive action to respond to the decision. Reversing the typical pattern of black students requesting access to segregated white schools, Robert and Gertrude Rempfer, a white Fisk University faculty couple, asked to enroll their children at then-segregated black Pearl Elementary. Lee Lorch, another Fisk professor active in both civil rights work and the Communist Party, and his wife, Grace, requested the same. (Looby initially represented the Lorches and Rempfers before the board, but he dropped the Rempfers from later litigation and the Lorches left town for Little Rock.)[36] Ennix, the board's lone African American member, argued that "in view of the decision of the Supreme Court we can allow these children to attend the Pearl Elementary School." The board's eight white members referred the matter to its instruction committee, on which Ennix did not serve. Superintendent W. O. Bass felt that "the sensibilities of both sides" had to be considered, and evoking delay, he suggested that the community "sit around and talk the matter over." Board member Elmer Pettit implied that the ongoing improvements to school facilities would reduce the need for actual desegregation.[37]

Superintendent W. O. Bass brought news of the 1955 *Brown II* decision to the city school board that June. Members appreciated the ambiguity of the opinion's call for "deliberate speed," voting to "study and report" on the question of desegregation. The vote was again eight members to one, with Coyness Ennix calling for immediate desegregation. The board placed the study in the hands of the standing instruction committee, and let drop Ennix's motion to meet with community groups to discuss desegregation.[38] The instruction committee was tasked with surveying how other southern cities were responding to *Brown*, and the board planned to wait until the next state census of schools, done every six years, to act. They asked the state to expedite their survey, but the state refused.[39] Quietly, the county school board commissioned a report on the geographic distribution of its black students, keeping this information at the ready but not using it in any proactive fashion.[40]

Cecil Sims embodied the nexus of government, business, and elite society in Nashville, and became a key architect of Nashville's approach to desegregation. He was the most successful attorney in town, leading his firm in representing Ford, Western Union, and Nashville's biggest local businesses. A member of the Vanderbilt Board of Trust and the elite Belle Meade Country Club, he also served on the Davidson County school board. Sims made *Brown* a focal point of legal study, and produced an intricately constructed position on desegregation that threaded explicit resistance with the barest minimum of compliance. It was resistance in the name of moderation.[41]

As other districts managed desegregation by focusing only on high school, or only on working-class areas, Sims helped frame a way for Nashville to at once claim compliance and achieve minimal desegregation. Before an audience at an American Historical Association gathering in Memphis in 1955, Sims argued that it was no great surprise to have the Supreme Court declare segregation unconstitutional. The "predictions of dire consequence" from *Brown* were misguided, in Sims' view, and arose from "a gross misunderstanding" of the actual decision. *Brown* addressed "compulsory segregation," interpreting the impact of segregation to come from being "*compelled* to attend a separate school." Recounting reports from northern schools, Sims assured his listeners that student habits limited actual social contact between black and white students, so that even where desegregation happened, integration did not.[42]

Sims did not believe that anyone would want integration, aside from "the most zealous of crusaders." Once compulsion was removed, individuals and families would choose segregated schools. Sims assumed that such a thing as choice "free from coercion" existed for both black and white families in the mid-1950s South. His comments reflected ideas about "free choice" that ran through the nascent discourse about de facto segregation as originating in individual choice rather than state action.[43]

While the city school board studied and Sims advocated resistance while claiming to comply with legal mandates, civil rights attorneys in Nashville mobilized. Z. Alexander Looby took the lead. Looby partnered with a younger attorney, Avon Nyanza Williams Jr., as well as with the NAACP's local branch and colleagues in the NAACP's Legal Defense Fund. Williams had been practicing law in Nashville since 1953. He hailed from Knoxville, where out of a working-class and financially unstable family background an older sister finished college, got a teaching job, and put Avon and his brother through college. Beginning Johnson C. Smith University in Charlotte at the age of fourteen, Williams graduated and continued on to law school at Boston University. In his choice of law he followed the path taken earlier by his first cousin, Thurgood Marshall. Williams came to Nashville—a place the white business elite sometimes characterized as a "son-in-law town" for the number of young men in elite banking and insurance who gained their positions by marriage—as a son-in-law himself: Williams had married Joan Bontemps, the daughter of noted poet, Fisk administrator, and Nashville school board member Arna Bontemps.[44]

Looby and Williams identified black families whose children would attempt to register at segregated white schools. Alfred Z. Kelley, father of four and a long-term NAACP member, was a self-employed barber to black clientele and thus was less vulnerable to economic reprisals than others. His residence in East Nashville, close to segregated white East High School but across the river and downtown from segregated black Pearl High School, dramatized the geographic consequences of segregation.[45] Kelley attempted to register his son Robert at East High School in September 1955. In the next weeks, twenty-one other black students applied with their families to three other segregated white schools, where administrators refused to register them despite the fact that they lived within the school zone.[46]

With these test cases in hand, Looby filed a complaint in federal court against the Board of Education of the City of Nashville. The case made its way slowly through the courts. In March 1956, board attorney Edwin Hunt offered vague assurances that the board was "making plans looking toward the abolition of compulsory segregation." In October 1956 hearings, Judge William E. Miller ordered the school board to submit a desegregation plan by January 1957. Well before that deadline but more than a year after Robert Kelley and others were denied registration at several schools, the school board's "Instruction Committee on Abolishing Compulsory Segregation" outlined its plan. It desegregated only the first grade starting in September 1957, using a new zoning plan "based upon location of school buildings . . . without reference to race," while making no provisions for desegregation beyond the first grade.[47] The board passed the plan with an eight-to-one vote, over Coyness Ennix's dissent.[48]

With desegregation shrunk to first grade alone, the board curtailed its reach even further by using an idea promoted by Cecil Sims. Sims advocated what he called "intelligent zoning." Although claiming to function "without reference to race," "intelligent zoning" meant creating new geographic school zones squarely upon the foundation of previously explicitly segregated ones. City schools director W. O. Bass asked each elementary school principal, all of whom operated segregated schools at the time, to conduct a "census" of their school's student body—in essence, to map where the schools' current students, who had been assigned to the school on a segregated basis, lived. Then he asked principals to plot geographic zones to match their existing (segregated) student population. New school zones thus used segregation to locate and define their boundaries, and then called the results desegregation.[49] The principals (both black and white) creating these zones had an investment in the segregated status quo. Black principals reasonably feared that changes to their schools' student population would lead to lost positions.[50] On the basis of the new zones, only six of the thirty-six Nashville elementary schools had potentially desegregated student populations.[51]

Nashville school administrators managed desegregation in spatial terms, superficially complying with *Brown* while ensuring desegregation remained token. Although they produced no report on the geographic distribution of black students as had their Davidson County colleagues,

Nashville City Schools administrators used principals' local knowledge to the same end. In the city, administrators reported that if black residents were assigned to school based on the previous geographic zones for segregated white schools, fully three-quarters of the schools in the city would have some black enrollment. In the county, this proportion was even higher, although in many cases there would have been only one or two black children living in each zone.[52] The residential landscape was much less segregated than its schools. This is a point that would seem obvious to the families of Linda Brown of Topeka, Kansas, or the elder Hubert Dixon or young Robert Kelley in Nashville, or the generations of black students who reported walking or riding past white schools to get to their segregated black school.[53] To create the preponderance of single-race schools that operated into the 1960s, school administrators had to manipulate zone lines to create the kind of segregation in schools that they would later claim resulted only from residential patterns. School administrators translated the imperfect boundaries of a Jim Crow landscape into tighter bonds between segregated residence and still-segregated schools.

Nashville City Schools' approach to rezoning, like that of other cities, targeted poorer white neighborhoods for desegregation and exempted wealthier ones.[54] In city neighborhoods, many working-class and poor white families lived in closer proximity to middle-class and poor black families, making complete gerrymandering impossible. Of the six schools with new zones that included both black and white first graders, two sat adjacent to segregated white low-income public housing projects, one in North Nashville and one in East Nashville.

When white local leaders used "intelligent zoning" to limit desegregation, they not only kept black students away from their own children in schools serving wealthier neighborhoods, but away from the suburban neighborhoods they thought were appealing to relocating executives. The leaders managed desegregation in light of growth agendas, and used these agendas to further justify limited desegregation. After concerted recruiting efforts on the part of the chamber of commerce and local officials, the Ford Motor Company decided to open a new facility to manufacture car windshields in Davidson County northwest of downtown. Newspaper coverage announced the extraordinary half-mile-long facility and the estimated 2,000 to 2,500 new jobs at the plant, and asserted that quality schools facilitated Ford's choice of Nashville. Cecil Sims took the Ford decision as proof of the importance of schools in industrial development: "Good schools bring industry."[55] Ford officials explained in more detail that "key personnel" would have to move to Nashville with the new plant, and would be less likely to do so if the schools were not up to their standard.[56] Schools had become a factor in recruitment of industrial managers. Later coverage cited the "educational stability" that arriving professionals valued.[57]

Via gradualism and gerrymandering, the Nashville school board had reduced the mandate for desegregation stemming from *Brown* from the roughly 37,000 students in the district to its 3,367 first graders, then reduced to six the elementary schools with zones that included both black and white students.[58] These zones gave only 115 black students the option to attend previously segregated white schools, and 55 white students the option to attend previously segregated black schools.[59]

Each of these students' families then confronted the question of whether they would act in favor of, or against, desegregation, because Nashville's plan also allowed parental choice to further limit desegregation. The school board's outside legal counsel, Reber Boult and Edwin Hunt, worked with superintendent Bass and his assistant William H. Oliver to create extensive transfer options within the first-grade desegregation plan.[60] (In addition to representing the school system, Boult was also lawyer to inveterate and loud racist James [Jimmy] Stahlman, publisher of the Nashville *Banner*.) Boult's and Hunt's plan allowed any parent or guardian to receive a transfer if their student had been assigned to a school that had previously served a different racial category than their own, or if the majority of students in the school or grade were of a different race.[61] Students could not transfer to further desegregation, but they could transfer to avoid it.

All the white parents residing in zones now linked to previously segregated black schools took these transfer options or otherwise avoided desegregation. Although geographic zones made it most likely that poorer white families in integrated neighborhoods would experience school desegregation, the choice provisions provided them a way to opt out. The exercise of parental choice decoupled neighborhood and school for white families for the first time. Unlike the much-bemoaned decoupling that came later with busing, this one was welcomed and embraced. Of the 115 black students eligible to attend a previously segregated white school, nineteen did so.[62] Through the combined means of zoning and parental choice, Nashville administrators shrank the immediate impact of the *Brown* decision to a change in schooling for fewer than twenty black children and the few hundred white children in school with them, from a total school population of over thirty thousand. The district leadership and its attorneys had achieved what it had earlier assured the over two hundred community groups they met with to discuss desegregation: that some degree of desegregation was inevitable, but that the planned program would make little change in patterns of segregation.[63]

Support for free-choice provisions to restrict desegregation came from other state and local voices as well. Governor Frank Clement, a Democrat with national ambitions, wanted above all else to maintain calm. Going even further than Nashville's parental choice provisions, Clement proposed allowing parents to leave schools where black students attended and allowing school boards to maintain segregated schools for parents who wanted them, to avoid "friction or disorder among pupils or others."[64] Dr. Henry Hill, president of Nashville's Peabody College, a leading teacher-training institution, opined that desegregation should be facilitated by "a minimum of compulsions and a maximum of options."[65]

A network of well-known Nashville residents also organized against desegregation. Founded in the summer of 1955, the Nashville-based Tennessee Federation for Constitutional Government gathered Vanderbilt professor and Agrarian defender of the South Donald Davidson; attorney Sims Crownover; and local writer, artist, and later attorney Jack Kershaw, among others. The organization at times embraced massive resistance strategies. Its more practically minded offshoot, the Parents Preference Committee, ran a petition drive to push the board of education toward Governor Clements's model.[66] They called for "establish[ing] separate schools for pupils whose parents or guardians voluntary elect that they attend school only with members of their own race," legitimizing segregation as a parental choice.[67] With six thousand signatures from the group, Judge Miller allowed them to make their case in his courtroom, creating uncertainty just two days before school would open on the following Monday.[68] Miller responded unequivocally that the state's school preference law, on which the petitioning parents were relying, was "patently and manifestly unconstitutional on its face."[69]

The school board majority and segregationist groups like the Tennessee Federation for Constitutional Government demonstrated indigenous forms of resistance to school desegregation. Their decisions to minimize desegregation to the greatest degree possible, and to frame for the public the process of desegregation as a burden for which the area was "not psychologically ready"—as the board would continue to assert in 1958—opened the way for other forms of street-level and public resistance.[70]

The central figure in both organizing white protest against desegregation in Nashville and in the constructed memory of resistance is John Kasper. A New Jersey native, executive secretary of Washington, DC's Seaboard Citizens' Council, and itinerant white supremacist organizer, Kasper came to

Nashville in August 1957. His organizing work in Tennessee began in the fall of 1956 in the town of Clinton. Within a matter of days of arriving there, he organized picketing at Clinton High School, where earlier twelve black students entered the previously segregated school. Kasper's allies threatened black families by phone and participated in an attack on one black student outside the school. Waves of local efforts to quell Kasper's activities—including restraining orders, jail time, and intervention by the National Guard—failed to end the protests and violence. Calm came only once the US Department of Justice charged and secured convictions for Kasper and six colleagues.[71]

Kasper sat in jail in Clinton in July 1957, but made his way to Nashville by August. There he formed alliances with both local and itinerant organizers. Kasper called his organization the Davidson County Division of the Tennessee White Citizens' Council. At least nine Nashville residents joined as lead organizers. Locals who helped spread Kasper's message came chiefly from the working-class neighborhoods of East Nashville and from the Germantown neighborhood just north of downtown, and included the head of the Davidson County Ku Klux Klan organization.[72] This distribution suggests a working-class orientation to Kasper's recruiting efforts, but also logically follows from the geography of school desegregation in Nashville. The six schools slated for token desegregation under the board's plan were in the same East Nashville and North Nashville neighborhoods from which many of Kasper's organizers came. The geographic design of desegregation matched the protests' working-class accent.

In August, Kasper and his organizers held near-daily rallies in neighborhoods around Nashville, focusing chiefly on working-class white areas not far from centers of black residence. Protest rhetoric mixed themes common to massive-resistance discourse: demands that the school board, whose members they portrayed as puppets of Mayor West, "exhibit fullest manhood" by refusing to enforce standing court orders; calls for the sale of schools to teachers and administrators who would operate them on a private and segregated basis; cries that "race-mixing" and "miscegenation" were certain outcomes of school desegregation; and criticisms of school board and other civic leaders who urged compliance as "pinkos, red devils, Vanderbilt-Fisk Socialists and the political scum of Nashville."[73]

Kasper and colleagues led rallies in response to Judge Miller's hearings on Friday, September 6, 1957, and the weekend following, when Miller overruled the Parents Preference Plan. A Nashville police officer working undercover within Kasper's organization reported gatherings of 350 people at the downtown War Memorial Auditorium on Friday the 6th and 500 on

2.5. Segregationist activist John Kasper, pointing, September 1957.
Courtesy of Nashville Public Library Special Collections.

the grounds of segregated white Fehr School, where Grace McKinley and others registered their students, on Saturday the 7th.[74] This working-class protest threatened elite Nashville's ability to approach, and resist, desegregation in ways that respected the bounds of the local image of moderation. School board attorney Edwin Hunt earlier helped draw up the parental-choice provisions that offered Nashville ample routes away from desegregation, but then worked through the night to secure injunctions against Kasper and his organizers in the days before school opened in 1957.[75]

On Monday, September 9, the first day that black students attended previously segregated white schools, one thousand people gathered at the War Memorial and moved to the Capitol building, listening to speeches by Kasper and Rev. Fred Stroud, another traveling organizer from Albuquerque, New Mexico. Kasper called for a boycott of high schools, in sympathy for elementary school children attending token desegregated schools as of that day. Attendance at schools was down, but no massive boycott occurred.[76]

Official voices offered weak to no support for desegregation. The segregated white PTA refused to sponsor meetings to discuss desegregation, while the school board continued to portray desegregation as an unfortunate development to be managed grudgingly.[77] The board described *Brown*, which applied the nearly century-old Fourteenth Amendment to local schools, as offering a "new interpretation" of the constitution or challenging "deepseated convictions which motivate people" and favoring "abstract theories of sociology, political science and constitutional interpretations." The board worried that the contest between these two would damage the public school system, but appealed to citizens of "good will" to "reflect credit upon the City of Nashville." The segregated white teachers' union echoed the call, asking "'all people of good will' to assist us in making in our schools the adjustments that may be demanded by this 'monumental change.'"[78] The school board also did as little as possible to communicate about its newly desegregated structure, hiding resistance under a veil of neutrality. It did not contact families directly, but shared the news of student assignment only through newspaper announcements and in response to individual queries. Superintendent Bass explained that the board did not communicate to avoid seeming to "influence parents one way or another as to where they sent their children to school."[79] Reinforcing the geography of segregation, the *Banner* published a map showing school zone lines and marking historically and still-segregated black schools with a (C).[80]

No strong pro-desegregation grassroots movement had the vigor of John Kasper's. Modest liberal efforts, led by the Nashville Community Relations Conference, called for accommodation and "law and order." Supported by the United Church Women, the Federation of Jewish Women, and the Nashville Council of Churches, the Conference held two workshops to "build some constructive opinion" about desegregation and hear stories of previous experience in St. Louis and Baltimore. They circulated a memorial with signatures from six hundred individuals, and sent representatives to school board forums and other venues to express support for desegregation.[81]

With weak support from the official bureaucracy, encouragement for the families of students desegregating Nashville's schools fell to community organizations as well.[82] The local NAACP organization received assistance from the small Nashville CORE chapter as it helped inform black parents of the option to attend previously segregated white schools. Some families resented the calls they received from "Negro professional people" asking them to take up the cause and its risks. Some "professional people," including Rev. Kelly Miller Smith, in fact did enroll their own children as well.[83]

Despite the school district leadership's stated desire not to appear to influence parent decision making, the board's policies very much directed parental choice. In the fall of 1957, some black parents transferred their children out of the formerly white school to which they had been newly zoned, but then later changed their minds and attempted to register their child at the formerly white school; the superintendent interceded to stop these retransfers.[84] Echoing the suspicious and patronizing attitude many school administrators took toward black families seeking access to formerly segregated white schools, assistant superintendent Oliver denied the transfers because he felt that the families had been "put up to the task," did not in fact want the transfer, and lacked sufficient reasons to want to attend the previously segregated school.[85] No such careful inspection or roadblocks faced those black and white families alike who chose to remain in segregated schools.

*Brown v. Board of Education*, like many civil rights rulings, was not self-executing. To bring the Supreme Court's opinion that segregation was unconstitutional into practice in school districts, local figures like Z. Alexander Looby and Avon Williams had to act affirmatively to apply the ruling to their district. Once Looby and Williams achieved a court order for desegregation, the work of desegregation continued to devolve, to become the responsibility of less and less powerful people. The school district not only scaled desegregation back to its most meager levels, but crafted opt-out provisions that passed the question of whether to desegregate to the parents of six-year-old children. In *Brown*, the justices acknowledge education's tremendous collective import, but in Nashville as in so many school systems, made realizing its value the responsibility of very young children and their families working against, rather than with the support of, local institutions and officials. Not only did these families confront the social and economic pressures and fears of violent retribution rooted in years of experience with segregation and the mechanisms of white supremacy, but they were even more vulnerable when state action cast desegregation as a matter of their choice.

As the school board majority and district officials modeled quiet bureaucratic resistance to desegregation, the days leading up to the opening of school also brought fiery individual and group acts of violence. Incidents ranged from verbal threats against parents and their children to assaults and destruction of public and private property. Mrs. H. M. Watson committed to send her daughter Barbara Jean to previously all-white Jones Elementary School. When callers threatened to set her house on fire, she worried about how to protect Barbara Jean, her four other small children, and her home. She called a local organizer, who agreed to escort Barbara Jean to school so that Mrs. Watson could mind her home and her children.[86]

The most dramatic and most publicized act of violence was the nighttime bombing of Hattie Cotton School in East Nashville after a single black student registered there. A dynamite blast blew a hole in one of the school's walls, causing $71,000 in damage and temporarily shutting the school.[87] No one was injured in the blast, which was eventually tied to the organizing efforts of John Kasper.

As striking as this act of violence was, however, it was only the most extreme example of the pervasive sense of fear stirred up by white segregationist activists throughout the first week of school. On Monday morning, September 9, black first graders and their parents walked gauntlets of shouting and taunting white bystanders as they entered Buena Vista, Fehr, Glenn, Caldwell, and Jones schools. At Glenn School in East Nashville, principal Mary Brent reported that the three black children attempting to begin school there "huddled" inside the school office as crowds gathered outside. At eleven o'clock in the morning, Brent and the children's parents decided that they should not stay. Police officers escorting them home led the children out a side door of the school. The crowd realized where the children and their families were exiting, and shifted to threatening positions at the side door. Police officers guided the students away from the school and safely home.[88]

Margaret Holt Conquest, one of Kasper's lead organizers, entered Glenn's office with a group of two women and three or four men and demanded to know where in the building she could find "the Negro children."[89] At Fehr School, a black mother registering her child became visible to crowds outside through a window. A white woman lunged through the office doors at her. Fehr's black janitor, Richard Hancock, was in his car leaving the school when he realized he had a flat tire. As he left his car to check the tire, he was chased by a group of white men until he jumped over a fence and ran a block to safety. The crowd gathered at his car, poured coal oil on it, and set it afire. The family of a new black student at Fehr found the outbuildings at their home burned on the second day of school.[90] This level of violence prevailed despite Nashville Police Chief Douglas E. Hosse's promise to arrest anyone who attempted to intimidate children or parents.[91]

After the Hattie Cotton bombing, both black and white parents around the district kept their children home from school. Administrators blamed a concerted boycott effort linked to John Kasper, but basic fear for children's safety likely played a role as well. Attendance on the first day of school was already approximately one-third below registration; it then fell dramatically after the bombing. Of Fehr Elementary School's 383 registered students, fewer than twenty finished out the week. The other desegregated schools had participation rates that were slightly higher. The boycott was short lived, as were fears over safety severe enough to merit withholding students from school. Three weeks later, attendance at Hattie Cotton and other schools returned to normal.[92]

If the bombers hoped to galvanize resistance to desegregation, their actions did the reverse. The Hattie Cotton bombing helped cement many residents' attachment to the idea of Nashville as a moderate city and to tamp down public expressions of resistance. Nashville's business elite had hoped to weather desegregation without the kind of negative attention gathered by the showdown between state and federal power on the steps of Little Rock Central High School, begun just a few days earlier; the bombing shattered that hope. Yet the Hattie Cotton explosion overreached, pushing local leaders to define segregationism as extreme, violent, and rooted outside of Nashville. On the day after the bombing, the *Banner*, the more conservative paper whose front-page editorials earlier stopped just shy of endorsing massive resistance, called John Kasper an "uninvited evangel of mischief" who had "sown the malevolent seed for this harvest of terrorism."[93] With segregationist resistance defined by the extreme bombing, anything short of that became "moderate" and compliant. When Davidson County superintendent J. E. Moss remembered the bombing decades later, he argued that it had helped desegregation overall to proceed more smoothly, as many locals may have been against desegregation but could not endorse "bombing little children."[94]

Asked to choose between the kind of violence the bombing represented or acceptance of minimal desegregation, the vast majority of Nashvillians chose the latter. Lajuanda Street, a black first grader whose family registered her at a formerly segregated white school that September, recalled that after the bombing "suddenly things got instantly better," that she sensed a turn in sentiment toward accepting desegregation.[95] John Seigenthaler, a local newspaper reporter at the time, recalled that "Nashville's civic body felt [a] shock of ice-water" because of the bombing and another contemporary observer felt that the extremity of the bombing meant that "people who wanted to stand up and do their best to try to prevent integration, were almost put in the position of not being able to do so because of such a terrible thing."[96] With yet another metaphor, schools administrator Hugh Waters likened the result to a "dew settling over the community," bringing people together, calming emotions, and reinforcing a sense of commitment to law and order.[97]

That very commitment to order, which emphasized *Brown's* letter rather than its spirit, was both a moderating force and part of Nashville's indigenous, segregationist tradition. Contrasted with the bombing, institutional and bureaucratic resistance seemed to be "moderate." In December 1957, after three months of operating five minimally desegregated elementary schools, the board's instruction committee explained that its meetings in the community regarding desegregation "have convinced the members of your Committee that an overwhelming majority of the people of Nashville are deeply and conscientiously opposed to compulsory integration."[98] Popular (white) opposition implied disorder, which in the circular logic of the time justified arguments against desegregation.

Even if the bombing did enable a climate more accepting of token desegregation, what was happening for Nashville's children was far from "moderate." As of the second year of the plan, only 23 black first and second graders attended formerly segregated white schools. In 1959 the number was 43, and in the fall of 1960, 157. Ten years after the Supreme Court's ruling in *Brown*, fewer than 5 percent of black children in Nashville attended previously segregated white schools. No white students attended previously segregated black schools.[99] While five elementary schools opened with desegregated student populations in 1957, that number had increased to only seven by 1963, when two junior high schools also desegregated as the grade-per-year plan reached seventh graders.[100]

"Intelligent zoning" greatly slowed desegregation. So did the practical difficulties of what CORE labeled "partial desegregation." When grade-per-year desegregation unrolled slowly, it divided younger students at one school from their older peers at another. This division not only forced parents to choose between desegregation and the familiarity and support brought by having siblings at school, but also created logistical difficulties for those who relied on older children to walk younger siblings safely to or from school.[101]

Parents who nonetheless chose to participate in desegregation, like Grace McKinley or Mrs. H. M. Watson, weighed benefits against risks. Iridell Groves, mother to first grader Erroll Groves, shared her view of the situation: "I didn't think they taught the black kids as much as they taught the white kids. And I was determined that he was going to learn as much as he could. I felt like they couldn't teach them without teaching him." For other families, the scale tipped in the other direction. Hesitant families resisted making "their child a guinea pig." Others worried not only about the violent hatred demonstrated in the first days of desegregation in Nashville, but the stories carried in newspaper and television reports of the mistreatment of the Little Rock Nine even with a soldier assigned to each black child.[102] One parent was "in awe of the hatred" on display in these years.[103]

Vanderbilt professor Eugene Weinstein conducted a study of black families living in zones that offered desegregated schools and found that "better-educated, more stable, lighter-skinned parents chose to desegregate," while "segregation-choosing families [regarded] society as more threatening and chaotic."[104] As of 1960, roughly two-thirds of black families given the choice in Nashville continued to send their children to segregated schools, and in that year less than 1 percent of Nashville's black students attended desegregated schools. Given the district's manipulation of desegregation to affect as few schools as possible, even had all black students and their families chosen to put themselves daily within the desegregation struggle, that figure would have reached only 3 percent.[105]

What enrollment did occur resulted from extensive local efforts to persuade black families to choose desegregated schools. CORE members worked in interracial teams of two to reach out to and support families in their neighborhood in the first year of desegregation. In the summer of 1960, the NAACP branch asked Nashville ministers to exhort their congregants to enroll. The national NAACP helped recruit families and students. June Shagaloff, a member of NAACP attorney Thurgood Marshall's staff, spent much of the summer of 1960 working on the ground in Nashville, providing the "full time professional" leadership that branch secretary Vivian Henderson credited with a fourfold increase in black students' enrollment in desegregated schools compared to the previous school year.[106]

Some leading figures in the desegregation struggle faulted not only the Nashville plan, but black Nashvillians themselves, for the limited reach of desegregation. Attorney Avon Williams described limited black participation as evidence of deep psychological barriers. In his characteristically bracing tone, Williams spoke to an organization sympathetic to desegregation in June 1961, and criticized black families who chose to keep their children in segregated black schools.[107] Williams felt that segregation facilitated "substandard Negro education which is seldom openly and honestly recognized as being substandard" by black or white Nashville residents.[108] More baldly, Williams spoke of a "substandard subculture in the Negro community," one that a few leaders like himself who, having "escaped" its "crippling effects" on their "initiative and intelligence," could not bring to an end.[109] That subculture had grown up with different standards in part because of segregation, with its "residential, social, and even religious ramparts" that provided a "shield" from "the light and censure of the com-

munity at large." Those who "refused to accept the advantage" of desegregation did so out of ignorance and fear, Williams believed: "A man can
remain in a dungeon for so long that he is reluctant, fearful, and momen-
tarily unprepared to meet the beauty of the sunlight."[110]

By focusing on culture and individual fear, Williams turned a blind eye
to the various practical factors that informed black families' hesitation or
resistance to desegregation. On transfer cards filed with the superintendent, the most frequent reason given by black families to move out of a desegregated school was the desire not to separate siblings by sending them
to different schools. White parents, however, "seldom assign reasons for
transfer other than the racial one," Weinstein found.[111] Combined with remembered violence against desegregating students in 1957, ongoing images of attacks on student civil rights protesters in downtown Nashville,
and the deep allegiance to some schools as cherished community institutions, Avon Williams's juxtaposition of segregation as "the dungeon" and
desegregation "the sunlight" was too stark.

The small numbers of involved students, the starting point for Williams's frustration, in fact made Nashville's desegregation plan popular with and frequently imitated by school districts around the South. As
the plan was replicated elsewhere, imitation and acclaim traveled back to
Nashville, where it reinforced the self-image of moderation and the idea
of successful desegregation as evidence of the city's moderation. Historian Benjamin Muse wrote in 1964 that Nashville was in the "forefront of
Southern cities in the elimination of segregation in the public schools."[112]

## Pedagogy, Homogeneity, and Resistance to Segregation

If Avon Williams was frustrated by the limits of local support for desegregation among black families, he likely was doubly frustrated by how many
ways resistance could be expressed. As in previous and later phases of
Nashville's educational history, discourse about curriculum—and particularly ideas about homogeneity in teaching contexts—proved another space
to do so. In the late 1950s and early 1960s, many Nashville educators—
like many of their colleagues nationally—believed that sorting students
into classes or groups by both age and perceived ability eased teaching and
aided student learning. As Dr. Henry H. Hill, the president of Nashville's
George Peabody College for Teachers, put it, "Regardless of religion or color
or general conditions, children do learn somewhat better when the group
is relatively homogenous."[113] Nashville superintendent William H. Oliver
left the question more open, saying that "most educators feel that homo-

geneous grouping is wise as far as it is practical," but that "we don't know what is the best thing to do. . . . The question of homogeneous grouping will . . . continue with us."[114]

The discourse about homogeneity in Nashville and elsewhere stemmed from a genuine curricular dilemma, in both philosophy and practice: how should teachers and schools respond to the reality of wide ranges in student ability, achievement, and interest?[115] One approach was to sort students to create as much homogeneity in ability and level of achievement as possible. Segregated schools of course had contained a wide diversity of student ability and achievement, but the divisions and distances created by segregation and the ideas of fundamental inferiority it reinforced allowed many white educators to generalize that white students were achieving more and were capable of more than their black peers. In Nashville, some educators made the idea of homogeneity into a defense of continued segregation, or used it to call for the most limited of gradual desegregation.

Talk of homogeneity never got far from the well-worn insistence on fundamental inferiority, or superiority, knowable by skin color. Even educators who imagined themselves supportive of desegregation were reluctant to deny the possibility of innate differences in aptitude. Mary Brent, principal of previously segregated white Glenn School when two black students enrolled in the 1957–58 school year, offered only a qualified denial of the idea of fundamental inferiority. Z. Alexander Looby, the plaintiffs' lead attorney in the Nashville desegregation case, *Kelley v. Board of Education*, asked Brent, "Insofar as the aptitude is concerned, there is no difference between the races, is there?" She responded that she "cannot see any difference with those two [black pupils at her school]," but "that's . . . the only experience I have had." Cecil Sims likewise could raise the question, but not yet answer it. "It may or may not be true that the Negro is inferior by nature. I don't know."[116] For educators unwilling to rule out the possibility of differences in aptitude by racial category, the idea of homogeneity provided ample space to resist desegregation and manipulate continued segregation. In a time when white store owners and managers still prohibited black men and women from eating at lunch counters or trying on clothes, thick layers of public and private practice linked segregation and claims of innate inferiority.[117] Lackluster denials issued within courtrooms where officials hoped to present an unbiased image did more to strengthen racist thinking about schooling than to change it.

The use of curricular ideas of homogeneity to argue against desegregation was on particular display in Nashville's court hearings on desegregation. *Kelley* hearings in 1958 addressed how Nashville would proceed in its second and subsequent years of desegregation, having desegregated only the first grade in the 1957–58 school year. Plaintiffs asked Fisk University sociologist Herman Long whether he agreed with Peabody's President Hill that students learn more when in a group that is "relatively homogenous." Long felt that children of "relatively equal ability" did achieve "better," but Long went to lengths to explain that such a view did not imply grouping by race. "Obviously this is not a racial factor," Long explained, distinguishing grouping by ability from grouping by race. Attorney Hunt disagreed, though. If, as Hill had explained, "Negroes in the South as a group rank below the whites in health, in general educational achievement," then arguing for classroom homogeneity was "talking of race."[118]

On the stand, witness Long tried to school Hunt in basic statistics, explaining that even if white students had higher average test scores than black students, grouping students by skill level did not mean dividing them by skin color. Long hoped to explain that the range of achievement among white students was large, the range of achievement among black students was large, and that these ranges overlapped substantially, even if there was a gap between average scores by racial category. Hunt continued to resist. On behalf of the City of Nashville Board of Education, he argued that effective schooling depended on dividing students by skin color as a proxy for academic achievement or ability.[119] While serving as the board of education's attorney, Hunt had taken a question in play among educators concerned about curriculum and combined it with racist assumptions to create a rationalization for segregation based ostensibly in the grounds of good pedagogy.

Nashville superintendent William H. Oliver explained that valuing classroom homogeneity suggested very gradual desegregation. If desegregation came immediately, rather than through grade-per-year gradualism, then "you'd have students put into classes together who had a very different background in the community, in the home, in social life, and in the school." These diverse backgrounds, Oliver argued, meant that some students would be "competing with others at a disadvantage," and some would be "held back because of others who were not on the same achievement plane with them." Oliver made the link between classroom homogeneity and gradualism in desegregation clear: "If homogeneous grouping has any value, then we can get the greatest value out of it by a gradual plan."[120] If pedagogical notions could support gradualism, Oliver did not see any incentives for speedier desegregation (or for desegregation at all). To Avon Williams, Oliver commented: "Frankly, I don't think we are gaining anything educationally by putting [black and white students] together. . . . Of course," he added, "I think that we must respect the Supreme Court's decisions. I don't advocate ignoring that."[121]

Given a more sympathetic reading, Nashville schools' arguments for homogeneity could have been simply an attempt to moderate the disruption of desegregation by avoiding bringing together students who had been in segregated school for several years and who, educators believed, would have sharply different levels of achievement. Administrators might have been attempting to do desegregation well, so that black students joining white schools could be introduced gently to new institutions—to make sure, as Mary Brent put it about her two black first graders, that "they have a foundation that will prepare them to go along . . . with the white children. . . . There will be no differences in their (shall we say) background."[122]

Whatever the motive, gradualism was in effect an argument against desegregation. It continued segregation permanently for the eleven grades of students who had moved beyond first grade as of 1957, including all those who sued in *Kelley*. And, of fundamental importance in understanding the trajectory of curricular thinking as desegregation unfolded, the debate revealed among some a persistent—if only quietly spoken—belief in racial inferiority.

A new desegregation case in Davidson County became a venue for more talk of classroom homogeneity and gradualism. Three years after the City of Nashville public schools began to desegregate, in 1960 the surrounding Davidson County Public Schools remained fully segregated. Attorneys and partners Z. Alexander Looby and Avon Williams initiated a desegregation suit targeting the then-separate county in 1960. The named plaintiff in the suit, Henry C. Maxwell, was a farmer living seven miles south of downtown Nashville in the area known as Providence, with four children enrolled in segregated county schools. His older children were of age to attend high school, but doing so meant twenty-mile bus rides each way to and from school. Their route was long because they had to circle much of the city of Nashville to get to Haynes High School, the county's only school for black students, located a few miles north of downtown Nashville.

*Maxwell et al. v. Davidson County Board of Education* proceeded more quickly than had the *Kelley* case, in large part because of precedent established by *Kelley* and similar suits elsewhere. But Davidson County's board was no less recalcitrant than the city's. After Nashville NAACP chairman M. W. Day attended a county school board meeting in 1954 to request a prompt response to the *Brown* decision, the board said it would establish a committee to study the issue. It made the same promise again in spring 1955 and spring 1956, but no such committee was in fact established by the time Looby and Williams brought suit on behalf of the Maxwells.[123]

In the Davidson County proceedings, Nashville became a case study and exemplar. Davidson County school administrators appreciated what Nashville had accomplished in limiting the scope of desegregation. Davidson superintendent J. E. Moss argued that the city's grade-per-year approach, its version of "non-racial" zoning, and the parental-choice provisions that allowed families to stay in previously segregated schools had "worked so well there that we [in the county] would like to follow that example."[124] They sought not only to follow the city's zoning method but also to draw on what white city administrators claimed to have learned about black students' educational needs and capacities.

In preparation for testifying in *Maxwell*, Moss took two full days from his responsibilities running a school system of more than thirty thousand students to visit previously segregated white Nashville schools that now included a few black students. The city school administration and principals at schools like Fehr and Glenn Elementary opened their student records to Moss, who examined the academic progress in general, and in some cases had taken the time to read the individual mathematics assignments of each black student in the school.[125]

Moss interpreted the evidence he found to support gradual, limited desegregation. Moss asserted that where black students entered "in the first grade they tend to do very well and their progress is satisfactory," while those that shifted to formerly segregated white schools in later grades "didn't do quite as well," although he offered no support for this generalization. Nashville City superintendent William H. Oliver agreed with Moss on this, not only defending his districts' gradualism but suggesting that the only successful entry point for black children in previously segregated white schools was at first grade.[126]

As Moss and Oliver argued for gradualism, they shared test score data that revealed deep inequality in the education their schools were providing. Yet they read this evidence through their assumptions that racial categories described differences in ability rather than opportunity. County school psychologist Emmett (Bob) Pettie explained that using aggregate measures, both black and white students "came out within the average range" on first-grade readiness tests, but that a gap between their achievement opened gradually wider each year. That is, the longer students stayed in school, the larger the test-score gap became. Black eighth graders' test results showed reading skills that were a year and a half behind the norm, while white students tested a year and a half ahead.[127] Davidson educators used these results to argue for only gradual desegregation, because they said introducing older black students into previously segregated white schools would mean setting them up for difficulties keeping up with their peers, or the likelihood of tracking into lower ability groups within classrooms.[128] County educators and cooperating witnesses from the city had clear evidence of unequal educational experience—despite starting at equal points, the more years black students stayed in school, the further behind their white peers they fell—but left that inequality unacknowledged.

Attorney Avon Williams and his expert witnesses tried to work against this line of argument, with Fisk University sociologist Herman Long returning to his point that in-group variation in achievement test scores was greater than that between groups. For Avon Williams, such evidence proved, as he put it yet again, that "this really does not constitute a problem of race relations at all."[129] There existed ample evidence of inequality in facilities, in transportation, and in resources, which could help explain patterns of inequality in student achievement. Nonetheless, with either indifference or willful disregard, Nashville and Davidson County administrators turned to evidence of inequality to argue for gradualism and against desegregation.[130] At times, they read differences in achievement created by uneven opportunity and resources, both in school and outside, as differences in innate, even natural, characteristics.[131]

Davidson County's attorneys argued vigorously in court that their schools should desegregate on the same year-at-a-time pace in effect in the city, to begin with first graders in the fall of 1961. After four days of witness testimony in late October 1960, Judge William Miller ruled that Davidson County could follow Nashville's plan but on an accelerated timeline. Miller ordered Davidson schools to open on a desegregated basis in grades 1 through 4 as of January 1961. This arrangement brought the county into line with the city, where the grade-per-year plan reached fourth grade in that year. From then on, both the city and county would allow black students to enter one additional grade per year until all grades would be desegregated as of 1968. Although a victory for the plaintiffs' side, the resolution galled Henry Maxwell and his children. Only one Maxwell child was young enough to attend a desegregated school. In January 1961, 42 black children enrolled at previously segregated white schools in Davidson County, a number that increased to 110 at the opening of the September 1961 school term, out of a total of 2,427 black students.[132]

The reality of wide ranges in students' preparation for school, previous academic background, ability, and personal ambitions created a genuinely thorny problem, not simply a manufactured one, for Nashville educators. It is one that educators continue to struggle with in schools both visibly diverse and seemingly homogenous to this day. Yet the problem of diver-

ras not taken up in Nashville on these terms. Instead, some school ministrators read innate differences in ability from evidence of unequal ational outcomes. That these outcomes stemmed from disparate treatment in schools and in many other aspects of life in Nashville fell out of the discussion, and evidence of disparate educational outcomes became justification for desegregation delayed.

## Conclusion

Z. Alexander Looby and Avon Williams pushed hard and consistently to bring *Brown* to Nashville, exploiting every tool the law offered them. Their efforts drew the support of parents like Grace McKinley and Iridell Groves, willing to make the uncertainties of desegregation part of their children's very first days at school. These children and their families did the work that the Supreme Court could approve but could not accomplish itself.

Nashville's white elite responded to *Brown v. Board of Education* by manipulating time and space to limit desegregation, while at times reinforcing racist approaches to curriculum that had long accompanied segregation. Figures like Cecil Sims and Edwin Hunt policed the boundaries both of protest and of desegregation to foster a public narrative of Nashville's moderation, to accomplish both formal compliance and meager actual desegregation. In this way, neither desegregation nor the response to it would tarnish the carefully guarded image of business- and growth-friendly moderation that Sims himself had helped shape as an advocate of metropolitan consolidation. Multiple modes of resistance flowed through single communities like Nashville, both with citizens and officials differently positioned using government power in a variety of ways. Few Nashville officials used their power toward an ambitious or positive view of desegregation, but they put government force behind ensuring limited desegregation and avoiding disruptive white resistance.

From their work as attorneys in matters of employment and housing discrimination, police brutality, and more, Looby and Williams confronted many of racism's manifestations. Over the decade after their initial victories in *Kelley*, they saw new forms of inequality take shape amid desegregation, often through manipulations in the spatial or curricular organization of schooling. At times, inequality emerged out of forthright neglect of black students, and at times out of efforts to better serve them. Early 1960s courtroom discussions of homogeneity turned out to be only one portion of a broader discourse about curriculum, segregation, and inequality.

# CHAPTER THREE

# The Curricular Organization
# of Segregated Schooling

*Brown* created a legal prohibition against dividing students by skin color, but as the boldface listings of "Colored" and "White" in Nashville's school directory for the 1960–61 year indicated, Nashville schools continued to make explicit divisions between students by racial category. The district's curricular approaches in particular embraced the idea that black students were fundamentally different than their white peers. This idea shaped both thinking about students in the immediate term (regarding remedial needs or compensatory education) and the long term (regarding future occupation and vocational education). It had impact on educational practices in the 1960s, and for decades after.

At times, ideas of student difference were expressed in racist resistance to desegregation, as discussed in chapter 2. They took root as well in deeply well-intentioned efforts by black and white educators to link schools to student need and future economic mobility. In practice, however, ideas of difference tended to reduce the vast range of actual individual variation in need and ability to false assertions that difference could be known by skin color.[1] The curricular organization of schooling became a powerful venue for the making of segregation and educational inequality in the same years in which desegregation efforts in schooling and in public accommodations began to challenge explicit categorizations of people by race.

Whether seeking to meet student need or shape future employment, Nashville educators and advocates were engaged with what Martha Minow has called "the dilemma of difference." Minow explains that Americans and American institutions like schools have struggled to answer these questions: "When does treating people differently emphasize their differences and stigmatize or hinder them on that basis? and when does treating people the same become insensitive to their difference and . . . stigmatize or hinder them on *that* basis?" Minow usefully points out that the dilemma is complicated by how individuals come to inhabit or bear particular categories—often not out of their choice, but through the judgments of others in power.[2] Vocational education and compensatory education discourse illustrate what Minow identifies as an unstated assumption beneath the dilemma of difference—that differences are inherent, rather than in fact both relational and environmental.[3] Many forces create differential need among students—from poverty and racial and economic segregation to systematic and generational neglect in education and other policy venues. These forces were amply visible in Nashville. Yet discussions of difference tended to locate "difference" in the person of the child and his or her categorical descriptors—race, class, address—rather than in his or her experience of differential treatment by both governmental and private actors.

Much of the discussion of difference occurred in the context of attempts to better serve black and poor students and to remedy historic inequalities of opportunity in schooling and in work. This goal animated the work of economist and civil rights advocate Vivian Henderson, who sought to bring more black Nashville workers into skilled and semiskilled employment. In the early 1960s, Henderson suggested that schools provide targeted vocational education for black students to expand their career prospects. Doing so involved predicting students' future occupations—what turn-of-the-century psychologist G. Stanley Hall called students' "probable destination."[4] Such predictions were inseparable from the surrounding, highly discriminatory labor market. Some approaches to vocational education, like Henderson's, sought directly to challenge this discrimination, while others accepted or even reinforced it.

Ideas of difference also guided the local educators (and their allies in national philanthropy) who helped shape "compensatory education" in Nashville. Targeting what they perceived to be the distinct needs of poor children in segregated black neighborhoods, black and white educators created some successful interventions in a few Nashville schools. Yet their work conveyed the needs of poor and black students as separate from those of the white, middle-class students the district treated as normative. Compensatory education and its accompanying language of "cultural deprivation" attached notions of student difference to particular geographic spaces in the city as well.

Meanwhile Nashville educators also saw increasing pressure from local business leaders to link curriculum—and especially vocational education—to local growth agendas. The chamber of commerce, the mayor, and various business leaders who had earlier championed urban renewal and metropolitan consolidation as routes to growth now turned to schools toward the same end. Doing so involved the complex and often troublesome work of thinking about students in terms of "probable destination." To meet both expanding enrollment and business demand for vocational education, the first consolidated Metro Nashville director of schools John Harper Harris made large comprehensive high schools with extensive vocational offerings the model for his district. Comprehensive high schools became the key venue for high school–level desegregation in Nashville during the 1970s and beyond, and a key site for the working out of the dilemma of difference in the era of desegregation.

Over the 1960s, compensatory education programs invested in city schools and in the idea that city students—and especially poor and black city students—were different than others. In the same years, vocational education's expansion also framed student need as more divergent than unified, which endorsed sorting students not only by pedagogical but economic interest, and shaped the high school model that would dominate in Nashville through the desegregation decades. These ideas guided the curricular organization of schooling in Nashville in the decade before busing for desegregation.

## Respecting or Challenging a Segregated Labor Market

At the turn of the twentieth century, black intellectuals and educators confronted a quandary: What should schools teach when their students faced a racist labor market upon graduation? This question of educational philosophy and practice nested within the larger question of how black Americans could advance themselves and their communities. Was it Booker T. Washington's vision, to "cast down your bucket where you are," a vision of the most gradual of reform that aligned with the industrial education programs Washington developed at Hampton and Tuskegee? There, the experience of menial labor became part of the training (or subjugation) of black students, including those who intended to launch themselves into careers as school teachers. W. E. B. DuBois took sharp aim at Washington for this approach in *The Souls of Black Folk*, offering a more assertive vision of democratic justice that needed education to challenge—rather than reconcile black students to—the realities of a segregated South premised on racial proscription.[5] The debate, over whether vocational education might open or restrict opportunity for black students, continued in mid-twentieth-century Nashville.

Vocational education was far from a simple good. Not only did school districts distribute vocational offerings unevenly, but the benefits of those offerings were uncertain at best, especially for black students. From its earliest iterations in the 1910s, vocational education programs had failed to prepare students for specific yet shifting skill needs amid changing labor demand. Yet the allure of the "education gospel"—that targeting schooling to vocational preparation could create opportunity—remained strong.[6] In Nashville as in other cities South and North, vocational education, where offered, pointed black students at lower-skill occupations than those in better-resourced vocational programs for white students.[7] And resource inequalities were crucial in vocational education, with equipment and staffing needs much greater than traditional academic courses.[8] Gaps in public education mattered more when industry- and union-based training programs, and many private vocational training schools, continued to exclude black students.[9] Yet even when black students completed training in skilled work, they often faced racist hiring practices that made becoming vocational educators themselves the only way to use their skill.[10]

Historically the field exemplified separate and unequal as well. In 1941, war production needs led to the creation of the only dedicated vocational school in the city of Nashville and Davidson County, Hume-Fogg Technical-Vocational High School. Opened with a focus on aviation mechanics to serve the local Vultee Aircraft (later AVCO) factory, Nashville city schools operated it as a segregated school, serving only white students from both the City of Nashville and Davidson County. In 1942 the Fair Employment Practices Commission found Vultee to have excluded black workers from manufacturing jobs. Only twenty black employees—less than 1 percent of the company's payroll—worked at Vultee, and they did so in janitorial and kitchen positions exclusively. Vultee managers used segregated training schools such as Hume-Fogg as an excuse. Vultee representatives told the commission that they hired from "pre-employment training schools" that produced only white trainees. A school administrator countered that it was nonsensical to train black workers for aircraft jobs since Vultee, like so many manufacturers across the nation at the time, refused to hire them.[11] This circular logic linked both schooling and labor market discrimination to keep black students in Nashville from opportunities in skilled manufacturing.[12]

Pearl High School was the only segregated black school in the city or county with vocational offerings in the mid-1950s. Pearl offered fewer vocational education courses to its black students (nine) than white students could find in other district schools (fifty-eight) at a moment when black students made up over a third of the district's high school population.[13] While Hume-Fogg and other segregated white high schools offered courses in drafting, refrigeration, electricity, electronics, IBM operations, and other highly skilled trades, Pearl focused on trades such as "general metals, foundry practice, and hosiery looping," which pointed students toward less-skilled work available in the local segregated labor market.[14] Some vocational programs at Pearl targeted employment niches available to black workers, as in multiyear courses in tailoring, or bricklaying and cabinetmaking. Despite the limited offerings, one observer noted that "Negro pupils avail themselves of vocational training more extensively than do white pupils" when it was available.[15] While Pearl offered vocational courses, the program there was "antiquated and not compatible with the demands placed upon our youth competing for jobs in an urban economy."[16] Even if Hume-Fogg's program remained "far from what it should be," it still outpaced Pearl's.[17]

Vocational curricular offerings had their own post-*Brown* rush to equalize. The architect of "intelligent zoning" in Nashville, Cecil Sims, pushed to create a county-wide vocational training center for black students, as well as more immediately to add vocational courses in the building trades at Haynes High School. Pearl gained new courses in plumbing and electrical work, and the newly expanded Cameron had an industrial co-op program.[18] Despite the expansions, school administrator W. H. Oliver admitted that "training has not been provided in the past years as well for the Negroes as for the whites." Oliver explained that the programs followed (segregated) labor demand.[19]

In the peak years of local direct-action campaigns for the desegregation of public accommodations, some organizers focused on getting black students access to more and better vocational education. Vivian W. Henderson made vocational education central in his investigation of economic opportunity in Nashville. He and his colleagues wrote, "After twenty years of technological change and in the face of changed manpower demands, Negro youth are still being offered vocational training to prepare for employment as cooks and maids." This was no hyperbole. Proudly framed and displayed photographs of the "cooperative training program" at Pearl High School over the 1950s and early 1960s showed black girls and some boys in housekeeping uniforms unloading dishwashers, cooking, and pushing the strollers of their employers, or working in local cafeterias.[20] Throughout the early twentieth century, southern vocational programs in segregated black schools provided training for "black jobs," devoting school resources to preparation for positions for which no formal training was previously required.[21] Where students participated in semiskilled occupations, they did so within the narrow sector of black-owned businesses. Pearl photographs documented students working as clerk-typists, file clerks, or electricians with black supervisors and in black-owned businesses or institutions, not in the larger number of local white-owned businesses and institutions.[22]

With a greater range of more highly skilled crafts taught at Hume-Fogg, the school became a target of desegregation activism. While Vivian Henderson and other local leaders encouraged black test enrollment there in 1960, the school remained segregated until 1962. The NAACP petitioned the board to desegregate, which it did in advance of other area high schools still waiting for the grade-per-year plan to reach their level.[23]

Local leaders like Henderson were at once aware of the flawed local history of vocational education and hopeful that schooling for particular job opportunities could become a mode of opportunity for black students. They wanted to chip away at the joint oppression by race and class that W. E. B. DuBois articulated and that Henderson addressed in his own work as a University of Iowa–trained economist. Henderson had arrived in Nashville in 1952 to teach at Fisk, where he began his ascent to prominence in his field and later to the presidency of Clark Atlanta University in 1965. In Nashville, he quickly became involved with the local chapter of the NAACP, where his economic expertise informed local activism. Estimating black purchasing power at 30 percent of downtown retail sales, his research encouraged a 1960 boycott of retailers who refused to employ black salespeople. The boycott cost downtown retailers a quarter of a million dollars in March 1960 alone.[24] Under this pressure, downtown businessmen sought to end the boycott, and negotiated with Henderson and Rev. Kelly Miller Smith to do so by agreeing to hire black workers in sales, clerical, and office positions.[25] The boycott was one among other efforts to end racist exclusion in employment, including targeted campaigns at Southwestern Bell, aircraft manufacturer AVCO (formerly Vultee), and Western Union.[26]

Barriers to fair employment were high. Henderson's Community Conference on Employment Opportunity (CCEO) documented a three-part pattern of limits on employment for African American workers in Nashville. First, black professional or skilled workers found employment only in businesses "devoted almost exclusively to serving Negroes," such as Nashville's historically black colleges and black church publishing firms. Second—and despite the strength of the local black middle class—more than 80 percent of Nashville's black workers occupied menial or unskilled positions. And third, there was "very little absorption of Negro manpower in the occupational middleground" of semiskilled work.[27] As of May 1962, Henderson counted "only one (1) Negro licensed plumber in Nashville and only two (2) Negroes licensed as electricians," yet saw predicted growth in the area economy over the next decade in "pipefitting, plumbing, air conditioning, refrigeration, electricity, and other . . . areas where apprenticeship training is the key to learning the skill and qualifying for employment."[28] The economist who saw black purchasing power as a lever for hiring in downtown retail hoped to find in job training another lever to opening new categories of work to black employment.

Henderson identified opportunities particular to the early 1960s. Henderson had led his field in articulating how black economic progress had stalled in the late 1950s, in part because "technological improvements" threatened jobs "previously 'reserved for Negroes.'" Technological change threatened black unskilled jobs, but Henderson hoped to make the development of new semiskilled positions a point of entry for black workers, a way of addressing the gap he saw between unskilled employment, which was poorly paid but available, and the limited opportunities in professional fields.[29]

Government employment became a site of opportunity as well. President John Kennedy's March 1961 Executive Order 10925 required nondiscriminatory hiring by the federal government and its contractors, which included many semiskilled positions in clerical and construction fields. Although segregated education had provided municipal and state-level employment for highly educated black professionals, state employment remained relatively closed to black workers. Henderson and Herman Long (the Fisk sociologist who testified about student achievement scores in the 1960 *Maxwell* hearings) found that 7.1 percent of state agency employees (primarily headquartered in Nashville) were black, while black people made up 16.4 percent of the state population.[30] Black workers were at once proportionately underrepresented and confined to less than a tenth of the total 1,216 job types in state employment.[31] Black workers made up only 1.5 percent of the state's clerical workers, 13.6 percent of their technical and skilled workers and craftsmen, and less than 10 percent of professional workers, concentrated almost exclusively in education, social services, and corrections.[32] Explicit state practices (such as the employment service's keeping of separate listings of Negro and white applicants from which department heads could select candidates) and implicit ones (such as phone operators steering some job postings to the office on Jefferson Street, in the heart of the black commercial district, and others to the downtown office near more white firms) indicated the extent of small-scale but consequential supports for segregation within the state bureaucracy.[33]

Henderson hoped that black youth could be "channeled into" government agencies and contracting firms.[34] Doing so meant first ensuring that potential employees had the skills these jobs required. It was here that Henderson and his colleagues argued for the "right to participate" in the schools and programs that could offer this preparation. The logic of exclusion that appeared in World War II–era discussion of vocational education and discriminatory hiring continued in public contexts, as when southern school boards justified offering limited vocational training to black students "on the grounds that jobs in the crafts and technical areas are not opened to Negroes so why train them for such jobs."[35]

Henderson imagined that major transformations in black workers' economic status could be rooted in specific skills taught in school. Working with the CCEO and Fisk, Henderson planned a workshop for Nashville guidance counselors, with the goal of informing them of new requirements and opportunities for employment. It was a nuts-and-bolts session, including a panel on "teaching test content" geared at the civil service examination.[36] The state's employment application blank offered another promising point of entry. The form asked only one question about quantifiable skill: how many words typed per minute.[37] Could answering with a high number be sufficient to launch an African American worker into a previously unavailable job category?

Despite his hopeful pragmatism, Henderson's interest in vocational training was neither naive nor unaware of the history of vocational education for black students. He clarified that he was not endorsing the "poor quality vocational and technical training programs that serve as *dumping grounds* for problem students," nor with programs that prepare black youth for "traditional Negro jobs." Henderson remained hopeful that "constructive programs" that combined the "best of vocational, technical, and academic curricula" were possible, but he doubtless knew that vocational education had been at best a very imperfect tool to advance black economic opportunity.[38] Privately, Henderson reminisced that his forefathers had made great sacrifices in the hopes that education would make opportunity. Yet he feared that "education does not of itself open doors . . . in addition to an education, you should have a white skin."[39]

If those doubts came out in private, Henderson's public voice offered less-qualified advocacy for education as the route to individual and collective mobility. Education would "pay significant dividends to the economy of the South" and create "more manpower potential" to "help eliminate poverty and the burden of low-income dependents."[40] Adopting James Bryant Conant's descriptor for urban students, Henderson predicted that failing to meet youth's educational needs would "set the stage for a southern type of 'social dynamite'" among "unprepared Negro urban youth . . . unemployable because the school system failed to fulfill its obligation to provide them with training and skills commensurate with the demands of the economy."[41] These remarks conveyed at once an economist's confidence that growth could raise all boats and labor markets would be responsive to worker skill. The mutually reinforcing cycle of segregation by skin color in schooling and segregation by skin color in employment had long shaped vocational education, in both southern and northern contexts. But Henderson called for trying, again, to make vocational education a less-conflicted educational good.

Vocational education opened doors for sorting not only between vocational educational programs at black and white schools, but within them as well. All of Nashville's high schools remained formally segregated in the early 1960s, with desegregation at that level beginning only when the school board accelerated the grade-per-year plan and incorporated high school grades in 1966. Vivian Henderson, like the majority of the leadership of the local NAACP and their university-affiliated supporters, was a middle-class professional; teachers at schools such as Pearl composed the backbone of the local black middle class. Pearl drew much of its local reputation from the strength of its college-preparatory programs. When Pearl alumni and later Rev. Amos Jones recalled his years at the school, he explained what it felt to sit outside of Pearl's college-preparatory ethos. As a student from a poor family who was "just thinking about working on the print line, just like . . . Daddy," Jones felt he left Pearl having lacked the "enthusiasm and guidance" that he needed as motivation to learn.[42]

Henderson navigated a complex reality, seeing schools as both a historic force in the limiting of black employment opportunity and a potential venue for expanded opportunity. His vision of strengthened education was one part of what he felt was needed to address the subjugation of black workers as a race and a class, including job creation and a higher minimum wage. Locally, vocational education became the favored route not just of activists like Henderson but Nashville's business elite and its leading educators. Without careful protections in place to attach it to Henderson's hopes of expanded opportunity, vocational education ultimately fed a curricular logic of segregation and restricted opportunity.

## The Paradox of Compensatory Education

As businessmen and some civil rights leaders advocated designing schooling to suit future employment, 1960s-era compensatory educational programs for the "culturally deprived" further demonstrated the dilemma of
difference. Compensatory education brought new ideas and resources to
bear on the problem of unequal education. Seeking to address the disproportionate failure of poor students—and often focusing on students who
were both poor and black in selected Nashville urban neighborhoods—
these programs reinforced the notion that some students, identifiable by
geography, income, and skin color, had different short-term needs and
long-term prospects than their peers. Paradoxically, compensatory education sought to aid particular groups of students yet created new obstacles
for them and their communities by deepening the impression that they
were fundamentally different than others. In an unequal and racialized
landscape, these ideas of difference could at times merge too easily into
support for segregation and inequality. This impact would have been important even had compensatory education provided significant gains for
targeted students. But as most programs failed to do so, that legacy is all
the more important.[43] Compensatory education, alongside vocational education efforts of the period, conveyed often racialized ideas of difference
on the eve of more extensive desegregation.

In 1963, prompted by metropolitan consolidation, Nashville's transitional board of education hired consultant Francis G. Cornell to offer his
assessment of the newly joined city and county school systems. Cornell
documented a "sharp decline in Negro achievement in the upper grades"
in Davidson County, and lower achievement for black students in the city
system as well. In Cornell's view, "the new Metro School System will most
certainly fail" to create "equal educational opportunity" if it continued to
offer substandard facilities and neglected to tailor schooling to the "peculiar requirements" of "less fortunate neighborhoods."[44] Nashville schools
served many "less fortunate" white students, but the district's most substandard facilities sat in historically black city neighborhoods or previously
white neighborhoods experiencing black in-migration.[45]

Cornell's attention to the "peculiar requirements" of schools in "less fortunate neighborhoods" echoed the developing national attention among
academics and policy makers to students living in poverty, many in segregated urban neighborhoods, and faring poorly in school. This concern was
the focus of attention-getting national studies such as James Coleman's
*Equality of Educational Opportunity* (often known as the Coleman report)

and contributed to the passage of the Elementary and Secondary Education Act of 1965. Its Title I aimed to provide additional resources to schools serving students from low-income families.[46] The language of the day—describing poor and black students as "culturally deprived"—also reflected national trends. The label originated in early-twentieth-century efforts to shift from innate characteristics and racial categories to culture as an explanation for difference. By the 1960s, however, the usage reinforced ideas of black pathology that gave a new gloss to old claims of inherent difference and inferiority. The discourse continued to locate the causes of poverty and low educational attainment not in institutionalized and structurally supported racism and inequality, but in individual and group characteristics.[47]

Even the semantics of the term reflected this problem. The idea of "deprivation" implies an actor, someone doing the depriving, but does not specify who this actor is. When Harold Stinson, a Nashville administrator, drafted a district proposal to the Ford Foundation in 1965 for a compensatory education program, he noted that new education efforts had to overcome the effects of "serious neglect in the past." Differences in achievement levels were the "outgrowth" of this neglect, and proved only that "equalizing efforts on behalf of the educationally and culturally deprived will not suffice."[48] Stinson thus linked compensatory education to structural neglect. Yet Stinson's diagnosis fell away as both philanthropic and federally funded efforts took shape in Nashville. Emphasis shifted from deprivation, with its hint at actors responsible, to culture, located in individuals or groups and separate from forces of policy, politics, or economics.

Even as contemporary discourse shifted from a structural to individual orientation, poverty-focused education policy did not in fact treat individuals as individuals. The programs relied instead on categorical ideas of student need, amalgamating young people under headings like poor, black, urban, inner city, or disadvantaged. Efforts to define programs for "peculiar" needs became in fact programs that rhetorically portrayed—and often treated—large groups of students from a neighborhood, a school, or an entire socioeconomic category as a homogenous mass.

Three compensatory education programs at work in Nashville show this pattern, and demonstrate the troubled impact of defining and targeting specific populations of students. A cluster of Nashville schools participated in a Ford Foundation project working with a small group of cities to address the limits of desegregation to that point—which had, in Nashville as elsewhere, proceeded slowly and left many black students in still-segregated and still-substandard schools.[49] The Ford initiative, called the Nashville Education Improvement Project (NEIP) within its broader Great

Cities School Improvement Program, began in 1964 and focused on eight schools. Carter-Lawrence, Fall, Napier, Johnson, Murrell, and Clemons elementary schools were either previously segregated black schools that remained all black or had become majority-black through recent shifts in local demographics. The two participating junior high schools, Cameron and Rose Park, had been segregated black schools and had no white students as of 1964.[50] All were located in South Nashville, an area notable both for its concentration of poor black residents in public and private housing and for extensive displacement from urban renewal and highway construction.[51]

NEIP brought more resources, connections with local expertise, and manpower to the participating schools. The program's many facets included remedial reading and math instruction in elementary schools, in part through an experimental program for teaching reading developed at the local school of education, George Peabody College for Teachers.[52] Teachers participated in summer and yearlong training institutes emphasizing remedial instruction and "special programs" for superior students. The program promised "better instructional materials geared to the needs of students from deficient cultural backgrounds."[53] Ford officials visiting the program in Nashville described a "big and impressive impact on students five to seven years old in the participating schools," and an "almost narcotically high" morale among project staff. The organizational structure remained "shallow," however, typical of programs based on external funds but lacking deep support in the local school district.[54]

The program conceptualized black students' need with an emphasis on exceptionality at best, pathology at worst. Black students tended to perform more poorly than white peers, explained by "deprivation which is the outgrowth of past neglect." Quickly the language of deprivation slipped from concern about what students had been denied historically, to fundamental or prescriptive views of difference, asserting an "inability of the group to profit from academic experiences. . . . The most immediate implication is that these children cannot learn," program documents asserted, but then would latter reassure with suggestions that different kinds of educational experiences could prove successful. NEIP's early planners moved away from distinguishing their students by class, shifting to a racialized view of difference. The needs of students in South Nashville's poor black communities were "not very different, on the average, from the general Negro population in the metropolitan community."[55]

NEIP and subsequent programs in Nashville also demonstrated a merging of thinking about compensatory education and vocational education, usually considered as separate educational phenomena, under the banner of the development of students' "economic competency." Compensatory education programs offered special instruction in reading and enrichment areas but also offered vocationally focused programs for "slow learners" at the junior high school level. The "Work Education Experience" program operated within the two junior high schools involved in NEIP, and continued via Model Cities and Title I once Ford funding ceased.[56] NEIP program administrators described their interest in vocational education in expansive and positive terms, characterizing their contemporary moment as one in which "race and parental socio-economic status" were losing power in determining occupational possibilities, and that students could benefit from knowing more about a "wider array of occupational specialties."[57] Despite the optimistic rhetoric, in practice vocational programs continued to emphasize less-skilled occupations and encouraged preadolescents to make consequential career choices.

Many of the project leaders in NEIP and Model Cities were educators who were deeply committed to improving opportunity for their students. But many came from and carried the perspectives of a black middle class in Nashville that was becoming more disconnected from the poorer communities they served as teachers and administrators. In the 1950s and 1960s, black schools were very economically diverse, with the children of Fisk professors and bank officers in school with those of domestic workers and the unemployed. By the mid-1960s, movement to new suburban developments for black families in Nashville's northern suburbs, or into neighborhoods white families had left, meant fewer black middle-class residents lived in urban North Nashville. Poor black students became an exceptional and distinct group for both black and white middle-class educators. Some educators may also have been responsive more to the needs of their employer—the school district—than the students and communities involved, as a Ford Foundation observer worried was happening in NEIP.[58]

The basic conceptual geography of compensatory education in Nashville added a spatial dimension to the dilemma of difference. Both NEIP and the Model Cities program that began in 1967 and extended beyond NEIP's end shared a view that black children in the targeted South and North Nashville neighborhoods were different than their peers in other parts of the county-wide district. Model Cities sought the "particularizing [of] the regular school experience for the needs of the students of the area through curricular revision and re-design."[59] The program generalized across students based on geography, and asserted that particular types of students were found in particular places. (Like their peers nationally, however, program leaders stopped shy of asking one further question, about how these places came to be as they were). NEIP and Model Cities then provided more resources for these targeted schools, working within the logic of *Plessy* more than *Brown*.[60]

When the Ford Foundation ended funding for NEIP in 1969, MNPS did not provide ongoing support. But the program was not without a local legacy. One community organization that had become formalized under NEIP continued to work in the same vein, and several individuals grew into leadership positions in other compensatory education programs in Nashville through their NEIP work. Principal Mary Craighead rose from NEIP coordinator to principal at Carter-Lawrence Elementary School and continued on as a principal in Nashville's first decade of busing. Buford Drake moved from NEIP to the educational component of Nashville's Model Cities project. The project's legacy continued into Nashville's use of its federal dollars from the Elementary and Secondary Education Act's Title I funds.[61]

In the Model Cities neighborhood area in North Nashville, the connection between programs was particularly tight, as Title I funds supported the education components of the Model Cities program administered by a former NEIP teacher.[62] Title I brought new dollars to Nashville's schools—and unlike other venues in Title I's first years, it appears that those dollars did in fact make their way to the district's high-poverty schools.[63]

Title I practice in Nashville encouraged both a racialized and spatially concentrated vision of poverty, despite the reality of a quite varied landscape of economic need. School board members and administrators labeled the Title I–participating schools with the spatially resonant "Project Higher Ground," and referred frequently to "project" or "project area" schools.[64] An administrator explained that students had to live in "the project area" to be eligible for Title I assistance, even though there was no contiguous geographic area—other than the whole county—that contained all of the district's Title I–eligible students or schools. More than a third of Metro Nashville's schools qualified in the first five years of Title I, many of them majority white, even as sixteen of the twenty schools with the highest concentration of poverty were historically segregated or all-black schools. Yet within Nashville's historically segregated or all-black schools, economic diversity appeared as well. Historically segregated Cameron High School, like several of the surrounding South Nashville schools, had upward of half of their students living in severe poverty. But by contrast, only 21.8 percent of Pearl High School's students did.[65] On this measure, Pearl was more comparable with segregated white East High School than with Cameron. Although Title I provided Nashville educators help in addressing student need for black and white urban, suburban, and rural poor students, the program reinforced associations between black and poor students and the urban landscape.

During the 1960s—in the same years in which business leaders and administrators explored how to sort students at the school level, based on predictions of future career path and in hopes of opening economic opportunity and making growth—compensatory education sorted and divided students by race, class, and geography in the name of addressing student need. Educators, community members, and school administrators who advocated for compensatory education programs were concerned about the visible problem of low educational achievement at several Nashville schools that served predominantly black and poor students. These educators faced an embedded quandary: how to meet student needs without simultaneously deepening inequality by reifying difference and asserting that demographic categories were fair proxies for the real range of student need and ability. Although many of its local advocates sought to challenge inequality, the compensatory education strategy emphasized the exceptionality of poor black students—often as a precondition for securing resources available as a matter of course to wealthier white students. As educators, federal policy makers, and philanthropists emphasized the "cultural deprivation" of their students, they made a case that secured these resources but simultaneously defined their students as fundamentally different from more privileged others. The image of exceptionality pushed against desegregation in the same late-1960s years in which litigation began to refine new approaches to integrating students. It also coincided with other views of difference anchored in the local economic structure.

## Educating for Growth: Business and the Vocational Push

Predictions about students' expected futures had long informed thinking about schooling and curriculum for white students as well as black students. How did the needs of the boy on his way to college, the girl who would get married and stay home, the kid assumed to be headed for the assembly line, with or without a diploma, differ? In the same years in which Vivian Henderson and his colleagues called attention to inequalities in vocational education and hoped to use curriculum as a lever for individual economic mobility, Nashville business leaders took up the topic as well. They invested in efforts to connect students to the labor market, in the hope of generating workers to fuel economic growth. Their interest in vocational education perpetuated and strengthened sorting based on presumed occupational future, but with much less attention to challenging labor market segregation than in Henderson's work.

Vocational education promised all things to all people, and yet was relatively inexpensive compared to other job-creation or antipoverty approaches. An emphasis on education fit well within social programming—like the era's War on Poverty efforts—that claimed broad goals but lacked the tools to intervene more assertively in the labor market. Doing so was judged too far reaching by many Americans of the era, and labeled unnecessary by contemporary neoclassical economists.[66] Vocational education could promise a lot without troubling the narrow bounds of local liberalism by focusing on young people and emphasizing their individual characteristics and readiness for the job market. Various local actors were invested in connecting students to the labor market. All supported the basic premise that schools could sort students based on interest (whether expressed or ascribed) and future workplace destination, and could design curriculum accordingly. This sorting often overlapped with racial and class categorizations as well, and helped construct ideas of difference.

Even as Nashville's schools offered black students fewer opportunities in vocational education than white students under formal segregation, programs for white students remained meager. A 1945 study of vocational education in the state found it to be "not adequate," and that "the public high school of Tennessee was still largely a college preparatory institution . . . largely composed of students who never intended to go to college." Nearly half of Tennessee's schools offered no vocational education courses.[67]

In the immediate post–World War II years, business groups like the chamber of commerce did little to encourage specific skill training for students, focusing instead on spreading free market ideology via teachers and schools. In the 1950s, the chamber ran Business-Education Day, an annual event in which teachers visited participating businesses, partaking of a "full program of economic education" to "study the operation of the American Free Enterprise System," and take what they learned back to their classrooms.[68] The chamber also supported a curriculum unit that urged students to "discuss the personality traits that are helpful in getting and holding a job" and "make a list of the characteristics of a good workman in a democratic country." After students viewed a film titled *Productivity—Key to Plenty*, the guide called for them to "discuss the implications it has for individual workers in the country."[69] Much less consistently than it sponsored Business-Education Days, the chamber hosted mirror-image Education-Business Days, in which businesspeople visited schools for the day to study curriculum, teaching procedures, and survey facilities. Although the teachers-visiting-businesses program continued to grow after desegregation began in 1957, the businessmen-visiting-schools program withered. Desegregation shook the chamber elite's interest in local schools, but the organization turned to new visions of what schools should do for business.[70]

During the 1950s, the chamber's discussions about schools as worker-production venues shifted. In the early 1950s, they emphasized maintaining Nashville's low wage–inducing labor surplus and ensuring against the "raiding" of local labor by other locales.[71] By the second half of the decade, chamber organizers and other leaders began to call for schools to prepare future workers more effectively, and heard their calls echoed at the state level. Worker preparation neither implied increasing expectations for all students, nor an assault on the inequalities in vocational education. Much of the business rhetoric about worker preparation sought to simultaneously raise skill levels and limit expectations, with both white and black future workers in mind.

Mayor Ben West carried a newspaper clipping with him to the January 31, 1957, meeting of the chamber's board of governors and provoked more local attention to vocational education. The clipping described a survey conducted by the Indianapolis Chamber of Commerce and the state's Employment Security Office, on local demand for skilled workers. West suggested that the Nashville Chamber organize a similar study, to provide information about the local supply and demand for skilled workers for use within the school system. Describing Hume-Fogg, Nashville's one "technical" high school, as a "semblance" of a program because it served only three hundred students, West called for an adequate training program at the high school level.[72] West's proposal met with "considerable favorable comment and much expression of enthusiasm" among the city's business leaders and employers on the chamber's board. Some chamber members recalled that industrial recruitment efforts had taught them that at firms like General Electric and RCA Victor, "All are concerned with the availability of labor and trained personnel." The chamber moved quickly to involve the city and county boards of education, representatives of local labor, industry and the University of Tennessee, who "underscored need for expanded vocational facilities as the key to continued growth of the Nashville community" and launched a local labor survey.[73] Nashville's local interest in education as training had a state-level corollary as well. Governor Frank Clement organized a 1958 conference emphasizing the centrality of education to economic growth efforts.[74]

When schools promised more directly to prepare students for work, they had to engage a changing labor market. Nashville's 1950s and 1960s business advocates made broad predictions about growth, but often lacked specifics about which sectors would grow. They themselves came from a range of industrial and service sectors, and their uncertainty reflected national efforts to think about changing "manpower" needs and what "automation" meant for work.[75] Frequently, organizations like the Tennessee Municipal League linked higher worker skill and economic growth: "The State's greatest opportunity lies in the development of [its] potential labor supply into a trained labor supply."[76] This emphasis on increased skill fit squarely within the southern—and broader Sunbelt—hopes for a shift from lower-wage industries like textile production to higher-wage, consumption-boosting jobs in defense or more technical production.[77] Added to the challenges of a historically and still-segregated labor market, vocational education faced the challenge of linking schools to the moving target of the labor market.

Whether attached to new or old forms of industry, vocational discourse spoke at once of increased worker skill and limited educational aspirations. After quoting General Electric or RCA's interest in highly trained workers, chamber leaders at times suggested that "there is a need for more Indians and fewer chiefs."[78] Vanderbilt's vice chancellor, C. Madison Sarratt, active in the chamber, commented that there was "no hope in the world of sending all bright youngsters to college."[79] Buford Ellington opened his 1958 gubernatorial campaign with a speech that echoed the high-flying rhetoric of the era of Sputnik and the National Defense Education Act. He called for training in math, science, and "even space exploring," but then urged educators not to ignore the majority who needed "practical training in the less spectacular fields" like welding and electricity.[80] With fewer than 40 percent of local students finishing high school within four years in the 1950s, concerns about tamping down expectations were overblown.[81]

If the chamber explored education and economic development, business remained attracted to the South's antiunion environment and its low taxes. These factors likely outweighed the draw of worker training. Nonetheless, Nashville and Tennessee leaders thought that training could be a prime factor in bringing industrial development, and they pursued growth via major changes that mattered for schooling even if they ultimately had limited economic impact.[82]

Nashville's business leadership sought to use schools to prepare workers in the same years in which they embraced growth in gatherings like the chamber's "New Cities for Old" conference or exhibits of downtown urban renewal. Thinking of worker training opened the complex question of what kind of economic growth they thought, or hoped, would develop.

Vocational education discussions remained attached to specifically industrial or craft occupations; as Davidson County superintendent J. E. Moss put it, the goal was in part returning "dignity to work with the hands."[83] In keeping with the changing profile of Sunbelt economic development, the chamber itself officially shifted in 1955 from discussing industrial recruitment to a broader interest in all "new enterprises." Yet talk of vocational education demonstrated continued attachment to industrial or craft work that privileged white (and usually male) workers while reinforcing underemployment of black workers, who secured less than 4 percent of newly created local manufacturing jobs as of 1960.[84] Without a history as a strong manufacturing center, but with a mixture of industrial ambitions and awareness of the power and growth potential of local finance, insurance, and real estate sectors, defining what kind of worker Nashville needed was not a simple task.

Using Indianapolis's model, the Nashville Chamber of Commerce cooperated with the Tennessee State Department of Employment Security—with funding from the US Department of Employment Security—to survey more than 1,700 Nashville employers on their current and projected labor needs. The July 1957 *Nashville Metropolitan Area Skill Survey* reflected prevailing and enduring patterns in thinking about Nashville's economy.[85] Appreciating the higher wages often paid in manufacturing, the report inaccurately emphasized these positions as the source of Nashville's long-term economic future and the best focus for its vocational education efforts. The *Skill Survey* acknowledged that, even in a sample admittedly skewed toward large manufacturing companies, the largest single employment field in 1957 was clerical and sales work, and that this field's anticipated growth of 24.5 percent by 1962 would mean dramatically more new jobs there than in the slightly faster-growing but much smaller "skilled" employment sector. The survey defined feminized clerical work outside of the "skilled" category, and missed the opportunity to evaluate whether more workers should be trained in this area. Focusing on manufacturing continued business leaders' and educators' fondness for speaking of "work with the hands," full of masculine overtones when juxtaposed against increasingly feminized clerical work.[86] Local business leaders seemed enamored of vocational education as a prompt to economic growth, but they were far from certain about which careers fit their growth ideal. If they struggled with that question, they remained silent on the matter of whether vocational education might challenge labor market segregation.

Nashville's local-level discourse aligned well with 1960s-era thinking about how education and growth related. Not only did schooling seem key to economic growth—as southern boosters had been arguing for decades—but it could be central to eradicating poverty as well. President Lyndon Johnson's War on Poverty chose job training rather than job creation, early childhood education rather than full employment, taking the more politically palatable approach. The irony was this: emphasizing education as *the* route out of poverty located the responsibility for poverty in the skills and capacities, in the very bodies, of poor people. It seemed to be an individualizing, rather than a structural, approach. Yet at the same time, echoing similar tensions in thinking about compensatory education, the programs designed to offer new skills and capacities to poor individuals tended not to see them as individuals per se, but as representatives of categories—of blackness, of poverty—that homogenized more than they individualized. These ideas at times authorized racism, reinforcing segregation and sustaining inequality.[87]

## Embracing the Comprehensive High School Model

While Vivian Henderson and the local chamber of commerce saw in vocational education routes to their own (different) goals, Nashville schools director Dr. John Harper Harris added his own. Harris came to Nashville in 1963 from Des Moines, Iowa, an experienced school administrator hired by the transitional board of education to take the reins of the newly consolidated Metro Nashville system. Harris was a formidable, if not widely liked, character known for a brusque, imperious demeanor and what one observer described as "a reputation for being an automaton" concerned with "administrative tidiness" over "human concerns."[88] In a 1964 speech to the Kiwanis Club, Harris assured his audience he understood that the lack of vocational education facilities and curriculum was a serious local problem. He argued that "there is dignity in work" and that "we must realize that every boy can't be a doctor or a lawyer or a PhD. Industry needs young people with training and we must be prepared to provide them." Before receiving a standing ovation, Harris suggested that linking children as young as twelve to exploratory programs in careers could "save boys and girls."[89] These ideas aligned with others circulating in elite Nashville, as when insurance executive and Peabody trustee David K. Wilson hoped to start a program to place emphasis on "the dignity of work, upon the importance of individuals regardless of their employment and nature of work, and upon pride in quality of workmanship."[90]

The federal Vocational Education Act of 1963 facilitated Harris's interest in vocational education. The act both increased vocational education dollars and lessened prior constraints on their use in particular fields or occupations. Federal funds had flowed to secondary vocational education since the 1917 Smith-Hughes Act and subsequent measures, but educators like Harris saw in the new act's $255 million appropriation (with requirements for a one-to-one match) the opportunity for course offerings more relevant to local labor markets.[91] Harris had new dollars to put behind the vocational education programs of interest to the Nashville business community.[92]

Expanded federal funds were helpful, but not determinative, of Nashville educators' interest in vocational education. Nashville schools in the 1960s, like their southern counterparts, were completing the transition from elite to mass institutions that had happened decades earlier in the North.[93] The majority of northern white students attended high school since well before World War II, but Tennessee and other southern states saw much lower high school enrollment rates. In 1950 Tennessee, the figure was 45 percent overall, and for black students, 41 percent. By 1970, however, 69 percent of the age cohort, black and white, attended.[94] Sorting by occupational destination had earlier occurred between students who were attending high school and those who were not; progress toward universal high schooling brought the question of sorting into the school program. Skills- and career-focused schooling seemed to fit students who increasingly stayed in high school, but would not continue on to college.

Vocational education also promised to help administrators address the "dropout crisis" that emerged once high school attendance became normative. As early as 1958, local press portrayed high school dropouts as part of a growing trend both locally and nationally. A local reporter profiled "Frank A.," a white eighteen-year-old who was "already dissatisfied with life." Frank had dropped out of school not because he was failing, but because he felt "There was just nothing there for me."[95] Nashville school administrators knew that a large portion of their students never completed high school, a point that became more noticeable as high schooling became more typical in these decades. The City of Nashville reported a 1963 dropout rate of roughly 50 percent, higher than the figures for Davidson County or the state overall.[96] When asked why a large number of students dropped out, Nashville principals listed "inability to do the work" as the primary cause. Next came economic conditions, such as the need to work and contribute at home, and marriage or pregnancy third.[97]

While local liberals organized conferences and immediate interventions for students deemed at risk, Harris took a more systematic and curricular view.[98] Dropout rates stemmed from too little curricular diversity, too few vocational offerings, and too little guidance counseling. More of these, Harris implied, would leave "Frank A." feeling that school did have something for him. Nashville high school principals agreed with Harris, identifying vocational education courses as the fix for both "the slow learner" (one principal even specified an IQ-point range to determine who took vocational classes) and "those in financial need." Principals of both segregated black and segregated white high schools made similar suggestions for vocational offerings as well as vocational counseling to ensure that the right students, in educators' estimation, took the classes.[99]

Dr. Harris and his colleagues at MNPS considered vocational education a fix for younger students as well. Harris aimed to divide students into vocational and academic tracks as early as age twelve. If vocational education was the cure for dropouts, and if the characteristics that suggested dropping out, including lack of interest, having failed a grade, or "resentment toward authority," could be discerned in the last years of elementary school, then "trade school centers beginning at the 7th grade level" would help keep students in school. Clarifying the purposes of these centers, administrators explained that they prepared students for "service oriented work," at a less-skilled level than in a vocational training program. Their proposal suggested courses in "food services, hospital aides, carpentry, masonry, house wiring, plumbing, cosmetology aides."[100] These proposed offerings simply recast existent offerings for black students in Nashville.

Nashville leaders advocating for vocational education did so for different, yet broadly related, reasons. From Vivian Henderson to chamber representatives, all thought that it was both possible and appropriate to link what happened in classrooms to the particular skill needs of employers. They thought such efforts could benefit Nashville by preparing students for employment, providing employers labor, and, more broadly, laying the groundwork for economic growth. And all were concerned with the question of how high school could be useful not only for college-bound students, but for those who, in earlier decades, would not have attended at all. Each of these approaches depended—whether for purposes of expanding or limiting opportunity—on sorting students by presumed future path and determining their education on this basis. Doing so provided wide openings for discriminatory practice inside schools.

Even as the district was embracing expanded vocational programs, some local educators in existing ones suggested cautions. Clara Mae Benedict served as a guidance counselor at the segregated white Cohn High School, where she established a job placement office in 1958. The office's work included visiting local employers to survey their hiring needs. Benedict made over two hundred such visits with colleagues in the job placement office's first five years.[101] From 1958 until 1961, her office at Cohn placed one-third of its male graduates and two-thirds of its female graduates in their first jobs, the rest marrying or attending college. In a retrospective study, Benedict showed how white vocational graduates experienced the local labor market, as well as gender-based divides in that market. Likely because it lacked traditionally male trades and industries courses available at Hume-Fogg, Cohn's vocational program served three times as many female students as males. Of the female students placed in jobs, 44 percent were placed as typists, an additional 22 percent as clerical workers, and another 21 percent as stenographers, making clerical jobs the overwhelming employer of white girls coming out of Cohn's vocational courses. Benedict was confident that employer interest in girls trained in clerical skills would continue to be strong into the 1970s.[102]

Benedict saw, though, that "prospects for male high school graduates were not as bright as for girls."[103] For employed white boys, no single occupation dominated: 20 percent went into sales, 18 percent into factory work, and 13 percent into clerk positions. The rest took jobs as delivery boys, apprentices, maintenance, or office workers. Benedict explained this pattern: even when jobs were available in manufacturing or other industries, most companies required workers in these fields to be at least eighteen years old (older than some high school graduates), and in some cases twenty-one.[104] If this was the case, could male high school graduates be industry-ready workers? If not, why direct them there through vocational education?

Some education officials at the state level had similar concerns, including Commissioner of Education Quill Cope. Cope was concerned that "the wrong kinds and types of programs with the wrong type of training" would still seem attractive to local political and business groups, thus creating a large financial burden for the state "without compensating results."[105] Business leaders at a state conference on "Education beyond the High School" offered that "industry does not encourage technical training. Instead, industry prefers sound and thorough basic education in English, mathematics, and sciences." Similarly, another employer had commented in the 1957 *Skill Survey*, "Our greatest difficulty is finding young men who can write legibly, do simple arithmetic correctly, and THINK."[106] But other businesspeople at the state and local level continued to call for secondary-level vocational education, even as there was no consensus on whether vocational schooling worked as worker preparation. Many Nashvillians seemed to think that vocational education was an educational good, but it remained a thorny one even without trying to address a discriminatory labor market.

The history of industrial education and vocational training in the South might suggest that Nashville's new interest in vocational education was a direct response to desegregation. After all, the chamber's involvement in this issue neatly coincided with the announcement of grade-per-year desegregation. Yet the actual story, like desegregation itself, is of more embedded and pervasive forms of inequality. Nashville business leaders seem to have been talking about white students even more than black students when they spoke of increased vocational education. They imagined vocational courses to prepare students for the skilled industrial positions dominated by white male workers almost exclusively. As the school district crafted programs with model white male students in mind, however, they created parallel but unequal variants for black students. Advocates for black children thus faced two kinds of inequality: one based on racist exclusion from educational opportunities, and the other rooted in the notion that schooling should be pegged to future employment, and thus bounded by racist divides in the local labor market. Vocational education invited into school ideas of difference based in the dynamics of class and race oppression that characterized the local labor market. Authorized and encouraged to sort students based on "probable destination," vocational education contributed to a curricular logic of difference and segregation.

John Harper Harris merged multiple strands of local interest in vocational education into a proposal for a new prototype of high school education for Nashville. In a seventy-page proposal to the board in 1966, Harris suggested that all Nashville high schools become comprehensive high schools, incorporating significant vocational and academic offerings within the same institution.[107] Harris spoke about the plan in sweeping terms, suggesting that comprehensive schools could reflect and shape the cultural climate in which they existed, and contribute to a "a sense of order, unity and efficiency" in society.[108] Harris sought to bring order to the divergent interests and needs at play in secondary education in Nashville.

Harris's comprehensive high school had new scale and its reach, but in some respects simply renamed and expanded on the mixture of vocational and academic courses long present at a few Nashville schools. Cohn, in a working-class white area, and Pearl, serving black students in North Nashville, were already "comprehensive" in Harris's definition, if smaller than he envisaged. Meanwhile, many of Nashville's historically segregated white schools at least imagined themselves as single-class institutions. Some had been developed that way intentionally, as Davidson County superintendent Bass opined earlier in the decade.[109] The proliferation of smaller schools, as well as the fragmentation of students between black and white schools, city and county systems, kept the idea of the larger comprehensive high school from developing as fully in Nashville as it had already done elsewhere. When James Bryant Conant's 1958 *The American High School Today* brought more attention to the idea, consolidation was under discussion but not yet resolved in Nashville.[110] Neither city nor county systems wanted to take up new construction until it was clear who would pay for, and who would own, new facilities.[111]

Local and national civil rights efforts influenced Harris's ideas. He wrote acceptingly of "different ethnic, racial, and cultural groups . . . struggling for recognition, full rights, fair employment practices, nondiscrimination in housing, and higher levels of living." Having come to Nashville after the emotional peak of the sit-in movement but amid an ongoing direct action campaign to secure desegregation in public accommodations, Harris might have had this local struggle—or national examples of growing urban unrest of the mid-1960s—in mind when he disapproved of "pressure tactics, emotional displays, and florid propaganda" instead of "reason and the exercise of sober judgment."[112] On desegregation, Harris offered neither moral appeals in support nor screeds against. Desegregation was, for Harris, another bureaucratic challenge to be managed rationally and within moderate boundaries. Comprehensive high schools could help, by making "reason dominant over coercive force in every walk of life."[113]

Looking at an educational landscape in which about one-third of all students continued on to college, one-third received a terminal high school diploma, and one-third left school before graduation, the comprehensive high school promised at once to bring students together and keep them separate. Unlike in the smaller high schools that dotted Nashville's landscape and "divide[d] the population along social and economic lines," in comprehensive high schools, students would come together to develop as citizens and members of a community, and yet move toward separate work and academic paths. Comprehensive schools' large size (in Harris's view, roughly two thousand students) enabled this coming together and a wider range of classes than was fiscally viable in a smaller setting.[114] In the comprehensive high school, those headed to technical college would mingle in the lunchroom, the playing field, and the student council with college-bound students and those considering dropping out of school altogether. The comprehensive high school seemed to be a way to have it all—to adjust to swelling enrollments of baby boomers more likely than ever to remain in school up to and through high school, while accommodating a variety of life trajectories and plans.[115]

When Harris opined that comprehensive high schools could help "keep democracy working in the years ahead as well as it has worked in the past," or when he criticized earlier generations of educators for assuming "that all youth can profit by the same program," he revealed the chasm between his vision of school and society and the actual experience of black students in Nashville. Their history proved Harris's vision of uniformity never to have existed.[116]

Local discussions about vocational education that predated Harris's arrival helped him realize his vision. In the late 1950s, when Ben West and the chamber explored vocational education, the city council approved a large allocation for a new technical and vocational high school. Intended to serve both the city and county populations before consolidation, the proposal faced political and personal conflicts between city and county that delayed agreement on a location. Nonetheless, a multimillion-dollar allocation sat at the ready in the Metro capital improvement budget.[117] Harris's vision of a comprehensive high school provided a new approach to expanded vocational education while steering around previous conflicts; the board agreed to shift the technical-vocational school allocation to a new comprehensive high school. Board member Harlan Dodson suggested that more than one such school would ultimately be needed.[118]

Despite Harris's emphasis on a diverse student population, the school board chose comprehensive school locations that ensured segregation. While planning the first new comprehensive high school—ultimately named McGavock and located in a suburban area with a nearly all-white student population—the board also discussed a central-city comprehensive school for a South Nashville neighborhood home to an increasingly segregated black population.[119] The board and MNPS also took steps to expand vocational programs at the all-black Pearl High School.[120] To the extent that board members shared John Harris's vision of a comprehensive high school to serve a diverse range of students, they imagined diversity of class, income, and aspiration, if not race.

By 1968, planning for what would become McGavock Comprehensive High School was well under way, to the applause of local business leaders and the great hopes of many educators and administrators. The new institution sought to sort students more assertively, if putatively in a less constricting fashion, than had the "traditional" high schools it replaced. It aimed to encourage participation in vocational education by removing the stigma implied in separate vocational facilities, to help students find the "post-high school studies better suited to their natural interests and gifts."[121] Although McGavock's location and initial zone made it inaccessible to the students of North and South Nashville who were the targets of simultaneous compensatory education efforts through Ford Foundation, Model Cities, and Title I dollars, the comprehensive high school shared with these programs a basic commitment to a curricular logic of difference in ways that ultimately encouraged segregation in practice. The new school housed various classes, programs, and tracks ready to absorb and divide students on the basis of their "probable destination."

### Conclusion

Over the 1950s and 1960s, calls for segregation bolstered by outright claims of inferiority based on skin color gave way to a new discourse of sorting based on student need and predicted future life course. At times this discourse was motivated by educators' and activists' efforts to craft compensatory education to target student need, but in the process it reinforced ideas of inherent racial difference. At times, as in the work of Vivian Henderson, it sought a benevolent and opportunity-creating use of vocational education and prediction of future employment, imagining education as a lever for individual and collective black economic mobility. And at times, this discourse found support from a different direction, with ideas of curriculum and difference in student need aligning with the rhetoric of local economic growth that made claims of benefits for all, but which included few actual mechanisms to ensure the distribution of these benefits or to confront still-dominant patterns of labor market discrimination. Across these multiple, simultaneous efforts, Nashville educators and community leaders shaped the curricular organization of schooling in ways that, in their own years and for many following, helped make segregation and inequality. The curricular embrace of the idea of student difference along categorical rather than individual lines more often encouraged the reproduction of inequality instead of its undoing.

In some aspects of compensatory education discourse, educators conceptualized student difference in relationship to the racialized geography of the city. In doing so, they were participating in a small portion of a broader conversation about that geography—about which sections of the metropolis were appropriate for, or deserving of, schools, and about which would bear most directly the burdens of local growth agendas.

# CHAPTER FOUR

# The Spatial Organization of Schooling and Urban Renewal

By the late 1960s, student organizers had waged and won major civil rights struggles in Nashville. Coming from Fisk, Tennessee Agricultural and Industrial (now Tennessee State), Pearl High School, Meharry Medical College, American Baptist Seminary, and at times with allies at Vanderbilt, they held sit-ins, marched, and arranged myriad acts of civil disobedience to counter the pervasive segregation in Nashville's commercial spaces. They faced ugly insults, absorbed sharp punches, and spent nights in jail. Leading voices both in defending student activists and litigating school desegregation were involved, and became targets: Z. Alexander Looby's home was bombed (without causing injury), while Avon N. Williams accustomed himself to threats and frequent petty harassment—an unordered load of concrete delivered and billed to his home; a large funeral wreath sent to the office, "In Loving Memory of Avon."[1]

Despite real victories in court and in the streets, Nashville remained a deeply divided city in the second half of the 1960s—in fact, even more divided than a decade before. In 1957, at the initiation of school desegregation in Nashville, working- and middle-class black parents like Grace McKinley walked a few blocks through a working-class neighborhood of white families to take their first graders to school.[2] Ten years later, most of those white families had taken the well-trod and well-subsidized path to the suburbs. Increasingly, black families with means had done the same. Black real estate developers offered suburban developments starting in the early 1960s, but families with means saw new incentives to move—or found themselves compelled to do so—when urban renewal and highway construction brought another round of property expropriation and dislocation for black residents as the decade progressed. Multiple federal policies, from suburban home finance subsidies to highway construction, helped demarcate a band of suburban privilege. Meanwhile, the city neighborhoods long home to Nashville's poorest families saw ever more concentrated need for infrastructure improvements and faced the brunt of the era's displacement and disruption.

Against this backdrop typical of the American post–World War II city and metropolis, Nashville shows how local and federal decisions in the spatial organization of schooling also furthered the neglect of urban areas and the privileging of the suburbs. Planning and education officials committed local capital improvement dollars to suburban spaces in the 1960s, enabled in doing so through consolidation and encouraged by federal agency statements that endorsed suburbs as the right places for schools. Meanwhile, the urban school construction that did occur depended upon federal urban renewal subsidy more than local investment. In other black urban neighborhoods where school overcrowding had long been visible, schools remained over capacity. Through their long-lasting choices about school location and closures, planning officials helped make segregation and inequality through the spatial organization of schooling.

Judgments about school location, highway construction, and many other 1960s interventions in the metropolitan landscape involved demarcating distinct areas of the now-consolidated municipality. Joined since 1963 in a single jurisdiction and government, metropolitan Nashville existed in the minds of local planners and officials as a collection of distinct zones of land use, population, resources, and power. Consolidation had promised to bring more services and resources to new suburbs, and it did so via the expansion of sewer, road, lighting, police, and fire services.[3] Consolidation helped not only by linking the suburbs to the greater administrative capacity of the city government, but to tax revenues that came from the city and county together. Local revenues flowed to the suburbs while city neighborhoods saw improvements chiefly through federal funding. Rather than committing local dollars to necessities like separating storm and sanitary sewers to ensure that downpours did not bring human waste into the streets, local officials turned to urban renewal funds. In a unified metropolitan government, revenues found their way more frequently to the band of suburban privilege, while growth-minded redevelopment placed additional burdens on the urban core. In many metropolitan areas fragmented by municipal lines, distinct land uses often had coincided with jurisdictional boundaries.[4] Yet in Nashville, these divisions occurred within a single jurisdiction, and buttressed unequal distributions of resources in metropolitan space.

Meanwhile, the burdens and dislocations of urban and metropolitan growth remained unequally distributed as well. Ongoing and new urban renewal projects, alongside the construction of three interstate highways that met in Nashville, produced a period of extraordinary spatial disruption in city neighborhoods. By the late 1960s fully one-quarter of the land area of the former City of Nashville came under one urban renewal program or another, without counting additional acreage involved in highway construction and Model Cities efforts.[5] Urban renewal funds helped Nashville planners build expressly segregated schools close to high concentrations of poor black families in public housing. Residential clearance and displacement pushed black and white middle-class families out of city neighborhoods, adding economic isolation to racial segregation in black neighborhoods.

A broad range of federal policies, managed by local officials, reconstructed urban and suburban Nashville over the 1960s. As they had been in earlier eras of planning and urban renewal, schools remained important nodes in this work. As the first phase of court-ordered desegregation came to an end, the spatial organization of schooling and the broader scope of urban renewal and other interventions in the city's geography helped shape the uneven metropolitan landscape across which desegregation's buses would later roll.

## Schools for the Suburbs

The 1963 consolidation of the city of Nashville and Davidson County prompted the newly formed metropolitan school district to take stock of its facilities. Jointly the Metropolitan Planning Commission (MPC) and Metropolitan Nashville Public Schools surveyed the school system and projected future need. Their efforts resulted in a more than three-hundred-page report titled *Schools for 1980*. The report set forth "principles" and "objectives" to guide future school construction, location, and closures.[6] *Schools for 1980* reflected the main currents at work in Nashville school construction planning in the 1960s. First, it drew from federal reports and guidelines that issued ideological justifications for choosing suburban over urban locations for schools. Second, it served the interests of local real estate developers who had long interacted with the planning commission around school construction, as discussed in chapter 1. Third, it partook of categorizations of metropolitan space that linked neighborhood, school, and homogeneity, in keeping with contemporary planning theory. The explicit and implicit beliefs reflected in the *Schools for 1980* report reveal the crucial influence of planning professionals on the making of the educational landscape—a landscape that, despite Nashville's metropolitan organization, featured investment in the suburbs and neglect of the city.

During the decades after World War II, federal policies in housing and transportation encouraged the dispersion of white middle-class families into the suburbs.[7] Education officials also reinforced the pro-suburban bent of federal policy. In 1958, the Department of Health, Education, and Welfare (HEW) published a guide to school-site selection that reveals official federal assumptions that quality education should be found in suburban settings. Emphasizing the school site as "an educational tool itself," HEW argued that "schools should be located in an environment that stimulates love and appreciation of the beautiful in life." Such a statement might have allowed multiple interpretations of "the beautiful," but the report consistently narrowed this definition to suburban locales as it set out criteria for school-site selection and gave examples from around the country.[8]

The images in HEW's *School Sites* report made the point powerfully. Fourteen of the seventeen illustrations show a newly constructed school in what can only be described as a pastoral setting—rolling lawns, an occasional stand of trees or a more densely wooded background, and possibly even a lake in view. Only three showed any other sign of development, and that development was limited to detached houses. The text elaborated, cautioning against noise, dust, and congestion and suggesting that schools needed "clean air and abundant sunshine." Therefore, areas with "high buildings" should be avoided "if at all possible." School sites and any commercial or industrial development were also incompatible, as were "crowded neighborhoods." For federal officials, these were not trifling considerations. Factors such as smoke and noise and the presence of tall buildings were "depressing and annoying, and there is little or no justification for selecting sites that subject persons to irritations from these sources. . . . School boards should give careful consideration to the health and safety of students . . . as they examine prospective pieces of land for the location of schools, because the lives and welfare of young Americans are at stake."[9]

HEW's *School Sites* guidebook likely originated in the department's repeated efforts during the Eisenhower administration to secure federal funding for school construction, as the baby boom generation swelled beyond the capacity of existing school facilities. As of January 1955, the Eisenhower administration estimated that the national shortage of classrooms ran to 340,000. Despite these dramatic figures, Eisenhower's ambitions faltered on the rocks of segregation. Representative Adam Clayton Powell attached riders to each of the school construction bills that would have required any state receiving funds to prove that they were operating desegregated

4.1. One representation of a "school site in an attractive environment," from James Taylor, *School Sites: Selection, Development, and Utilization* (US Dept. of Health, Education, and Welfare Office of Education, special publication no. 7, Washington, DC: Government Printing Office, 1958).

school systems. Southern representatives found this measure unacceptable, and thus blocked the legislation. Even though the nationwide school construction program never materialized, HEW published the pro-suburban guidelines in *School Sites* at a moment when the agency could reasonably imagine national responsiveness to its ideas.[10]

Unlike clearly segregationist policies such as federal lending standards, *School Sites* issued seemingly commonsensical calls for the health and safety of children. But adding federal pressures for suburbanization to a housing and schooling landscape already divided by Jim Crow meant further segregation. Like pro-suburban mortgage policies, these federal influences were far from neutral even as they portrayed themselves as such.[11] Suburbanizing schools deepened the concentration of poor black families in the center city. Following the "de facto segregation" narrative would suggest that school construction in the suburbs simply followed residential housing patterns. Tracing school construction decisions to their roots in politics and ideology shows instead that public officials—federal as well as local—explicitly privileged suburban space in education policy and understood the power of schooling to influence local housing markets. Education policies also drove housing patterns.[12]

At the local level, real estate interests were well represented on the planning commission and land-use bodies. They had long interacted with planners to secure the school construction and zoning that allowed them to promise new schools among their communities' amenities. Cooperation between the school board, planners, and real estate developers to plan and build new schools in suburban developments merged market-driven incentives for school construction in suburban areas with state power.

As they had in the 1950s, developers continued in the 1960s to seek and secure connections between new suburbs and new schools. H. G. Hill Jr., a grocery-chain operator turned real-estate developer and banker, built a group of subdivisions in an area called Hillwood, which stretched southwest into a previously rural quadrant of Davidson County. Hill donated land for two schools to serve his new neighborhoods.[13] As enrollment in the area grew, the Warner Park Estates Company, working in the same area, had "more or less reserve[d]" a plot for "school purposes" and sold the land to the school board at a price one-third below the appraised value.[14] In this way, suburban developers secured modern schools for their subdivisions, and effectively chose school sites before the school district and its planners acted. Acting out of profit motive more than planning theory, they enacted their own support for the "neighborhood unit" concept.[15]

Having encouraged the building of schools in their neighborhoods, developers and real estate agents then used schools as important elements of their marketing and advertising efforts. In Hillwood, claims that homes were "walking distance to H. G. Hill Elementary School" or were zoned for Hillwood High School frequently appeared in real estate advertisements in the 1960s.[16] Other ads shouted "Rosebank School Area" or "Prestige Overton High!" amid descriptions of a house's bathrooms, bedrooms, acreage, or the age of the roof.[17] Real estate agents touted proximity to a wide range of schools, typically listing more than 20 schools by name in a given day's classifieds, a significant portion of the roughly 130 schools in operation in the 1960s.[18] City planners and real estate interests understood the power of schools to determine home values and steer the suburban residential development that benefited a web of interests from sales agents to mortgage banks.

The Metropolitan Planning Commission was often frustrated by its inability to bring a broader vision of urban planning to fruition because of its lack of control over key government activities related to growth. For example, the state's highway construction plans—including where the new roads would cut through existing Nashville neighborhoods and business districts—became known to the planning commission only after the plans had been finalized.[19] As massive funding streams flowed to the Tennessee Department of Transportation for interstate highway construction and to

the Nashville Housing Authority for housing construction and urban renewal, the Metropolitan Planning Commission had no analogous source
of funding to leverage its vision for the metropolitan landscape. As Domenico Annese of the consulting firm Clarke and Rapuano recalled it, the
MPC was "good at making plans but not good at actually accomplishing
any of them."[20] School construction, however, did offer the MPC a place
to build things, and to determine where not to build. School construction
offered an accessible field of action for the planning commission around a
topic that tended to be politically popular at a time of growing enrollment
and explicit demand for new facilities.

An MPC staffer, Joe Williams, explained that a core planning function
was deciding where schools fit as "piece(s) in an urban jigsaw puzzle," with
planners uniquely suited to "coordinate the parts of the whole."[21] When,
in 1963, a national school administration conference met in Nashville, the
planning commission made their case for planners' roles in school construction. Williams emphasized the need to build, and at times to prevent
building. He described a "central area" of Nashville where past enrollments had been growing alongside residential construction. The school
board proposed adding facilities in the area, but planners "revealed other
factors which eventually proved decisive . . . not to further develop [per-
manent school facilities] in this particular area."[22] Williams was vague, but
most likely he was speaking of crowded North Nashville areas that planners, if few others at that point, knew that the state had slated for interstate highway construction and the accompanying demolition of houses
and businesses.[23] Williams congratulated himself and his agency for having successfully argued against the school board's plans to provide a new
school for the children of this area.[24] By 1971, whatever changes Williams
envisioned had not yet come about, although highway construction in the
immediate area was near completion. Portable classrooms stood around
a still-overcrowded and increasingly run-down Early School that operated
even more significantly over capacity than when Williams issued his confident projections.[25] Highway construction, which brought multiple forms
of destruction to North Nashville, meant further neglect in school facilities
as well.

Reflecting each of these influences, from the federal to the highly local,
the Metropolitan Planning Commission's 1964 *Schools for 1980* captured
the agency's pro-suburban focus and shaped school construction in Nashville for decades. *Schools for 1980* outlined supposedly impartial criteria
that revealed the depth of metropolitan government bias toward suburban
spaces and against schooling in urban ones. After broadly stating that the

board should plan for "harmonious relationships between school sites and surrounding land uses," the planning commission more specifically asserted that "areas with objectionable features [such] as dust, noise, odors, smoke, congested traffic, busy highways and railroads should be avoided as site locations," as "these nuisances destroy the proper environment for teaching and learning." In the same manner as HEW's *School Sites, Schools for 1980* issued commonsense calls for quiet and safe school sites that implicitly required suburban over urban school location. The preference for suburban space was even more explicit by 1970, when a school construction policy that reiterated the principles in *Schools for 1980* added that "locating schools in areas zoned for commercial or apartment use should be avoided whenever possible."[26]

*Schools for 1980* also suggested that schools get ahead of the suburbanization trend, to achieve economies as well as respond to shifting demographics. Calls for "advanced procurement of [school] sites" suggested that the district build schools and wait for students to move to them, assuming development of new suburban population centers. This "principle" of advanced procurement would go unmentioned when it was expedient to downplay the coordination of school construction and residential development, as when attorneys for the school system stood up in court and asserted (in keeping with the developing de facto narrative) that continuing school segregation was simply the product of residential segregation patterns that the school district followed and which were out of their control.[27]

*Schools for 1980* provided a table comparing "core" (city) and "frame" (county) enrollments over this time period. The three columns of the table indicate total enrollment in core and frame combined, the percentage of the total in core (city) schools and frame (county) schools. This presentation of the data can easily be misread as indicating a decrease in city school population, rather than a decrease relative to the size of the suburban and rural population. It is too much to suggest that such a presentation endorsed divestment in city schools, but it is reasonable to consider such figures to be implicitly suggesting a shift of energy and resources away from a shrinking "core" to an expanding "frame," even when in absolute terms no fewer city students were to be educated in city schools in 1963 than a decade earlier.[28]

The Metropolitan Planning Commission and board of education adopted standards for school-site size that required at least ten acres for an average elementary school and more than thirty for an average high school, with an acre covering roughly the area of a football field. The system's new flagship comprehensive high school, planned along the outlines offered

4.2. Aerial view of McGavock Comprehensive High School. Courtesy
of Metropolitan Archives of Nashville-Davidson County.

by John Harper Harris in 1966, barely met these guidelines. It opened in
1971 to house 3,200 students on a 44-acre parcel and fell within suggested
size standards by including adjacent park acreage. Site requirements necessitated new school construction in the suburbs. Where else would such
extensive tracts of land be available and affordable? *Schools for 1980* set an
ideological and practical direction for school construction that the district
continued to embrace into and through the next phase of school desegregation, and that in fact played a part in shaping that desegregation.

Engaged in planning schools facilities in Nashville, planners partook
of different ways of rationalizing the complex demographic, political,
and educational landscape before them. First crafting seemingly objective
categories to apply across a varied landscape, they then deployed these
categories with widely varying effects in city as opposed to suburban settings.[29] After setting out the pro-suburban principles and standards out-

lined above, planners divided the metropolitan area into ASAs, standing for analysis (or, sometimes, analytic) service areas. Planners explained in *Schools for 1980* that the concept of the ASA stemmed from the planning commission's previous work with planning units (as discussed in chapter 1). Planners calculated the projected school population for each ASA by using demographic projections to 1980 based on the planning unit structure and their categorization of each unit as growing, declining, or stable.[30] Elementary schools, with smaller enrollments, had smaller ASAs, while high schools needed much larger ones that drew from multiple planning units. Although it is impossible to determine how closely the ASAs related to the boundaries of the planning units, it is nonetheless clear that *Schools for 1980* embraced the planning unit logic that linked neighborhood, school, and homogeneity. As the report's authors restated it, planning units were "delineated by economic, social, ethnic, geographic, and topographical criteria."[31] If they approached ASAs as they had planning units, their work reinforced segregation by identifying a homogenous population and identifying (or constructing) a school for that population. Focused directly on schools, planners worked in the tradition of practices that constructed and reinforced segregation. Planners continued to use the ASA as a basic dividing unit for the metropolitan school district for years after the 1964 report.[32] As in the ideal neighborhood unit as drafted by Clarence Perry, and its local equivalent, the planning unit, the ASA also idealized locating a school at its geographic center.[33] If ASAs were drawn to respect segregated population patterns, this added provision would make desegregation even more difficult.

By beginning with divisions of the landscape based on future population estimates rather than present need, the planning commission created a rational structure from which to identify areas that needed new schools and sites where schools could be "deleted."[34] The ASA structure, which assumed a single school was or would be sufficient to serve a geographic area, flattened the reality of greatly varying population densities in the metropolitan area. Although ASAs in the central city were smaller than those in the surrounding suburbs, the use of the ASA oversimplified metropolitan space and obscured the fact that planners were calling for closures of several urban schools, under the heading of simply providing one school per ASA. The Metropolitan Planning Commission opened *Schools for 1980* with the assertion that they would not neglect school facilities in the city center, where they saw a "definite need for a program of replacement, rehabilitation and new construction at both the elementary and secondary levels."[35] Despite these claims, the implicit message of the ASA scheme pointed in the other direction, as did the report's pro-suburban principles and standards for school sites. Writing in 1959, Irving Hand acknowledged that the absence of churches, schools, and playgrounds was among the "principal characteristics" leading to neighborhood blight. When MPC neglected city schools, they helped feed neighborhood decline.[36]

Both before and after *Brown*, Nashville's city planners and school administrators adopted school construction practices that favored segregated white suburban spaces and often left urban, primarily poorer black students in crowded and inferior schools. From 1960 to 1972, Metro Nashville Public Schools opened twenty-four new schools, or more than one-sixth of the total schools in operation in 1972. The overwhelming majority of these new schools sat in areas of established or new suburban development and served predominantly or exclusively white populations, in keeping with national trends. The one school planned for a predominantly black urban neighborhood was smaller in capacity than many of its suburban counterparts, and its construction was subsidized by urban renewal grants for the area.[37]

The suburban construction boom extended to the new comprehensive model as well. McGavock Comprehensive High School was the first to open. The school enjoyed a $7.875 million construction budget, with additional subsidy for its thirty-acre land acquisition from federal open-space funds.[38] Having the first comprehensive high school in the suburbs seemed fitting for a superintendent who had bemoaned "the strife, turmoil, and ugliness of the city" that outweighed the "cultural treasures" available there.[39] The school board named the new school McGavock, after the once slave-owning family on whose 1,100-acre former plantation the school would sit.[40] School district officials in charge of construction jokingly exchanged notes as they evaluated the site. Revealing the casual bigotry running through the district office, an administrator in charge of school construction sent his surveyor to check the site "to see if there are any bad sinkholes or good niggers buried there." "All clear," the surveyor reported.[41]

John Harper Harris deemed the school's location "favorable"; however, its placement in the predominantly white eastern suburbs undercut his claims that comprehensive high schools would serve broadly diverse student populations. The location helped produce a class-diverse but racially homogenous (98 percent white) student population.[42] School planners boasted that the location at the junction of a circumferential road and an interstate would facilitate access for students from around the county, but the district did not provide transportation. Nashville's first comprehensive

## School Construction, 1960-1980, and 1970 Black and White Population
Metropolitan Nashville-Davidson County, Tennessee

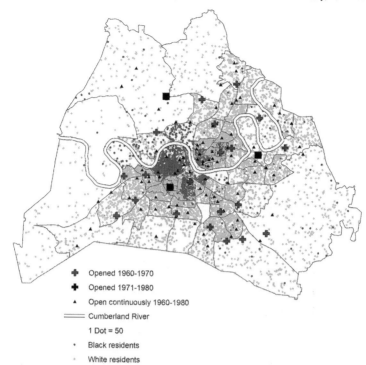

＋ Opened 1960-1970

✚ Opened 1971-1980

▲ Open continuously 1960-1980

═══ Cumberland River

1 Dot = 50

· Black residents

· White residents

4.3. Data for this map comes from: MPC, *Schools for 1980*; School Directory, MNPS, 1979–1980; City of Nashville Public Schools Directory, 1960–1961; "Pupil Enrollment," 1969, Kelley, box 11, file 4; "Fifteen Year Analysis of Enrollment Trends, Metro Nashville Public Schools," 1984, *Kelley*, box 21, file 1984; and John Egerton, "Analysis of Data From Interrogatories Submitted to Metropolitan School System," 1970, *Kelley*, box 11, file 4 (1 of 2). Population figures for 1970 are from the 1970 Decennial Census, available from Minnesota Population Center. National Historical Geographic Information System: Prerelease Version 0.1. Minneapolis: University of Minnesota, 2004, at http://www.nhgis.org. Assistance with GIS from the staff of Columbia University's Digital Social Sciences Center.

school was formally open to black students, but lacked structures for substantially equal access and inclusion.

At the same time that the school district engaged in extensive building in the suburbs where enrollments were rising, several existing urban schools were enrolled over capacity, using portable classrooms or nonclassroom space to house as many as two hundred students. Planners acknowledged overcrowding, but turned to vague language about "land use [in the area] being in flux" or predicted that an urban residential area would be "converted to use for other purposes through public action as well as through private initiative" in order to avoid calling for new facilities in the city. When they did make such a call, they failed to identify where a suggested new school would be built.[43] Instead, they focused on new building in suburban areas.

The principles and standards in *Schools for 1980* amounted to more than rhetoric. Four years after the report was published, school board attorneys asserted that it guided all school construction decisions; and six years after that, the district proposed a school construction policy that clearly echoed the report's principles and standards.[44] The impact of *Schools for 1980* is evident in the breach as well. Beneath the statements of principles at the front of the report, planners did slate some urban schools for repair or expansion. They were at times motivated, like many other southern districts in the 1950s and 1960s, by the hope that eliminating the most dire examples of inequality in segregated schools would lessen calls for desegregation. Yet segregation and the unequal power it reflected continued, and many promised repairs still did not materialize. A few years after the report, the conditions in several urban schools remained poor. Clemons School had cracking plaster ceilings and walls, broken windows, and exposed heating pipes inside classrooms, while the four-story wood-frame Pearl Elementary lacked fire escapes.[45]

In court, school administrators used their adherence to the principles and standards in *Schools for 1980* to claim unbiased decision making regarding school construction. Even if such remarks were sincere, the disparate impact remained. Pro-suburban approaches to distributing public resources such as schools, drawing on national trends and rhetoric, were layered on top of existing Jim Crow patterns to deepen segregation and inequality.[46] Instead of responding to a segregated landscape in housing—often erroneously understood as "de facto segregation," the product of private rather than state action—both local and federal school officials helped build this landscape by binding together housing and schooling in the process of suburban development. Their pro-suburban planning visions deemed urban neighborhoods inappropriate for educational investment and later helped strip schools from urban spaces. More immediately, highway construction and urban renewal brought displacement and dislocation to urban residents and institutions.

## Displacement in the City

While school construction patterns represented the confluence of suburban growth and pro-suburban views that encouraged resources to flow to the suburbs, it was city residents who faced burdens, disruptions, and at times property expropriation via highway construction and urban renewal. Nationally, most urban renewal projects focused on urban jurisdictions fragmented from their suburban core. As a metropolitan jurisdiction that vigorously pursued and used federal dollars, Nashville illustrates how urban renewal worked within a political structure responsible to both city and suburban constituencies. Nashville may even have seemed like an ideal case for federal officials of the day, including for Robert Wood, chair of President Johnson's Task Force on Metropolitan and Urban Problems in 1964 and then undersecretary at HUD, who argued that the problems of older cities would "only be solved in the context of metropolitan area-wide strategies."[47] Despite the metropolitan framework, urban renewal and other interventions in the landscape distributed their opportunities and their costs unequally.

Federal and local dollars met in urban renewal projects in Nashville's urban core at many points over the 1960s. Two of these—urban renewal's reshaping of the Edgehill area and the extension of Interstate 40 through Nashville—resonated well with the city's growth agenda by expanding the city's commercial reach via the highway, rendering distant suburbs more accessible and carving out new areas for commercial development not far from downtown. Nashville planners designed urban renewal in ways that placed its harsher consequences (for example, property value expropriation and destruction, residential displacement, extreme concentration of public housing, and geographic isolation) on black communities in both North and South Nashville.

Nashville's black leadership did not reject urban renewal outright; some thought it "the only hope" for desperately needed infrastructure improvements. Unpaved streets, housing without indoor plumbing, and dangerous conjoined storm and sanitary sewers persisted in some areas years after the collective hand-wringing over the Capitol Hill slums a decade earlier. Federal dollars could help address these conditions. Leaders like Mansfield Douglas III sought to "improve the plan" to better recognize and meet the needs of current and future residents.[48] The highway proved immovable, but local black and white activists who organized against Edgehill's linked housing and school segregation found some success in limiting that project's impact.

Earlier urban renewal projects, as in East Nashville, demonstrated initial linkages between schools, housing, and segregation. Other urban renewal projects in Nashville further refined these connections. In the Edgehill project, the NHA refined its entrepreneurial use of federal funds and funding formulas to link housing and schooling further.

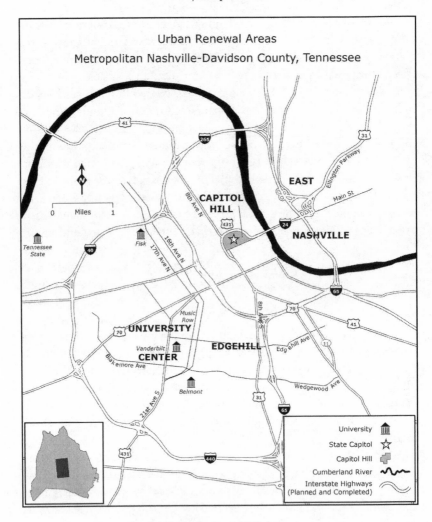

4.4. Map by James W. Quinn.

Edgehill was an established residential area immediately south of Nashville's downtown business district. The NHA long ago identified the area for public housing construction, building the Edgehill Homes as a segregated black public housing project in 1951.[49] Local activists later described the area as "the heart of the vast South Nashville ghetto," one that had been formed through public housing construction forcing relocation of working- and middle-class families (some of them homeowners) as well as through the relocation of displaced Capitol Hill residents to Edgehill

Homes.[50] By the early 1960s, Edgehill housed a mix of "low and middle income Negroes," in homes ranging from decrepit to well maintained, rented and owner occupied. The Nashville Housing Authority reported 88.5 percent of the land in residential use.[51]

In 1962, NHA's Gerald Gimre announced plans for the Edgehill Urban Renewal Project, to cover 1,130 acres and displace 2,175 families. The project received federal approval in 1966. Dislocation came from Edgehill's plans for expanded public housing and school construction, as well as clearance of residential land for commercial uses. Like other urban renewal projects "planned with industry in mind," the Edgehill project cleared residential land and set some of it aside for business expansion—here, for more space for a religious publishing house, and in one of Nashville urban renewal's more pedestrian and unaesthetic uses, the body shop and storage lots of a car dealer.[52] Edgehill residents experienced additional dislocations from nearby transformations in the landscape—another urban renewal project focusing on Vanderbilt University and Music Row to the west, Interstate 65 to the east, and a new downtown redevelopment effort just to the north.[53]

In the early 1950s, the school board built a new elementary school in South Nashville to serve the then-new Edgehill Homes.[54] A decade later, urban renewal's one-third local, two-thirds federal funding formula helped motivate Nashville school planners to build a school within the new Edgehill project boundaries. School construction became a vehicle through which to meet the local funding requirements and leverage additional funds. For the Edgehill project, the NHA counted $2.6 million of expenditures on school sites and school construction as expenditures credited toward their local share of urban renewal dollars, possible because the school served primarily or exclusively students from the urban renewal area.[55] Building a school for an urban renewal area could leverage funds for public housing in the same area. Urban renewal's fiscal requirements created a disincentive for building a school that might desegregate by serving Edgehill and a nearby white neighborhood. In court in the *Kelley* desegregation case a few years later, NHA executive director Gerald Gimre explained that "when school facilities are lacking for a planned public housing project, the board of education provides a school for that project."[56] Board of education attorneys presented Gimre's comments as proof positive of the school board's innocence in fostering segregation.

The Edgehill project was not Nashville's largest nor its most expensive, but it was the first to provoke a persistent opposition movement critical both of displacement and segregation. By the fall of 1966, a long list of local organizations came together as the Edgehill Committee to oppose the NHA plans. The Tennessee Council on Human Rights, the Tennessee Commission on Human Relations, Nashville's NAACP branch, the Nashville Christian Leadership Conference, the Nashville Community Relations Council, and the Davidson County Independent Political Council all weighed in, as did neighborhood-based organizations such as the Edgehill Citizen's Organization, the South Street Community Center, and the Edgehill Methodist Church. These groups emphasized the destruction and displacement that would come to the neighborhood, pointing out that "not all of the houses . . . are substandard," and that many homeowning families in Edgehill would "be forced into becoming renters" when the NHA bought houses for less than replacement value given the restricted pool of housing available to black purchasers. The gathered organizations asserted that via the project "an aspiring middle-class segment in the Negro population in Nashville is being destroyed."[57]

For some families, forced movement out of Edgehill was only the most recent link in a chain of displacements through urban renewal and state action. Willa Clark, who had moved within the Edgehill area when her house was taken for the enlargement of a local (and segregated) school, bought a new house that urban renewal then claimed. Clark worried that the $5,750 she received—on a house for which she had paid $7,000—would not cover a new residence. The chain had yet another link for nearly half of those who relocated from Edgehill to "standard private homes" south of the project area. Their homes fell to the construction of the Interstate 440 loop in the 1980s.[58] The combined effects of urban renewal and highway construction in the Edgehill area alone displaced nearly four thousand families over ten years.[59] The whole process must have rankled even more when homeowners realized how much local realtors, whose professional organization consistently opposed and encouraged noncompliance with federal fair housing measures, earned from property transactions within urban renewal.[60]

The Edgehill Committee focused on segregation as well as displacement. The NHA planned to add 640 more units near the existing 500-unit Edgehill Homes. Edgehill pastor and neighborhood organizer Rev. Bill Barnes argued that if he had been seeking to "guarantee segregation, [he] would have chosen this kind of location" for public housing.[61] The committee also identified NHA's enterprising linkage of school construction and public housing construction as a force for segregation in both. The local segregated black school would "be a strong influence in producing all-Negro occupancy" in housing.[62]

Both critical activists and housing administrators agreed that locating more public housing in Edgehill would further the concentration of black residents already present in the area. What they differed on was whether this was a problem. Robert Crownover, director of housing for the Nashville Housing Authority, acknowledged that "the placing of housing in any particular neighborhood in the city" determines whether it is occupied "predominantly" by black or white residents, "one or the other."[63] Crownover's agency earlier had acted more assertively to maintain segregation, using a "free choice" tenancy program that involved applicants meeting with a counselor and determining their choice of projects. This practice ended after a federal investigation in 1968.[64] Other NHA administrators saw housing development specifically for black families as a necessary response to contemporary criticisms of urban renewal. Charles Hawkins, NHA's director of urban renewal, explained that since "urban renewal was being dubbed Negro removal," the project design needed to ensure that "the families will remain Negro" so as not to further the impression that urban renewal pushed some people out and put others in.[65] Director Gerald Gimre's attempt to reassure residents likely failed: "We intend to rebuild the ghetto."[66]

Fighting housing segregation remained challenging as the local housing supply remained "wholly inadequate," particularly for lower-income black families, a problem exacerbated when highway construction and urban renewal destroyed more than 17,000 units.[67] The Edgehill Committee crafted a multipart campaign of letter writing, appeals to federal officials, and legal intervention to keep housing development but reduce segregation.[68] Before US Secretary of Housing and Urban Development Robert Weaver visited Nashville in November 1967, local activist Martha Ragland wrote to enlist his help in pressuring the city to enact an open housing ordinance and "decongest" the Edgehill housing plans.[69] After Weaver's visit, the Edgehill Committee worked through the Atlanta regional office of HUD and ultimately won revisions to shrink the planned 320 units on each of two sites to a maximum of 180 each. They also advocated dispersing housing throughout the project area, including in the predominantly white University Center area.[70] The Edgehill Committee had tried, with some success, to moderate the segregationist impulse that guided planning for public housing.

While South Nashville did the work of housing Nashville's poor, North Nashville became the link between Nashville's downtown and the interstate highway network stretching gradually across the country in the 1960s and 1970s. The ribbons of concrete that formed I-40—ultimately binding

4.5. Mayor Beverly Briley (r) and Nashville Housing Authority head Gerald Gimre (l) at a ribbon cutting. Courtesy of Metropolitan Archives of Nashville-Davidson County.

eastern North Carolina to Southern California by way of Tennessee, Oklahoma, and Arizona—flowed right through North Nashville. State planners and their consultants from Clarke and Rapuano chose the highway's ultimate route among others that came close to privileged residential enclaves in Belle Meade or the Vanderbilt campus. State highway planners and their consultants chose the route in the late 1950s, but it remained shielded from public view in state agency documents and hearings poorly announced or misannounced. In the mid-1960s, property acquisitions in the North Nashville area began. Avon Williams and his longtime political ally and friend Edwin Mitchell, a professor at Meharry Medical College, still called the area home. With other North Nashville residents they pushed to stop and revise the construction plans, including filing suit and pushing the litigation all the way to the Supreme Court. Even this mode of appeal proved unable to shift the momentum.[71]

I-40 bisected Jefferson Street with a towering overpass and its concrete support columns, destroying new and old buildings alike and casting long shadows. North Nashville's Jefferson Street commercial and recreational corridor had taken on even more significance for black commerce after the Capitol Hill redevelopment destroyed much of the black business district there. Highway construction seized or devalued many middle-class, owner-occupied homes nearby, taking new and old absentee-owned rental housing as well. Some home owners may have wished that the state had acquired their property, as the construction of access ramps just feet from their homes expropriated value if it left owners still holding title.[72] And the highway severed the previously nearly contiguous campuses of Tennessee State, Fisk, and Meharry. Clarke and Rapuano planners knew that the highway would form a "Chinese wall" dividing and destroying the neighborhood.[73] Local activists and some allies in the federal highway bureaucracy pushed for mitigating features, including improved pedestrian access, but few of these came to pass. It was, in the words of federal administrator Lowell Bridwell, an example of "atrocious" planning.[74]

Advocates like Edwin Mitchell saw not only the immediate but the spiraling impact on North Nashville. Houses previously serviced by a local fire station were now cut off from it by the highway, and lost their fire insurance for inaccessibility.[75] Previously integrated into the basic grid that carried cars and pedestrians into downtown, North Nashville now had few through streets. Mayor Beverly Briley admitted that the road formed "a barrier to the Fisk and Meharry area isolating it like a ghetto."[76] The distribution of resources and burdens in the metropolis went beyond pro-suburban development and urban neglect to active destruction.

A few years after the Edgehill struggles, as Nashville planners heard public outcry over yet another urban renewal plan, Edwin Mitchell and Mayor Briley shared the stage at a debate organized by the predominantly white West Nashville Cherokee Citizens Organization. Mitchell described urban renewal as a process "most often manipulated against poor people." Briley excused urban renewal's previous struggles with a quick remark: "When you're doing things, you're going to make some mistakes." He was interrupted by a member of the audience: "Why is it the mistakes always result in the wealthy people getting the property?"[77]

North Nashville lost a lot of property, but at least in Mayor Briley's eyes, he had offered some recompense by making the area the focus of Nashville's federal Model Cities application. Once funded, Model Cities became the centerpiece in a tug-of-war between Edwin Mitchell and his allies still fuming over the violation that was I-40 and a mayor baldly opposed to both the principal and practice of "maximum feasible participation as promised in the urban revitalization effort."[78]

Model Cities' education programs carried forward the curricular emphasis on difference, while the broader public rhetoric around the Model Cities project marked the North Nashville area as a whole as troubled and exceptional. Mayor Briley referred to Model Cities as a program to address the neighborhood's "sociological problem."[79] The very process of applying for a Model Cities grant and deciding which portion of the city would receive it became a performance in deficit theater, one that added to a February 1967 bus tour in which local business leaders explored a close-to-downtown area well known for its unplumbed, unsafe, but inhabited shacks.[80] These events and the press coverage they garnered taught white suburbanites who increasingly lacked even drive-by familiarity with city neighborhoods about urban conditions and poverty. Except for occasional mention of the highway's consequences for North Nashville, Model Cities discourse most frequently left readers to apply their own ideas about what caused these conditions.

Urban renewal, highway construction, and school construction policies helped make the deeply segregated landscape that later efforts at school desegregation would struggle against. The extraordinary dislocations of the 1960s for central-city residents in Nashville also form an important backdrop for the busing plan that began in 1971. Busing became yet another spatial disruption to neighborhoods already fundamentally reorganized, dispersed, and in some cases entirely deconstructed through federal and local policy.

## Desegregation in a Divided Landscape

By 1968, school desegregation in Nashville had advanced beyond tokenism in some respects, but the making of educational segregation and inequality continued through linked school and housing policy. The numbers of black students attending previously segregated white schools inched upward, from the dozens in the late 1950s to the hundreds by the early 1960s, and to the thousands toward the middle of the decade. Teaching faculties had made less progress. A voluntary and small-scale attempt at faculty integration began under John Harper Harris in the mid-1960s, so that many schools with nearly all-black student populations had one or two white teachers, and vice versa, but most facilities remained far from desegregation.

Desegregation advanced differently in each school context, but two patterns emerged. In outlying suburbs and formerly rural areas, very small numbers of black students began to attend previously segregated white schools. They faced receptions that included the quietly and the loudly hostile. Michael Tribue, the first black student at Donelson High School, felt as though he was "parting the Red Sea," walking among white students lining the hallways. Norman Braden remembered his beginning at Antioch, including a first-day assembly at which the principal greeted the school, "Welcome you all, and welcome you niggers." Braden stood up. "The word is Negro," he offered. The principal called Braden a troublemaker, and from that day on, Braden recalled, "It was like hell was put on me."[81]

Braden and a white student he had been fighting with both found themselves suspended, spent the day hanging out at the creek behind the school, and from there formed a lifelong friendship. White students at still nearly all-white schools, like Cindy Acuff, noticed a few black students appeared in their classes, or on cheerleading squads, and at times friendships formed there as well. Athletic competitions between black and white public high schools began in 1966. Game days—sites of tension between rival schools—became explosive. Braden recalled fans throwing rocks and fights all around the field as all-black Cameron High School played nearly all-white Litton. Everything calmed, Braden remembered, when the lauded Cameron band took the field and all eyes turned to them.[82]

In centrally located schools, statistical desegregation came more quickly via residential succession, with black families moving into city neighborhoods that many white families left. At Cohn High School, educators and community members worked intentionally to sustain ideas of community into and through demographic change at schools. Cohn had long served a working-class white urban population. The school's teachers and administrators attributed relatively less conflict at their school to intentional programming about desegregation, decisions to establish black-white quotas within each classroom to mirror the school overall, and democratic school governance practices. At Cohn, the majority-white school community still claimed the school as their own despite substantial desegregation.[83]

By the late 1960s, desegregation was advancing, but largely in spite of school district policies. Informal methods of student enrollment and zoning stymied desegregation even where residential changes seemed to make it more possible. In 1968, Samuel McDonald lived with his family at 1816 Hillside Avenue, close both to Cameron, a historically segregated all-black school, and to Central High School, previously Davidson County's segregated white flagship high school, alma mater of current and first Metropolitan Nashville Mayor Beverly Briley and his predecessor as mayor of the City of Nashville, Ben West. On the maps for the "geographical, nonracial" zones set out in the late 1950s and early 1960s, the McDonald family lived within the zone for Central. Many families like the McDonalds had taken opportunities provided by white out-migration to the suburbs to move into previously proscribed areas of Nashville, including those not far from Central. But Samuel did not attend Central. When he finished junior high school, his guidance counselor sent his file to Cameron, effectively registering him at the school. His mother recalled that "some lady" visited their home to tell her that Samuel could attend Cameron or Central. Mrs. McDonald wondered, "How could we live in two different zones?"[84]

In the early 1960s, a choice between schools like Cameron and Central was formally available under the "freedom of choice" provision that allowed parents to opt out of their zoned school if it required their child to join a student population where they would be in the racial minority. Considering a group of districts with parental choice plans, including Nashville, the Supreme Court found such plans unconstitutional in 1963 in *Goss v. Board of Education of Knoxville*.[85] It took nearly two years, however, before the newly created Metropolitan Nashville Board of Education responded to this ruling and changed district policy. Choice as a mechanism to avoid desegregation persisted in Nashville through the 1964–65 school year.[86] In 1965, the board accelerated its grade-per-year desegregation plan to extend through high school, three years ahead of schedule but eleven years after *Brown*. As appointed by Mayor Beverly Briley, like Mayor West before him, the board contained eight white members and one black member.

The board kept the zone lines drawn in the first years of desegregation static as areas of black residence expanded gradually outward from the historic city core, in some cases producing increased desegregation at area schools. This added to the expansion in desegregation that came with the culmination of the grade-per-year desegregation plan. Along the measures that later desegregation scholars would use to characterize "highly concentrated" schools, segregation decreased notably in some portions of Nashville in the mid-1960s. Both black and white Nashville students became less likely during the 1960s to attend a highly segregated school with a minority (black or white) population of less than 10 percent. In 1963, 96 percent of black children attended a school that was more than 90 percent black; 100 percent of white children attended a school that was more than 90 percent white. By 1968, desegregation had increased markedly, yet segregation remained the norm for most black and white students. More than a third of the school system's white students attended schools without a single black child, and nearly all the central-city historically black schools had no white children. Two-thirds of Nashville's black students and 85 percent of its white students attended schools with a black or white minority of less than 10 percent.[87]

As Avon Williams observed, in some neighborhoods desegregating schools quickly became resegregated, as black people's movement into some inner-ring suburbs and formerly white city neighborhoods was matched by quick and often total out-migration by white residents.[88] And in the outlying suburbs, real estate agents, developers, and homeowners maintained strict boundaries in residential space, boundaries that could not be overcome by class.[89] Black professionals moving to Nashville to work in Christian denominational centers or higher education found themselves shut out of white neighborhoods they could otherwise afford.[90] A black banker recalled that families moving into previously white neighborhoods had been "burned out" of their homes.[91] Blockbusting tactics in evidence in other cities were also at work in Nashville. Real estate agents made false reports that a house on a given street had already been sold to a black family to push another homeowner to sell, or real estate agents rang doorbells in neighborhoods with the effect of "just frighten[ing] people to death" to get them to "sell right away," ushering white families out at suppressed prices and black families in at inflated ones.[92]

Real estate practices that pushed white homeowners to sell in fear also publicly marked some areas of Nashville as newly defined black neighborhoods. Before 1968, classifieds in the *Tennessean* and *Nashville Banner* daily newspapers marked selected classified ads as "COLORED," or sometimes, somewhat ironically, as "Integrated." After the 1968 Fair Housing Act, which had been publicly opposed by the Nashville Association of Realtors, the same practices continued, in more veiled language. By the early 1970s, some classifieds invited "Anyone."[93] School enrollment statistics and residential patterns often moved in tandem, with school zone lines an important determinant of whether white families would stay in a neighborhood with black families moving in, or would leave. As *Tennessean* reporter Rob Elder put it, "Even if they resist the pressure to sell, white families in the area find that its school zones place them in a difficult position. Several say they would leave their children in integrated schools, but do not want their children to go to schools where whites are a minority."[94] In one case, Nashville schools helped a group of white families avoid that fate. The district bused a group of white students away from majority-black Johnson School, walking distance from their home, to nearby and 90 percent white Margaret Allen Elementary. The school board rejected this practice immediately upon learning of it from the administrative staff, yet allowed the Allen students to stay for another year.[95]

As mentioned above, Samuel McDonald became a Cameron student chiefly through the actions of a junior high school guidance counselor who sent his file to that school rather than Central, linking him to a historically segregated school rather than a desegregating one. McDonald's counselor might have made a reflexive decision to continue categorizing and segregating students, a small-scale one that aligned with the powerful broad-scale decisions that had shaped school zones and housing locations for decades. Or the counselor might have actively chosen Cameron, possibly valuing the sense of tradition and community attachment that many students expressed about the school even as successful pressures to desegregate lunch counters and public accommodations over the 1960s cast its continued segregation into sharper relief.

In Nashville and other communities, black students' experiences with their segregated schools had multiple facets. Students, as did their teachers, recognized the shortage of material resources, the obligation to pay for their own sports uniforms or the dispiriting message carried in studying from re-bound (and at times racist-graffiti-laden) textbooks discarded from white schools.[96] They resented the poorly built—or poorly maintained—classrooms that the district continued to tolerate but local reporters described as "firetraps."[97]

Despite these enduring frustrations, historically black schools as both physical and social institutions remained central spaces for students and families navigating a segregated metropolis. Recalling growing up in both South Nashville and North Nashville some years earlier, Gena Carter centered her childhood idea of neighborhood on the school she attended and its proximity to her home. Segregation marked some not-too-distant corners or blocks as off limits to her as a young black girl, but home and school were consistent nodes in her idea of community and neighborhood. Carter had, like family generations before her, attended Pearl High School. Into the late 1960s, other students spoke similarly of Cameron as a place deeply interwoven with the local community, a place that fit into family histories, with teachers that "taught your mother, your brother," or, for some students, established a clear feeling of being known and appreciated. Some students' firm attachment to Cameron extended even after they moved outside of the immediate area. Semetta Coure Pulley opted to remain at the school into high school because she wanted to continue in the program for academically advanced students she had earlier benefited from, even though her family moved to a more rural section of county. Segregated black schools like Cameron and Pearl were known institutions, familiar and often supported by tradition, symbolizing at once ideas of community strength and the inequalities of segregation.[98]

Students' sense of attachment to the school as a community institution was not always uncritical, however. Rev. Amos Jones, who in the late 1970s and 1980s became a leading advocate for maintaining Pearl High School against a threatened closure, recalled the Pearl of his youth as far from perfect. Not only did it still reflect what Jones felt to be an overemphasis on white culture, he did not find there the encouragement and motivation he needed to pursue his studies, rather than "circumvent them" by choosing less challenging courses. Jones felt he was missing the broader course offerings and the motivation he felt students at segregated white schools enjoyed.[99]

Strong community attachment to schools characterized some white communities as well. Litton High School, which served an inner-ring, almost all-white suburban area of East Nashville, functioned as a community hub for residents of the area who also reported generations-long connections to their schools.[100] This pride of attachment expressed by white families endured at Litton, as at Cohn and Central, as the schools became gradually more statistically desegregated in the late 1960s.[101]

Thus in the late 1960s, Nashville's desegregation picture was a complex one—modest change in some venues, while overall segregation continued through recent state action and the enduring effects of earlier policy choices. Without the pressure of further litigation in the federal courts and the strengthened calls for active desegregation via *Green* and *Alexander*, these patterns would likely have continued for years, if not decades, with Nashville remaining closer to statistical segregation than desegregation.

### Conclusion

Looking across federal influences on the city, rather than at schools alone, helps highlight the ways that federal dollars and federal power worked both for and against segregation locally. Beyond the important general effects of federal mortgage policy that subsidized the making of white suburbia, Nashville had been unusually well attuned to Washington's ideas and offerings. In school construction, local officials made direct use of the ideological justifications for suburban school construction coming from the Department of Health, Education, and Welfare. In urban renewal, the city capitalized on personal relationships, well-positioned representatives in Congress, and its own history with urban renewal efforts to create an extraordinary density of projects that shaped urban space.[102] Funding formulas that allowed enlargements of segregated schools to leverage further federal dollars for segregated public housing meant that federal funds subsidized segregation in housing and schooling together more than a decade after *Brown,* and years after the passage of the Civil Rights Act. Federal school construction guidelines clearly embraced a pro-suburban vision that, in jurisdictions like Nashville with both urban and suburban areas, helped steer local resources toward the suburbs and away from the city center despite demonstrated need there.

The federal government helped build a landscape of segregation and inequality. They did so not only in ways that set the context for schooling in Nashville, but in connection with residential segregation. As they had in earlier phases of city planning discussion and practice, schools became factors in the shaping of the segregated metropolis.

### Coda

In October 1967, Edwin Mitchell stood before a breakfast meeting of the Nashville Chamber of Commerce to deliver an invited address. A radiologist at Meharry and longtime political collaborator of Avon Williams, Mitchell spoke at the invitation of David K. Wilson, the chamber president and head of a regional insurance company. Wilson thought that he might "dramatize" the lack of communication between "leaders of the Negro and white communities" with the invitation, but on seeing Mitchell's planned remarks, Wilson had cold feet. The night before the talk, he called John Seigenthaler, the publisher of the *Tennessean,* asking if Mitchell might be persuaded to tamp down his comments. Seigenthaler thought not—and in fact had already set the type for the full remarks to appear in the next day's paper.[103] Mitchell delivered his speech in full. One newspaper photographer documented the event by shooting over Mitchell's shoulder to capture the audience he faced: a room packed with men (and a few women) at formal cloth-covered tables, nearly all of them white, many with their arms crossed in closed, almost hostile, poses.

Looking across 1967 Nashville, Mitchell had much to be critical of. The student-led organizing campaigns of the early 1960s brought victories in desegregating downtown lunch counters, retail shopping, movie theaters, and other public accommodations. But Nashville's black leadership repeatedly confronted entrenched power that continued to privilege the white suburbs and overburden or destroy historically black urban neighborhoods. A voice for metropolitan consolidation only a few years earlier, Mitchell now saw how the metropolitan structure segmented and distributed resources within the metropolis unevenly. Mitchell made it clear that he held the city's business leadership to count for failing to consider black Nashvillians' opposition to their various growth-minded plans, the construction of I-40 chief among them. When the chamber of commerce endorsed these plans alongside state and local officials, Mitchell said, "YOU DID NOT SPEAK FOR US."

Mitchell offered a multifaceted critique of metropolitan inequality beyond the highway. He looked out at his stern immediate audience, and he looked beyond it, at an economic landscape in which jobs and commerce "leap-frogged" over city-dwelling black residents to new locations in the privileged white suburban belt and even beyond the county boundary. The neighborhoods that opportunity jumped over held nearly three-fifths of the county's poor people, and almost half of its unemployed. They lived in substandard conditions not because of "the ravages of those within" or an often-assumed "inherent failure due to race," but because landlords maximized the profit they could squeeze from their investment properties and their tenants. "The people who live here are truly *consumers* of the slum rather than *producers*," Mitchell clarified.

If a few years earlier Vivian Henderson had been comfortable appealing to education as a route toward economic opportunity, Mitchell feared calls for further education as a diversion. "But you tell us education is the answer to the problem; the Negro is unprepared! . . . Now where is the market for Negro labor outside those vocations that serve his own people?" Listing federal Equal Economic Opportunity Commission data on occupation after occupation in which black workers were radically underrepresented, Mitchell returned to the question of what education could undo. "In municipal employment, even all of the drivers of garbage trucks are white! How much education and what kind of a test does that job require?" Leveling a charge at those who made facile assertions of curriculum as sufficient to transform deeply entrenched labor market segregation, Mitchell added: "No, *education* is not the answer. Education plus *opportunity* is the answer!"

Mitchell addressed the chamber at a tense moment locally as well as nationally. A few months earlier, Stokely Carmichael's speeches at Vanderbilt and Fisk highlighted a black power discourse that the white elite found especially discomfiting, and gave the final push to turn long-simmering student and youth unrest into violent confrontation in April 1967. Modest by comparison to others, the Nashville riots came amid more extensive mid-1960s rebellions from Watts to Harlem to Detroit. Chamber president Wilson no doubt knew that many in the audience would hear Mitchell as offering a local explication of the causes of the 1967 unrest, from a respected man who himself had wandered the streets that night, trying to urge participants toward nonviolence.

Mitchell's remarks might have offered the local elite a rationale for the kind of frustration and anger that motivated unrest, but they work also as a catalog of the varied forces that had helped make educational inequality and segregation in the city over the postwar decades. Mitchell highlighted the role of city planning choices—immediately, highway construction and public housing location—that had decades-old roots in how planners saw the metropolis and bound schools and neighborhoods together with segregation. His emphasis on the shape of segregation in the local labor market highlighted the difficulty—and the limitations—of organizing curriculum to make economic mobility when so many sectors remained sites of racist proscription. And when Mitchell took on the chamber's "Forward Nashville" booster campaign, he recognized the city elite had never designed its growth agenda to move all of the city's residents forward. Their favored rhetoric of their city's "moderation" in desegregation in schools and beyond did more to obscure than to reveal the hard and multiple realities of segregation and inequality Mitchell saw all around him.

Mitchell's remarks came not long before new Supreme Court decisions in *Alexander* and *Green* provided Avon Williams new opportunities to address the slow progress of school desegregation in Nashville, to open the door to more assertive desegregation via busing. Williams launched a decades-long legal challenge to win a busing plan that produced statistical desegregation in Nashville unmatched by most American school districts. But whether such statistical desegregation could unmake the inequality made by so many deeply rooted and varied processes remained an open question.

# PART TWO

# Remaking Inequality, 1968–1998

# CHAPTER FIVE

# The Road to Busing

In 1968, Nashville schools saw levels of segregation typical of the American South at the time, with the vast majority of white students attending schools that were nearly all white, and black students attending schools that were nearly all black. Segregation persisted in most schools despite increased desegregation in a few others, brought about by the extension of the district's grade-per-year desegregation plan to all grades combined with the impact of residential succession in some neighborhoods. Three years later, in 1971, the district began to operate under an extensive desegregation plan that used busing to achieve significant statistical desegregation in more than two-thirds of the district's schools.

Avon Williams and his NAACP Legal Defense Fund allies pushed for this remedy on a new legal and historical foundation. Williams recognized the power of narratives about segregation and inequality as forces in their making. He sought to reject an established and nationally influential public and legal narrative: the idea of "de facto segregation." The term mischaracterized segregation in schooling as the product of housing policy, and cast both as the result of private rather than state action. Rejecting "de facto segregation," he indicted the intertwined roots of segregation in housing and schooling. Williams's arguments succeeded in securing more desegregation, via crosstown busing, but did not overcome distorted local understandings of segregation's roots.

Nashville accomplished much more statistical desegregation than most American cities that lacked busing plans, or had plans that operated exclusively within city boundaries and exempted the suburbs. Yet busing, from its initiation, remade rather than challenged educational inequality. Nashville's approach to busing resulted from both local and federal decisions and continued to treat black and white students—and increasingly, suburban and urban students—differently. The spatial organization of schooling in the era of busing was a key aspect of remaking inequality within desegregation. Regarding decisions about which students rode buses, to which schools in which places, busing worked to favor the suburbs and their residents and to devalue central city neighborhoods and their residents. Although these inequalities were quite visible to leaders like Avon Williams involved in advocating for busing, core questions of busing's design were made in closed bureaucratic and federal official spaces, rather than in connection with broader democratic debate. Thus contesting the ways in which busing remade inequality became that much more difficult.

## "With Each Reinforcing the Other": Avon Williams against "De Facto Segregation"[1]

Local and national developments set the stage for the plaintiffs in *Kelley v. Metropolitan Nashville Board of Education* to return to court in the fall of 1968. The *Green v. County School Board of New Kent County, Va.* case tested whether freedom-of-choice plans that did not rely explicitly on race were constitutional (unlike Nashville's earlier plan, which had, and had already been found unconstitutional in *Goss*). The Supreme Court's May 1968 *Green* decision stated that school systems had an "affirmative duty" to formulate desegregation plans that would eliminate discrimination "root and branch." Avon Williams believed that choice remained a significant, if sub rosa, practice in Nashville; both *Green's* specific finding against freedom of choice and transfer practices, as well as its broader call for assertive desegregation, provided new legal openings.[2]

Local events in the spring and summer of 1968 provided a sense of urgency as well, and highlighted the porous boundaries between the matter of segregation and broader concerns about ensuring fair treatment for black students. At a basketball tournament game at the downtown Municipal Auditorium, violence broke out between supporters of all-black Cameron High School and previously segregated white (and still majority-white) Stratford High School. Despite the fact that fights had long been a post-game feature at high school athletic events in Nashville, this event stood out for its scale, location, and message of conflict between black and white students. After several rounds of district-level hearings, the state athletic association responded by suspending Cameron from all interscholastic competition for a year. Cameron community members argued the suspension evidenced continued inequality in the board's treatment of black communities. For Avon Williams, the fight itself showed one cost of segregation. It produced social distance and unfamiliarity between black and white adolescents. Williams added the incident to his pleadings in *Kelley*, but Judge William E. Miller ruled that there was "no material relation" between the fight and the broader desegregation effort.[3]

Again, developments in other courtrooms prompted reconsideration of desegregation in Nashville. The *Alexander v. Holmes County* ruling of October 1969 held that the *Brown II* standard of "all deliberate speed" was no longer permissible and called on "every school district . . . to terminate dual school systems at once and to operate now and hereafter only unitary schools."[4] Williams and his NAACP LDF counterparts came before Judge Miller again, asking that he apply the new *Alexander* standard to review Nashville's progress on desegregation.[5]

On February 2, 1970, Judge Miller opened nearly two weeks of hearings in Nashville. A Yale-trained attorney, Miller had presided over *Kelley* since its inception in 1955. He had also supervised the district-court proceedings in the famous *Baker v. Carr* case that established the one-man/ one-vote principle in legislative representation. After being elevated to the Sixth Circuit Court of Appeals by President Richard Nixon, Miller continued to hear the *Kelley* case by special designation as a district judge through 1970.[6] Miller structured the hearings around three questions framed by the plaintiffs (and following *Alexander*'s standard): Had the school board met its duty to use school zone lines to reduce segregation? Had it met its duty in faculty integration? And had it used school construction decisions to further desegregation? Even before the hearings, Miller enjoined the school board from "purchasing new sites, building new school structures, or expanding present school facilities," pending a full consideration in court.[7]

Avon Williams used witness testimony to argue that the school board failed to meet the new *Alexander* standard of affirmative desegregation and to build a multipart narrative about the forces that crafted and sustained segregation and inequality in Nashville's schools. He drew not only on official school district policy but on the interactions among school policy, local city planning policy and practice, and property markets. In making these arguments, Williams confronted the increasingly powerful narrative of "de facto segregation." In the northern context, rights advocates beginning in the mid- and late-1950s turned to the idea of de facto segregation as a legal strategy to focus attention on the effects of segregation when causes remained veiled or difficult to prove with specificity. Yet having embraced the idea of de facto segregation for the openings it created in the north, organizations like the NAACP then saw the concept picked up by their typical foes, and by judges, at times to limit action on desegregation.[8]

5.1. Avon Williams, 1979. Courtesy of Nashville Public Library Special Collections.

Imported to a southern courtroom involved in reappraising the nature of segregation after the ostensible end of Jim Crow, the idea of de facto segregation offered a convenient way for local officials to stake out their own innocence in matters of ongoing segregation and to distance themselves from the historic and ongoing policy decisions that continued segregation in Nashville.

Williams argued that schools had been deeply implicated in Nashville housing and urban renewal policy, with segregating impact, and schools had been tools in shaping population growth and producing value in residential markets. That is, he recognized and named key aspects of the story set out in part I of this book. The intersections between schooling and housing policies and markets were not hidden, but a live part of the way that Williams understood the origins and contemporary practices that shaped and sustained segregation. In taking this approach, Williams supported Judge James T. McMillan's view in Charlotte's desegregation case, *Swann v. Mecklenburg County*, in 1969. McMillan explained that school location decisions as well as segregating actions in zoning, public housing construction, and beyond showed that "there is so much state action embedded in and shaping [these policy areas] that the resulting segregation is not innocent or '*de facto*,' and the resulting schools are not 'unitary' or desegregated."[9] Williams perceived not only state-sanctioned segregation in housing and schooling, but the construction of the two together. The narrative of de facto segregation, premised in part on a strict division between housing segregation and school segregation and the privileging of the first as determinative of the second, obscured the interactions between housing and schooling that Williams appreciated.

Drawing on a varied (if not always deep) base of documentary and testimonial evidence, Williams sought to establish a three-part analysis: private real estate actors encouraged segregation, and school administrators reinforced these judgments; planning decisions about school location had the power to encourage residential development and heighten real estate value in segregated suburbs; and urban renewal projects relied on a funding formula that allowed municipalities like Nashville to convert local spending on school construction to a subsidy for nearby, segregated housing construction.

To illustrate in court that segregated housing resulted not simply from myriad separate, individual decisions, but reflected systematic practices that worked across housing and schooling together, Avon Williams introduced Joyce Beisswenger, the wife of a Vanderbilt divinity professor and a newcomer to Nashville. Beisswenger testified that she asked her agent to show her properties in an "integrated neighborhood," but reported that she was "strongly discouraged" from this goal and ultimately unable to find a real estate agent to meet this request. Having located one potential home, Beisswenger inquired at the local school to confirm that their children would attend if they bought the house. The school employee who answered the phone—in Beisswenger's impression, the principal—explained that "it was his personal advice" that "I think you should not move into this neighborhood." As Beisswenger recalled, the school official explained that he would "not like my white children to go to school with Negro children," and promised to disavow these remarks if quoted.[10] Beisswenger's tale implicated not only local real estate agents, but a local school administrator operating in his official capacity.

Williams argued also that school construction and location decisions made new (usually segregated white) suburban developments more attractive, simultaneously increasing their property value and accelerating movement to these suburbs. Williams understood the centrality of public schools to private real estate markets, challenging the tidy housing versus schooling, private versus public dichotomies on which the idea of de facto segregation rested. To illustrate this point, Williams introduced as an exhibit a recent section of the *Tennessean* classifieds. The ads, he pointed out, listed schools along with other attractive elements of local properties.[11]

Metropolitan Planning Commission Director of Planning Robert Paslay, a witness for the defendant school board, offered surprisingly frank support for Williams's view of linked schooling and real estate development. Paslay agreed with Williams that "the location of schools influence[s] residential land use patterns," as school construction made areas "much more attractive for residential settlement." Consumer and developer interest increased in areas close to new schools. He continued on to explain the power of planning to affect residential growth, confirming that "by the adjustment of the size of a new school, one can control, to some extent . . . the residential growth of the area." Paslay, one of several Nashville planners with previous experience in other cities, held a view of schooling shaping the metropolitan landscape that was in stark contrast to the one implied in the paradigm of de facto segregation. There, schools appeared as strictly public institutions reacting to separate, private residential markets over which they had no influence.[12]

Williams built his case chiefly on the ways schools helped construct white suburban neighborhoods and black urban ones, but also criticized the planning commission for failing to take stock of visible patterns of racial concentration in new black suburban development. Robert Paslay insisted that the planning commission would not and could not predict whether it would be black families or white families who would occupy a planned Trinity Hills Village subdivision. The community—planned to hold as many as five thousand residences, according to its developers—abutted other recently built suburban areas, some of which had housed black residents exclusively from opening or had, in the late 1960s, undergone a quick transition from white to black occupancy. In Williams's view, Trinity Hills represented a potential concentration by class as well as racial category—the development received federal Section 235 funds and aimed to provide affordable accommodations to low- and middle-income families. Williams saw this development in suburbanization as another opportunity to make intentionally desegregating choices in school location. Instead, Robert Paslay insisted that he and his colleagues—who typically based their planning actions on projections of future population—were unable to predict the future racial composition of the area. Supposedly without consideration for the racial composition of the school, the planning commission approved a new school abutting Trinity Hills Village, expressly for the children of the new development.[13]

Avon Williams used urban renewal finance as another example of linked housing and schooling segregation. As explained in part I, Nashville planners had skillfully maximized federal urban renewal dollars via local-federal matching requirements. One way they did so was by locating new school construction or expansion within an urban renewal district—where it was often needed, but where it would also produce a segregated student population. The incentive to build schools specifically for segregated housing came from the formula for federal urban renewal funding. Municipalities had to provide a one-third local contribution to match two-thirds of federal dollars, but the local contribution could come in the form of construction of other municipal facilities in the area.[14] With corroboration from planner Robert Paslay, Williams explained that school construction subsidized public housing construction, even as public housing remained actively segregated in Nashville into the mid-1960s.[15]

Rather than contesting Williams's claims fully in the areas of zoning and construction, the Nashville school board, through its attorneys, made inaction their defense. According to Floyd Detchon, the school systems' head of zoning, plaintiffs' descriptions of continued segregation were false because in numerous instances where residential demographics had changed, the school board had left zone lines unchanged. Describing the Caldwell School—an East Nashville elementary school that had served an all-white population from the surrounding neighborhoods and segregated public housing projects until the late 1950s, and continued to serve the area once those housing projects became all black a decade later—Detchon explained that "many blacks were moving in, and we did not attempt to cut this off in any way."[16]

This was exactly the kind of inaction that *Alexander* found wanting, and that produced resegregation rather than stable desegregation. Many of the previously segregated white schools enrolling black students for the first time under the 1957 grade-per-year plan had become majority, but not exclusively, black by the late 1960s. All were located in working-class white residential areas close to areas of black residence. Other segregated white schools where gerrymandered zone lines had prevented any black enrollment in the late 1950s and early 1960s began to enroll black students by the middle of the decade. The school board did not change zone lines as more black families moved in and white families left, so some of these schools moved quickly to a large minority, and in some cases a majority, of black students.[17]

After two weeks of intensive hearings and evidence offered by the plaintiffs and school board, Judge Miller held that Nashville schools had not acted affirmatively to ensure a unitary, desegregated system. Miller explained that the Supreme Court's recent rulings required school boards to use school zone lines to "maximize pupil integration." Instead, in Nashville, zone lines that had been "drawn . . . with the aim of maintaining segregation" remained in place, and that despite some demographic shifts in residence, they generally continued "to serve quite well the segregative purpose for which they were originally established."[18]

Judge Miller used illustrations of a few close-by clusters of schools to prove his point. Maps showing both residential demographics by racial category and school zone lines demonstrated how, in one contiguous group of seven schools, four schools had only black students, one had 90 percent black students, and two had 99 percent or more white students.[19]

A map of five schools in East Nashville used shaded areas to show that black residences were often neatly contained within school zone lines. Judge Miller characterized the lines as "drawn to enclose" black students. Only one of the five schools with white students was also home to a significant proportion of black students.[20] Inglewood was the exception. This previously middle-class segregated white area became a destination for middle-class black families leaving more urban neighborhoods in other parts of East Nashville. Robert W. Kelley's family made this move, as had others as early as the late 1950s.[21]

Judge Miller took the school board to task for its zoning and construction policies, in which he saw evidence of intentional segregation of the sort often labeled "de jure." And he acknowledged forces that constrained housing market opportunity for black buyers, including "relatively weak

Table 5.1  Student Enrollment for Seven Nashville Schools with Contiguous Zones, 1970

|  | White enrollment | Black enrollment | Percent black students |
| --- | --- | --- | --- |
| Ford Greene | 0 | 887 | 100 |
| Head | 0 | 791 | 100 |
| Carter-Lawrence | 0 | 516 | 100 |
| Murrell | 0 | 328 | 100 |
| Clemons | 51 | 519 | 90 |
| Ransom | 355 | 2 | 1 |
| Eakin | 487 | 5 | 1 |

Source: Kelley et al. v. Metropolitan Nashville Board of Education, July 16, 1970, 317 F. Supp. 980.

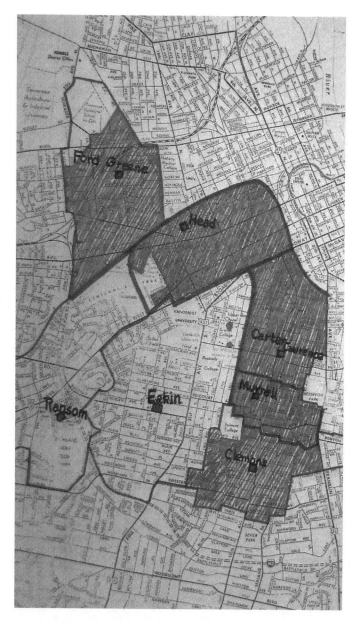

5.2. Judge William E. Miller included maps to illustrate the segregative school zones lines in use in Nashville in his 1970 opinion in *Kelley et al. v. Board of Education of Metropolitan Nashville*, July 16, 1970, 317 F. Supp. 980. Shaded areas indicate black residence.

economic strength and discriminatory real estate practices."[22] Yet Miller did not adopt Avon Williams's overall argument about the interrelationships between housing and schooling policy. Instead, he returned to familiar ground. Miller emphasized how school segregation followed housing market patterns, which he characterized largely as the product of the private market rather than state policies. For Miller, school segregation followed from the separate domain of housing segregation. Earlier, he had characterized residential segregation as "natural." Now he portrayed schools as the recipients of demographics beyond their influence. When "segregation is purely the unavoidable result of bona fide racial residential patterns," schools with segregated enrollments were permissible.[23] Miller did, however, support the plaintiff's charges that MNPS had organized school construction to respect residential segregation rather than challenge it. He thus ordered the school system to cease all projects planned but not yet in active construction.[24]

The *Tennessean* excerpted short snippets of the opinion, bringing Judge Miller's thinking into more public circulation. They chose to publish passages that portrayed housing and schooling as separate matters but also promised to challenge segregation. "It is true that a school board can do nothing about where the pupil population is located, but it is equally true that a school board can most certainly do something about where pupils attend school."[25] The evidence Williams introduced about how school practice in fact had influenced where "the pupil population is located" went missing. Desegregation that followed Miller's view could address where students were assigned to schools, but need not do much to reverse the use of school construction to enable suburbanization or the deepening of urban segregation by race and class.

Judge Miller's decision in *Kelley v. Metropolitan Nashville Board of Education* applied increasingly assertive legal doctrine on desegregation. *Alexander* and *Green* said it was insufficient to open the doors of schools to black students but not alter existing segregated attendance patterns. Avon Williams was a skilled and well-informed attorney looking for a way to build on these rulings and accelerate Nashville's movement toward the kind of plan that Charlotte's Judge McMillan first ordered in *Swann* in 1969. McMillan ordered busing across school zone lines to achieve educational desegregation despite residential segregation.

In arguing for busing, Williams also opposed the dominant ways of thinking, in both legal and public circles, about persistent school segregation a decade and a half after *Brown*. Judge McMillan agreed in part. He understood continued segregation to be the result of formal policy, and thus formal education policy could and should be designed to overcome it. Yet Williams went a step further by more explicitly linking housing and schooling. He wanted to break down the assumption that residential segregation developed independently from school policy. Williams assembled partial yet significant evidence that governmental and private action made housing and school segregation together.

Williams won a new remedy, but he did not succeed in toppling the narrative of de facto segregation that rested in part on a false separation between housing and schooling. Judge Miller instead reasserted the "de facto" view, describing patterns of housing segregation as the cause of persistent educational segregation. Miller did not explain why he took this route. He might have found Williams's evidence insufficient to establish full legal causality, or he might have been persuaded by the frequent arguments from the school board's attorneys that segregation in housing and urban renewal was separate from and beyond the purview of the defendant board. The very structure of legal advocacy in school desegregation and beyond encouraged this argument, as cases targeted the actions of a single defendant entity and sought to hold that entity, not others not represented in court, responsible for past actions or future remedies.[26]

Judge Miller's reliance on the de facto paradigm limited possible solutions to the problem of persistent segregation, and contributed to (or at least left unchallenged) a powerful public narrative about the root causes of segregation. The multilayered, dynamic interactions that Avon Williams portrayed in court emerged from the legal process tidier, thinner, and less true. Even as Miller ordered more extensive desegregation, he reinforced familiar but false dichotomies—between housing and schooling, between public policy and private markets or interests, between state action and individual choice. Had Miller challenged the de facto narrative, it would not have revolutionized local conversation about segregation. But it would have offered a small step toward a fuller history of segregation's deep and broad roots, a step away from misleading narratives that helped—and continue to help—remake inequality.

## Local and Federal Plans for Desegregation

Issued on July 16, 1970, Judge Miller's order gave the school district thirty days to assemble a new plan that would create more desegregation. He did not specify the use of busing, which the courts had ordered in Charlotte but was still under review by the Supreme Court. Miller charged the Nashville board with developing a policy for school construction and site selection that would favor rather than hinder desegregation. Having been persuaded by Williams's evidence that Nashville's teaching faculty remained desegregated only in a token sense, Miller also called for faculty integration to meet a target of 80 percent white teachers and 20 percent black teachers in each school.[27]

For even the most organized districts with developed infrastructure, this task would have been a large one. For Metro Nashville Public Schools—which had operated without a superintendent for six months after the sudden death of John Harper Harris in January 1970, and with the newly hired Dr. Elbert Brooks in the post only two weeks at the time of Judge Miller's order—the task was beyond daunting.

Brooks, an Arizona native and the former principal of a large Tucson high school, recalled a warm welcome to Nashville by the local business leadership, including from growth advocate Victor Johnson, who hosted a luncheon for him at Aladdin not long after he arrived in town. Faced with the question of how to devise a new plan for desegregation of a district he was still getting to know, Brooks decided to appoint a large citizens committee to help design this plan, and turned to a well-regarded local business leader to head up the effort.[28] Dan May, the second-generation owner of a local textile mill and former chairman of the City of Nashville Board of Education, became chairman of the newly founded Citizens Advisory Committee.[29] May, who was white, was joined by a vice chair who was black—Dr. Matthew Walker, of Meharry Medical College. Beneath an eighteen-member advisory committee, each of three sixteen-member subcommittees had a chair and cochair, one black and one white.[30] Brooks likely hoped that the committee structure would convey community investment and consent, especially given his short tenure. In fact, the subcommittees and the committee as a whole were too large to work effectively, held public hearings but found them often weakly attended, and voted to approve a plan for submission to the board with less than a majority of members present.[31]

The committee leadership also highlighted the boundaries of "moderation" among the city's white leadership. Dan May was a respected, frank-speaking pragmatist with a reputation for involvement in causes of concern to Nashville's black community. But he was more often chosen by white leaders than black ones to represent black community concerns. He had been Mayor Briley's pick, over an experienced black minister, to chair the body that managed War on Poverty programs in Nashville.[32] May felt that court orders subordinated "all other considerations in the development of the child to the one problem of integration" and explained that the "primary purpose of the schools is to educate, not to be used to further any sociological concept," such as desegregation.[33] These views made May less than inclined to go beyond minimal compliance.

Presenting its plan to the board on August 14, 1970, the committee called for some pairing of schools, linking majority-black and majority-white schools to achieve desegregation in both. This strategy, in use in many other districts nationally, meant students from both schools' earliest grades would attend the previously majority-white school, and those in the later grades the previously majority-black school, or vice versa.[34] The school board balked at the idea of pairing, arguing that the district did not have the buses it would require. In a public hearing with an estimated six hundred parents in attendance, parent Peggy Davis explained that "we are not against integration. You can send us to [the local majority-black school]. But please don't pair us." She may have been concerned over the ways that pairing divided students within a given family between different schools when each school served fewer grade levels. Her concerns reflected a preview of the family-logistics-based concerns that many mothers, both white and black, expressed over the course of desegregation.[35]

Although the school board rejected the pairing idea, school district officials had offered few real alternatives. Committee member and Vanderbilt professor Bradford Brown complained that the administration presented the citizen's committee only one possible plan, and rejected all suggested alternatives as "unsuitable."[36] On August 17, 1970, just minutes before Judge Miller's deadline, the school board passed a muted version of the plan suggested by the citizen's committee.[37] Elbert Brooks later admitted that the committee's initial proposal would have led to more desegregation than the version later passed by the board.[38] The board's plan modeled slippery bureaucratic phrasing, pledging to "implement planning that will move toward the assurance that each child during his or her educational preparation . . . will have the opportunity to attend an integrated school."[39] It tried to achieve more desegregation by tinkering with zone lines, increasing integration in twenty-four of the district's schools. Nineteen others already met the integration target the committee used, of between 15 and 35 percent black students in each school. They rezoned most of the district's remaining ninety-eight schools—but with little impact on desegregation.[40] The plan continued the district's earlier conversation about using large comprehensive high schools to aid desegregation.[41]

The committee also proposed, and the board approved, nine school closures. That these schools were nearly all in Nashville's urban core added a spatial twist to the pattern visible in communities both north and south where desegregation meant the shuttering of historically black schools. In Nashville, most (but not all) of the targeted schools were previously segregated black institutions. The threatened closure of two of these, both previously segregated white schools—Central High School and North High School—received such immediate public outcry that the board reversed itself on these sites. Both the citizens' committee and the board agreed to cancel expansion of a crowded all-black city elementary school, Murrell, and to abandon plans to expand Rose Park Junior High School—a previously segregated black school—into a comprehensive high school for the city, because high school facilities dollars should be "spent at a new location which would maximize integration for students at these grade levels."[42] The proposed school closures and curtailed construction in city neighborhoods foreshadowed what would become the prime struggle over the implementation of desegregation in Nashville over the next decade and a half. In the context of desegregation, which communities needed, and which communities deserved, local schools became a focal question. The spatial organization of schooling remained a key aspect of the remaking of educational inequality under busing, just as it had long been central to the making of inequality and segregation.

Amid the talk of urban school closures, Avon Williams raised a different and broader question. In the 1970 hearings before Judge Miller, Williams tried to convince the court that the school board and planning commission together had aggressively supported suburban school construction even when classroom seats were available in city classrooms. The board argued that no such seats existed, but Williams continued to focus on how the planning commission and board so readily assumed the burden of building new suburban schools to meet suburban population growth, rather than extending zone lines for existing schools outward to the suburbs. In essence, he asked, why was it the school system that had to move its schools to follow suburban migrants, rather than the suburban migrant who could, as a result of their move, travel farther to existing schools? This was an important question that, as it went unanswered, revealed how public services accommodated and facilitated choices, such as the move to the suburbs, often portrayed as strictly private. Williams likely knew, of course, that this line of argument ran up against decades of city planning and popular thinking that made schools part of residential property rights and value and put schools at the center of definitions of neighborhood and community.[43]

The new district policy on school facilities and construction asserted again the assumption that school facilities needed to follow the students. It conveyed pro-suburban messages familiar from *Schools from 1980*, but took them even further in presuming and facilitating continued suburban development. The new policy emphasized that the board should purchase suburban school-site locations in advance of suburban development, while urban spaces remained proscribed for schooling: "locating [school] sites in areas zoned for commercial or apartment use should be avoided when possible."[44] Avon Williams called the policy "vague and indefinite," with no protections for existing urban schools or limits on suburban school construction.[45]

For faculty desegregation, to meet the court-specified 80 percent white/ 20 percent black teacher ratio in each school, MNPS planned to use a mix of voluntary and involuntary transfers, and to place new hires in schools in which they would be in the racial minority on the faculty. Advisory committee members noted that the prescribed ratio meant much more disruption for historically black schools with predominantly black faculty—which stood to lose up to 80 percent of their teachers in a single moment—than it did for historically white schools. The committee suggested a transitional year in which previously segregated black schools could have between 35 and 50 percent black teachers. At first, the school board overruled this as unacceptable to the court, but ultimately, through adjustments and resistance, many schools opened with faculties of up to 40 percent black teachers.[46]

Williams shared the committee's concern, but (as he would continue to do over the next decade in *Kelley*) pushed for faculty ratios to track the racial composition of the student population at each school, rather than the district faculty composition overall. Williams was arguing for more black teachers to be hired (as there were proportionally fewer black teachers than there were students in the system). He also hoped to add "official policy and legal safeguards for black children subjected to white classroom teachers" to ensure that "black cultural differences will not be viewed as a reflection of inferiority," that intelligence testing "not be systematically interpreted to the detriment of black students," and that black students receive "adequate, sympathetic, and non-discriminatory academic or vocational counseling."[47] Although they may have had some influence on "human relations" programs in Nashville schools, these concerns received no legal or formal policy response. Williams also worried that the pattern visible in other districts, where faculty integration brought job losses and demotion for black teachers, would come to Nashville.[48]

With zoning, construction, and faculty desegregation proposals in place, administrators began frenzied preparations for opening school in less than two weeks. Officials worked constantly, over nights and weekends, to make necessary changes to facilities and faculty rosters implied by the plan. Portable classrooms had to be relocated, and 705 teachers had to be reassigned to new schools (165 who had volunteered, 540 who had not, selected by random lottery).[49] In the end, the frenzy was pointless. Faculty desegregation did begin in the fall of 1970, but developments outside of Nashville caused delay in all other elements.

As Nashville educators scrambled, the Supreme Court agreed to hear arguments in *Swann*, to assess whether Charlotte Judge McMillan's busing plan was constitutional. School board officials in Nashville argued, and persuaded Judge Miller, that beginning a new plan in Nashville would be ill advised until the resolution of the legal question posed by the Supreme Court's review of *Swann*. On August 25, Miller stayed the implementation of the school board's recently devised zoning plan until the Supreme Court ruled.[50] After scrambling to open under a new desegregation plan, the district now chose to scramble to return to the status quo ante. Newspaper photographers captured images of trucks carrying portable classrooms away from schools where they had just arrived, back to where they had come from.[51] Nashville students returned to school on the basis of geographic zones drawn in 1957 on the principle of "intelligent zoning" to limit desegregation—zones that Miller identified as intentionally segregating.

Avon Williams appealed Judge Miller's stay to the Sixth Circuit Court of Appeals, where the judges agreed that, in this case "growing hoary with age," and despite the pending legal questions raised by *Swann*, the district court was in danger of "denying justice by delay." The appeals court quoted liberally and supportively from Miller's July 1970 opinion, and reasserted the judge's statement that "affirmative action to maximize integration in all feasible ways" was what was required. The Sixth Circuit sent *Kelley* back to Nashville, ordering Miller to proceed in evaluating the board's plan against the plaintiffs' and others' objections and, ultimately, work toward implementation.[52]

Despite his opposition to the stay, Avon Williams and his colleagues had numerous objections to the board plan. Tallying its impact on desegregation, Williams argued that the plan meant "continued segregation in virtually all of the Metropolitan system," while underutilizing central-city black schools and continuing construction in majority-white suburban spaces. Together, as Williams argued again over the coming years, the result was black children and parents bearing "the major burden of integration without substantial change in the condition of near total segregation which continues to exist in the inner-city all-black schools."[53]

One group of white parents complained to the court about their children's assignment to the previously segregated black Rose Park School. The parents—reflecting a mix of university professors, clergy, and others who identified in favor of desegregation—protested the plan for treating their children differently than those in other rezoning arrangements, where white children would have remained in the majority. The parents, organized under the name Citizens for Unitary Education, described the 1970 plan as "piece-meal, inconsistent, and arbitrary," and one that would desegregate by "injecting a substantial white minority, through busing, into a previously predominantly black school."[54] The reverse, with a black minority "injected" into a predominantly white school, was the more typical model for busing, and within a year would be the most common approach in Nashville as well. These parents opposed the selective application of desegregation to some rather than all students in MNPS, and did so based on the historically grounded notion that zone lines had originated in segregationist gerrymandering and thus should be dismissed across the board, not simply tinkered with.[55] They were just the first of many (most much less supportive of busing than this group claimed to be) to take up the mantle of fairness between white communities as a key consideration in busing. Their actions also hinted that not even white liberals would tolerate the idea of schools that put white children in the minority.

By the time the case returned to Nashville from the Sixth Circuit, *Kelley* had passed to a new federal judge in Nashville, Hon. L. Clure Morton. A Knoxville native and former FBI agent descended from a long line of East Tennessee Republicans, Morton was a Nixon appointee to the bench and was known for his quick wit and sometimes sharp tongue.[56] In early March 1971, attorneys for the defendant school board, the plaintiff parents, and two new groups that aspired to intervene in the case were back in court to debate how to move forward, aware also of the potential that the Supreme Court would affirm *Swann* and thus raise the pressure to bus for desegregation. Morton worked forward from Judge Miller's 1970 decision, and did not reopen the earlier discussion of segregation's causes.

In April 1971, the Supreme Court affirmed Charlotte's use of busing.[57] Deeming neither the school board's plan (stayed by Judge Miller) nor a hastily assembled alternative submitted by the plaintiffs to be sufficient, Judge Morton requested the Atlanta regional office of the Department of Health, Education and Welfare, Office of Education (HEW) to craft a plan for Nashville. Later sections detail the process through which the plan was created. In sum, it accepted most of the school board's decisions on school closure and the exemption of thirty-three schools in the outer suburbs. It adopted the school board's suggested desegregation target of 15 to 35 percent black students in each school. In some neighborhoods, intentional zoning could create more desegregation. More frequently, HEW used pairing (as the citizen's committee had proposed in 1970) or clustering (like pairing, but with more than two schools) to group together students from previously segregated schools and then divide them by grade level rather than by race. In inner-ring suburbs and other areas with black and white neighborhoods in close proximity, pairing or clustering could work with a group of schools near to one another. But many black residential areas in Nashville were too far from white ones, and vice versa, so pairing or clustering had to work with "non-contiguous" zoning. The paired or clustered schools often were at quite a distance from one another. Buses would transport students from black neighborhoods into white ones for certain grades, and then white neighborhoods into black ones for others.[58]

Legal scholars have distinguished the early years of desegregation as a time of formal equality—the school doors were open to all—but without substantive equality, as most schools remained firmly segregated. Busing in Nashville, with its prescribed and often achieved 15 to 35 percent black student ratio, can appear to evidence substantive equality. No longer were the school doors just open; black and white students were going to school together. Yet in fact, what developed was a new formal equality—of statistical desegregation and racial ratios—that did not guarantee substantive equity in the process or outcomes of schooling. The spatial organization of Nashville schooling, crafted over decades of school construction planning and through recent school closure decisions, meant that most black children from urban areas rode buses out of their neighborhoods for at least nine of their twelve years in school. White children from the suburbs rarely did so for more than three. Travel distances were great. The plan distributed students differently at elementary, junior high, and high school, and sent black students to a greater number of schools over their school years than white students. The plan contained wide variations, but it consistently placed its greatest burdens on the shoulders of black urban students.[59] Assigning grades 1 through 4 to suburban schools kept the youngest white students at home in the suburbs while their black age-mates rode buses. Plaintiffs' attorneys raised many of these points in 1971, as they protested the disparate burden in the busing order.[60] Attending to how busing allocated burdens forces recognition of inequalities within busing itself.

For a six-year-old living in a racially isolated white suburban area—yet not close enough to the county line to be exempted from busing entirely—her education would be structured as follows:

Grades 1–4: Suburban neighborhood school, short travel distance (usually less than thirty minutes)

Grades 5–6: Urban neighborhood school, long travel distance (six to ten miles, up to fifty minutes on bus each way, in some cases up to eighty minutes)

Grades 7–12: Suburban junior and senior high schools drawing from multiple urban and suburban neighborhoods, short to medium travel distance (In some areas, one year of grades 7–9 occurred in an urban neighborhood.)

This pattern was reversed for students (the majority of whom were black) living in racially isolated urban areas. This was the plan that shaped Hubert Dixon III's schooling beginning in 1971:

Grades 1–4: Suburban neighborhood school, long travel distance (six to ten miles, up to fifty minutes on bus each way, with some cases up to eighty minutes)

Grades 5–6: Urban neighborhood school, short travel distance

Grades 7–12: Suburban junior and senior high schools drawing from multiple suburban and urban neighborhoods, long travel distance (six to ten miles, up to fifty minutes on bus each way, in some cases up to eighty minutes) (In some areas, one year of grades 7–9 occurred in an urban neighborhood.)[61]

Dixon attended two suburban elementary schools in second through fourth grade before returning close to home briefly for two years of junior high, and then heading outward again to a suburban high school. The same schema, only slightly altered, guided Hubert's niece Brittany's experience twenty years later, when she attended six schools before graduation. She went to school close to home or traveled via bus to distant schools near the county line, depending on whether she and her family lived, as they did for portions of her schooling, in the suburbs, or in her grandparents homestead just across the river from North Nashville. Both generations of Dixon students attached positive gains to their experience with desegregation, as it opened opportunities for later learning and fostered relationships with peers both black and white. Yet for both, there was the uncertain feeling of being part of a "methodology that was taking place" as

5.3. Students board a school bus to return home after their day at Percy Priest Elementary School in suburban Nashville. By Nancy Rhoda, the *Tennessean*.

Hubert Dixon put it—a methodology that valued some measures of equality, and some communities, more than others.

White resistance to busing proved quite vociferous. Yet most white families, particularly those living in Nashville's band of suburban privilege, did not experience their own children's busing across town until fifth and sixth grade, and possibly only then. These white families lived close enough to the city core to be bused, but not so close that desegregation could be arranged through zoning shifts alone, and not so far out as to be in one of the thirty-three schools exempted entirely from court-ordered busing. Busing seemed to fundamentally disrupt the general correlation between housing location and schooling location, yet the experience of busing was a highly contingent one, where student assignment depended not only on the racial composition of a given neighborhood, but its urban or suburban positioning. Beyond the initial assignment, the family experience of busing was further conditioned by economic resources, by social networks, and to some extent by simple chance. Busing was at once a policy shift that was quite drastic, and one that left ample space for old inequalities to continue in new forms.

The particular shape of Nashville's busing plan resulted only in part from vivid courtroom and curbside debate. Quietly moving bureaucratic practices and ideological commitments—some decades old—located students and schools in the metropolitan landscape.

## Shaping Busing: Predictions and Depictions
## of Metropolitan Space

The spatial organization of schooling in Nashville during busing turned on narratives about the past and present, including concepts like "de facto segregation," as well as on ideas about the future. The questions seemed simple enough: Where were the students now, and where would they be in the future; where were the (acceptable) schools, and where should they be in the future? Planners' and educators' answers to these questions often engaged ideology as much as empirical reality. They focused on ideas about the metropolitan landscape divided, as in earlier planning efforts like *Schools for 1980*, into regions of "growth" (in the suburbs) and "decline" (in the city). In the process, they informed material and consequential choices about where students went to school and which communities kept or lost their local schools.

The Metropolitan Planning Commission had chief responsibility for collecting and sharing area demographic information, and making projections about future trends. Collaboration between the MPC and school board brought planning information and ideas into the work of shaping a detailed desegregation plan. As chapter 4 illustrated, pro-suburban thinking about metropolitan space and schooling had been visible in Nashville for years before busing was on the horizon. Planning ideas celebrated suburban spaces as appropriate for schooling. Planners' representations also emphasized suburban growth and urban decline, and together these ideas fed directly into planners' work with school administrators. Both representations and projections of demographic change thus helped lay the foundation for desegregation plans that disproportionately burdened black students and separated urban communities from schooling.[62]

In the late 1950s, planners cautiously documented both the persistence of dense central settlement and low-density suburban expansion. Maps that focused on areas of growth and decline in percentage terms came with disclaimers that the percentage change over differently sized, differently dense regions could be misleading, either by exaggerating growth or overstating decline; planners included maps that displayed the same data differently as a useful counterpoint.[63] A decade later, the planning commission's focus on ascertaining where growth was happening overrode care to provide multiple interpretations of the data, and planning maps distorted population data and projections. In population projects issued by the MPC in 1969, dozens of maps showed all demographic changes in the county in percentage-change terms. A layperson looking at these maps would notice

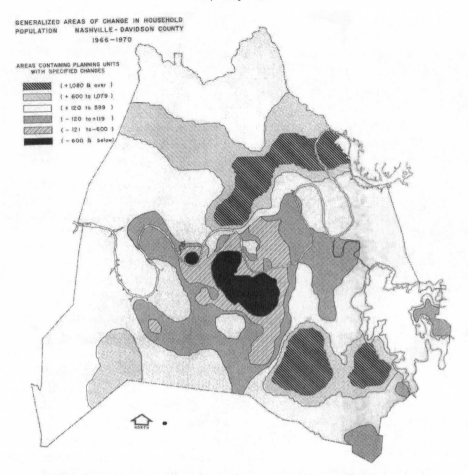

GENERALIZED AREAS OF CHANGE IN HOUSEHOLD
POPULATION    NASHVILLE - DAVIDSON COUNTY
1966 - 1970

AREAS CONTAINING PLANNING UNITS
WITH SPECIFIED CHANGES

( + 1,080 & over )
( + 600 to 1,079 )
( + 120 to 599 )
( - 120 to +119 )
( - 121 to -600 )
( - 600 & below)

5.4. "Generalized Areas of Change in Household Population, Nashville-Davidson County, 1966–1970," selected map from "Projected Distribution of Residential Population in Nashville-Davidson County to 1985," Metropolitan Planning Commission, 1969. Original color image edited for legibility in black and white, with thanks to Seth Erickson.

areas of growth and decline. Asked to answer the question of where schools were needed, they would reasonably conclude that developing schools in the city—with areas of 20 percent or more population decline—would be wasteful, and that all building should happen farther into the suburbs, where growth would exceed 30 percent. Throughout this period, with a focus on suburban growth and development, planners overlooked or even made invisible the needs of inner-city students, who remained present and often underserved by educational facilities. They were poorly represented

## 1970 School-Age Population
### Metropolitan Nashville-Davidson County, Tennessee

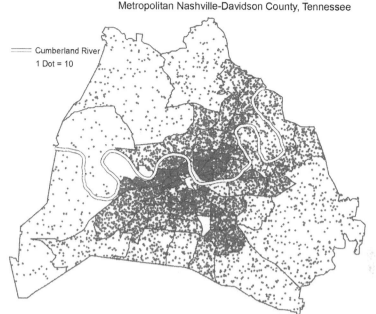

5.5. 1970 Decennial Census, via NHGIS, http://www.nhgis.org. This map uses census categories for ages 5–9 and 10–14 as the measure for school-age students. The county outline in figure 5.4 differs from this figure because it uses a different but equally valid method of projecting the three-dimensional earth in two dimensions.

in percentage-change terms, which reinforced instead the changes planners took to be inexorable—rapid urban decline and displacement of urban residential areas by commercial development, and fast suburban growth.[64] These planning maps provided the basis for school construction planning well into the 1970s, as confirmed by planner Robert Paslay in hearings in *Kelley*.[65]

Nonetheless, school administrators and planners (and in some cases, attorneys for both sides in *Kelley*) remained focused on urban decline. Despite both bureaucratic discourse and planning representations that made this fact hard to perceive, as of 1970, Nashville's school-age population was distributed across suburban areas *and* remained densely concentrated in urban areas. Significant migration out of the city core by white families in the 1960s had been accompanied by major population increases for black families.[66] Planning maps obscured this dual dynamic even as they influenced busing plans. Estimating population change from 1966–1970, planners assumed an inner-city population decline nearly three times greater than that which occurred. Those estimations had figured a loss of 8.4 percent for the inner-city area, when in fact the 1970 census revealed only a 3.6 percent decrease to have occurred. As school-age children made up 48 percent of the inner-city population, this undercount missed around 4,000 children under age 18.[67] Simultaneously, the planning commission had overestimated suburban growth—which came in at a significant 12.1 percent, still "well below" the predicted 18.9 percent increase.[68] By 1973, after the fundamental outlines of the busing plan had been formed in part through assumptions of urban decline, planners acknowledged that "the so-called flight from the inner city is certainly less than dramatic" as of the early 1970s. There was in fact a 1 percent net gain over the decade in city dwellings, despite the destruction or conversion of more than 17,000 units through interstate highway construction, urban renewal, and commercial and industrial expansion. In a shift from their earlier emphasis on decline, the planning commission belatedly acknowledged that developers and financial institutions continued to have "faith" that "the inner city will continue to house a large proportion of the county's population."[69]

In schools like Washington Junior High and Wharton Elementary, which had been sites of parent protest in earlier years over overcrowded conditions, classrooms remained over capacity.[70] In the decade that saw sharp decline in white school-age residence in the city, the black school-age population increased even more sharply, by 42.5 percent.[71] There were fewer white urban residents, but still many thousands of urban residents. City-dwelling children remained a similar proportion of the county's overall school-age population.

Images of central-city neighborhoods as increasingly depopulated easily coexisted with—and could be reinforced by—other public images of inner-city Nashville circulating at the time. With a suburban population increasingly connected from urban residential neighborhoods, press depictions carried increasing weight. Both the planning for Nashville's Model Cities project and the coverage of the "riots" around Tennessee A & I's campus in the fall of 1967 conveyed litanies of pathology about crime, decrepit spaces, and unemployment.[72] They offered little to counter an image of a declining, even depopulating, urban core.

The question of how, and whether, to represent local school demographics visually became a point of intense debate within *Kelley* hearings before Judge Morton. Before Morton turned to HEW to design desegregation in Nashville, he requested plans from the school board and the plaintiffs. To assist in making a plan, Avon Williams requested what came to be

Table 5.2  Nashville School-Age Population, 1950, 1960, and 1970

A. School-Age Population in City of Nashville Areas, 1950–1970, by Census Racial Category

|  | White 5- to 14-year-olds | Percentage change | Black and other 5- to 14-year-olds | Percentage change | Total city 5- to 14-year-olds | Percentage change |
|---|---|---|---|---|---|---|
| 1950 | 14,912 |  | 7,302 |  | 22,214 |  |
| 1960 | 16,010 | 7.4% | 11,532 | 57.9% | 27,542 | 24.0% |
| 1970 | 12,754 | −20.3% | 16,431 | 42.5% | 29,185 | 6.0% |

B. School-Age Population in City of Nashville vs. Surrounding Davidson County, 1950–1970, by Census Racial Category

|  | City 5- to 14-year-olds | County (not inclusive of city) 5- to 14-year-olds | Total 5- to 14-year-olds | City 5- to 14-year-olds (as percentage of total) |
|---|---|---|---|---|
| 1950 | 22,214 |  |  |  |
| 1960 | 27,542 | 47,952 | 75,494 | 36.5% |
| 1970 | 29,185 | 57,160 | 86,345 | 33.8% |

Note: Census racial categorizations change over time. Here I use the label "Black and other" to represent what the census labels "Nonwhite," "Black and Other," or "Black," "Hispanic," "American Indian," and "Asian and Pacific Islander." I use children ages five to fourteen to measure school-age population, despite its exclusion of older students, as it allows for consistent measure across all four decades in the census. Using school-age population rather than school enrollment leaves out the impact of departures from the public school system.

Source: US Census, via NHGIS, http://www.nhgis.org.

called a pupil locator map—a map, to be created by the school board, indicating the home, grade level, and race of each child in Nashville schools.[73] Williams argued that neither he and his colleagues, nor the school district, could craft an appropriate desegregation plan, nor would anyone be able to evaluate competing plans, without such a map.[74] The school board resisted, though, and the fight over Williams's request for a map, in arguments that moved beyond the courtroom to the *Tennessean*, revealed that much was at stake in empirically based representations of space, with the power to contest or at least complicate local mythology about segregation, school policy, and urban depopulation.[75] The school district's reluctance to create such a map seemed to suggest investment in keeping understandings of metropolitan residential distribution fuzzy or fungible.

Certainly, preparing a pupil locator map would mean a great deal of labor in the days before desktop computing. One school board argument against preparing the map was its estimate that doing so would cost

$8,000 in materials and time, particularly as there were "no such maps in existence"—the 1970 board plan had apparently been created without one.[76] The result of this expensive process would be a map of thirty-five by thirty-five feet, one board official claimed.[77] Earlier, Judge Miller found these arguments persuasive and allowed MNPS to produce tables, but not spatially organized displays, of student residence, race, and age. But Judge Morton—and before him, judges on the Sixth Circuit Court of Appeals—believed the map to be necessary in preparing a detailed desegregation plan and ordered the board to submit one.[78] The resulting creation was a mammoth ten-by-ten-foot map that dominated Morton's courtroom through the spring and early summer of 1971.[79]

Once created, the map highlighted the absence of such information in earlier discussions of zoning and desegregation. Previously, spatial information had been casual and highly local, or presented in more-difficult-to-digest tables or metes-and-bounds zone descriptions. As a knowledgeable councilmember noted after he had struggled to understand proposed 1970 desegregation arrangements without clear visuals, the "average parent" would be "almost lost" when confronted with the details of a desegregation plan without a map.[80] Vague information also circumscribed who could participate in informed debate about desegregation. And without a map, preexisting cognitive maps of the city—like those that equated central-city neighborhoods with decline—remained unchallenged. Preconceptions filled the spaces where information was lacking, and ready simplifications of metropolitan spatial patterns could even more powerfully influence desegregation policy.

Even with the pupil locator map, federal and local officials as well as Nashville residents traded on simplifying categories of metropolitan space in their discussions of possible desegregation solutions. One approach involved building what education officials referred to as midpoint schools—schools intentionally located at the midpoint between areas of black and white residential development. In other cities, and in national education discourse beginning in the mid-1960s, advocates suggested midpoint schools be "education parks" or "great high schools": remarkably large educational complexes including as many as 18,000 students in a single area, drawn from a huge (and thus presumptively diverse) geographic zone. Expert witnesses for the plaintiffs—and to a more limited extent, witnesses for MNPS—had discussed midpoint schools as a tool for desegregation. The comprehensive high schools Nashville educators had proposed since the late 1960s, occasionally referred to as "great high schools," fit neatly within this conversation, if at more modest size.[81]

But what was the midpoint? Where was the boundary between racialized black and white space in Nashville? Judge Morton's 1971 hearings provided the opportunity for one senior school staffer to identify such a line and plan hypothetical school locations, in relationship to it. In court, Morton asked Bill Wise, MNPS's assistant superintendent for facilities, to use what he knew of the city landscape, and draw where he would locate schools with the goal of maximizing integration. Borrowing a blue pencil from Avon Williams, Wise proposed that large comprehensive high schools on the model of McGavock be located in a ring around the city. School sites would follow the route of a still-under-construction ring road called Briley Parkway. A few decades later, Wise remembered himself as not yet "dry behind the ears, let alone competent" to do long-lasting school construction planning on the fly.[82]

When he later adopted Wise's suggestion as part of Nashville's desegregation plan, Judge Morton added the explanation that Briley Parkway marked the division between "inner-city" and suburban Nashville, and between black and white populations. The parkway was clearly a convenient marker, a bright line dividing the metropolis. But with a radius of seven miles from downtown, the circle Briley Parkway formed poorly matched the actual boundary between black and white residential areas (see map, p. vii). By 1971, black residents lived in new suburban developments near the parkway to the northwest of downtown, but in the rest of its route, white suburban developments sat on both sides of the road's actual or projected path.[83] Thus when lay residents and professional planners asserted that Briley Parkway *would be* such a boundary, they revealed their projected image of where black residence would expand to. Briley Parkway itself was a prediction of sorts, as it remained only partially constructed as of 1971, but it came to represent a new bright line between inner-city black and suburban white Nashville, one that could even come to seem another "natural" division in metropolitan space.[84]

Within both popular discourse and in the planning profession, the term "inner city" remained fungible, yet reflected the identification of black Nashvillians with a particular section of the city and the idea that the inner city would expand outward. Schools located on actual boundaries between black and white residential areas would aid equal access for both communities. But when the boundary used to plan Nashville's high schools was drawn between a projected image of where the black inner city would expand to and white suburban space, the result was more suburban construction, and disparate burdens for black schoolchildren.[85]

As school administrators and expert witnesses in court focused on dividing lines between inner-city and suburban Nashville, a small citizens group entered *Kelley* as intervenors to offer a different interpretation of the geography of segregation and the path to desegregation. Concerned Citizens for Improved Schools (CCIS)—as the group of black and white liberal residents, academics, and clergy named themselves—organized in 1969. Their first successful action secured the redrawing of the school zone for a new junior high school, to ensure a small, rather than nonexistent, black population there.[86] After this success, CCIS became involved as intervenors in *Kelley* and forwarded their own desegregation plan. Focusing on the idea of the "neighborhood" as a constructed rather than naturally occurring phenomenon, CCIS acknowledged "long and enduring attachment" to the idea of neighborhood schools. The adherence to the notion of neighborhood schools had, they argued, "aided the general public in convincing itself that placement of children in schools within their 'neighborhoods' . . . is right, proper and almost constitutional. Such is not the case."[87]

CCIS sought to redefine the concept of neighborhood, first by discarding all existing zone lines "drawn years ago to assure and perpetuate segregation." In their place, CCIS suggested dividing all of Davidson County into a set of "expanded neighborhoods," each of which contained urban, suburban, and rural areas.[88] Their interest in including the whole county was not without self-interest, and picked up a theme that would continue: to distribute more evenly the "burdens and benefits" of desegregation (implicitly across the county's white population), desegregation needed to reach the whole county. This was a particular concern for many CCIS members who lived in inner-ring suburbs and some integrated neighborhoods, and thus feared resegregation if their communities experienced busing while others were exempt.[89]

Although CCIS members moved radically away from the existing geography of school zones and cognitive maps, most participants in legal debates over school desegregation remained focused on the growth-and-decline geography of the city, a geography that for many seemed to align with boundaries in racialized black space and racialized white space. These conceptions of the metropolitan landscape, even if inaccurate, remained powerful in shaping the ultimate form of busing for desegregation in Nashville.

As maps and tables tried to answer the question of where Nashville's students were—and would be—other efforts focused on what the district's school facilities looked like. Here, too, seemingly objective representations could convey deep and influential bias.

When director Elbert Brooks assembled the citizens' committees to propose a 1970 desegregation plan, he also called for a district-wide study of school facilities and programs. Brooks assembled a team of consultants from universities in a range of southern and midwestern states, who together visited Nashville and provided a report on the school systems' facilities and its future needs. They completed their work just as the busing plan was under debate. The *Building and School Improvement Study* (BASIS) created a superficially objective measure of Nashville's school facilities, but included value judgments about where schools should sit in metropolitan space. The 174 criteria for evaluating schools, such as the size of the restrooms and the library's illumination, also included the "age" and "condition" of the surrounding neighborhood. Using this matrix, a recently constructed, modern facility in a poor neighborhood would be marked down for its surroundings. This was one criterion among many, but it implied continued doubt about the possibility of excellent schools in a poor neighborhood. HEW planners accepted the BASIS designations without review, although they did make a driving tour of most of the district's schools.[90]

BASIS marked nearly all of Nashville's urban schools as "inferior" or "inadequate." Some of these schools were in fact in poor repair, due to lack of appropriate maintenance over decades—a fact that underscored how, even after post-*Brown* efforts to equalize facilities to stave off desegregation, real inequalities remained. Other schools were in decent condition but were simply outmoded compared to the pro-suburban standards for school locations discussed in chapter 4. BASIS authors also echoed the binary growth versus decline structure visible in planning commission maps and population reports, grouping schools and the geographic areas they served into "high growth" and "high loss" categories. The school board asked HEW officials not to include those schools marked "inferior" or "inadequate" and located in "high loss" areas in their planning, anticipating their closure. Desegregation, systemic neglect, and cognitive maps of the city's present and future combined to sever local school-community connections in some urban contexts.[91]

In developing their plan, HEW planners confirmed five urban schools (close to home for the area's poorer African American residents) for closure and downgraded four other urban schools, either from high school to middle school, or from elementary school to special education school. Although these downgraded schools remained open, their historical relationship to the community around them changed significantly through this shift. Closures did not simply follow school condition, however. Not all schools in poor condition were shuttered, and HEW praised one school's condition but terminated it because highway construction had cut it off

**School Closures, 1960-1980, and 1970 Black and White Population**
Metropolitan Nashville-Davidson County, Tennessee

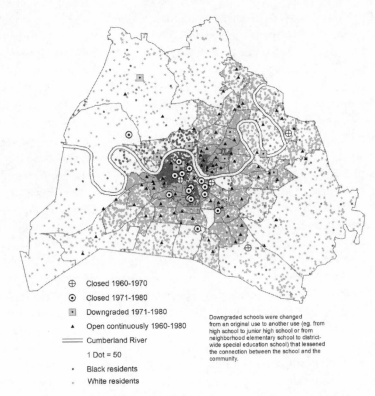

⊕  Closed 1960-1970

⊙  Closed 1971-1980

▣  Downgraded 1971-1980

▲  Open continuously 1960-1980

══  Cumberland River

1 Dot = 50

•  Black residents

◦  White residents

Downgraded schools were changed from an original use to another use (eg. from high school to junior high school or from neighborhood elementary school to district-wide special education school) that lessened the connection between the school and the community.

5.6. Data for this map comes from: MPC, *Schools for 1980*; School Directory, MNPS, 1979–1980; City of Nashville Public Schools Directory, 1960–1961; "Pupil Enrollment," 1969, *Kelley*, box 11, file 4; "Fifteen Year Analysis of Enrollment Trends, Metro Nashville Public Schools," 1984, *Kelley*, box 21, file 1984; and John Egerton, "Analysis of Data From Interrogatories Submitted to Metropolitan School System," 1970, *Kelley*, box 11, file 3 (1 of 2). 1970 population figures are from the 1970 Decennial Census, available from Minnesota Population Center. National Historical Geographic Information System: Prerelease Version 0.1. Minneapolis: University of Minnesota, 2004, at http://www.nhgis.org. Assistance with GIS from the staff of Columbia University's Digital Social Sciences Center.

from its residential zone.[92] In fact, from HEW's perspective it was uncertain that *any* urban schools would remain open in Nashville. The agency's team outlined options for desegregating the city; second on the list was "Closing all of the inner-city schools and busing of the students to the outer-suburban schools." The HEW team did not consider the inverse. Logistics ultimately helped to keep some city schools open, because shuttering them would have meant increased busing and overcrowding until school construction could catch up in the suburbs.[93] When these decisions about school closures took place in the pages of the BASIS report or in conversations between school district officials and HEW staffers, they occurred out of the reach of community advocates who would have contested them.

Nashville's busing plan had great variability, but it consistently remade inequality by privileging suburban space. Many layers of planning practice and education rhetoric had long pointed policy makers to attend to the needs of suburban rather than urban residents. In the early 1960s, when schools in both the suburbs and city were strikingly overcrowded, suburban communities got new school buildings, while urban areas were assured that cramped conditions would be relieved, ultimately, through conversion of residential to commercial land. By the late 1960s, the near certainty with which planners described continued suburban growth and urban decline authorized continued neglect of the schooling of significant numbers of urban students, most of them black. These strains continued into HEW's desegregation plan, rather than being stopped by it.

Once busing for desegregation began in Nashville, Avon Williams and other black leaders referred to it as a "necessary evil."[94] Federal court intervention, in the form of Judge Miller's and Judge Morton's rulings, had been necessary; the persistence of segregation to 1968 as well the meager plans of the 1970 citizens' commission suggested that little statistical desegregation would have happened otherwise. Continued segregation would have further enabled the sort of resource inequalities and political disempowerment long evident in Nashville's historically black schools. Yet the "evils" of busing for desegregation were real as well. The federal role in Nashville's schools of the 1970s and 1980s was contradictory—at once a needed lever in rooting out continued segregation and producing statistical desegregation, and a force in the remaking of inequality.

### Conclusion

If *Brown* shrank the problem of inequality to the problem of segregation, later litigation and its reinforcement of the idea of de facto segregation separated segregation from its full history, and thus distorted thinking about desegregation. Avon Williams's efforts in Judge Miller's and Judge Morton's courtrooms succeeded in securing more assertive desegregation via busing, but failed to shake the judge's attachment to de facto segregation as both a contemporary description and historical explanation. De facto segregation defined the problem of segregation as a product of individual choices. The narrative of de facto segregation allowed desegregation remedies to be understood as separate from the broad, deeply rooted, and multipart policy campaign that built segregation. Busing's discomforts and disruptions appeared as novel interventions rather than as an attempt to use state power toward equality after decades of its use for inequality.

As of fall 1971, Nashville had a busing plan that protected white suburban students from many of busing's burdens. Most black urban residents saw their children travel further, and for more years of their schooling. This important inequality came about through a series of interlocking policy decisions, with their roots reaching back to the early 1960s, when planning and education officials together selected suburban space as the site of educational investment. The spatial organization of schooling helped remake inequality in the process of desegregation.

Although planning maps, frameworks of growth and decline, and intricate population projection may seem quite distant from the lives of individual children, the first days of school under Nashville's desegregation plan proved how linked they could be. As the local press paid attention to how many white children were not attending school as part of an organized boycott, Nashville's young black students told another story with their very presence. Suburban schools that received first through fourth graders from city neighborhoods found themselves with many more black students than their enrollment plans projected; a few city schools for fifth and sixth graders did as well. Multiple schools needed zone readjustments to prevent overcrowding after the first weeks of school. Far more black children lived in Nashville's city neighborhoods and its housing projects than projections had shown. Invisible in maps and projections and planning schema, these children came to school.[95]

# CHAPTER SIX

# Busing Resisted and Transformed

In July 1971, Judge L. Clure Morton ordered busing for desegregation across most Nashville schools, increasing by roughly 15,000—or 44 percent of the previous total of 34,000—the number of students who rode buses to school. The increase was the steepest for black central-city residents. Now four times as many Nashville schools achieved statistical desegregation, meaning that they had at least a significant minority of black students, and a targeted 15 to 35 percent black student ratio.[1] Roughly one quarter of Nashville's schools, all of them almost entirely white, remained exempt from desegregation, deemed by the school board too distant from areas of black population.

Prior to the school year's opening in September 1971, thousands of Nashville residents made their opposition to busing known with highly visible protests. Yet the full story of resistance to busing not only extends into the first year after Judge Morton's order, when parent protests continued and conditions at schools were often unsettled, but ran through busing's first decade, when a range of decisions crafted in bureaucratic corridors rather than at curbside protests or church-basement meetings shaped desegregation's implementation. School board, local government, and state as well as federal officials made choices that furthered white suburban privilege and worsened the burdens for black students and families created in the initial busing plan of 1971. Not unlike the first wave of response to desegregation in the 1950s, formal governmental resistance to busing paralleled the more visible street-level, often working- and middle-class white protest against busing. Some of this resistance—as in local official refusal to procure enough buses—worsened the experience of desegregation and earned it new opponents. In other cases, officials used state power to manipulate schooling in favor of continued segregation. Few official voices spoke in favor of desegregation, choosing to convey instead either outright opposition or obliged compliance. When one of the school board's white liberals issued mild comments in favor of desegregation, joining the single black board member in this position, the mayor tried to force her from the board.[2]

In busing's first decade, the curricular organization of schooling intersected directly with the spatial organization of schooling. John Harper Harris's late-1960s embrace of the comprehensive high school model included an emphasis on vocational education that resonated with long-term efforts to link education to local and state economic growth; it also quietly reinforced the long-standing and false notion that desegregation meant a broadened range of student ability and interest. New sources of state funding for vocational education, secured through appeals to education as a lever for collective economic growth, helped Nashville open or expand several new comprehensive high schools. Sited intentionally in the suburbs, the new high schools furthered white suburban privilege in the process of desegregation while offering new ideological and pragmatic routes for resisting busing and sorting students between and within schools. Together the spatial and curricular organization of the comprehensive high school helped remake educational inequality alongside statistical desegregation.

Many early-1970s white Americans, in Nashville as well as elsewhere, framed their opposition to busing as an intrusion into cherished realms of family authority and property rights. From this perspective, resistance to court-ordered busing strove to keep state action within its proper limits. White citizens criticized and fought hard against state involvement in areas they termed, derisively, "sociological" (even as they benefited from many layers of state action). Yet they embraced an expanded state role when it related to the economic arena—or more specifically, to the promise of economic growth. Resistance to busing in Nashville continued white conservative opposition to programs that aided historically disadvantaged groups while demonstrating growing support for those uses of state power that targeted economic growth and claimed that doing so meant universal benefit. Understanding desegregation as resisted and as transformed helps illuminate the complex mix of tendencies in evolving 1970s politics, in which opinions on state intervention were not monolithic but depended heavily on the purpose of that intervention.[3]

## Resistance from the Fairgrounds to
## the Country Club to the Mayor's Office

Nashville's schoolchildren joined 350,000 others who began to ride buses for desegregation in the US South in the late summer of 1971, only a few months after the Supreme Court's April decision in *Swann v. Mecklenburg* upheld the strategy.[4] Each district had its own distinct plan, and each had its own forms of public debate about, advocacy for, and resistance to busing. Compared with the violent forms of protest in cities like Boston and Denver only a few years later, busing in Nashville and most of the involved districts began more peacefully and with smaller-scale instances of disorder. In this respect, Nashville continued the tradition of moderation that city leaders claimed for themselves and their city. If relatively less violent than in other locales, resistance to busing in Nashville ran both broad and deep. Grassroots citizens' organizations, elected and aspiring politicians, and officials in both local and federal agencies pushed back against busing in a variety of ways, and made decisions that shaped how busing was carried out.

The most visible and voluble of this resistance, led by local politician Casey Jenkins, had an effect similar to the Hattie Cotton bombing of 1957: clarifying the boundaries of protest beyond which most Nashville residents would not go, while sanctioning resistance in other forms. Any action that qualified as law abiding came to seem a moderate, reasoned response.[5] Little active pro-desegregation advocacy could take hold or be sustained in this climate. A veneer of local compliance offered thin cover for extensive, if nominally moderate, resistance.

By the time Judge L. Clure Morton issued his July 1971 order, anti-busing white citizens had become a significant political force in Nashville. The frankly racist and hostile themes of the 1957 protests remained visible, joined by the rhetoric of property-rights-based, purportedly color-blind conservatism like that evident in other cities. Some of the same figures most active in 1957 remained very visible, but by early 1971 Casey Jenkins was the most influential. Jenkins became the head of organized resistance to busing in Nashville via the Concerned Parents Association (CPA), whose local branch he helped found.[6] Nashville's CPA was born in a parents' meeting at Tusculum Church of Christ in Nashville's working- and middle-class white southeastern suburbs. A group of parents there asked to speak to local franchise businessman and Metro Councilman Jenkins about busing. Jenkins, then thirty-five years old, had been in Nashville only since 1968 and on the council since late 1970. In this short time, he had established his reputation by opposing a few pro-desegregation zone changes. But most of Jenkins's short time on the council had been focused on smaller-scale issues like increasing the price of beer permits.[7] Busing provided Jenkins a rich opportunity to define himself politically and claim a position of leadership on an issue of broad popular interest.

After the Tusculum church meeting, Jenkins moved quickly to mobilize an anti-busing movement. The CPA organized four hundred protesters to go to the federal courthouse on March 12, 1971, as hearings in *Kelley* were under way. The group filled the limited spectator seating in Judge Morton's courtroom and spilled into the hallways. After thirty minutes of disruption from their protest, Morton adjourned court and warned against continued disorder. When hearings resumed four days later, they did so behind locked doors, with twenty-five extra marshals and other federal agents forming a tight circle around available entrances. CPA had again organized a large contingent, estimated by newspapers at between four hundred and six hundred, to attend the hearings. Barred from entering, the group spilled onto the sidewalk, briefly blocking traffic on Nashville's main downtown thoroughfare. Meanwhile, the suburban area of Madison, to the northeast of downtown, was home to another kind of protest, as "hundreds" of students stayed home from school in an expression of their parents' or their own opposition to the prospect of busing.[8] In Mayor Beverly Briley's mind, these weeks were key in shaping desegregation in Nashville. When Morton later ordered busing, Briley understood it in personal terms. He felt that protesters had "angered" the judge and thus provoked him to issue "the worst busing order in the country."[9]

On the evening of March 16, the CPA organized a rally at the War Memorial Auditorium in downtown Nashville, where local councilmen, several state legislators, and leading attorneys railed against busing before an audience estimated by the *Tennessean* to number five thousand. Amid supportive comments from other elected officials, Jenkins spoke of busing for desegregation as "discrimination against all people" and reasserted his intent to use all lawful means available "until the will of the majority is done."[10] The event gained quasi-official imprimatur through its location—in a public building across a plaza from the state capitol—and the presence of a dais full of Nashville's elected leadership.[11] CPA managed to seem both grassroots and official at once.

Soon after CPA led these large protests, rumors began to circulate that Casey Jenkins would run for mayor in the August 1971 election. The nonpartisan format of Metro's mayoral elections made it more possible for a new figure like Jenkins to mount a serious challenge.[12] Jenkins announced his candidacy in early May, and made opposition to busing the primary focus of the campaign. He promised that "not one child will be bused," without legal footing to make such a claim.[13] Once Judge Morton had issued the busing order, Jenkins claimed that he would delay the opening of school in September 1971, until the Supreme Court had had a chance to review the school board's appeal of Morton's directive.[14]

In hundreds of letters and phone messages to their mayor while busing was under consideration in court, and over its first year, Nashville citizens expressed their concerns, their fears, and in some cases their hopes for busing. White homeowner conservatism came through clearly in many letters, with mothers and fathers writing to complain that busing disrupted the property rights they felt extended to their suburban school as well as their suburban home.[15] Although the actual contours of the busing plan proved quite the reverse, some saw the policy as evidence of municipal neglect of suburbanites.

The exemption of the outer-suburban areas from busing had divisive impact. One resident of a suburban area included in busing explained, "We all feel so alone because so many who were not affected by this law have taken the attitude that they are lucky because their children were not bused."[16] This was one expression of class differences in experiences of and opposition to busing. Working- and middle-class letter writers typically experienced busing differently than did wealthier families with more resources who often lived in areas exempt from busing. Casey Jenkins built on these class divides, cultivating a working- and middle-class orientation in his campaign and contrasting his supporters with those who lived in wealthier sections of Nashville more likely to be exempt from busing, and where private school attendance rates were higher and private tuition less burdensome. Speakers at CPA rallies also "took verbal punches at educated men" who were "messing things up," as one observer noted.[17] In the weeks before the election, Jenkins released polling numbers showing his strength in working- and middle-class areas like Tusculum and declared his weakness in both black North Nashville and wealthy white Belle Meade.[18]

Nashville's business and governmental elite also called or wrote to Mayor Briley in support of his resistance. Sanders Anglea, a former Nashville vice mayor and then Metro councilmember, suggested to Briley that "the people of this community are on one side and the courts are on the other," and urged the mayor to delay school opening until the community could "get its sovereignty back."[19] Briley did, in fact, write to "direct" the school board, "within the powers that he had." He felt that "threatened violence" over busing was real and that school should be delayed in hopes of a stay of the busing order. Schools director Elbert Brooks did not comply.[20]

If, in private, incumbent Mayor Beverly Briley felt "caught in the middle" between taking a stand against busing or conceding the need to desegregate, his public remarks and letters to constituents were firm in their opposition.[21] Briley was a capable observer of American urban politics, with a reasoned early critique of how federal policy had facilitated suburban out-migration and deepened segregation while weakening the white in-town neighborhood he had grown up in.[22] With this awareness, Briley might have been better positioned than most to understand busing as an attempted repair of past inequalities. Yet he chose, in both public statements and private letters, to emphasize his opposition, calling the practice "nonsensical," one that prioritized "sociological" over educational factors. His letters to constituents promised to continue "the same fight" he had been fighting since "the 1950s," implying opposition even to the earlier struggle against formal segregation itself.[23] When politically liberal or moderate locals wrote in encouraging the mayor to stand for rather than against busing, he dismissed their comments as "completely out of . . . touch with reality." He emphasized instead his fear that busing would produce "a complete diffusion" of public support for education.[24] This kind of concern motivated policy choices that favored white suburbanites and worked against an equitable approach to desegregation.

As Nashville schools readied themselves for busing's start, and antibusing activism continued in the late-summer heat, both incumbent and rival newcomer leadership competed in the August mayoral race. Each candidate campaigned to prove himself more committed to opposing desegregation, with rhetoric that detached busing from the long history of state-sponsored segregation.

Briley's active if less vitriolic opposition to busing, against Jenkins's more heated approach, left many black Nashville voters feeling that they lacked a viable candidate in the 1971 mayor's race. Dr. Edwin Mitchell, head of the Davidson County Independent Political Council, called on black voters to "ignore" the mayoral race. As Mitchell put it, he would "just like to tell my people to vote 'no.'"[25] Casey Jenkins made a late-in-the-game attempt to draw black voters to his cause. He promised to fight to keep Cameron High School—the historically black high school in South Nashville—open alongside three smaller, previously segregated white schools that were slated for closure or conversion from senior to junior high status under the 1971 plan. Jenkins went on at length about Cameron as a "symbol of pride to the people of South Nashville. . . . It will destroy the morale of the people of South Nashville," he declared, if Cameron was closed as a high school.[26] Many black Nashville residents concurred with the concern for Cameron's fate, but likely few found Jenkins to be a convincing spokesperson.

In the August 1971 general election, Briley, Jenkins, and two longtime Nashville political figures competed. Briley and Jenkins advanced to the runoff two weeks later, and there many black Nashville voters chose not to vote, but enough supported Mayor Briley to help ensure his reelection with just over 54 percent of the votes. Precincts in the predominantly black areas of North Nashville and Edgehill had unusually low turnout, which Mitchell's DCIPC credited to their unusual calls for nonparticipation, but not all black voters stayed away from the polls. Those who voted supported Briley over Jenkins at roughly ten to one.[27]

Among largely white precincts, the results of the August 1971 mayoral election revealed the clear class orientation of CPA's version of resistance to busing in Nashville. In the "silk stocking boxes," as local newspaper reporters labeled wealthier voting precincts, Briley won by ratios ranging from three-to-one to eight-to-one. By contrast, working-class and lower-middle-class white suburban areas south and east of downtown—including the district around Tusculum Church of Christ, where CPA had been launched—polled heavily for Jenkins. These "blue collar boxes" went more than two to one for Jenkins.[28]

Even if an ultimately unsuccessful candidate, Jenkins had remarkable success in organizing and fomenting anti-busing fury. At a rally at the Tennessee State Fairgrounds in Nashville, a capacity crowd of 15,000 gathered in the racetrack stands on the night before schools opened for the first time under Judge Morton's busing order.[29] Flyers circulated with the baldest of racist rhetoric, little changed from the 1957 threats of interracial sex and "mongrelization." The next day, CPA pickets at dozens of schools greeted buses and parents dropping off their children, hostile to both black children riding in the buses and white families who had chosen to defy CPA's call for a boycott.[30] Hubert Dixon III recalled seeing picketers on his arrival by bus at previously segregated white Brookmeade Elementary, and thinking at first that there was a "welcoming" or a "celebration taking place," having not yet seen the lettering on protesters' signs.[31] After ten or so days of protests, and as attendance gradually rose close to stable levels in most schools, Jenkins called off the pickets. He first redirected energy to protests at school board meetings but ultimately was unable to shift the early momentum into a large or long-lasting movement. He gestured toward and ultimately helped start a statewide anti-busing effort, but by the mid-1970s his influence faded, and not long after he left Nashville.[32]

6.1. Casey Jenkins and anti-busing protesters meet an arriving school bus at Rosebank Elementary, September 1971. Signs read, "Bus the Supreme Court, Not Us!" and "Exchange Federal Funds for Neighborhood Schools." Courtesy of Metropolitan Archives of Nashville-Davidson County.

While Mayor Briley and Jenkins tousled to prove their anti-busing credentials, they left a space wide open for other community leaders to claim a moderate position—one that offered no support for busing in principle or in practice, but declaimed threats of violence and disorder to foster and preserve an image of Nashville as a compliant and calm city. Of the three local hubs of influence for the city's elite—the Nashville Chamber of Commerce, the Belle Meade Country Club, and the Vanderbilt Board of Trust—it was the most growth-minded of these, the chamber, that took the most public stance on busing. (The Vanderbilt board was dominated by the brash racist James [Jimmy] Stahlman, author of the *Banner*'s front-page anti-busing editorials, and the Belle Meade Country Club was itself a segregated white, exclusively Christian institution for the rich). The chamber of commerce published a full-page advertisement in the *Tennessean* and *Banner* on June 21 and 22, 1971, explaining they felt a "moral obligation" to do all that they could to ensure that "the city does not suffer from possible violent reaction." The city's reputation and civic culture were at stake, threatened by the possibility of "high emotion" and "extremists," and the chamber spoke up for "the preservation of a calm, law-abiding community."[33] They struck themes that ran through business-led calls for moderation from Little Rock in the 1950s onward, but simultaneously stayed away from the more supportive elite stance, or even rhetorical cooptation, of busing visible in cities like Charlotte.[34] Whether conversations in the chamber and in other elite circles included voices willing to take a more affirmative position on desegregation, the ultimate message remained tightly constrained, avoiding any positive recognition of busing or desegregation, or of the core inequalities these interventions tried to target. The moderate message was still too much for some. Casey Jenkins chose to publicly split with the chamber of commerce and criticize the ad, likely to burnish his anti-elitism.

A few groups of Nashville citizens worked hard to push beyond the resistance of their fellow citizens and to embrace busing. When Casey Jenkins called for a "Lights On against Busing" protest, Rabbi Randall Falk, Rev. Bill Barnes, and fellow desegregation supporters declared it "Lights On" for quality integrated education. In the end, as Rev. Barnes recalled, the day was foggy and yet most lights were off. One resident of the Edgehill neighborhood found the many media images of anti-busing protesters to be disturbing, and felt spurred to action. With a friend, she organized area mothers to greet school buses as they arrived in the community from outlying suburbs, offering each student a few school supplies and a note with a telephone number for an area resident willing to help in case of an emergency or difficulty at school. Concerned Citizens for Improved Schools continued its work but shifted to offering youth programs to support busing in practice. They received federal funds for their Volunteers in Action program, which trained student leaders in desegregating schools.[35]

Other organizations formed to claim a "middle-ground" position on busing—which meant raising "legitimate" concerns about travel time or student safety at ad-hoc bus stops. They also traded in well-worn racist stereotypes, as when raising concerns about what they presumed to be a new "diversity of student ability," that, they feared, would impede the progress of advanced students.[36]

Black Nashville leaders who had supported Avon Williams's and the NAACP's litigation remained vocal supporters of busing. Some strains of black community criticism of busing emerged. As Hubert Dixon Jr. observed his son's experience, he was generally appreciative. Yet there was a circularity to busing that bothered him. Remembering his own elementary and high school classmates' trips past segregated white schools to get to their segregated black schools, he noted, "Blacks had already been bused all their lives, and now they were being bused again."[37] A survey that collected some evidence of black opposition offered Mayor Briley and other busing opponents the pretext under which to decry busing as generally unpopular among both black and white Nashvillians. Veteran civil rights activist Rev. Kelly Miller Smith and colleagues in the First Baptist Church Capitol Hill's Social Action Committee sought to clarify, asserting that they "enthusiastically" favored busing "in preference to the conditions to which they have been subjected in the past." Noting improved physical conditions in statistically desegregated schools and access to better educational resources, they decried the efforts of local leaders to present "greatly exaggerated negative views" of busing: "The problem is not busing. We do not need to find a remedy for the busing situation. Rather, the problem is racism. . . . Busing is necessary because our neighborhoods exhibit the racist practices of our society at their very worst." North Nashville's Rev. Amos Jones made the same point in Biblical terms: "Open housing is not a reality . . . and therefore I am for busing for racial balance. . . . Whatever you sow, thus shall you reap."[38] Nashville residents like Dixon Jr. and others who had witnessed earlier decades of busing for segregation likely heard this remark with added layers of meaning.

Avon Williams's legal practice—which extended beyond school desegregation to a variety of matters often but not always relating to racist discrimination—gave him a close-up view of the ways in which open housing was not yet a reality in Nashville, and of the ways school desegregation featured in how some white Nashville residents thought about housing segregation. After only reluctant, stuttering, and partial opening of the local real estate market following the 1968 Fair Housing Act, most Nashville suburbs remained overwhelmingly white in the mid-1970s. Formal means—such as lingering and colloquial use of restrictive covenants preventing sale to black buyers, or mortgage lender agreements not to approve black applications, as well as intimidation and even violence against the first black families to move into previously white areas—maintained the boundaries of all-white communities. Williams represented local black educator Dr. Sammie Lucas and his wife in their effort in 1972 to buy a house nearly across the street from McGavock High School. Decades after the 1948 Supreme Court ruling in *Shelley v. Kramer* holding restrictive covenants unconstitutional and unenforceable, the white sellers claimed that a "color clause" restricted their sale to white people exclusively. The Lucases had to sue to convince the owners that such covenants no longer had legal authority. The sellers explained their refusal to sell to the Lucases as a matter of school segregation as well as housing segregation. They did not want to sell to a black family in part because they did not want to further increase the black population at the local school, already desegregating via busing.[39]

In its first years, busing prompted a wide and varied flurry of resistance, from fairground rallies of thousands to kitchen-table discussions about to whom to sell a home. White leaders like Beverly Briley and his elite supporters rhetorically reduced the diversity of views about busing to a homogenous mass of resistance, black and white. In fact, while the majority position was one of resistance, other insistent voices supported desegregation in principle and busing as a mode of achieving statistical desegregation in practice. Nonetheless, Mayor Briley and other local officials put their weight behind resistance in ways that heightened the difficulties of busing and thus broadened opposition. These acts of official resistance became much more powerful than the meager calls for compliance from the powerful and organized local business elite.

## Busing without Buses

If busing is what we need, we need to start doing it right. The politicians of Nashville may be complying with the letter of the law—but certainly not with its spirit.

—Roger Richardson, *McGavock High School student, 1976*[40]

Sparked by opposition to busing, the Concerned Parents Association and Casey Jenkins's run for mayor exemplify the kind of reactive popular organizing that contributed to the making of suburban conservatism in the late 1960s and 1970s. Mayor Briley used his podium to endorse and further this resistance, again hearing supportive responses from white Nashvillians from all walks of life. From Ralph B. Owens—financier, member of the elite Vanderbilt Board of Trust and the super-elite and secret Watauga Association—who called to let Mayor Briley know that he was "with him 100%"—to the minister of a working-class white East Nashville church, calls and letters poured in.[41]

Yet resistance continued in legal and bureaucratic spaces as well. A key matter was the question of buses—how many the district needed as it increased the number of students riding to school by roughly 40 percent. In the Metro council, the majority of members opposed busing and refused to pass the school system's proposed budget for 1971–72 if it included funds to purchase buses to aid desegregation. The council was willing nonetheless to purchase eighteen buses to transport students to the new McGavock Comprehensive High School.[42]

This resistance made the basic operations of busing much more incon-venient—and in some instances, more dangerous—than it needed to be for all Nashville residents with students in public schools. To transport students without sufficient buses, MNPS staggered school start times from as early as 7:00 a.m. to as late as 10:00 a.m., with the school day ending at a variety of points from 12:30 to 4:30 p.m. This schedule, which ill matched many parents' work schedules, left children home in the morn-ing unsupervised or had them walking home from the bus stop after dark (in the winter) on suburban streets that lacked sidewalks. It also shrank the content of students' education, as MNPS cut the length of the school day from seven to six hours—again, to cope with insufficient buses.[43] The school board applied to the Department of Health, Education, and Welfare for federal funds to purchase new buses rather than locating the needed amount (less than 1 percent of its operating budget) internally. In keeping with the Nixon administration's stance on busing, which ranged at times from the ambivalent to the expressly oppositional, this request was denied by agency officials.[44]

One mother working outside of the home, Nashville principal Aldoro-thy Wright, recalled a last-minute rush to find her son a place in a Catholic school with a more conventional schedule so that he would not be left alone at home in the mornings. Another mother and homemaker, preg-nant with her fifth child, wrote to Mayor Briley to explain that she rose at 5:30 to begin a four-hour stretch of readying children for school, with the eldest leaving at 6:20 a.m. and the youngest not until 9:30. Mayor Briley, seeking to keep civic anger focused on the courts rather than the local gov-ernment, built upon stories like this in his anti-busing addresses. Nowhere did he acknowledge that these were optional, the result not of busing, per se, but of underfunded busing.[45]

Judge Morton took the school board to task for not pushing hard enough to secure the buses they needed, describing their efforts to counter Briley and the council's resistance as mere "lip service to the Constitution," and even wondering if their tepid efforts were in part designed to encour-age conditions favorable for appeal. Escalating the increasingly personal conflict between himself and Mayor Briley, the judge enjoined the council from any further discussion of busing. Morton sharply ordered the board immediately to find within their $65 million budget the $500,000 needed to buy buses and thus put in place the infrastructure to allow a less oner-ous busing schedule for Nashville children.[46]

Judge Morton's efforts toward a reasonable implementation of his bus-ing order became another hook on which busing's opponents could hang their criticisms. Mayor Briley lashed out against the judge's actions both in limiting council debate and requiring the expenditure of funds. Locals called Briley's office, describing Morton's actions as "asinine," "dictatorial," or an "attack on our freedom as Tennesseans and United States citizens," and evidence of Communism or "tyranny." The steady drumbeat of blunt racism continued, as when one anonymous author signed off as "A citizen troubled over the continued existence of the country, whose citizenship rights have been disregarded to favor a race of people retarded by nature."[47]

With Casey Jenkins's electoral challenge defeated, Mayor Briley made Judge Morton his chief target. Ray Blanton, a conservative from Western Tennessee running for Senate in 1972, called Morton "the busingest judge in the nation" and wielded him as a weapon against the incumbent Republican, Senator Howard Baker, who had recommended Morton to the bench (but had himself established a firmly anti-busing position). Morton received death threats, only heightened when local and state politicians often portrayed busing as an issue of the judge's personal discretion rather than one of constitutional requirement.[48]

Mayor Briley interpreted Judge Morton's refusal to tolerate local obstructionism as an indication that the judge was "personally biased and prejudiced," and, aggressively, Briley asked for Morton to recuse himself from *Kelley*. Briley premised the request on a technicality, that Morton had used sources from outside of the courtroom to develop his bias against the defendant school board (and metropolitan government) and in favor of the plaintiffs, and that Morton had spoken to the press about the case.[49]

In a highly unusual action among the federal judges who oversaw desegregation cases, Judge Morton did recuse himself. His reasons, though, were not those that Briley offered.[50] Morton deemed Briley's accusations of bias and misconduct "without merit" but chose to recuse himself in hopes that doing so would smooth feelings and facilitate progress: "Maybe emotions can be calmed so intelligence can have an opportunity."[51] Although Morton did not explain his later decision to move his courtroom from the federal courthouse in Nashville to the small town of Cookeville, eighty miles to the east, local lore held that he had been run out of town over busing.[52] Given both the social pressure Morton experienced—as when angry members of the city elite cornered him and his wife at parties—and his own ambivalence about busing as a remedy, his recusal is less surprising. Decades after leaving *Kelley*, Morton described himself as having been required to order busing by the higher court's rulings despite his personal opposition. "I think a man ought to be able to buy a house close to a church and a good school and be able to raise his kids in a good community."[53]

When Judge Morton left the case over the objection of Avon Williams, it passed to Judge Frank Gray Jr. Previously an attorney in private practice and the mayor of the small town of Franklin, Tennessee, about twenty miles south of Nashville in then-rural Williamson County, Gray was elevated to the bench by President John F. Kennedy in 1962.[54] Filed under Judge Morton but managed by Judge Gray, a new line of legal attack opened that illuminates how federal resistance to busing affected local cases. After earlier debates over funding for buses, three city councilmen now went to court to find other parties responsible for the failure to properly fund busing by buying buses. The councilmen sued HEW over their implementation of federal programs designed to assist districts in desegregation. In 1971, as Dr. Brooks and his colleagues had planned busing's implementation under the council-imposed constraints, they hoped for financial assistance under the Emergency School Assistance Program (ESAP). Although the legislative history of ESAP (and its successor, the Emergency School Assistance Act [ESAA]) showed that the congressional majority intended it to support both the logistical and programmatic implementation of busing for desegregation, President Nixon pressed for limitations on its use of funds, including bans on supporting busing's costs.[55]

Schools superintendent Elbert Brooks applied for funds via ESAP to purchase new buses. Shortly thereafter, however, the same local HEW officials who had encouraged him to do so communicated that his funding request would receive "zero priority," not because of a formal policy change but one that had come down by "word of mouth" from HEW's Washington office. As Judge Frank Gray explained it, federal officials (acting, by implication, under the influence of a White House opposed to busing) "played a substantial role in effectively impeding the process of desegregation in the Nashville public schools" by undermining the intended purposes of the ESAP. Nonetheless Judge Gray had little recourse, as he could order only that HEW consider application from Nashville for any unallocated ESAA funds.[56] Given the tone of HEW's defense in court, which one local attorney characterized as sounding "like some Alabama school board," as well as the late timing, such a reconsideration was not likely to yield any aid.[57]

Federal actors in the form of district court and appellate judges ordered busing in Nashville, but federal agency officials from HEW helped give busing in Nashville its unequal and burdensome shape, and later undermined one congressional effort to ease desegregation where it was happening. Nashville's congressional delegation stood opposed to the "judicial mischief" of busing, as Senator Howard Baker termed it, and reinforced anti-busing messages coming from the Nixon administration.[58] Their actions helped give busing a difficult start in Nashville, with unreasonable schedules and shortened school days. These conditions encouraged both black and white citizens with the resources to leave the public school system to do so.[59]

The loud official resistance coming from the mayor's office, and the school board's "hard-line" stance against desegregation (as Judge Morton characterized it) left school district officials like superintendent Elbert Brooks a narrow space in which to work. Brooks sought support for busing's implementation—as in his search for external funds for busing—or refused outright defiance, as in Mayor Briley's request to delay school's opening. Chiefly, his efforts focused inwardly, on matters of operations and implementation that, doubtless, took great time and absorbed much staff effort, but did not offer vocal public leadership in favor of desegregation. Brooks characterized President Nixon's opposition to busing as producing "one more kind of pressure for education people to bear," a sentiment that seemed to capture many school officials' approaches to busing.[60]

## Chasing White Middle-Class Families through Metropolitan Space

Although Casey Jenkins and his thousands of anti-busing protestors made the most noise against desegregation, and elected representatives reinforced the idea (if not the manner) of their opposition, quiet bureaucratic decisions also fundamentally determined the shape of busing. At times these policy choices undermined what busing might have contributed to greater equality. Some bureaucratic resistance likely responded to popular opposition, but resistance also flowed within the official channels of city agencies. As in the process of planning busing in Nashville, and as continued in each of busing's phases, school officials made ameliorating white suburban resistance a core part of their approach to complying with the court's desegregation mandates.[61]

After the first year of busing with too few buses, the school board petitioned the court to end busing at three junior high schools, seeking to return them to their previously segregated enrollments. Two would be all black, and one all white. If buses were not transporting students to these schools, more would be available at other schools, thus allowing the district to reduce the wide range of start times that had frustrated parents. Reflecting how superficially some officials imagined desegregation, the board proposed that the resegregation of these schools could be offset by one-hour-per-week exchange programs in which students from all-black and all-white schools would attend activities or tutorial sessions together. The letter also explained that Hillwood Junior High School, which would become all white under the new plan, would continue to share a campus with Hillwood High School, with a student population that was one-third black through busing, and thus there "still would be significant black presence on campus," although in an entirely separate institution.[62]

In many other American cities that began busing for desegregation, some white families expressed their resistance by enrolling in private schools or moving away from the school district.[63] In Nashville, because the initial busing plan also exempted some suburban areas, they had the option of moving to sections of the district where busing for desegregation did not reach. The boundary line between what the district termed "court-ordered" versus "non-court-ordered" schools—despite Avon Williams's rightful protest that the whole district was in fact covered by court order—allowed new forms of district-level resistance to, or lack of will in maintaining, desegregation. As with other aspects of desegregation in Nashville, this resistance worked through the organization and reorganization of schools in metropolitan space.

In southeastern Nashville, in an area exempted from busing, Cole Elementary saw its student population grow by nearly 25 percent from January 1971 to the start of school in September. Developers had opened new suburbs in the area, long in the works, but the school's numbers increased further via "migration" of families to the area to avoid busing via what the district's zoning official called "massive integration."[64] Developers planned even more single-family home and apartment construction nearby. The scale of growth at Cole rendered insufficient the district's typical strategy to accommodate white "migration" to schools positioned like Cole, of expanding class size beyond state requirements. Judge Morton's 1971 order prevented new construction or the addition of portable classrooms.[65] Choosing to accommodate white suburban resistance to busing, MNPS developed a new strategy at Cole. The district relabeled a school inside the busing boundary as an annex to Cole, assigning (and in some cases transporting) students who lived outside the busing boundary to a school within it, creating another school with a nearly all-white population. Thus the district facilitated white suburban interest in all- or nearly all-white schools, shifting the spatial organization of schooling to facilitate white suburban families' resistance to desegregation.[66]

Decisions like those at Cole—prompted in part by the pragmatic difficulty of managing increasing enrollment in some portions of the district—reveal the extent to which school administrators felt that they had to accommodate families' residential choices. Avon Williams earlier sought to question the district's commitment to following these choices, and wondered why it was always the district, rather than the families themselves, that had to absorb the expense and inconvenience of a decision to move to the suburbs. Although operating on metropolitan scale, with authority over schools across many neighborhoods, MNPS was unwilling to challenge the suburban expectation that each suburban (and usually majority-white) community have its own local school. As school-closure decisions revealed, the housing-schooling relationship proved more easily broken when the community in question was urban or majority black.[67]

Although Judge Morton's orders were quite clear in freezing construction in the areas of the county beyond the busing order, MNPS's formal school construction plans continued to emphasize suburban school expansion. Issuing a new long-range construction plan in 1973 (one that was reiterated in 1975), the school board continued to envisage more suburban construction, including supposedly "mid-point" but largely suburban schools along Briley Parkway, as suggested by the board and sanctioned by Morton. Frustrated by population shifts to areas outside of the reach of the busing order, the board by the mid-1970s was discussing the possibility of expanding busing county-wide. Such a move seemed to promise more stable desegregation and yet further emphasized the suburban family as busing's chief constituency.[68]

The school board designed and planned schools for largely white communities; how they would become desegregated was often an afterthought. A new comprehensive school to serve the communities of Goodlettsville and Madison had been imagined since 1968. After 1971, planning changed in two ways. The board chose a new school site closer to Briley Parkway, and it promised that the school population would come from Goodlettsville and Madison—nearly all-white areas—to which would be added enough black students to reach 15 percent of the school population. School planners often thought of desegregation in this way. A largely white suburban area needed a new school; black students (from what community or distance unspecified) would be bused to meet the required racial ratio for the school. With their travel and their bodies, black students enabled the construction of a school designed to meet the desires of others. This pattern repeated itself in neighborhoods across the city as declines in overall enrollment continued, and yet suburban school construction continued. The board moved black students to fill seats and racial quotas in outlying new or existing schools in predominantly or exclusively white suburbs. A few years later, an MNPS teacher protesting the closure of her inner-ring suburban school saw a similar dynamic: "Our blacks are needed else-where. Scatter them here, there, and yonder." Meanwhile, seats in schools close to home sat empty. As Avon Williams took pains to point out, the board repeatedly chose to build new schools in the suburbs rather than utilize existing central-city buildings.[69]

Some central-city facilities with aging buildings were scheduled for replacement, but most were not. School administrators explained these anticipated closures as the result of the court's freeze on school construction as of 1969, indicating that some buildings "had deteriorated physically" enough that it was no longer feasible to renovate them and that "the projected change of pupil population and current site-size requirements prohibit replacement on the same site."[70] Without stating it directly, MNPS was endorsing the closure of more central-city schools, using site-size requirements and the language of demographic decline as seemingly objective justification. Meanwhile, they ignored the history of disinvestment in city schools, a history worsened by how Nashville structured busing.

The board of education's attorney sought court approval for a new construction plan, but got no response from Judge Gray, who became ill not long after *Kelley* moved to his docket. After a first year of court inaction, MNPS decided to proceed with construction projects that its legal counsel deemed acceptable under their interpretation of previous court rulings.[71] Their choice of projects seemed to reflect some attempt to stay within the boundaries of the court order. Yet Avon Williams and his colleagues saw many of the board's construction plans, their manipulations of school facilities and boundaries (as around the Cole Annex), and multiple other policy choices as facilitating white flight and furthering the unequal distribution of the burdens of busing. This became one of the matters that Judge Frank Gray left unaddressed in his latter years on *Kelley*.

With increasing numbers of inner-city elementary schools closed—along with the plan's provision that first through fourth grade schooling was in suburban schools—central-city black students would travel even more, and even farther, to newly constructed suburban schools, placing what Avon Williams called an "unconstitutional burden of desegregation upon black schoolchildren."[72] Continuing early-established patterns visible in urban renewal and highway construction, metropolitan-scale policy often rendered the experiences of black central-city residents or students invisible.

Initial orders for desegregation set out crucial parameters for what followed, but as populations grew, contracted, and shifted location as other aspects of metropolitan politics pressed on school systems, districts made myriad decisions that gave busing its ongoing form and character. In some districts, like Charlotte, important aspects of these decisions were made under the supervision of the federal court that had ordered busing. Judge James T. McMillan remained engaged in shaping Charlotte's busing plan intensively for six years.[73] By contrast, Nashville's board of education operated under court order, but with a nearly empty bench. After Judge Morton's recusal, the case passed to a judge whose own record on civil rights made him appear a likely ally to the desegregation cause, yet the combination of his illness and his engagement with a consuming desegregation case at the higher education level meant that Judge Frank Gray left multiple aspects of *Kelley* unsupervised.[74] His absence favored the defendant school district over the plaintiffs, as the school district could act directly on Nashville schools, while the plaintiffs could act only through the courts.

## Vocational Education: Desegregation, Space, and Curriculum

Nashville's congressman Richard Fulton joined the local official consensus against busing, and added a new, curriculum-focused element to the discussion. Fulton, a Democrat and earlier a vocal supporter of the Civil Rights Act of 1964, spoke more favorably of desegregation in general than did his colleagues in the Tennessee delegation to Washington, yet also expressed "strong opposition" to busing "as it is being done under court order in Nashville." Fulton's opposition to busing carried criticisms common to the local and national debate, but he further proposed—ultimately unsuccessfully—a bill to fund "Emergency Educational Assistance and Construction." He hoped that expanded funds for school construction could achieve "quality integrated education without busing." In the same measure, Fulton called for targeted vocational education funding for "cities affected by integration-busing emergencies." Fulton likely saw vocational education as an appealing offer to working-class white communities who had been at once most vocally opposed to busing and had fewer opportunities to resist via withdrawal. Although Fulton's vision directly linking vocational education and desegregation was not realized at the federal level, vocational education did operate in Nashville with direct impact on desegregation.[75]

In earlier phases of schooling in Nashville, what students learned in school often tracked student demographics. School- and district-level decisions provided white high school students different course options than their black peers. Compensatory education programs suggested different strategies for reading instruction for black children and poor children than white children and middle-class children. Thinking about curriculum in these ways—assuming that skin color and class were proxies for student ability and need—implicitly authorized continued segregation, if not between schools then within them.

Once busing began, ideas about curriculum and about the broader purposes of schooling continued to intersect with thinking about segregation and desegregation. While Nashville and Tennessee residents divided sharply on the question of busing for desegregation, they were much more likely to agree about vocational education and the hope that schools could prepare students for jobs and leverage economic growth. In the early 1970s, Tennessee invested hundreds of millions of dollars to expand vocational education, and these dollars transformed both the curricular and spatial organization of high schooling in Nashville. Vocational education dollars allowed the district to build comprehensive high schools on the model first suggested in 1966 by John Harper Harris, and on the spatial plan—in a ring around Briley Parkway—imagined by Bill Wise in court and sanctioned by Judge Morton and HEW in 1971.

Locating these schools almost exclusively in Nashville's suburbs, the vocational curricular initiative had direct consequences for where black and white students attended school, as well as what they found within school classrooms and corridors. Where ideas about curricular differentiation had, in the 1950s and 1960s, worked in favor of segregation, continued thinking about vocational education became important in remaking educational inequality in desegregating schools in the 1970s and 1980s.

Nashville's vocational emphasis authorized educators to think of students as future workers in ways that deepened schools' sorting by race, class, and gender. Yet vocational education policy in 1970s Nashville and Tennessee did not stem from a conspiracy to use curriculum to fight desegregation. Tennessee's vocational education efforts reflected a shift from discussions of curriculum as a mode of increased opportunity for targeted groups of students, toward a focus on economic growth as the source of (often unrealized) benefits for all. It was a kind of thinking about education and the economy that opened the way for inequality, and conflicted with the more explicitly redistributive claims of desegregation.[76]

In other words, Tennessee's vocational efforts were not directly designed to channel black students in to, or white students out of, vocational courses. Vocational education appealed heavily to working-class white constituencies, as imagined job seekers. Congressman Fulton's endorsement of vocational education in the same constituent mailings in which he decried busing and pledged to oppose it suggests this targeted constituency.

Similarly, when Nashville's John Harper Harris first planned McGavock High School for the county's eastern, predominantly white suburbs, he had white students in mind. Skilled industrial production remained the dominant target for economic growth in the early 1970s, while jobs in this field remained overwhelmingly occupied by white men. As one observer put it years later, "The vocational act . . . that was for white folks." Making the same point in more abstruse language, a Nashville delegate to the state legislature recalled the effort as having "no sociological ambition."[77] If conceptualized this way, however, vocational education nonetheless proved to have major impact on Nashville's black students as well.

Like the Nashville businessmen, educators, and civil rights leaders who pushed for vocational education in the 1960s, state-level policy makers and economic development advocates took up similar arguments in that decade and into the 1970s. Governor Buford Ellington proclaimed proudly that the people of his state had "come to realize that personal fulfillment and individual and economic progress can go hand in hand" through vocational education.[78] Not only would trained workers fill jobs, but they would help create these jobs; "all efforts to build the economy of the state result in more opportunities for a better life for all Tennesseans," a state study commission on vocational education declared in 1973.[79]

This period of boosterism reflected decades-long efforts toward economic development. Throughout the postwar decades, Tennessee, like its southern counterparts, had focused a great deal of energy on economic development, by which state boosters usually meant luring new industry. Many localities, like Nashville, had sought out industrial relocations in the 1950s and 1960s, and found some success with new or expanded plants for Ford Motor Company, among others.[80] Cities and smaller towns competed with each other to lure business with free land, factories built at municipal expense and leased at very low rates, and tax exemption for all equipment and machinery purchases.[81] Delegates from cities or the state traveled in "team trips" to cold-call northern and midwestern businesses and seek out firms interested in relocating.[82] In these years, even as local advocates hoped to tailor school programs to suit employer demand and open new avenues for black employment, vocational training (especially at the secondary level) received relatively less attention in these growth-seeking processes.

Shifts in the industrial-recruitment game added to vocational education's import. By the late 1960s, Tennessee officials had learned that their state could not compete with Mississippi, Alabama, or other Deep South states on low wages. Instead, they hoped to lure industry with local skilled labor and state support for continuing worker preparation. In 1967, Governor Ellington expressed an evolutionary view of the state's new position, having "progressed" beyond offering only the "natural resources" of unskilled labor and raw materials to be able to support "higher stages" of industry, to be "choosy" in recruitment efforts.[83] Through vocational education, Ellington and fellow governors implied, the state could be more Research Triangle Park than rural Mississippi.

Governor Ellington claimed that it was "no longer enough to 'educate' people; we must educate for the particular jobs and responsibilities that our people will be required to perform."[84] State dollars flowed into vocational training programs for existing and new businesses, and state and federal support created area vocational training schools with similar goals.[85] Beginning in 1971, the "Industrial Training Service" commissioned three "mobile classrooms" that could be moved to the front gate of a factory under construction, and could hold selected students and a factory-approved teacher to teach a factory-approved curriculum. Asked to opine on developing state vocational education plans, some firms listed skills they sought regularly, including welding, tool and die making, or machine millwrighting; but for others, the core demands were for skills in basic math and reading, and "employability." Others explained that they recruited nationally for their skilled positions, limiting the impact of local training.[86] There were hints as well that payments to companies for "training" at times became "a sizeable wad of money with no strings attached," lacking any skill increase for local workers.[87] Nonetheless, state officials worried that Tennessee was moving more slowly on the industrial training front than had its Sunbelt competitors in North and South Carolina, Georgia, Virginia, Arkansas and Florida.[88]

The conversation turned to high school–level vocational education in 1972. After state-wide hearings, the legislature unanimously authorized nearly $200 million for construction and expansion of vocational education facilities for high school students, or over $900 million in 2010 dollars.[89] The Comprehensive Vocational Education Act (CVEA) pledged to fund the creation of at least one comprehensive vocational high school in each county in the state, toward the goal of making vocational training available to 100 percent of the state's students and enrolling 50 percent in vocational courses.[90] It gained unanimous support in the legislature in part because it promised so many positive outcomes at once (and in part, some participants recalled, because of the very well-organized vocational education lobby). Reinforcing the idea that more trained workers would bring more industrial development, the CVEA was the latest, and largest-scale, manifestation of the decades-long effort at industrial and economic growth, while also intersecting with educational and political concerns of the moment.[91]

As in Nashville in the 1950s and 1960s, state-level discussion of vocational education also emphasized vocational education as a means to keep students in school. Tennessee legislators indicated concern that "too many boys and girls are becoming school dropouts because of the lack of adequate vocational courses in our public schools."[92] State Commissioner of Education E. C. Stimbert emphasized vocational education as a means of decreasing the state's high dropout rate: in 1971 only 56 percent of those who had started first grade in 1959 made it to twelfth grade twelve years later (whether or not they then graduated).[93]

And also as in Nashville decades earlier, the anti-dropout rhetoric contrasted with a parallel discourse of diminished expectations. Tennessee's legislative study bemoaned "too many persons . . . entering colleges who really should be pursuing vocational programs." Speaking at a hearing on vocational education in 1971, a representative of the state teachers' union, the Tennessee Education Association (TEA), derided the high school curriculum as too focused on college, and thus ill suited to the needs of Tennessee students, only one-quarter of whom ultimately would attend.[94] He blamed the misplaced focus not only on the lack of vocational facilities (often due to small schools with limited funds), but on public attitudes that vocational education was only for the "slow" or unambitious. These attitudes and the labor-education mismatch that followed could be corrected, the TEA official urged, by vocational guidance counselors placed in, and actively guiding, students at the junior high school level. More students in vocational classes would mean more people graduating from high school, fewer "non-qualified people attempting college," fewer on welfare or in prison, and more gainfully employed.[95] Business representatives asserted the same concern. An executive at middle Tennessee industrial firm Heil/Quaker complained that "too much importance is attached to a college education in Middle Tennessee."[96]

These Tennesseans echoed a broader critique in circulation among state governors, business and industry leaders, and the federal Office of Education: that the American high school structure was too academic. US Commissioner of Education Sidney P. Marland drew on Department of Labor projections to assure educators that by 1980 only 20 percent of all jobs would require a college diploma. Marland encouraged high schools to prioritize the needs of students who would enter the workforce immediately, an approach he titled career education.[97] Unlike the educational rhetoric surrounding the federal vocational and manpower training acts of the early 1960s—which emphasized a changing economy demanding more skills and more education—early-1970s discourse about vocational and career education, with its criticism of a college-preparatory orientation, actually emphasized rearranging expectations for students downward.

Vocational education debates reveal the ways in which public notions of work were in flux in the 1970s. Official public figures in Tennessee and elsewhere linked discussions of work and education to cultural judgment. Ohio's governor James A. Rhodes penned a 1969 treatise against "educational snobbery" that required an "unnecessary yoke" of academic courses in high school. Rhodes worried that without sufficient vocational courses, "decadence" and unemployability would result.[98] Perhaps vocational education could offer a reassurance that work was still real and tangible, and masculine, akin to the prevalence of hard-hat imagery in national politics at the time. Yet vocational education could offer few real guarantees. Vocational education contained big rhetoric that brought little change on the measures it promised to address.[99]

Concerns about dropout rates, hoped for and real demand from industry for trained employees, and criticism of high school as too focused on college—all of these found their way into the Tennessee legislature's thinking about vocational education.[100] The tendrils reaching out from so many agendas and motives helped ensure strong legislative support for vocational education, crossing significant divides in Tennessee politics and bridging areas with distinct economic contexts. It offered something for the rural counties—hit particularly hard by agricultural decline and desperate for industrial development—as well as the state's larger cities like Nashville, facing the "astonishing paradox of shortage labor for specific jobs and high unemployment rates in inner city areas."[101]

That paradox was sharpest, as it had long been, for Nashville's black workers. Although Nashville's black leaders had been much less present in pushing for vocational education at the state level than they had been in 1960s-era local programs in Nashville, their delegates did support the CVEA. Representative Harold M. Love and Avon Williams, now a state senator, both voted in favor. Love, a Nashville Democrat, represented the Bordeaux neighborhood, where increasing numbers of black middle-class Nashvillians lived. An insurance salesman and Nashville native, Love graduated from Pearl High School and Tennessee A & I (later Tennessee State University), and held a master's degree from Fisk.[102] He was a member of Nashville's Urban League but not its NAACP, a mark of his relative conservatism when compared with the more activist agendas of fellow legislator Williams. Representing the North Nashville urban neighborhood he still called home, Williams exemplified the concerns of the state's cities. Love sponsored a legislative study of job training programs in Tennessee in 1971, arguing that "there are many citizens of our state for which improvement or an appearance of improvement in employment does not reach," by which Love likely meant his unemployed and underemployed constituents who struggled to find work in Nashville even amid lower aggregate unemployment rates (compared to other areas in the state). Their economic futures depended on "who they are, where they are . . . and what job training may be available."[103] Love, like Vivian Henderson and others before them, saw vocational education as a route out of poverty. Although Avon Williams's detailed knowledge of the limitations of vocational education in practice might have tempered his expectations, he also supported the act. Finally, that both of these legislators, who had earlier cast protest votes against proposed anti-desegregation measures, supported the state's vocational education measure suggests that at least to them, it did not have segregationist intentions.

The Tennessee CVEA anticipated construction on new vocational facilities to begin as early as 1974 and to be completed by 1977.[104] Such plans depended on actual appropriations, which saw less unanimity than the original legislation. Governor Winfield Dunn boasted of his own support for and leadership on vocational education—the promise of which he called "downright thrilling!" in his own notes—yet Dunn vetoed the first bond issue to fund vocational education facilities construction, arguing instead for a slower process and more effort to innovate within, rather than only expand, the existing vocational education system. Dunn later proposed an appropriation half as large as the one he vetoed, but he met a feisty response in the legislature. The vocational education bill's senate sponsor, David Copeland, a Chattanooga Republican, led a successful override vote and secured an additional bond, bringing the construction and equipment expenditures to $197 million over five years.[105]

State dollars financed 95 percent of the construction of expanded vocational wings at seven Nashville high schools, bringing into being over the 1970s the ring of comprehensive high schools first described in Judge Morton's courtroom in 1971.[106] In keeping with Morton's effort to limit construction that could impede desegregation or facilitate resegregation, he approved proposed comprehensive school construction or expansion only at what he deemed midpoint locations around the route of Briley Parkway, and theoretically between areas of black and white residence. Morton ordered the board not to expand one high school in a predomintly white suburb, and rejected the construction of another as too far ɔm Briley Parkway.[107] However, after Judge Morton had recused himself from *Kelley* and the case moved to Judge Gray's docket, MNPS forwarded its construction plans to the court for approval, including these projects. When Judge Gray proved unresponsive on district requests to approve new construction, the district decided to proceed anyway.

As the district built new seats in Nashville's suburbs, it furthered immediate and long-term pressures for administrators to assign more black students away from city schools like Pearl High School, and for urban students to travel away from their neighborhoods for high school. As Pearl's enrollment shrank, its local allies saw their argument weaken for the continued existence of their historically important school. The combination of state support through the CVEA and local implementation made the suburban comprehensive high school with its vocational and academic offerings the prototype for high school–level desegregation in Nashville.

Local figures could agree on vocational education—and the broader vision it implied of schooling targeting economic purposes and leveraging growth—even when deep divisions confronted the district via desegregation. As vocational education took form in practice, it proved to create new openings for inequality.

## Conclusion

Popular resistance to desegregation gave evidence of the depth of white commitment to defend the tight historic linkage between neighborhood, school, and segregation, a linkage challenged by busing. In Nashville, white resistance to busing became evident in a variety of forms—from aggressive picket lines at schools to begrudging and economically self-interested calls for compliance in elite circles. Even quieter processes of bureaucratic judgment and implementation, often working to shift the spatial and the curricular organization of schooling, remade inequality in busing's first decade. These decisions often prioritized the felt needs of white and suburban families, particularly as compared to those of black families in the city core.

If considered a kind of public pedagogy, official choices about busing communicated to white families that they should appropriately expect their felt needs and desires to be prioritized above others', to have their children deemed the chief focus of a school district's functioning. In this way, Nashville school officials were setting themselves up to compete for the affections of white families—to compete with surrounding and less demographically diverse exurban school systems, or local private schools—on terms on which the district could never win.

Vocational education, supported by a mixture of growth-minded and educational logics, made its mark on Nashville curriculum, but also transformed the spatial organization of high schooling in the city. Students who rode buses to high schools under court order for desegregation got off the bus at schools that grew larger and expanded their curricular offerings via state vocational funding. These schools sorted students between academic offerings and vocational programs. Inside schools, the state legislative encouragement to understand students as future workers set the context within which teachers made millions of decisions as they interacted with children.

The enlarged state role in worker preparation could seem to contradict the nearly simultaneous calls of anti-busing protestors for a less meddlesome state. Although anti-desegregation activism has rightly been portrayed as a seedbed of conservative politics—and local activists surely protested busing as an invasion into treasured realms of family authority and homeowner rights—pressure for vocational education in Nashville highlights the nuances of that conservatism. It was not bluntly anti-state, but reflected a recalculation of the appropriate uses and targets of state power. The more targeted and explicitly redistributionist claims of busing for desegregation drew criticism as an inappropriate use of state power, although various manipulations in favor of segregation and white privilege appeared unremarkable. Meanwhile, expansive or even intrusive state efforts to link students to jobs could be supported in the name of economic growth amid claims of benefit to all. A new trickle-down logic was gaining hold, one that opposed direct assistance to historically underserved individuals or groups, but supported a more expansive use of state power in the name of growth with purportedly broadly distributed benefits.

Between Judge Morton's 1971 order for desegregation and the experiences of tens of thousands of Nashville students and families lay crucial decisions—made as frequently out of the glare of public attention as within it—that shaped the basic structures and approaches of desegregation. These decisions both resisted and transformed busing in Nashville, helping remake educational inequality as Nashville students, teachers, and families experienced the next phase of desegregation.

# CHAPTER SEVEN

# Busing Lived and Imagined

What happened after the protests quieted, when buses carried tens of thousands of students across Nashville's streets and highways to new schools in often unfamiliar communities? Busing did create substantial statistical desegregation in the Nashville schools it reached under Judge Morton's 1971 order. More than 60,000 Nashville students—nearly three-quarters of the district's total enrollment in 1971–72—attended one of the 111 schools where busing and intentional zoning increased desegregation. The number of schools with highly concentrated (90 percent or more) populations of black or white students declined in 1971, from 101 to 30. All of these thirty sat in nearly or all-white outlying areas exempted from busing in the 1970s.[1]

Decades later, many Nashville students remembered desegregation's positive marks on their lives, while also recalling worrying and at times painful unfairness in their schooling. They paid careful attention to individual interactions with teachers and peers, but observed as well their district's approach to desegregation, querying their own position in the desegregation project.[2]

Desegregation involved not only bus routes and construction plans central to the spatial organization of schooling, but efforts to attach school curriculum to the labor market. State dollars flowed to vocational education in the 1970s with hopes of leveraging economic growth, a goal that many could agree on despite deep fissures over desegregation. Agreement on vocational education did not resolve the many complications and uncertainties involved in practice: How would schools determine and match changing labor market demands? Who would decide which students took which classes, and how? Vocational education implied that schools should view students in terms of their future occupation (within a still-segregated and unequal labor market). In practice, vocational education tended to further "second-generation segregation" and continued unequal educational opportunity even within statistically desegregated schools.[3] Vocational education also opened up new routes to resist desegregation and recreate segregation between schools.

How Nashvillians narrated their experiences and observations of desegregation helped shape busing and its inequalities as well. Over the 1970s, white middle-class families resisted desegregation and busing through their withdrawal from Nashville schools. Ten thousand fewer students attended Nashville schools for the 1971–72 school year than the previous year's enrollment predicted. Yet such dramatic resistance was in some ways not as important, ultimately, as the ways in which local educators, city planners, and judges decided to respond to it. So-called white flight, an oversimplifying label, became the dominating local narrative about busing for desegregation in Nashville. That narrative reached into how educators thought about the spatial organization of schooling in Nashville, and limited the visibility of and attention to black children and their families in negotiations over busing. Both the practice of busing and the narratives through which it was understood helped remake inequality by privileging those most likely to resist busing—white middle-class suburbanites—and minimizing the claims of those black urban families who were the district's most reliable constituents.

## Living Busing

From the perspective of the test-score-focused early-twenty-first century, the primary question about desegregation might seem to be its impact on Nashville students' achievement, measured statistically. Earlier, too, black and white parents alike worried about the impact of busing and statistical desegregation on their children's learning. Given the limitations of surviving and accessible data, more is unknown than known. Nashville test score data from the late-1970s show that desegregation's impact there aligned generally with contemporary national patterns—in which busing was more likely to accompany increases in student test scores than declines. In Nashville, the late 1970s saw a gradual improvement in the achievement test scores of black students, while white students' remained steady.[4] Data do not survive to allow a full examination of Nashville student achievement across the 1980s and 1990s, particularly at the school or classroom level. One snapshot, comparing 1971 achievement with 1991 figures, suggests that major gains for black students, and modest gains for white students, took place across the busing decades. Yet even those comparisons—much less full causal interpretations—carry many possible flaws.[5]

However, neither data about steady or rising achievement via statistical desegregation nor accounts of social learning via desegregation garnered as much public attention in Nashville as stories of popular resistance, particularly in the 1970s, and "racial tensions" in the 1980s. Nashville students speaking to reporters over the 1970s and 1980s, and in oral histories conducted well after high school, appreciated how busing brought unprecedented social contact with groups and places they had rarely if ever encountered before. This social contact was a key feature of desegregation that produced long-lasting, positive impact on students in Nashville as it had in desegregating districts nationally.[6]

As the court-approved 1971 desegregation plan left only a few small high schools exempted from Nashville's busing plan, the vast majority of Nashville's high school–age students did the daily work of desegregation in their schools. They met in classrooms, on athletic fields, in student clubs, and on the bus. They developed friendships, negotiated careful social treaties in hallways and cafeterias, and became careful observers of the shifting forms of inequality around them. For them, desegregation was less a large-scale political battle than a varied, complex daily experience whose nuances appeared in small-scale but consequential choices: which type of music a band director chose, which school ring you wore, whether you could find a ride home after school if you had practice or a club meeting. The universal questions of adolescence remained, refracted in new ways in the large comprehensive high schools that became the key setting for desegregation in Nashville.

Nashville alumni remember their high school years through stories that resonate with national patterns in desegregation. Amy Stuart Wells and colleagues conducted interviews with dozens of graduates from the class of 1980, in high schools in Pasadena, California; Charlotte, North Carolina; Englewood, New Jersey; Austin, Texas; Shaker Heights, Ohio; and Topeka, Kansas. These students recounted learning to appreciate and work with peers who came from different backgrounds, while also feeling frustration over inequalities in how busing burdened black and—where they were present—Latino students more than white students. They appreciated the comfort they later felt in interracial settings, comfort lacking for peers who had not attended integrated schools. They saw cross-racial contact as an independent good, not just a mechanism for access to nicer science equipment or higher test scores. Their comments indicate that they would have agreed with lauded Nashville principal Thelma Rucker, who explained that without statistical desegregation on the scale busing brought, "I and my teachers and my children would still be ignorant of the rest of the world, still hung up with misconceptions and false notions of superiority and inferiority."[7]

But these students did not romanticize busing as a cure-all, either. They noted how tracking within their schools constrained the opportunities of black and Latino students. Their stories point out what desegregation did accomplish, how it marked the lives of its students, and yet how it remained insufficient to change the unequal and racist landscape of work, housing, and social interaction that the students encountered after graduation.[8] Nashville students' stories share these complexities, with an additional appreciation for how the district's focus on large comprehensive high schools had distinct consequences.

Nashville students noticed how busing proceeded on unequal terms. White students appreciated that it was their black peers who traveled farther to get to school. Black students saw their large, suburban, majority-white comprehensive high school as just the latest in a long list of schools that they rode buses to, out of their own neighborhoods.[9] If not all districts shared Nashville's focus on suburban comprehensive schools, Nashville students shared with students across the country the observation that desegregation plans distributed busing's burdens unequally. When white students rode buses, it was more often to schools they felt to be both geographically and culturally accessible, places where they felt they belonged. In the worst cases, local observers in the 1970s wondered if frequent travel away from home via busing—as well as sometimes hostile school environments once students got off the bus—pushed later generations of students toward dropping out.[10]

Before busing for desegregation, students recalled sharp racial isolation. Asked to remember their pre-busing contact with students of a different racial background, some white students recalled pickup basketball games played alongside black and white players, or knew one or two black peers in their previous schools. But these experiences were exceptions to the norm for many white youngsters. Black students recalled even more limited contact. Charles Davis had no interactions with white children before busing took him to majority-white junior and senior high schools. Waverly Crenshaw remembered television as his sole exposure to white families before busing.[11]

In Nashville—and in keeping with the reports of students in desegregating schools nationally—the deepest and most egalitarian of cross-racial interactions occurred in extracurricular spaces, like band, student govern-

7.1. Students in conversation at Percy Priest Elementary,
1979. By Nancy Rhoda, the *Tennessean*.

ment, or athletics. Sports teams offered a common rallying point for students from diverse neighborhoods and previous school affiliations. Given the much higher status (especially in the 1970s) of boys' sports over girls', black boys found more routes into acceptance and power in their schools via athletics than did black girls. Sonya Ramsey had watched her brother achieve great popularity at McGavock through his athletic prowess. Yet when she attended Hillwood High School a few years later, she noticed not only the absence of this power for black girls, but how dating norms tolerated black boys dating white girls but not the reverse, further isolating black girls.[12]

Adult leadership remained crucial in these spaces. McGavock High School's championship basketball team illustrated how teachers and coaches could take the logistical difficulties of desegregation and craft them into opportunities.[13] Buses ran only once at the end of the school day, in part due to stinting local financing of the bus fleet itself. For students who relied on buses to get home, participating in extracurricular activities became more difficult. In McGavock High School's championship basketball program—which drew many of its star players from distant South Nashville neighborhoods—the coaching staff helped give students rides home after practice, or asked peers with cars to drive students home. Steve Flatt, a white student who lived in a suburban neighborhood close to the school, saw areas of the city that he had never before visited as he helped shuttle teammates home. Years later, Flatt wondered whether his coach's goals had been simply logistical, or had been designed to produce this learning. At a time when most white suburbanites knew central-city Nashville only through starkly negative and pathologizing local press coverage, these encounters productively challenged previous ignorance and helped overcome how segregation had "uneducated" white students, as Rev. Amos Jones put it.[14]

McGavock's Coach Joe Allen structured interactions between his diverse team, their neighborhoods, and their families. He held team meetings not only at school, but in gatherings that rotated among his players' homes. The team ate together in the modest public housing apartment of one teammate and the more expansive suburban home of another. When students gathered together in a Napier Court public housing apartment kitchen—one so clean that you could "eat off the floor"—assistant coach Milton Harris felt it sent a message to students: "It didn't matter *where* you lived, but *how* you lived in the place that you lived." Like Steve Flatt, player Charles Davis also had no previous experience with the kinds of communities his teammates came from. A Napier Court resident, Davis appreciated the introduction to communities beyond Napier that busing brought

7.2. McGavock High School basketball players, c. 1975. From McGavock yearbook.

7.3. Buses line up after school at Glencliff High School, 1979. By Nancy Rhoda, the *Tennessean*.

him: "It was like, 'wow, this is what I picture life being about' . . . that you have your own yard, your own fence, your private space that you can just enjoy." Davis cherished his "roots" in Napier Court, but also valued the new exposure to living conditions he had seen on television, but that he felt "just [weren't] in my neighborhood." Unlike other contemporary voices that emphasized differences between black urban and white suburban families to be the result of "cultural deprivation," Davis credited economic "resources" with fostering the leisurely dinnertime conversation and "family atmosphere" that he appreciated in his teammates' homes.[15]

Casual or incidental peer interactions carried evidence of continued and ugly stereotypes, as well as opportunities to challenge these. McGavock student Waverly Crenshaw joined the marching band, alongside a white girl who played the piccolo or flute. Waverly found his bandmate's wallet and returned it to her. Decades later he remembered the look of shock on her face when she realized that all her money was inside the wallet as Crenshaw returned it. In junior high school, Hubert Dixon III built a relationship with a white classmate around their shared interest in science fiction. The two phoned nightly to discuss stories they wrote together. When friendships did form, busing zones and assignments often changed, separating friends across different schools and "you would never see that person again." In general, white Nashville parents discounted the social interaction that busing made possible. A 1981 survey showed that 66 percent of white parents felt busing had not "improved understanding and acceptance" between black and white students. Forty-five percent of black parents felt it had, but 27 percent disagreed.[16]

Despite both intentional and happenstance relationship building inside statistically desegregated schools, the decades-long history of segregated schools linked to racially identified communities proved hard to shift. Students missed the sense of generational connections to pre-busing schools—the "I taught your mother, your brother . . ." feeling that Charles Davis associated with teachers at his neighborhood's historically black Cameron High School, or the experience of walking by pictures of grandfathers and grandmothers that lined the hallway at rural white Joelton High. Students also read meaning in the kind of music a band leader chose, for example, as a symbol of the school's cultural identity. Some black students encountered previously unfamiliar music and enjoyed it, while others arranged to transfer back to schools with black band leaders and a familiar repertoire.[17]

Under a busing plan like Nashville's, however, and like those throughout the country that closed black schools rather than desegregate them, more black students found themselves adjusting to white band music than

7.4. Glencliff High School, 1979. By Nancy Rhoda, the *Tennessean*.

the opposite. The court-approved busing plan either shuttered or converted to junior high school status all but one of Nashville's historically black high schools. As Nashville NAACP leader Mahlon Griffith observed, "[Historically black] Cameron's identity is gone, but [historically white] Hillsboro has the identity it always had."[18]

MNPS's approach to faculty desegregation—also under court supervision within *Kelley* and initiated a year before busing in 1970—furthered this feeling of lost identity for previously segregated black schools. With all faculties required to meet an 80 percent white/20 percent black ratio, white schools kept majority-white faculties; black schools lost the majority of their faculties (although the district at times interpreted the ratio flexibly). Black teachers did not suffer mass firings, at this phase of desegregation or earlier, as had been the case in some cities, but many black principals found themselves reassigned and demoted to assistant principal.[19] Mary Craighead, a skilled educator whose first leadership roles were within the 1960s Nashville Educational Improvement Project, moved in 1971 from segregated black Carter-Lawrence Elementary, where she had been principal, to take the same position at majority-white Glendale Elementary. Craighead's move captures some of the pros and cons of faculty desegregation. Having innovated in successful new programs at Carter-Lawrence in a high-poverty black community, Craighead was reassigned to majority-white Glendale when busing began. Her status and skill made her an attractive choice for a district seeking to avoid controversy where possible. Craighead spent the summer introducing herself to area families—sometimes with her foot strategically propping open a front door to force conversation, and despite epithets about the new "nigger principal." She became an important example for white and black students of black leaders in authority.[20] Yet her move from Carter-Lawrence to Glendale illustrated the diverting of talented black educators away from historically black schools.

For black teachers, faculty desegregation combined with busing in complex ways. As professionals, many black teachers mourned the loss of the long-established relationships with colleagues and community in historically segregated black schools. New colleagues in majority-white, often formerly segregated white schools were at times expressly hostile, or at other times caused hurt simply by ignoring new, possibly more veteran, black colleagues. Black teachers appreciated the resource equalization that came with desegregation—no longer having to subsidize school band uniforms, for example—but were far from certain that busing was serving their students well. Longtime Pearl High School teacher Anne Lenox was transferred to two suburban, majority-white schools. She resented the moves, but stayed in the job to be a guardian of black students. "I didn't ask to come here . . . but since I am here and I see what you are doing to my poor little black students, I am going to stay here as long as I can." Lenox was far from alone in her uncertainty about busing. In a 1980 survey, 36 percent of black teachers surveyed said that busing had improved educational achievement for black students, while 38 percent said it had not.[21]

Although district superintendent Elbert Brooks and his staff usually spoke in measured tones urging compliance and calm—acknowledging the presence of both resistance to and support for busing—and Craighead conducted patient house-by-house conversations, not all educators followed suit. A teacher at one majority-white suburban junior high school, to which black students were bused, recalled that her principal led prayers at anti-busing rallies. Another teacher, concerned about the treatment of bused-in students at her newly desegregated school, helped escort students to their buses when protesters lined their way; she did so over her principal's objections. School leaders' calls for calm also stayed far from any principled justification of either the project of desegregation or the mode of busing. Just as Mayor Briley and white business elites had earlier distinguished between the valid educational purpose and the invalid "sociological" one of desegregation, many white educators referred to busing as something separate from the district's core work of education. In 1973 senior district administrator Hale Harris remarked publicly that after the rocky first two years, "emotionalism" over busing had subsided, and now the district could "talk about what we are going to do about education." In his view, it was "time we stopped talking about" busing.[22]

Nashville's students heard a complex and contradictory mix of public messages about busing while experiencing individual interactions both supportive and discouraging in their schools. Even as they appreciated becoming more comfortable with interacting with diverse groups, black students particularly recalled their high schools as places that they never fully felt they belonged. Charles Davis, who capped off a stellar high school basketball career with a state championship in 1976, recalled that he never enjoyed "a sense of belonging" in the majority-white suburban junior and senior high schools he rode buses to. Everything felt different when, as he recalled with laughter, "I was . . . in charge of the basketball team." For Hubert Dixon, friendships with teammates or classmates mattered, yet "it was always very clear if you were a black student that you were in the minority, in terms of how you were referred to. . . . It was never really a sense of being integrated."[23]

The sheer scale of Nashville's new comprehensive high schools made the question of belonging—and desegregation in general—more chal-

7.5. Students at suburban Percy Priest Elementary during the 1976 bicentennial celebration. By Nancy Rhoda, the *Tennessean*.

lenging. When McGavock High School, Nashville's first post–World War II comprehensive high school, opened in the fall of 1971, it brought together nearly 2,800 tenth to twelfth graders, a newly constituted faculty, and an unfinished building with an incomplete sewage system. Approximately two-thirds of McGavock's students came from the surrounding working- and middle-class, predominantly white suburbs; just under a third came from predominantly black South Nashville neighborhoods. The first months included unsurprising hiccups—students lost in the vast thirteen-acre building, where directional signs had not yet been painted; conflict between groups of black and white students with no previous personal or group-level interaction. Administrators tried to smooth student interaction by carefully managing representation in the school, setting quotas for black and white cheerleaders, and assuaging frustration when 150 students from three previous schools aspired to the single basketball team. Negotiating all these issues was harder given the increased attention the school received as the new prototype for comprehensive education in Nashville.[24]

The first years of desegregation were the most tense and unstable, particularly when students who had attended largely segregated schools with their friends for years encountered other groups of friends who had their own attachment to their previous schools. The district's support for comprehensive schools not only brought black and white students together, but linked previously separate white communities. Cindy Acuff was a high school sophomore in 1971 when the new court order for busing closed her Litton High School and reassigned her to Stratford High. Litton was the hub of community life in her section of East Nashville's inner-ring suburbs, with "people who didn't have kids in school any more attending the football games" and students like Acuff herself long expecting to follow in her parents' footsteps and graduate from Litton. Litton's sports culture targeted feelings of rivalry between schools—and Litton's rival was Stratford. Litton students celebrated an annual "hate Stratford" week, and then months later found themselves assigned to Stratford.[25]

In McGavock High School's first year, numerous (and usually minor) fights broke out in the school's cafeteria and hallways. They were almost always, as one former student recalled, "not black-and-black or white-and-white fights," but "they were black-and-white fights." Racial slurs or other slights added to the social anxieties and tensions often present in high schools—tension that had for years before desegregation produced fights within schools. Any instances of violence had additional power in the context of desegregation. For students who already resented having to leave their previous schools to attend a new one, a sense of physical threat only added to their unease. Parents unsure of how to name their concerns about—or their opposition to—desegregation could comfortably unite behind the idea of protecting student safety. At McGavock, the first few years were the most unstable, with district administrators called in to provide extra supervision in the school's public spaces. The atmosphere calmed as the proportion of students who had begun their schooling at McGavock grew.[26]

Glencliff High School desegregated via busing in 1971 with 750 students, but expanded in 1978 to become a comprehensive high school with a population of nearly 2,000 under the state's Comprehensive Vocational Education Act (CVEA) funds. In one of the relatively few documented examples of organized student protest in the context of desegregation, Glencliff's black students initiated a nonviolent sit-in during the fall of 1978, protesting the lack of black nominees in the school's "superlatives" competition—for award categories like "best dressed" or "most likely to succeed." The students' modest protest was followed by a cafeteria fight the next day, and then a flurry of unfounded rumors about rape, assault, and weapons use at the school. Even seven years after the beginning of busing and at a suburban school in a white neighborhood, white students and their families boycotted the school for a few days, with attendance reduced by nearly half at its peak. Parents meeting with school administrators demanded rezoning that, school officials explained, would violate the

7.6. Glencliff High School, 1979. By Nancy Rhoda, the *Tennessean*.

district's desegregation plan. When a black parent expressed her concern to the school board that black students were "never really accepted" at the school, the comment drew boos from the audience. At a later gathering of white Glencliff constituents, the area's Metro councilman implied defiance of federal regulations tied to Title I funding when he asked, "How much money would we lose if we bused some of these students back to North Nashville?"[27] Another school administrator chalked up Glencliff's difficulties, like those he perceived at other high schools, to their being "overloaded with the worst [housing] project blacks." In fact, tension stemmed in part from the school simply being "overloaded," with four hundred students over capacity despite the existence of empty seats in other district schools.[28]

Difficulties like these accompanying busing's first decade helped to feed a general dissatisfaction with Nashville schools. Surveying public opinion about desegregation and education in Nashville, scholars Richard Pride and David Woodward found that "the general public, parents, and teachers were convinced that the costs of busing were high and the benefits incidental." In the same year in which 36 percent of Americans graded their public schools with an A or B, only 20 percent of Nashvillians did so.[29]

Nashville did have its desegregation success stories. Locally based writer John Egerton, who had covered desegregation nationally, wrote about Head Elementary's principal, Thelma Rucker. She had created an academically successful and demographically stable school where others (in Nashville and elsewhere) had failed to do so. In a formerly segregated black school building close to a North Nashville housing project, Rucker's Head School served fifth and sixth graders from the immediate area as well as those who rode buses from a more distant, and wealthier, white neighborhood. Rucker, characterized by Egerton as a "master chef" of a principal, prided herself on individual attention to her students' needs, which she linked to the school being "color-blind." "I don't care about color or class," she said, and later told the *Tennessean* that desegregation was a matter of "human relations, not race relations." Amy Stuart Wells and colleagues found students and educators around the country in desegregating contexts valuing the idea of color-blindness—one that seemed to foster calm, if not to guarantee justice. In Rucker's setting, it might have comforted white parents unsure of their place in an unfamiliar black neighborhood.[30]

Rucker's school grouped students by skill level at times—and doing so, Rucker acknowledged "unapologetically"—produced racially homogenous groups at times, given students' uneven previous schooling. But in other cases, teachers intentionally mixed students across skill level, or provided leadership roles to responsible and mature students regardless of academic prowess. Egerton reported that Rucker had created an atmosphere that middle- and upper-middle-class whites had come to trust, retaining students at the moment of peak resistance and withdrawal, when white students were first bused into city neighborhoods. And she had created a school where the reading skill of the school's neediest students rose appreciably. Head Elementary, as captured by Egerton, found remarkable success both in academic achievement and in encouraging a community ethos in a diverse institution.[31]

Around the twenty-fifth anniversary of the *Brown* decision, in May 1979, the Nashville *Tennessean* sent a reporter-photographer team into local schools to consider what desegregation looked like, seeking a "candid understanding of progress and problems." In an eleven-part series, reporter Saundra Ivey and photographer Nancy Warnecke captured a glimpse of life in schools in 1979. They told stories of students working together in classes, and sitting separately in cafeterias. (The images taken by Warnecke, now Nancy Rhoda, provide many of the figures for this chapter.) In the article series, student comments also underscored the slow pace of change, even after eight years of busing for desegregation, when high school students reminded the reporter that they had begun their own schooling in segregated elementary schools. These students pointed out that given these personal histories with segregation, they were "still learning" about desegregation. Students referred generally to peak tensions in the first years of desegregation, often worsened by the massive scale of new comprehensive high schools, which created feelings of anonymity that encouraged students to cling to old attachments to segregated school and community.[32]

Ivey and Warnecke visited Hillsboro High School, located in the affluent inner-ring suburb of Green Hills. During the reporters' visit, a fight broke out in the school's student smoking area, prompted by a white boy calling a black peer "nigger." Within seconds, the two students were brawling, and moments later, fellow students and teachers had intervened to stop the fight. Warnecke's camera captured each step in the students' confrontation, and the *Tennessean* ran four of them in large format, filling nearly a full newspaper page. The accompanying text used the fight to exemplify the close-to-the-surface tensions still present at desegregating schools. Read in the context of the other articles in the series, the article offered one piece of desegregation's story. Yet the images were large and striking, and likely drew many readers' attention, whether they read the accompanying text. Hillsboro students wrote letters to the paper and called for a follow-up meeting to clarify their story, furious at the depiction of the school that they described as constructively and positively integrated.[33]

Busing produced no single common experience, but myriad permutations based on a complex matrix of geography, class, and race. The largest dividing line fell between those students—most of them white—who lived in the outer suburban ring exempted (primarily at the elementary and junior high school levels) from busing entirely over the 1970s, and those in the one hundred urban and suburban schools desegregated by busing. Within the area served by those schools, the desegregation plan treated black and white students, and urban and suburban students, differently. Meanwhile, wealthier families had resources to choose private schools regardless of their address.

Among those participating in desegregation, both economic and social resources determined how families experienced and navigated desegregation. When Hubert Dixon III rode to suburban Brookmeade Elementary from his North Nashville home, his mother remained visible and involved in his school. Her frequent presence in the building—facilitated both by her not working outside of the home and by having her own car—combined with confidence that came from her family's social background. As Hubert's father remembered it, "We were educated enough to know, we're going to check [out their son's school]. And if we can't get satisfaction, we're going to go somewhere else."[34] Head Elementary principal Thelma Rucker recalled the many mothers who volunteered at the school in the first years of busing, offering their time and energy but likely reassuring themselves, too, that all was well.[35] Like it did for the Dixons, time, money, and access to school eased the experience of busing.

Many black families had neither the educational background nor the logistical access that the Dixons enjoyed. In years when 90 percent of white Nashville families owned cars, over 40 percent of black families did without, in a city with very limited public transportation. Lack of access created not only ongoing difficulties communicating, but trouble negotiating late developing emergencies when a child was sick or injured at school. Rev. Bill Barnes, whose Edgehill-area congregation included many families with children bused to the southeastern reaches of Davidson County, recalled being asked to drive mothers to outlying elementary schools to pick up their children. Sending children to an increased number of different schools via busing created extra complications for families with multiple school-age children. It became much less likely that children were at the same school as siblings, and so parents had more schools to try to connect with from a distance. One mother, unable to introduce her child to his teacher in person on the first day of school in a neighborhood far from home, sent him on the bus with a note pinned to his shirt. Hoping to convey her love and care—and a sense of the place and community to which her child was attached—she wrote: "My name is . . . and my mother's name is . . . and I live at . . ."[36]

As some families negotiated busing's logistical complexities with limited resources, these difficulties were somewhat mitigated for some of the small but growing black suburban population in Nashville. Their spatial position in the metropolis, largely facilitated by their class, meant they lived closer to other white families with school-age children. Thus black suburban children were more likely to attend local schools that, while within the bounds of busing under Judge Morton's order, could be desegregated through zoning without busing. Black suburbanization therefore provided one of the ways that—in Nashville as in other cities as diverse as Charleston and Milwaukee, Charlotte and Little Rock—class divisions within black communities became key variables in the experience of desegregation.[37]

Similarly, some elementary schools, particularly in East Nashville, could be desegregated by zoning, with both black and white students remaining in close proximity to home. At the high school level, of the five formerly segregated white high schools in the central city, four remained open under the 1971 busing order. White students in these areas, and some of the black students who lived around them, did not ride buses across town or far out of their neighborhoods.[38]

Nashville busing brought many variations based on geographic position and racial category, but across many settings, alumni and observers worried that segregation was shifting from divisions between schools to separation within schools. Scholars have identified "second-generation segregation"— racial segregation between academic tracks within statistically desegregated schools—in school districts nationally, whether under court order for busing or not. Racist judgments about academic ability appeared at each school level. Black elementary school students like Hubert Dixon III found themselves grouped, prior to any empirical assessment of their ability, with other black peers in the lowest-level reading groups. Steve Flatt, a white student at McGavock enrolled in honors courses, recalled noticing that black and poorer white students populated the school's vocational courses. As Waverly Crenshaw transitioned from Cameron High School, where he had been an honors student, to McGavock in its first year, a guidance counselor scheduled him, without consultation, into vocational courses. Black administrators like Dr. Aldorothy Wright noticed enough cases like Crenshaw's to consider it a pattern in student placement, an observation NAACP President Dr. Charles Kimbrough shared. Dr. Wright thought the pattern resulted from a lack of black guidance counselors and embedded racism in the choices the district's primarily white guidance staff made.[39] As historians and sociologists have demonstrated in other cases—and consistent with the larger trajectory of vocational education as a cap on more than a route toward, black academic opportunity—a significant portion of black students in Nashville found themselves shunted into vocational courses without specific choice or interest.[40]

Whether families could push back against unjust tracking often turned on their own social and economic resources. Both Hubert Dixon III and Waverly Crenshaw worked their way into more fitting placements—Dixon through excelling at periodic reading tests, Crenshaw through the intervention of a family friend and teacher who helped him move into college preparatory classes. But both also remembered friends and peers who lacked the supports they enjoyed and, as Crenshaw recalled, "didn't get re-steered, and didn't go on to college." With such children in mind, Head Elementary teacher Jimmie Lash felt that "for the majority of black children, desegregation has been a setback, because too many are unfairly labeled as unable to learn."[41]

Busing provided opportunities for Nashville students, like students across the country, to create new experiences, build new relationships, and learn new lessons. Students left their desegregated high schools more familiar with peers and communities that otherwise would have remained foreign to them. Yet even if many students saw busing in more nuanced and positive terms than the crisis-minded representations of local rumor, they did not romanticize the experience. Black and white students alike acknowledged continued inequalities in the experience and the opportunities schooling provided. Segregation within schools via curricular tracking became a major theme of their experience in Nashville, as it was in desegregating schools across the country. Yet in Nashville, that tracking resulted not simply from the unjust or stereotyping choices of adults in school. It traced back to the district's, and the state's, commitment to make economic growth through the large-scale, vocationally focused comprehensive high school.

## How Vocational Education Undermined Desegregation

Five years in the making, Metro's first comprehensive high school opened in 1971. . . . Though overshadowed by the year's top news story—busing—the event with time may rank equally in terms of lasting significance for the course of public education in Metropolitan Nashville and Davidson County.

—"Capitol Schools" brochure, Metro Nashville Public Schools, 1971[42]

Since World War II, vocational education in Nashville provoked many questions: how much power schools should have, through whose guidance, and with whose consent, to steer particular children to particular careers? Vocational education in the 1970s in Nashville and Tennessee expanded in part through the desire to facilitate economic growth through worker preparation. The program and the ideas on which it rested became a significant factor in shaping—and in multiple ways, undercutting—desegregation. However, Nashville's vocational education emphasis not only facilitated the suburbanizing of Nashville's high schools, as discussed in chapter 6, shifting the burdens of desegregation onto urban black residents, but expanding vocational programs also undermined desegregation's statistical goals. The programs did so by providing mechanisms for parents and students to resist busing assignments by claiming to seek different vocational or academic offerings. Additionally, even as some educators hoped earnestly to expand individual opportunity through vocational education, the district's emphasis on designing curriculum to match labor needs helped remake inequality within and between schools by encouraging tracking by racial category, class, and gender.[43]

White parental resistance to schooling in historically black neighborhoods was often bluntly expressed, and of all the high schools in Nashville, assignments to North Nashville's Pearl generated the most audible resistance. Two hundred and twenty families in the nearly all-white inner-ring suburban neighborhoods of Green Hills and Hillsboro found themselves zoned to Pearl, and petitioned the school board for the school's outright closure. If closure was not possible, then these parents suggested that *no* student be required to attend Pearl—an arrangement likely to lead, through slow attrition, also to closure. Other white parents attacked Pearl as an "unfavorable" school for their children specifically, but left open the possibility that other children could attend it because of the "strong sense of identity" between the school and community and its history of sustaining and encouraging Nashville's black middle and professional classes.[44] In either case, Pearl's physical location mattered greatly, as both a symbol of the school's historic identification with Nashville's black community and a source of immediate physical threat. One parent explained she feared for her children's safety when she recalled the violent protests in the neighborhood in 1967: "How can we be assured they won't riot again . . . ? Would you want your grandchildren in an all black neighborhood in school if this should happen? I do not want my child there."[45] Another objected to her daughter taking cosmetology classes at Pearl rather than at a majority-white school. She worried that her white daughter would learn only how to style "black hair."[46] The condemnation of the spaces in which many black Nashvillians lived continued even into the thinking of administrators who encouraged desegregation. One described his concern over children who "lived in a confined world of asphalt."[47]

Many school districts shuttered historically black schools like Pearl to dodge the question of whether or how they would assign white students to them. Others—like Charlotte, North Carolina—kept one historically black school open and channeled appealing resources and programs there. Doing so created a statistically stable desegregated student population, although some forms of segregation emerged anew between programs within the school.[48] Nashville took a noncommittal middle path, neither closing Pearl nor redesigning it to enable desegregation.

In fact, Nashville's vocational and comprehensive education policy helped siphon students away from Pearl and undermined the school's viability. Before 1977, MNPS allowed students to request to transfer out of their assigned school when they wanted to take a course not offered at their own school but available at another. If a student attested to their great interest in "Today's Consumer I," "Diesel Mechanics," "Keypunch," "Agriculture," or a particular language course, they received a transfer to their selected school. Typically they shifted to a school with a larger population of white students. At Pearl High School, the impact of curricular transfers was dramatic. The gap between anticipated white enrollment and actual white enrollment proved large each year after 1971. Departures from public schools overall as well as departures via transfers ensured that Pearl High School never met the court-ordered minimum of 65 percent white students. In 1971–72, the school had just under a thousand students, 62.9 percent of whom were black. The roughly one-third white student population shrank over the next five years to less than a quarter by the 1976–77 school year.[49] Nearly all students who applied for curricular transfers out of Pearl were white, and nearly all their requests were granted—whether they ultimately enrolled in the course they claimed to need or not. Some parents who sent their high schoolers to Pearl, out of choice or necessity, resented the "farcical" transfers they observed other families using, knowing that other parents had "lied through their teeth" to get their children transferred.[50] Just as with other modes of resistance to busing, transferring from Pearl was more available to those with more money, as transfer students had to provide their own transportation to their new school.

After 1977, the transfer floodgates opened even wider. A provision within the Comprehensive Vocational Education Act of 1973 promised that by 1977 all students in the state would have access to a comprehensive high school. Students who were zoned for traditional, noncomprehensive high schools (and in Nashville, Pearl carried this designation even though it had offered both academic and vocational courses for generations) had an option to transfer to a comprehensive high school. In 1977–78, 90 percent of transfer requests out of Pearl were approved, and the student population went from 24.2 percent white to 16.9 percent. The next year, the district granted 98 percent of transfer applications, leaving Pearl with a 3.6 percent white student population. Pearl was the most dramatic example, but other central-city, noncomprehensive schools with black student proportions above the 35 percent court-specified ratio similarly saw many transfer requests from white students.[51] At Pearl, vocational and comprehensive education thus became more than an affirmative curricular feature. It became a means for many white students to avoid desegregation.

As vocational education facilitated suburban school construction and created routes for students and families to avoid or manipulate busing, it had immediate impact on the students who took vocational classes in areas ranging from air-conditioning repair to child care, drafting to cooking. Although justified at the state legislature with promises that ready workers would spark economic growth, at the local level, Nashville's vocational programs struggled to meet the more modest promise of preparing students for available careers. When vocational education did translate to employment opportunity, it did so differently for black students than for white students, girls than for boys. Teachers and counselors worked to match students and courses to a broader (and still substantially segregated) labor market over which schools had no control, despite the grand claims of vocational and economic growth advocates.

Unlike Vivian Henderson's early-1960s advocacy for targeted training in semiskilled fields to expand black employment opportunity, the 1970s vocational push had a much less developed view of the distribution of economic opportunity or the reshaping of patterns of labor market inequality. Instead, it partook of a more generalizing trend—emerging in the 1960s-era War on Poverty programs but still powerful since—to "educationalize" poverty: to see in training (rather than more fundamental interventions in the economy) the path to employment and poverty reduction. Shaping schooling in this way found many adherents, as the broad support for the CVEA had demonstrated. In practice, many black educators as well as their white colleagues supported vocational education, identifying labor market preparation as an acceptable aim of schooling: one that worked within a flawed labor market, yet at times did open opportunity for some students.[52]

At the state level, the CVEA facilitated an expansion in the number of students taking vocational classes—doubling the number of participating students over the 1970s. At Nashville's McGavock, over 50 percent of the student body took at least one vocational class. Local observers noticed over-assignment of black students to vocational education. Tracing the specific demographics of vocational classes, at the local and school level, is difficult given limited extant data. State-level data, as well as sources like school yearbooks, can offer suggestive patterns. Across Tennessee, black students were somewhat over-enrolled in vocational courses in comparison to their proportion of the state's population (22 percent of vocational enrollees versus 15.8 percent of the state population).[53] While over-enrollment concerned some observers, it might have pleased others who wanted vocational education to target poor and/or black students previously underserved by workforce programs.[54]

For some students, simply being in—or out of—vocational education in general had consequences for how they understood their high school education or themselves. Yet other important designations *within* vocational education also shaped opportunity. Which particular vocational courses were taken by which students, and then how well these courses did or did not match actual labor demand, remained key determinants in whether vocational education expanded or restricted opportunity.

Agreement about workforce preparation as an educational good came more easily than success at actually meeting the demands of a changing labor market. This challenge had bedeviled American vocational education throughout the twentieth century. Meeting it became even more difficult amid a sharply gender-divided labor market. The state act transformed what kinds of courses students took, moving students toward more current trades, industries, and office occupations courses and away from the long-held attachment to agricultural courses as the sector waned. As the volume and distribution of vocational courses in the state changed significantly, historic gender divisions remained. Trades and industries courses—and particularly the "dirty shop" classes pro-industrial growth legislators had envisaged when they proposed the CVEA—remained overwhelmingly male. Office occupations, by contrast, as well as the smaller fields of health occupations and occupational home economics, remained heavily female. Gender divides reinforced damaging stereotypes about women and work, but they also served to position women to benefit more from vocational education at this moment than men, given that traditionally female offerings were more likely to point to growing sectors of the economy.[55]

Local vocational educators noticed as early as the mid-1960s that their male students had more difficulty finding work than did female students, a pattern only reinforced by the decline of the manufacturing sector strongly apparent by the 1970 census.[56] Male students placed in vocational education courses—by their own choice or someone else's—were not only tracked away from professional paths, but were more likely to learn skills without long-term economic value. By contrast, girls in office occupations classes (and the smaller number in health occupations courses) were learning skills for which demand was steadily climbing. Although the public rhetoric of vocational education, in Tennessee and elsewhere, highlighted industrial (usually male) work, most job growth in Nashville was in clerical and service fields, where female workers predominated.[57]

A labor market producing more opportunities for female workers than male created a conundrum for vocational educators. If educators respected conventional gender divisions, they set the stage for vocational education to benefit female workers more than their male counterparts, with courses for women in growing fields and courses for men in less promising ones. If they chose to challenge the link between female employment and clerical work, it meant a likely uncomfortable confrontation with the deeply held expectations of educators whose own career trajectories followed the male-industrial/female-clerical divide, and students and families who shared conventional expectations. Nashville's vocational educators chose the former path.

7.7. Vocational education, McGavock High School, 1976. From McGavock yearbook.

Within vocational programs that positioned women better than men, black women had particular opportunities to benefit. As Michael Katz and colleagues have documented in their study of the divide between black men and women in employment and life course in the post–World War II decades, the timing of each group's transition out of the agricultural labor sector and into others determined their success or failure.[58] Vocational education offered black women training for office jobs not only as the demand for these skills was growing, but also as hiring patterns became less discriminatory against black applicants. Governor Frank Clement publicly celebrated a state initiative to hire more "Negroes" in state government, increasing their number by 1,200 by 1965.[59] By the late 1970s, only 10 percent of clerical workers in Nashville were black, but the sector overall was growing while local business leaders who supported job training programs also identified new opportunities. Clerical and office occupations courses had long been available to students in Nashville's segregated black high schools, however, so access to these jobs was not an immediate product of desegregation.[60]

Geographic space also figured in making vocational training more productive for Nashville women, in ways that were largely consistent with the experience of those in cities from New York to Detroit. Newly trained clerical workers could seek positions in the finance and insurance offices that remained concentrated downtown. As a state capital, Nashville's downtown also included state and municipal offices. Public transit routes served the central business district and nearby areas of low-income housing. In contrast, by the late 1960s much of the male-employing manufacturing base of the city had relocated to suburban sites, often poorly served by public transportation.[61] This shift compounded earlier-established difficulty male vocational graduates had in gaining placement, especially in manufacturing and unionized trades, immediately after high school.[62]

Black men, who continued to face steep barriers to entry in manufacturing, found relatively more success in public sector employment, particu-

7.8. Vocational education, McGavock High School, 1975. From McGavock yearbook.

larly with the municipal government, which employed black workers at a rate much closer to their proportion of the Metro population. McGavock High School teacher Milton Harris recalled, for example, a pathway from the school's "trowel trades" or bricklaying courses to municipal employment.[63] Examples like this encouraged many black teachers and vocational educators as well as their white colleagues to remain supporters of vocational education.

If vocational education sorted students by gender, additional divisions between high- and low-skill trades compounded discrimination. High-skill courses served more white students, while black students were more likely to participate in lower-skilled courses. School yearbook photographs—one of the few remaining sources of demographic information on vocational course taking at the school level—indicate that most black students in Nashville vocational classes participated not in the higher-skill classes like computers, office occupations, or electronics, but in lower-skilled options including home economics, commercial foods, and the like. Clubs and classes focused on the traditionally female and lower-status fields grouped under home economics usually had a majority of black students, while black girls represented only one-third of the school population.[64] State-level vocational education statistics use the hybrid category of "disadvantaged" students—by minority racial status *or* class. Within these limits, they too indicate proportionally higher enrollment of disadvantaged students in lower-status service occupations than in office occupations.[65]

Thus Nashville's vocational enrollment may offer a story of segregation by class within a pattern of segregation by race and gender. The existing data suggest that African American students were more likely to take vocational classes than their white peers; the girls among them were more likely to take courses in traditionally female fields including office occupations and home economics–related domains, and the poorer of these girls were more likely to take occupational home economics (distinguished from regular home economics, as it targeted (often poorly) paid work in service in a private home). By contrast, office occupations courses increasingly opened routes to mobility due to historic and geographic factors. Some enterprising teachers worked individually to open employment opportunities for students within cooperative vocational education. A longtime vocational teacher at Pearl High School recalled going business to business in downtown Nashville seeking cooperative employment placement for his students, finding success at businesses as varied as the *Banner* newspaper, Baptist Hospital, and the local electric utility.[66] Even as some students benefited from some strands of vocational education, the vocational education emphasis within the structure and operation of high schools in Nashville remained a very limited tool for mobility or equality, and more frequently a venue for the remaking of inequality.

If vocational courses as they were carried out in Nashville reproduced rather than challenged stratification by class and race, institutional forces—like guidance counselors' roles in initiating course assignments—may not have been the only cause. Some patterns in vocational course taking may have stemmed from individual student and family preference. Student awareness of the segregated occupational landscape might have played a part as well. James Anderson's study of earlier periods in black vocational education noted that black students were aware in the early twentieth century that training in the trades would not overcome racism in hiring, leaving them reluctant to participate.[67] Such an awareness may have influenced students' notions of future careers into the 1970s, making it reasonable to choose lower-skilled courses like occupational home economics or commercial foods over higher-skilled ones in office occupations, electricity, or air-conditioning repair.[68]

As observed by both students and those who kept an eye on the system overall, guidance counselors made frontline academic placement decisions and at times contributed to tracking students by skin color more than actual interest or ability. But the forces favoring tracking were much broader. MNPS, having taken up a leading position in the expansion of vocational offerings and comprehensive high schools in Tennessee, set for itself the core task of preparing students for the local labor market. Whether Nashville educators channeled students into vocational courses equitably or not, their work to link students to employment always ran up against the firm reality that the local labor market remained highly unequal and unjust, with continued evidence of active discrimination in several sectors and very high unemployment rates for black men.[69]

Just as these inequalities in vocational education's functioning matter, so too do the program's overall limitations. As Governor Dunn may have worried when he tried to slow the funding of the CVEA, the expansion of vocational education in Nashville often replicated old-economy needs rather than met new demands. As Nashville administrator, and later superintendent, Charles Frazier recalled, vocational "educators led by memory," retaining a focus on older trades. In even more egregious cases, spaces planned for vocational education sat unused, new equipment still crated.[70] Even when unrealized, though, the district's and state's vocational education emphasis made ample marks on Nashville students' experience via school expansion and student transfers.

Even as it originated in efforts to serve white workers, visible in both Representative Fulton's 1971 plans and the local designs for McGavock High School, vocational education developed in ways that made it a significant force in the high schooling of black students in Nashville. Emphasizing students as future workers, when the surrounding labor market continued to segregate and limit labor opportunity by skin color, reinforced long-standing segregationist ideas even in desegregation's peak years. Vocational programs authorized teachers and school workers beyond the vocational track to make decisions about students based on judgments about the future, without safeguards to prevent unfair sorting and tracking of black and poor students in school-level practice. Nashville's vocational education story demonstrates the persistent and growing emphasis on schooling as worker preparation, and the many limitations and troubles of this emphasis. In Nashville, vocational education helped remake inequality in the era of desegregation.[71]

## "White Flight" and Images of the Metropolis

Students and families understood and narrated busing through their own immediate experiences, collectively recognizing both the accomplishments and difficult costs that came with desegregation and the policy choices that accompanied it, like Nashville's emphasis on vocational education and comprehensive high schools. Individual and family stories about busing were varied and complex, and shaped by multiple and quietly moving bureaucratic processes. Yet in public conversation, a more monolithic narrative about desegregation became increasingly audible in public discourse in Nashville and nationally over the 1970s. The narrative of "white flight" dominated the public story of desegregation, reinforced in national scholarly and political discourse, media coverage, and the comments of school leaders. It had roots in real and visible changes under way in Metro Nashville Public Schools, but it distorted a multifaceted reality, making one part of the busing story seem to be the whole. "White flight" anchored an understanding of desegregation that privileged white resistance and displaced attention from black families' and students' experiences, even at times rendering these families and children invisible. It allowed the story of busing to be dominated by the minority that refused to participate in desegregation rather than the majority that did.[72] The narrative of white flight helped remake inequality amid desegregation.

Together the courts, federal officials, and local administrators (sometimes with the aid of state vocational education dollars) defined busing to limit its impact on white suburban families. Yet white suburban families still resisted even the busing plan crafted to ease their participation. Approximately 18 percent of the white students enrolled in MNPS left the system—either by moving out of the county or choosing to attend private schools—in the first year of busing.[73] Political scientists Richard Pride and David Woodward studied patterns of white flight in Nashville and argued that while "some of these students would have left under normal outmigration, . . . it is clear that most left because of busing."[74]

Pride and Woodward identified patterns in departures by student age, showing that the particular shape of Nashville's busing plan influenced the specific form of withdrawal. White students in grades 1 through 4 who attended suburban schools close to home were relatively less likely to leave their schools. For fifth and sixth grade, however, the busing plan assigned two-thirds of the district's suburban white students to schools in central-city, historically black neighborhoods. At this transition point, the rate of white departures was "staggering." In the schools that were zoned to send students to North Nashville's Wharton Elementary School in grades 5 through 6, 49 percent of assigned white students left.[75] Pride and Woodward found that the key variables in determining white departures were assignments of white children to historically black neighborhoods and the wealth of the white families involved; at the high school level, when most schools were in suburban locations, white departures tracked the percentage of black students at these schools.[76]

The same pattern of white students' departures from public schools continued beyond the first year. In 1969, 9 percent of Nashville first graders were in private schools; by 1979, this number was at 20 percent, a figure that would have been even higher if measured as a proportion of white first graders, and even higher as a portion of white middle- or upper-class first graders.[77] White parents exercised a range of options in removing their children from MNPS schools, by moving to the outer reaches of the county exempted from busing; moving outside of the county line, enrolling in private schools; seeking (and usually winning) transfer out of a particular school on claims of curricular interest or hardship; or, less frequently, sending their children to live with relatives in other districts or even states.[78]

Massive shifts in enrollment destabilized MNPS's funding base by shrinking state and federal payments calculated on the basis of student population. But when local (as well as national) discourse portrayed these shifts as the result of white flight prompted by desegregation, it oversimplified the actual nature of the changes under way in two ways. First, it emphasized white mobility to the neglect of both black students' mobility and persistence in the school system and furthered the district's historic difficulty recognizing the presence of black students in urban neighborhoods. Second, it depicted all demographic changes in the district as a reaction to desegregation, when in fact the district, like so many others nationally, saw enrollment declines in part via the 1970s-era "baby bust."[79]

Over the 1970s, MNPS administrators observed significant over-enrollment and crowding in schools in the areas of the county exempted from busing by the 1971 order. This pattern, combined with under-enrollment in schools in central-city neighborhoods, seemed to reinforce the long-held idea of urban population loss and suburban growth. Census figures from 1980 show that the population of city-dwelling, school-age white and black children fell dramatically over the 1970s. The tracts that comprised the former City of Nashville—the most urban sections of the county—saw the number of white five- to fourteen-year-olds in the city shrink by 43.1 percent, while the number of black children in the same age category lost 34.4 percent, in part a result of opening opportunities for suburban migration. For white children, the 1970s continued the steep slide of the previous decade. For black children, however, the previous decade of the 1960s had produced such great growth that the 1970s decrease returned the population only to its 1960 levels. The decline was dramatic, surely, but there remained more than 18,000 children in Nashville's urban center, more than half of them black students. As with earlier city planning practices, emphasizing decline as a result of desegregation worked to obscure the presence of these students.

The white flight narrative highlighted enrollment declines and overshadowed other demographic trends of the late 1960s and 1970s that proved consequential for school district enrollment. Although schools in the outlying areas of the county experienced overcrowding, the county and the city both were part of a broader decline in school-age population. The county's overall school-age population fell by 25 percent over the 1970s, the same decade when the post–baby boom lull in birthrates led to a roughly 13 percent fall in that age cohort across the nation. US birthrates reached their slowest post–World War II rate in 1973, producing marked decline in the school-age population overall—not only the number in public schools, or the number of white children in public schools.[80] This population loss county-wide meant that even as the old city lost large numbers of students, the relative decline in the city as compared to the county was not as sharp as images of white flight and suburban overpopulation suggested.

The most dramatic and visible explanation for changing enrollment in MNPS over the 1970s was white withdrawal in protest over busing, and

Table 7.1 Nashville School-Age Population, 1970 and 1980

A. School-Age Population in Previous City of Nashville Areas, 1970–1980, by Census Racial Category

| | White 5- to 14-year-olds | Percentage change over the previous decade | Black and other 5- to 14-year-olds | Percentage change over the previous decade | Total city 5- to 14-year-olds | Percentage change over the previous decade |
|---|---|---|---|---|---|---|
| 1970 | 12,754 | −20.3% | 16,431 | 42.5% | 29,185 | 6.0% |
| 1980 | 7,251 | −43.1% | 10,774 | −34.4% | 18,115 | −37.9% |

B. School-Age Population in Previous City of Nashville Areas vs. Davidson County Outside of Previous City of Nashville Areas

| | City 5- to 14-year-olds | Non-city 5- to 14-year-olds | Total 5- to 14-year-olds | City 5- to 14-year-olds (as percentage of total) |
|---|---|---|---|---|
| 1970 | 29,185 | 57,160 | 86,345 | 33.8% |
| 1980 | 18,115 | 40,276 | 58,391 | 31.0% |

Note: Census racial categorizations change over time. Here I use the label "Black and other" to represent what the census labels "Nonwhite," "Black and Other," or "Black," "Hispanic," "American Indian," and "Asian and Pacific Islander." I use children ages five to fourteen to measure school-age population, despite its exclusion of older students, as it allows for consistent measure across all four decades in the census. Using school-age population rather than school enrollment leaves out the impact of departures from the public school system.

Source: US Census, via NHGIS, http://www.nhgis.org.

such withdrawal comprised a significant proportion of the district's enrollment loss. Yet that loss was exacerbated by a shrinking cohort of school-age children in Nashville and nationally. For a school district managing school buildings with too few students and too many expenses, the pressures of both kinds of enrollment loss mattered, even as only the former garnered the most attention. Even without desegregation, districts faced significant contraction after two decades of rapid growth.

Amid this complex reality—and just as they had in the years in which local educators and federal planners worked out Nashville's busing plan— the Metropolitan Planning Commission produced maps that tried to represent and simplify their area's demographic reality. Their representations showed student population in ways that visually minimized the presence of central-city students. Their maps tried to reckon with not only the changing school-age population, but changing participation in public schools within that population. In 1977 planners mapped each planning unit by proportion of public school students. The first clear message of their map was of the new and large concentrations of school-age children in areas just outside the boundaries of the 1971 busing plan. In the county's southwest and east, low proportions of public school students on the inside of the boundary contrasted clearly with high proportions just outside of it. The map offered clear evidence that the particular shape of the 1971 busing order had influenced residential out-migration—an argument white neighborhood activists just inside the border had been making since the early 1970s, and one that the school board began to make in late-1970s discussions of revising busing.[81] Yet the map also helped highlight other dense populations of public school students, including in a high-growth corridor running from north of downtown to the edge of the county in areas included in as well as exempted from the court order, containing both black and white suburban development. These areas all had between 23.1 and 43.8 public school students per one hundred residents, while the county average was 15.5. Central-city planning units that included significant proportions of black families in both public and private housing also remained densely concentrated with public school students.[82] The cartography of these maps—showing students as a proportion of the overall population, rather than in absolute terms—did not convey fully the particularly dense population of black students in the urban core.

City planners also represented the metropolitan landscape in ways that accorded with the white flight narrative and white families' rejection of urban and racialized black space. Continuing to describe and categorize urban space as they had for decades, the Metropolitan Planning Commission mapped their city according to "social types." City planners segmented the metropolitan landscape by describing, and judging, the people who lived there.[83] Using 1970 census data on educational level, race, overcrowded housing, and age, planners demarcated geographic areas of the city whose residents shared common characteristics along these variables—recasting in a new form the familiar "planning unit" structure of the 1950s and 1960s. The resulting multicolor maps divided Davidson County into twelve designated "social types," ranging from "Type 1: white, high income, middle and late childrearing families" to "Type 11: mobile, black, low income nonfamily," passing through "Type 7: racially mixed, middle-income, mixed family and nonfamily."[84]

The use of "family" or "nonfamily" as a geographic descriptor was new for the Metropolitan Planning Commission, and created descriptions of space that were both full of distortions and easy to apply to the question of where schools should or should not be. Of the three "social types" identified for black neighborhoods, two were categorized as "nonfamily," and the other "mixed family/nonfamily." Nonetheless, areas with high proportions of black residents had high percentages of overcrowded homes, single-mother-headed households, and a low median age—characteristics that point to the presence of families. In sum, the MPC labeled nearly half of Nashville's black, urban neighborhoods as "nonfamily," in spite of the presence there of thousands of school-age children.[85] In creating a language in which urban areas did not house "families," planners built an additional justification for educational neglect—by other families, or by school policy—of these areas.[86]

In a more generous reading, MPC efforts to divide and categorize metropolitan space came from an effort to identify who lived where, and to design facilities and programs accordingly. As demonstrated by Charles S. Johnson's earlier work in Nashville, or W. E. B. DuBois's in Philadelphia, mapping projects worked with these aims as well as more manipulative or segregationist ones. In court in 1970, planning officials took pains to explain that "race was not a consideration" in their use of planning units or other geographic categories built off of them. Yet they also acknowledged that planning units had been determined "some time ago," and it was unclear what steps, if any, the MPC had taken to disentangle the planning unit technology from this past. Instead, planning unit maps continued to be the background for school zoning and desegregation planning into the late 1970s.[87]

School officials and planning colleagues continued to think of suburban (and often racialized white) spaces as the most appropriate site for schools, and their representations of metropolitan space conveyed this bias. MNPS policies continued to favor suburban construction in an effort to make public schools attractive to those families who had left, or who were most likely to leave. In practice, the consequence was that more black students, and especially poorer black students, would travel farther and for more years, as many of their local schools closed. Until a new round of legal debates opened in *Kelley* in the late 1970s, the board's white majority continued to ignore black community leaders' complaints about unequal busing and calls for more equitable approaches coming from and on behalf of the increasingly class-segregated population of black students in central-city Nashville. Local advocates who wanted a more equal busing plan—one that would rely on schools in central-city neighborhoods as well as the suburbs—had not only to overcome the power of white suburban parents and their allies, but to recover the presence of black children in segregated black neighborhoods.

From HEW's planning to ongoing discussions between the planning commission and the school board over the 1970s about where students were and where schools should be, the official processes that configured busing rendered black students placeless. Not only was their claim on close-to-home schooling weaker as implied by the shape of the busing plan itself, but professionals' cognitive maps of the city continued to diminish or obscure the presence of these children. Busing became a continuation of earlier decades' urban renewal and highway construction decisions that stripped away black residential or commercial areas, authorizing kinds of expropriation and dislocation not expected for white residents.

The powerful local and national narrative of white flight simplified and exaggerated significant demographic shifts under way in the first decade of busing. For some observers, the white flight story served as a call to make desegregation more politically palatable for white families. But it was also just the sort of argument that local activist Eugene TeSelle feared: that "white suburbanites" who had the means to flee the system would "count for more" than city residents, black or white, "who may not have the means—or the will—to desert the public schools." Multiple layers of public rhetoric and planning representations continued to prioritize those white suburbanites over the district's consistent constituents in central-city neighborhoods.[88]

### Conclusion

Roughly 60,000 students continued in Nashville's schools by the late 1970s. These students learned from busing, at times in ways that helped them to bridge previously wide social gaps. And yet they learned as well how busing created new patterns of inequality within schools, or highlighted old ones, as students both black and white noticed disparate burdens for black students and disparate access to academic opportunities inside schools. What might they have said about how statistical desegregation and educational equality related to one another, or could relate?

In the somewhat crisis-minded and still deeply resistant public discourse about busing for desegregation in Nashville in the 1970s, that question was rarely engaged fully. Instead, narratives like white flight displaced attention from the compound set of inequalities at work, as well as from the clear opportunities and benefits of desegregation even imperfectly practiced.

For high school–age students in Nashville, most of whom attended the district's comprehensive high schools, vocational education defined their school's scale, location, and its physical design, even for students who did not participate in the vocational program. The district's emphasis on vocational education as a core aspect of the curricular organization of schooling worked to encourage schools to categorize students based on presumed life course, opening the way for compound inequalities along lines of race, class, and gender. The vocational emphasis, and the comprehensive high school model and economic-growth logic that supported it, diverted attention from the problem of remaking equality of opportunity within desegregating schools.

# CHAPTER EIGHT

# Busing Renegotiated

At the end of the 1970s and the early 1980s, Avon Williams, his colleagues, and the plaintiffs on the one side, and the Metro Nashville Public Schools staff and board majority on the other understood the district's desegregation accomplishments and challenges in fundamentally different ways. The school board's majority saw declines in white enrollment, which they perceived as their chief threat. They pushed to expand busing throughout the county, to preserve the statistical desegregation that they took as the chief measure of compliance with legal requirements and as a default indicator of equality of educational opportunity. Williams as well as new participants in the *Kelley* litigation took a different message from Nashville's first years of busing. They felt that the district's historic emphasis on statistical desegregation represented a too-thin notion of educational equality and came with costs greater than Williams and the plaintiffs wanted to bear. They sought not to end active desegregation, but to revise it toward more robust equality—valuing desegregation, black communities and their schools, and measures not just of student presence, but of student experience at school. The gap between statistical desegregation and equality of educational opportunity had become great enough to prompt a thorough reexamination on the part even of busing's historic supporters. As Williams's position on desegregation in practice evolved, he tested the bonds that tied local cases like Nashville's to national desegregation strategy as led by the NAACP Legal Defense Fund.

From the late 1970s through the early 1980s, Nashville saw five years of intensive litigation and public discussion of desegregation. The result, after another round of appeals all the way to the Supreme Court, was the 1983 expansion of busing for desegregation to reach all of Davidson County, incorporating Nashville's outlying suburbs for the first time and producing levels of statistical desegregation throughout the county well beyond that achieved in most districts nationally.[1] Yet extensive debate about how statistical desegregation related to educational equality made only modest marks on the shape of Nashville's new desegregation plan. In many respects, the 1983 plan continued the 1971 model. In the legal process leading up to the 1983 plan, school board representatives, attorneys, and community members framed the basic critiques that later guided the way to the end of active desegregation.

Nashville's local debates reflected a broader transformation under way in national civil rights discourse. Neither in Nashville nor nationally had there existed anything approaching unanimity on civil rights strategies or the problem of school segregation among African Americans. Yet by the late 1970s, several onetime desegregation advocates became its critics. Most famously, Derrick Bell argued in his interest-convergence theory that desegregation had served the interests of white people more than black people.[2] In many cities, the late 1960s and 1970s brought increasingly stark divisions between those who saw different routes to educational equality. These splits often accompanied increased interest in self-determination, nationalism, or community control. Brooklyn and Harlem activists pressed for highly local school governance known as community control, in part propelled by frustration at limited progress on desegregation.[3] In Milwaukee, black power–minded leaders fought against desegregation advocates to preserve two Milwaukee high schools in black neighborhoods.[4] In Atlanta, poor and working-class black women pushed for busing but lost to a biracial male coalition that favored substituting a black majority in the school district's leadership for desegregation of students.[5]

In Nashville, desegregation was not only debated or rejected in the abstract, as in Atlanta, Chicago, and elsewhere, or rejected by the courts, as in Detroit and Richmond.[6] Extensive desegregation happened, and through practice, ideas about desegregation changed. The experience of busing over the 1970s moved even the city's most ardent desegregation advocates at least to question how important statistical desegregation was in the pursuit of educational equality. They asked what alternatives existed when desegregation meant a spatial organization of schooling that privileged some communities and punished others; they at times reimagined curriculum in relationship to desegregation. It was the experience of busing in practice more than shifts in the rhetorical and political currents that prompted this reconsideration. No full-throated community control movement ever took shape in Nashville, where, contemporary observers agreed, the combination of white-majority, pro-suburban metropolitan politics and the centrality of school-system employment in the communities that produced Nashville's black leadership mitigated against its development.[7] With an eye more to local realities than national debates, Nashvillians evaluated what they had learned from busing, what narratives they would deploy in making sense of their experience, and how statistical desegregation did—or did not necessarily—foster educational equality.

## *Kelley* Back to Court: Public Debates over Desegregation and Equality

Avon Williams had long criticized the "punitive" nature of desegregation in Nashville and spoke of busing's burdens in terms of hours per day and years on the bus.[8] However, it was the possibility of closing Nashville's first and most distinguished black high school, Pearl, that cut especially close to the quick for a broad swath of black Nashville leaders. District enrollments declined over the 1970s, yet Nashville built thousands of new seats in expanded suburban comprehensive high schools. As a new set of comprehensive high schools neared completion in 1977, the board confronted the question of where the students to populate these schools would come from. One school board member put it simply: "[If] we build the schools we should send students to them."[9] To be filled anywhere near capacity (and desegregation targets), these suburban schools needed to pull students out of the remaining smaller, often strongly community-identified high schools in both black and white urban neighborhoods and a few white rural areas as well. The possibility of these closures animated much of the debate over desegregation's next phase.

In late 1976, the first hints emerged that the school board was reorganizing high schools and planning to close North Nashville's Pearl. The head of the local NAACP, Charles Kimbrough, and Rev. Amos Jones of the Interdenominational Ministers' Fellowship (IMF) appeared before the board to speak on behalf of the school. The IMF's Social Action Committee "condemn[ed] the current . . . plans as racist."[10] The IMF's charges had two prongs: first, that black city residents had borne disproportionately the difficulties of busing, including the travel and inconvenience and the inability to participate in extracurricular activities at schools distant from home. Second, they faced as well the costs of entering "hostile, sterile academic environments which negate" students' efforts and "alienate them from learning in general," forming a "racist pattern of psychologic, sociologic, and academic deprivation and destruction."[11] Without reference to the 1950s-era planning discourse that had earlier identified the loss of a school as a blighting factor in a community, the IMF leaders conveyed the same concern. The alliance of ministers emphasized as well how important schools were to communities, and thus how much "their absence" reflected the communities' "social disorganization."[12] Rev. Lester Stone read a clear message in Nashville's suburban school plan: "Putting high schools in suburbia suggests that education can't take place in the inner city, and I refuse to believe that."[13]

Concerns about Pearl flowed back to other historic injustices and losses for North Nashville as well. Referencing the previous damage done by the construction of Interstate 40 through the neighborhood's center, closing Pearl promised to be a "coup de grace" for a community that had already suffered extensively. A longtime teacher in Nashville schools described North Nashville's residents as "a group of people who suddenly find that everything that was once of great importance to them has gradually been eroded." With Pearl threatened, "What kind of pride can these good citizens have?"[14] Pearl felt like one of the last outposts of a North Nashville many of these middle-class community leaders remembered fondly, and one they defended vociferously against a deep history of calculated neglect and destruction brought by highway construction and urban renewal projects. The Jefferson Street business district had been twice severed by Interstate 40, one arm of which separated Fisk University from Tennessee State. The original First Baptist Church-Capitol Hill—spiritual home to many Nashville activists and the site of meetings to support the Nashville student sit-ins and other protest movements in the 1960s—fell to urban renewal in 1972. Pearl stood for a story of black Nashville that local development projects systematically stripped from the local landscape.

Over the next several years, local ministers, NAACP leaders, and representatives of the school's alumni appeared before the board to make their case.[15] For Pearl advocates, the closure of the symbolically important school was at the center of thinking about busing. When the school board proposed new uses for Pearl's historic building—as an adult education center, or as a facility for pregnant students, or for recent immigrants, or dropouts, or later, as an academic magnet—all defined the school away from its history of offering a comprehensive education for students headed to Tennessee State, Fisk, and local trades.[16]

It was the activism of Rev. Jones and others that "prodded" the *Kelley* plaintiffs to reengage with the case and push for alterations in the district's approach to busing.[17] North Nashville's churches had provided local leadership for decades. Yet the prominence of ministers in this fight made particular sense. The IMF membership included several churches, including

Jones's, located in North Nashville. If the community lost Pearl, it would be even harder for city churches to keep their communities vital amid the outgoing tide of working- and middle-class black families moving to the suburbs in the 1970s.

Some voices on the school board (and likely in the school administration) felt they could dismiss arguments for Pearl as rosy nostalgia: "People tend to look at things as they were in the past and not what they will be in the future," board chair L. C. Biggs opined.[18] Yet Pearl advocates also defended their school by suggesting that it be retooled and reinvented. Even as they celebrated aspects of the school's past, they imagined a different, if still related, future. IMF representatives had suggested that Pearl become a magnet school, drawing students not only from the neighborhood zone but throughout the district to programs in advanced languages and communications, fine and performing arts, health occupations, and/or community education.[19] The plans—particularly the most developed ones emphasizing health care—contained within them the same red flags for restricted opportunity visible in earlier phases of vocational training at Pearl. In the proposals for a health sciences magnet, for example, the proposed jobs were relatively low-skilled and poorly paid positions, such as "institutional home aides" or child care workers—ones often available without a targeted training program.[20] Although many IMF members were likely aware of the potential downfalls of such programs, they had incentive to be supportive. As the school board and Metropolitan Planning Commission demonstrated that there was no aggregate need for new high school seats in Nashville, given trends in both births and public school participation, they knew that "strictly based on the need for classroom space, this school may not be necessary at all."[21] A new curricular approach offered a basis from which to argue for the school's existence, as numbers alone did not.

Busing remained court ordered in Nashville throughout the 1970s, but the district lacked actual court supervision from 1973 to 1978. In 1973, when Judge Morton recused himself under pressure from Mayor Beverly Briley, the case moved to the docket of Judge Frank Gray, who soon became seriously ill and died in 1978. President Jimmy Carter appointed Judge Thomas A. Wiseman to replace Gray. Wiseman assumed the post in August 1978, where *Kelley* sat waiting for him. A native of the small town of Tullahoma, Tennessee, Wiseman made his career in Nashville and lived there with his wife and children, who were students in the Metropolitan Nashville Public Schools during desegregation. Wiseman brought political savvy to the case, having served as Tennessee's secretary of the treasury and competed for the Democratic nomination for governor in 1974.[22]

Once Wiseman was on the bench, Avon Williams re-initiated motions filed earlier, reprising his 1976 arguments that the school district should be held in contempt for violations of the 1971 court order. In a hot Tennessee summer, Judge Wiseman heard testimony on *Kelley's* long history and its current state, on a range of issues from school construction to student transfers. By the end of the summer, without waiting to compile a written order, Wiseman made a few rulings from the bench. He instructed the school district to end the transfer policies that facilitated white students' exodus from Pearl High School and thus undercut the school's chances of maintaining anything approaching the court's statistical desegregation targets. Wiseman also ruled that exempting thirty-three suburban schools from the 1971 order had produced white flight and resegregation. As those patterns resulted from the shape of desegregation policy, Wiseman labeled the results "a De Jure segregation." In light of these findings, a "complete reexamination of the remedy fashioned in 1971" was needed, one that would cover the whole of Davidson County.[23] When he called for a countywide desegregation plan, Wiseman wanted the board to start from scratch, assuming no aspects of the 1971 plan or later school board proposals.

Judge Morton's courtroom doors, locked against the large and disruptive anti-busing crowd in the spring of 1971, symbolized judicial oversight at a great remove from the community. Judge Gray's work in *Kelley* had been defined by inaction. By contrast, Judge Wiseman assertively encouraged public input and debate. Wiseman remarked, in comments widely disseminated in the local press, that the matter "deserve[d] the best efforts at resolution that can be mustered by everyone concerned."[24] This call prompted an outpouring of letters, plans, and appeals, in addition to the school district's public hearings in November 1979 and the contributions of dozens of witnesses in extensive court proceedings from 1979 through 1981. The flood of opinion and suggested solutions highlighted both the very broad range of concerns about busing and a fundamental lack of consensus about what the relationship between desegregation and educational equality was, or more simply put, what desegregation was for.

The terms in which Nashville residents expressed opposition to busing in 1979 and 1980 were many and varied. Public discourse had in some respects evolved from the era of Casey Jenkins's Concerned Parents Association protests in Nashville, although some themes persisted. References to government overreach and encroaching communism continued. So did claims that exclusive suburban schools, like exclusive suburban homes, were the product of individual hard work and merit, devoid of any policy influence or privilege.[25] A single mother wrote from suburban Goodletts-ville to explain that she had "paid to get out of the inner-city so my child could have a better environment. . . . There is no way that I am going to let my child be bused back in to what I just left."[26]

Many writers, often women, spoke of busing as a threat to their family unity and domestic economy, in both senses of the term. One mother first excused herself as "maybe . . . 'just a dumb housewife'" before explaining, "Sending my children to school with blacks doesn't bother me or my children," but that extensive time on buses meant a violation of her "right to be with her family."[27] Another mother described busing as one of several forces that were working to "pull the family apart."[28] Frequently, these fuel-shortage-era Americans juxtaposed uses of gas for busing with their own efforts to economize at home, and targeted busing as both socially and economically misguided.[29]

Other complaints specifically targeted the design of Nashville's busing plan, which exempted the most distant suburbs and made transfer requests ready routes of exit. Students wrote in to express their frustration with fre-quent reassignments that disrupted friendships, added to the already high number of schools a student attended over their career, or made it impos-sible to attend school with siblings. With exemptions available to some residents and not others, a few letter writers called not for less busing, but for fairer busing—which they defined as fairness for all white families. As one citizen put it, "If we are going to have forced integration at all then should it not be as Universal in the US as possible?"[30] PTA leaders from a suburban school within the boundaries of the initial busing area described the need to share the burdens of busing equally across all suburbs, or, as another writer put it, for all "to share" in providing a white student popu-lation for Pearl.[31]

Sitting as it did at the powerful nexus of ideas about family, future, and property, busing drew criticism from many angles. Powerful evidence in support of busing would have been needed to counter such criticism, yet evidence of any sort was often absent from debates about desegregation in Nashville. How desegregation had benefited Nashville students received much less attention in letters to Judge Wiseman, as well as in court pro-ceedings. At the request of the school board, Vanderbilt professor Richard Pride compiled an analysis of student test scores since 1971. His results showed that, in keeping with national trends in this period of extensive desegregation, Nashville's African American students had improved in both reading and math during the 1970s, and that white students had made modest gains but, despite the tenor of public complaint, had not slid. Busing had not cost white students in terms of test score–measured achievement, and had helped black students—points rarely conveyed in public rhetoric about busing. If achievement-related evidence was present, the accounts of social learning that Nashville students like Steve Flatt and Charles Davis had valued in their years at McGavock was almost wholly absent, with the important exception of the *Tennessean's* 1979 series on busing discussed in chapter 7.[32] In Nashville as nationally, key debates about desegregation unfolded without solid findings on desegregation's impact on students' social understanding.[33]

Amid all the voices writing in to Judge Wiseman and debating busing, elite businesspeople were conspicuous in their absence. Neither direct involvement in desegregation planning (as in the 1950s) nor calls for calm compliance (in the nervous early 1970s) continued once busing began. Surely, some business figures did engage with busing in other ways. Busing and the housing movement that resistance produced could be a profitable opportunity for those in property and housing markets and the finance industry that served them. But local elites had little incentive to recognize this publicly; they largely remained quiet on desegregation. Perhaps business leaders did exercise influence, but in closed channels that left few historical traces. Business leaders continued to talk of the importance of schools for their city's growth prospects, and a local business magazine named Charles Frazier, new superintendent of schools as of 1980, the "most powerful man in Nashville" in 1982. This sense of importance, however, did not mean deep involvement. Court supervision curtailed business involvement, and business leaders had diminishing connections to schools as parents, with increasing private-school going rates among not only the wealthiest, but the managerial class as well.[34]

Business silence on or disengagement with education, and particularly desegregation, was not atypical for the late 1960s through the 1970s, but it was a different path than that taken by local elites in desegregating metropolitan settings like Charlotte or Raleigh. Unlike Charlotte (where business leaders helped build a positive ethos around busing and claim desegregation as part of their city's growth-friendly image) or Raleigh (where business support was crucial in creating metropolitan consolidation in the mid-1970s), Nashville did not engage busing on positive terms. It seemed instead an outside imposition, an obstacle to local growth to endure and outlast.[35]

## "Desegregation with Moderation":
## A Revised View from the Plaintiffs

When Avon Williams returned to court in 1978, he was joined by a young associate, attorney Richard Dinkins. Dinkins had first begun to contribute to *Kelley* as a law student, working in Williams' office alongside his studies at Vanderbilt. While Williams managed both his law practice and his work as a state legislator, Dinkins joined the firm after graduation and became deeply involved in the case. He ultimately saw it to its completion in 1998.

Avon Williams argued in 1971 to extend busing throughout the county, and he sought a more equitable approach to busing, more evenly balancing the burdens of travel time, changes between schools, and local school closures. But the experience of the seven years that followed helped him understand even more vividly how initial inequalities in the busing plan could become magnified over time. Together, Williams and Dinkins called for the court to hold the school board in contempt for violating the earlier desegregation plan. Rather than simply looking for a revised plan, they called for the district to "divest themselves of the . . . facilities they had constructed in white suburban areas in an effort to preserve segregation and provide a preference to white students and parents." Without relinquishing this hope for busing equitably executed, Williams moved gradually away from commitment to the racial ratios that had guided Nashville's desegregation since 1971. He hoped to move toward more equality in the experience of schooling and desegregation—of more equally distributed travel time, of the preservation of historically black as well as historically white schools.

Williams also hoped to end what the plaintiffs and their allies increasingly understood to be the damaging public pedagogy of desegregation in practice. They felt that Nashville's busing plan was teaching the community that black institutions were inferior and that only in the presence of white students could black students learn. Williams, unlike some of the more vocal African American opponents of busing speaking nationally, remained assertively committed to integration as a goal: "In the long run the advancement of our people requires competition in the main stream, and . . . racial segregation is inconsistent with that competition."[36] Yet over time he had developed an even firmer sense of what busing should *not* do.

Williams's choice of expert witness for this phase of *Kelley* indicated how his views were shifting. Dr. Hugh Scott became a key—and ultimately controversial—figure in how the plaintiffs' legal team advocated for revised busing. Scott directed Hunter College's school of education in New York City, and previously had been superintendent of the Washington, DC, public schools. Chosen for that post at the age of thirty-six, after earlier work as both a teacher and administrator in Detroit, Scott was the first black person to serve as superintendent of a major US school system.[37] Scott effectively linked Williams's Tennessee-focused practice to the evolving national discourse about how desegregation and equality related.

On the stand in Judge Wiseman's courtroom, Scott drew from prepared notes to articulate his view of the relationships among desegregation, equality, and inequality. He was most direct in questioning the 1971 court order's racial ratio requirement, that schools achieve a 15 to 35 percent black/65 to 85 percent white ratio. This ratio conveyed the troublesome notion that "schools[with predominantly black student bod[ies] are detrimental to white students," while "schools with predominantly white student bodies are good for black students."[38] Challenged on the stand by the school board's attorney, William Willis, to clarify just what racial ratio he thought minimally acceptable, Scott spoke of roughly 12 percent as an acceptable level for a black *or* white student minority. But he also explained that it was not the ratio itself that he valued—instead, he chose the ratio to allow for the preservation of historically black schools that, through white resistance, had not been able to achieve larger white student populations.[39]

Williams's and Scott's views did not align identically in all respects, but the fact that Williams chose Scott—whose ideas would have been well known to Williams before Scott testified in court—reflected Williams's shifts in thinking and helped push him further toward a revised view of busing. Scott summarized his view: "A desegregation plan that accepts a majority white school must be prepared to accept a majority black school. That is what I'm saying."[40] Challenging the requirement that all schools be majority white had multiple aims: the preservation of Pearl High School as a historically black school in a historically black neighborhood, as well as increased contact between black students and black teachers (by shifting away from the faculty ratio that also enforced a white majority). Williams and Scott, alongside leaders in Nashville's African American communities, hoped that a formal court-ordered plan that permitted the existence of historically black and black-majority institutions could help undo the damaging public message conveyed in desegregation's closures of black institutions. Pearl's fate had broad meaning, for Scott as an observer as well as for local participants: "If desegregation means ultimately that [schools] that have long traditions of service to blacks have to be evaporated, desolved

[sic], eroded, terminated, that somewhere along the way black people got taken for a ride in terms of desegregation."[41]

What the school board's counsel framed as "white flight," Williams, Dinkins, and Scott viewed as the result of desegregation practices that systematically undermined institutions like Pearl. After implementing a 1971 desegregation plan that clearly privileged suburban over urban schools, the board continued to move students away from central-city schools by shrinking the zone that fed Pearl, providing unmonitored transfer options, and speaking of possible closures in ways that reinforced uncertainty about these schools' future. These actions helped produce shrinking enrollments at schools like Pearl, which the board then used to argue for its closure.[42]

On the witness stand as an expert, Scott emphasized not only the facial unfairness of a plan that sent only black six-, seven-, eight-, and nine-year-olds out of their neighborhoods—and never white children of the same age—while closing local city elementary schools. He also underscored the particular consequences of shifting schools and moving to new settings at this, the "worst age," he said, for such discontinuities. As kindergarten programs had not been covered by the 1971 court order, black kindergarteners shifted schools between kindergarten close to home and their first- through fourth-grade assignments farther away. School closures in city neighborhoods in the early 1970s also rendered kindergarten programs unstable.[43]

Listening to Scott on the witness stand seemed to pleasantly surprise Judge Wiseman, who heard in Scott's comments a novel approach to an issue that Wiseman felt had been considered too narrowly. Wiseman even asked (likely rhetorically) if "Dr. Scott would want to help us with a plan."[44] But when Scott took up the question of revising the district's 80 percent white/20 percent black faculty ratio at each school in order to allow schools with larger black student populations to have more black teachers, Scott found out how easily his arguments could be construed as rejecting rather than revising desegregation. Scott argued, as had Williams before him, for allowing black students more contact with black teachers so that students could benefit from professional role models and shared understanding of the "essential cultural things" that distinguished black people from white people, in Scott's view.[45] For Scott, the valuable relationships between black students and black teachers exemplified the "things that were good in blackness" that should not be "cast out in the struggle" for equal opportunity and access to "schools where whites are."[46]

Judge Wiseman heard in Scott's remarks a sharp change in tenor of the proceedings. Wiseman was, he explained, "saddened" by remarks that "underscor[ed] racial division and separateness." Scott tried to reject this notion, explaining that he was arguing for "solidarity," not separateness, and that more generally, "Regardless of how severely I may criticize what I consider to be some inequities in the desegregation plan, I must never let my criticism persuade me not to support that concept of desegregation and equal opportunity with all the [fervor] and strength that I can. Because that right is what it is all about."[47] He explained that he felt that his "responses [were] sometimes misinterpreted as a movement to resegregate," but in fact he was asking for "desegregation with moderation." From this point on, Judge Wiseman seemed to view Scott as an expert against desegregation more than for its revision. He asked, somewhat sarcastically, if the school board's attorney might like Scott's testimony so much that he would choose not to cross-examine. The middle position Scott and Williams sought to maintain—critical of aspects of desegregation but refusing to abandon the project—did not fit easily into the narrow contemporary categories of advocacy for or resistance to desegregation, nor did it accord with the dominant if flawed national narrative of an integrationist civil rights movement challenged by a destructive separatism.[48]

Through Hugh Scott, Avon Williams introduced a reordered approach to desegregation. In 1971, Williams fought hard for desegregation measured by racial ratio, and then, unsuccessfully, pushed against the inequalities within the court-accepted HEW plan to achieve this ratio. After seven years of busing in practice—years that had provided the plaintiffs and Nashville's black leaders ample time to consider busing's specific practice and its symbolic heft—Williams reversed the order, seeking first equitable treatment of students, and of schools in relationship to communities. If doing so meant a shift away from the long-established white-majority ratios, that was a shift Williams and many others in the city were willing to make. Williams, Wiseman, and most school board members agreed that busing needed to reach across Davidson County, but they shared little ground on what principles would guide a new plan.

## A Divided School Board and the Problem of White Flight

Nearly from the moment of Judge Morton's 1971 order for desegregation via busing, the Metro Nashville school board debated how to remain compliant with it. More than a third of Nashville's schools within the geographic boundaries of the busing order had more black students, and fewer white students, than the court-specified 15 to 35 percent black student standard.[49] Over the 1970s, the board authorized several adjustments to the desegregation plan Morton approved. The board and administration felt these remained within the terms of the order, yet they often pushed at its boundaries. Avon Williams had long felt that the adjustments—as in opening new facilities for suburban areas exempt from busing under the label of "annexes" or as part of the comprehensive high school plan— were simple violations of the order. Neither view ever was confirmed by the bench, though. With Judge Gray's silence, there was no comprehensive judicial review of busing in practice over its first seven years.

Over the decade, the composition of the school board shifted as Mayor Richard Fulton, formerly Nashville's US congressman, took office in 1975 and added his own appointments to the board. Fulton created a more representative board, breaking from Briley's practice of appointing seven white people and one black person, seven Christians and one Jew.[50] The new board's six white members and three black members represented a range of histories and commitments on the matter of desegregation.

The board's majority thought of white flight as the core desegregation problem, and the district's main problem overall. Not only did falling white enrollment challenge efforts to maintain a white majority in each school, but white flight threatened support for public schools, as Nashville's more politically powerful citizens backed away from the system.[51] Yet the obstacle was as much the idea of white flight as the demographic pattern. By 1977, MNPS enrolled roughly 19,000 fewer students than it had in 1970. Resistance to desegregation was not the only cause of that decline, though, as the 1970s' birthrate was influential as well. Yet in public discourse, each tick down in the enrollment figures was a student "lost" to white flight.[52] Both the board's own consultants and expert witnesses in Judge Wiseman's courtroom tried to nuance the discussion, but they were not able to dislodge the hold the idea had on the board's thinking. The board's majority continued to make mitigating white resistance and departures their first priority in ways that skewed desegregation's practice away from equality.

Without substantive discourse of the potential or real benefits of desegregation, one of the few affirmative statements suggested that placating white families was the best way to serve black children. As the board's attorney explained it, "If . . . white children are the primary educational resource for black children, the possible development of a poor and black public school system alongside a middle and upper class white private school [system] is the *ultimate* in burden for black students."[53] Nashville's administrators and its school board majority defined desegregation in ways that made white students their chief constituency.

The white board members who saw themselves as liberal on desegregation shared a view with most of the school district staff, that busing needed to be improved through expansion throughout Davidson County in order to expand the pool of white students involved in desegregation and limit opportunities for white flight. In a 1977 proposal from MNPS staff to this effect, the approach to more busing only worsened the disparate burdens of the 1971 order, with most black students from the city center now bused to the suburbs for nine or ten of their twelve years of school; for students zoned to two clusters of schools, the figure was all twelve years. The dominant position among white board members and educators who supported desegregation was to expand busing, but to prioritize the racial ratio and not address inequalities within the plan. Board members George Cate and Cynthia Morin most frequently took this position, which put them at odds with representatives of outlying suburban and rural communities who, like advocates for Pearl, often valued preservation of their small local high schools over involvement in desegregation.[54]

MNPS veiled continued inequalities in the practice of busing in fuzzy numeric representations. Describing a later version of a similar plan, school board attorneys claimed that the "percentage of students [to be bused] are approximately equal by race, with 74.2 percent of black elementary students compared to 66.5 percent of white elementary students on buses."[55] Yet students were on buses for different reasons: the vast majority of white students bused in the earliest elementary school grades rode from their suburban homes to their nearest suburban schools—for what Judge Wiseman later called "non-integration" purposes.[56] By contrast, nearly all the black elementary school students on buses were riding out of their neighborhoods for the purpose of desegregation.

The popular idea that desegregation served only the interests of black students further impeded attention to disparate burdens. On the witness stand before Avon Williams, suburban parent leader Richard Duncan explained that unequal burdens in the busing plan were fair "in the [sense] that the court order was instigated for the black children." In his view, the burdens could reasonably fall on the beneficiaries.[57] Duncan could not perceive what board member DeLois Wilkinson called "discrimination in the process of desegregation."[58] The board's attorneys dismissed the matter as they wrote, "certain costs are associated with almost any plan for the desegregation of a public school system, which costs must be balanced against the benefits sought."[59] By implication, disparate burdens were the price of desegregation.

Longtime Nashville teacher, later principal, district administrator, and board consultant Nathaniel Crippens was one of the few to explicitly reverse the question, noticing the extent to which busing plans had aided white resistance. Crippens explained to Judge Wiseman that black students had attended the schools to which they had been assigned in white communities, whereas white students had not done the reverse. Yet it was black students who were penalized for white resistance when black schools were closed. Crippens asked, "If blacks somehow find the resources to enable them to refuse to attend the high schools to which they are assigned in white communities, will the white high schools be closed and the white children be sent to a school in the black community?" How did these situations differ "in terms of equity" Crippens wondered.[60]

From late 1979 until nearly the moment of Judge Wiseman's February 1980 deadline to submit a new plan, the board and its Citizen's Advisory Commission wrestled over its shape, meeting for many hours, often with three outside consultants.[61] Within those meetings, the board debated the parameters for a new plan. Most board members were supportive of the same remade approach to racial ratios that Avon Williams introduced through Hugh Scott—that a 12 percent minority presence, black or white, would be sufficient to mark a school desegregated. Yet consultant Donald Waldrip felt that this would not be acceptable to the courts, and persuaded the board instead to stick to the white-majority racial ratio. They modified the 1971 15 to 35 percent ratio to 12 to 52 percent black students (using the updated 32 percent black student population of the district as a target, with a twenty-point range on either side).[62]

After marathon meetings, the board approved a new desegregation plan early in the morning of February 5. As had been threatened intermittently over the preceding five years, the new plan gradually phased out the smaller high schools in outlying rural or exurban areas. Pearl and Cohn, the urban high schools whose advocates pushed forcefully on their behalf, would also close. But their communities received a consolation prize from the board, which planned its first urban comprehensive high school for a location between the two schools. Some of Pearl's advocates celebrated that decision, seeing it as the manifestation of a message long missing in board policy: "This would say to inner city children—white and black" that "you are first class citizens, you really matter." This was a message that they had been present "verbally but not *operationally*."[63]

The board's plan set a limit on busing for first and second graders of no more than thirty minutes in either direction and called for reopening a few central-city elementary schools to serve only first and second graders. This move, which the board explained as intended to reduce the disparate burden experienced by black urban students, increased the number of transitions between different schools these students faced—a frequent source of complaint for both black and white parents.[64] By expanding the boundaries of busing, and through rezoning, the school board's plan promised to bring 82 percent of Nashville students into schools that were predicted to have between 12 and 52 percent black students. Before, roughly 58 percent of students had been in schools in this range.[65] The plan continued to define desegregation on the basis of the percentage of black students in a school. In sum, the new plan made minor adjustments directed at the problem of burdens and recognition of Nashville's urban spaces, but kept intact the core approach of the 1971 plan, extended to the whole county.

This plan proved short lived. Just a few weeks after its approval, the three black members of the board together signed a statement effectively withdrawing their support. The African American board members—Chair Isaiah T. Creswell, Barbara Mann, and DeLois Wilkinson—had often disagreed over how much to prioritize Pearl's continued existence, among other issues. Now they came together to oppose the continued shuttering of city schools, including the decision to remove the "last vestige of Black educational tradition and culture at the secondary level" by closing Pearl. They rejected the notion, previously supported by Mann and consultant Crippens, that a new comprehensive high school combined with Cohn would be sufficient compensation. As had earlier versions of county-wide busing suggested by the school district staff, the new plan exacerbated the disproportionate burdens of busing, often involving black students traveling for ten of twelve years of schooling, rather than the eight of twelve the board usually cited. Creswell, Mann, and Wilkinson noted also that in some sections of the district, black students never attended a school close to home.[66] James Haney, the head of the Pearl High School Parent-Teacher-Student Association, wrote even more forcefully that his community wanted a plan to "minimize busing and give more consideration to the neighborhood school."[67]

Wilkinson had been Pearl's strongest advocate on the board for years, often voting to protect Pearl even when it meant joining with white board members who wanted to curb desegregation to preserve their local, majority-white schools. Contemporary observers sometimes labeled hers a "separatist" position, and could see in her own biography a conventional civil rights narrative of integrationism giving way to separatism. Wilkinson was a longtime member of Nashville's First Baptist Church, a hub of organizing in the early 1960s sit-in and boycott movements. She had, with her young children, been the first to cross the color line at the Monkey Garden children's restaurant within a major downtown department store.[68] One of

8.1. Members of the Metropolitan Nashville Board of Education on a school bus, c. 1980. Clockwise from left: Isaiah Creswell, Ted Ridings, Cynthia Morin, DeLois Wilkinson, Barbara Mann. Courtesy of Metropolitan Archives of Nashville–Davidson County.

those children later attended a largely white private school, where he struggled and felt like a "zombie," as Wilkinson recalled, making neither friends nor academic progress. After hiring a reading tutor who helped him catch up over the summer, Wilkinson moved her son to majority-black Wharton School, where she worked, and where he made friends and flourished. She explained the change as a matter of "getting into a place that he felt he belonged."[69] By the late 1970s, Wilkinson described herself as in favor of integration, but "not in favor of it when those in positions of authority do not enter wholeheartedly into the plan to assure the intended benefits are reached by all the children."[70] Wilkinson emphasized equality and belonging within desegregation; she sought to balance concern for white students' experiences with that of their black peers. This was an effort that frustrated some of her white colleagues on the board. Wilkinson remembered one representative—not an ally of the desegregation project—asking her to "stick to the ratios and the percentages and the things that I can deal with." As she recalled, he complained that he could not "deal with all of that humanitarian stuff. . . . We're here to formulate a desegregation plan."[71]

Barbara Mann's path to the school board was through the League of Women Voters rather than direct action organizing. Suggested for appointment by the league, she was a consistent, pro-integrationist voice on the board. Her decision to dissent from the February 5 plan represented a break from her long history of supporting desegregation even when its costs were high, a position that board chair Isaiah Creswell had often taken as well. It was frustration at the tenor of the board discussion and the public pedagogy of desegregation in Nashville that moved Mann toward Wilkinson's views. In Judge Wiseman's courtroom, both board members recalled the board discussion of the fate of the Caldwell School in East Nashville, located next to the Sam Levy public housing development. The school itself had a lauded program and faculty, but white board members argued for its closure because the surrounding area had a high crime rate: white parents would not tolerate sending their children there. Mann explained that she did not "think that black people live in places that are not fit for schools." She felt that the shape of desegregation was "continually say[ing] to black youngsters that, 'In order for you to get something that is good, you have to move into another community.'" This carried "the impression and perception of inferiority," making "a psychological impact on the youngsters who are moved outward."[72]

DeLois Wilkinson situated the closure of Caldwell within Nashville's longer and multipart disinvestment in urban neighborhoods. She suggested that instead of closing the school due to concerns about crime in the surrounding area, the city could try to address the crime.[73] Wilkinson might reasonably have been concerned that, without worries over school safety as a point of leverage, a community like Sam Levy was even more weakly positioned to demand help in reducing crime. Mann and Wilkinson (along with Creswell, who did not speak publicly about his dissent from the board's plan) had reached a point of frustration with inequalities within busing not only in the area of student experience, but as an indicator of the metropolitan government's refusal to value city neighborhoods within the metropolis.

Mothers residing in the Sam Levy Homes with children at Caldwell agreed with Mann and Wilkinson that it should remain open, but from a more intimate perspective. Writing to Judge Wiseman to preserve their school, they described it as "the heart of the community." Some documented their support for the school, and their success in raising money to air-condition Caldwell's classrooms. Others asked the fundamental and poignant question many parents faced when their children rode buses to distant schools and their families lacked cars: "How could we come after them if they are a long way from home?"[74]

Caldwell School sat at the center of its community in ways invisible to those board members who saw urban schools chiefly as barriers to white participation. Despite months of intensive debate, the school board had been unable to agree on an approach to desegregation that could at once acknowledge Caldwell and placate white parents. After Barbara Mann, Isaiah Creswell, and DeLois Wilkinson issued their statement of dissent, Judge Wiseman understood that the board's proposal was a plan without a consensus, supported only by the white moderates on the board and the district staff.

In the 1950s and 1960s, Nashville city planners defined and designed neighborhoods and communities around the presence of schools, and had for years reinforced the notion that spaces without schools were not communities. Doubtless, busing had confused—and in some cases appeared to sever—the school-community link. "Neighborhood schools" activists, resisting busing for desegregation, surely told the story that way. But in fact, most white Nashville neighborhoods in the 1970s continued to enjoy open schools that, if not defined by the neighborhood boundary, were at least proximate institutions at which students would attend for most of their years in school. When supporters of schools like Pearl and Caldwell defended their schools, they sought the same recognition of their communities—a recognition that planning policy as well as school policy and the process of desegregation had often denied them. The idea of the school-centered neighborhood unit, decades old at this point, lived on. Advocates for schools like Pearl, unlike earlier adopters of the neighborhood unit, wanted their schools to serve their communities, but did not require a racially or geographically exclusive definition of that community.

## The Interveners: Small High Schools, Limited Desegregation

In early 1980, as school board members met late at night to devise desegregation plans, a new coalition of Nashville citizens and some educators formed around the defense of the older, smaller high schools that the school board planned to close. In light of the district's emphasis on comprehensive high schools since the late 1960s, these schools stood out to many administrators as holdovers that no longer fit. Two of them, Pearl and Cohn, sat within city neighborhoods. Advocates for both appeared at board meetings and formal hearings at various points, beginning in 1976, when closures were on the table. Representatives from both communities argued for their schools not only as important fixtures in their communities, but as crucial to the continued existence of strong urban spaces. Four other small schools served outlying rural and nearly all-white exurban communities previously exempt from the 1971 busing order. As did advocates for the urban schools, representatives from these communities argued that their high schools were crucial community institutions. For both advocates of urban and outlying schools, the fact that large comprehensive high schools were under-enrolled while yet more were planned for construction proved only that Metro government, thought of skeptically across these communities but for distinct reasons, had gone too far in favoring already favored suburban precincts of the metropolis. That error, the small high schools' advocates insisted, should not force further neglect of their communities through school closures.

This common terrain allowed organizers from six quite diverse communities to join together in a coalition to defend the "jewels of the community" that were their high schools. Doing so meant engaging with the ongoing *Kelley* litigation and suggesting a place for their schools in what they depicted as a new strategy for desegregation.[75] Judge Wiseman granted the group the formal status of an intervening party in *Kelley*, with concerns distinct from either the plaintiffs or defendants.

Coalescing across "different, and often differing," parts of the county, the interveners were a markedly diverse group. The middle-class identity of a small-town turned suburb like Bellevue contrasted with the blue-collar white community around Cohn, the middle-class black leadership that spoke in support of Pearl, and the rural, small-town ethos of Joelton, where three thousand community members signed petitions and wrote letters conveying their attachment to their school that had served generations of locals.[76] The interveners' opponents in court, and at times on the bench, would accuse them of defending narrow parochial interests, but some of the group's leadership had extensive experience around schools and desegregation with national perspective. They included a former president of the National Education Association teachers' union, a community organizer with experience in school planning in Brooklyn in the heady years around the Ocean Hill–Brownsville community control controversy, and a former leader of the Atlanta NAACP chapter during that city's desegregation negotiations. Their Nashville work was distinctly local but aware of its national position.

In the winter and spring of 1980, Leo Lillard emerged as the chief architect of the interveners' approach to desegregation. A Nashville native and Pearl alum, Lillard had a long organizing history dating back to his high school days in the early 1960s, when he helped bring Student Nonviolent Coordinating Committee Freedom Riders home to Nashville after they were stranded in hostile Alabama.[77] After college at Tennessee State,

Lillard left Nashville and moved northeast, ultimately to Brooklyn. There he worked with young people, including bringing a group of students to a summer program at Malcolm X University in Greensboro, North Carolina. Lillard identified as a pan-Africanist by the time he returned to Nashville in 1976, where he was shocked to see the extent of school closures in his old neighborhoods in North and South Nashville. Lillard argued for historically black Pearl's survival alongside fellow interveners who defended historically white high schools, and acknowledged that it was a not-always easy alliance. Some worked against further desegregation "for the wrong reasons," in his view. Lillard drew on and felt motivated by the national discourse of community control, but tamed it to fit a political context he felt was too constrained by southern norms to consider community control directly.[78]

At Cohn High School, alumnus and Nashville councilman William Higgins, former teacher and national educational leader Helen Bain, and the alumni and booster clubs advocated for the continuation of their school. Cohn advocates argued that schools like Cohn were central to their communities, and that these urban residential communities were worth defending. They replied to the school board's request to define "unitary education," as "oneness of opportunity for all children . . . and oneness geographically centered at and emanating from the heart of the inner-city." This kind of defense of the city was more familiar coming from black advocates who had been frustrated by decades of urban renewal and disinvestment that both predated and then became exacerbated by white flight. Councilman Higgins voiced a continued attachment of white city residents to their communities, despite mass suburbanization and out-migration, and a recognition of the importance (symbolic as well as economic) of institutions like Cohn for these communities' survival.[79] Schools director Elbert Brooks, attached to the comprehensive model, wondered why Cohn community members would not prefer greater access to new vocational courses.[80]

If Cohn's supporters felt that board policies and metropolitan politics had neglected city neighborhoods, Bellevue High School's community felt that they, too, fell outside of the privileged, pro-growth suburban mainstream. Doug Underwood published the small-town weekly paper the *Westview*, which gave him a ready platform for his views on all matters Bellevue. The area was "in the path of metro growth" and suffered from insufficient control over its own destiny—as zoning and infrastructure fights revealed—in Underwood's view.[81] Underwood's columns often celebrated and defended the benefits of what he saw as the community-oriented high school at Bellevue. That a resident of the wealthier, more suburban area of Hillwood represented Bellevue on the school board further fed the claims of outsider status.[82] Tired of feeling that Bellevue was Metro's "stepchild," Underwood and other local residents explored incorporating as a town within Metropolitan Nashville–Davidson County—which would heighten local control over functions like zoning, although not over schooling.[83]

Doug Underwood founded Save Our Schools, an organization to fight for Bellevue High School, and then ultimately joined forces with Lillard and Cohn's advocates as interveners. The Save Our Schools cochair, Mary Vowels, brought to the group a much shorter history with Bellevue, but a longer experience with school desegregation. Vowels moved to Bellevue when her husband transitioned from a deanship at Atlanta University's business school to an economics professorship at Tennessee State. She described herself as ready to "hibernate" in the Nashville area, fatigued from her involvement in Atlanta's school desegregation struggles and local campaigns for economic justice.[84] She had served as the cochair of the Atlanta NAACP's education committee in the years when the local branch agreed to end calls for active desegregation in return for black leadership positions in school administration and board governance. This arrangement, called the "Atlanta Compromise" by those who derided it in connection with Booker T. Washington's conciliatory 1895 speech of the same name, earned the Atlanta chapter expulsion from the national NAACP. In Vowels's view, the Atlanta story brought middle- and upper-income black and white families back into public schools by keeping students close to home.[85] In addition to the experience she brought from Atlanta, her visible leadership as an African American woman gave Save Our Schools a ready, if superficial, defense against the not infrequent claims that its support for neighborhood schools like Bellevue was nothing but thinly veiled racism.

Bellevue's ground-level organizers, most of whom were women homemakers, turned out their constituency in numbers. So many residents attended one school board meeting that the board relocated to Bellevue High School midmeeting, where they met an audience of two thousand. Frustrated by what organizers felt to be dated knowledge about the size of the African American population in Bellevue, and with a year to go before the release of 1980 census data, three hundred volunteers worked to produce their own door-to-door census of the area, counting 16,464 residents and tallying a black population of 5 percent.[86] This level of energy was difficult to sustain, though, and fell off once the interveners' efforts began to focus on Judge Wiseman's courtroom.[87]

Students, parents, and community representatives from Nashville's remaining small high schools—Joelton, in the steeply hilled northwest of the county; Antioch, in the once rural but quickly growing, suburban southeast; and DuPont, in the working-class community around the textile plant of the same name, in eastern Davidson County—met with representatives from Pearl, Cohn, and Bellevue over long hours to develop their philosophical and legal stance. Once Judge Wiseman became increasingly interested in their ideas, they sketched their vision of a desegregation plan. The group was represented by Cecil Branstetter, Bellevue resident and noted labor lawyer, and gained signature support from a range of council representatives and community organizations.[88]

Over the winter of 1980 the interveners offered what they described as a wholly new plan for Nashville desegregation. They divided Davidson County into six zones, each of which included at least one comprehensive high school and at least one traditional, noncomprehensive, smaller school. Each family would choose between schools within their zone, with magnet programs placed at some schools to ensure that they would draw at least a 10 percent minority of black or white students, the threshold the interveners used to define a school as desegregated. Any school that did not meet the 10 percent threshold would close.[89] Motivated primarily by the desire to maintain their local schools, the 10 percent ratio was, in the view of lead planner Leo Lillard, a necessary concession to the contemporary focus on statistical desegregation.[90]

Under such a plan, schools like Pearl (which in recent years had between 5 and 15 percent white students) and Bellevue (which had 12 percent black students) could remain open, safe from the threat of replacement with a new comprehensive high school that would have no specific community identity.[91] The interveners' plan also was less aggressive about efficient use of school facilities and marked fewer schools for closing than had school board representatives. The schools that were closed were more evenly distributed across both city and suburban Nashville.[92] The plan placed the decision of small versus large comprehensive high schools in the hands of families, as each cluster would have one of each type of school; provisions for choice also effectively promised parental discretion in which schools' racial composition they preferred.[93]

The interveners' plan cohered around the idea of the community school, whether that community was white or black. After various phases in the spatial organization of schooling in Nashville, these communities wanted at minimum the option of approximating the old school-centric neighborhood-unit design. The coalition was further united by an antibureaucratic sentiment, explaining that they acted "without the slightest deference to local governmental power and without the slightest concern for protection of and personal growth of a large educational bureaucracy not involved in personal service of children's educational needs."[94] These were anti-busing activists on a model quite different than Casey Jenkins's 1971 allies, who made loud claims about property rights in home, school, and segregation together. The basic anti-government sentiment the interveners expressed was present in many places beyond Nashville, but the interveners shared a sense that they had to act to defend communities—whether rural, exurban, or rural—that fell outside the favored band of suburban privilege.

Avon Williams and the NAACP leadership at first responded coolly to Leo Lillard's efforts with the interveners. Williams never acknowledged the more than superficial similarities between his efforts to keep Pearl open by sanctioning a 15 percent minority (black or white) school as desegregated, and the interveners' commitment to do the same but with a 10 percent minority (black or white) minimum. Other members of Nashville's civil rights community did, however. In early February 1980, Nashville's Operation PUSH chapter voted to endorse what they referred to as "Leo Lillard's plan," calling it a "realistic" means of achieving, if not "optimal," at least "significant integration." The Nashville NAACP chapter earlier made a similar endorsement.[95] By 1980, there was a significant consensus—at least among organized black participants—that the white-majority racial ratio represented a thin version of educational equality, where a more robust vision would attend not only to desegregation, but to the relationships between schools and communities and the character of students' experiences within schools. They would choose to constrain the former in hopes of achieving the latter.

In his closing arguments before Judge Wiseman, Avon Williams reflected a bit on the transformation in his own thinking. He again proposed a minimum desegregation standard of 12 to 15 percent black or white students. "What is sauce for the goose is sauce for the gander," he said, meaning that any school—majority or historically white or black—could be judged desegregated if it contained a small minority student population. Williams broke from his usually controlled and formal courtroom demeanor to share in a bit of introspection, revealing his view not only of the problem with racial ratios as they had influenced *Kelley*, but a broader critique of how Nashville's white leadership had approached desegregation. Williams wished that the school board and other leaders had "just [told Nashville residents] what they need to do and then . . . go ahead and let them do it, and then when they start complaining, just explain the reason for it." Rather than trusting citizens to adjust to new circumstances and be able to reason through new arrangements, the board—and certainly Mayor Briley's office—had instead devoted itself to acknowledging and even crediting white resistance and trying to mitigate it: "The philosophy of the school board plan is to say that white people have got to be in the majority all the time, and that if white people run away from us, we have got to chase them and try to get them back."[96]

Having come together around the defense of their small high schools, the white communities represented by the interveners directed their energy not only at the legal process, but at a political change that they hoped would make school policy more responsive to their views. In the early 1970s, the anti-busing Concerned Parents Association had called for an elected school board, a departure from the appointive model used on most Nashville boards and commissions.[97] Now, representatives of outlying suburban communities organized first an unsuccessful legislative effort, and then a successful referendum on a charter amendment to make the board of education an elected rather than appointed body. The leadership of the existing school board stood against the transition to election, arguing that quality candidates would not subject themselves to the labors of an election.[98] The nine seats and the geographic districts they served remained, but in the eyes of superintendent Charles Frazier, in office at the transition, the board's politics "changed overnight." The first elected board, taking their seats in 1982, had more representatives from outlying communities like those represented by the interveners; it also now had two, rather than the previous three, black representatives.[99]

## Wiseman Revises Busing

Judge Wiseman presided at dozens of days of public hearings from July 1979 through April 1980, proceedings that yielded over five thousand pages of transcripts and box upon box of supporting exhibits. He received hundreds of letters from citizens, many of them conveying a blend of hopes for desegregation, resistance to it, and complaints over implementation. On May 20, 1980, the judge issued a sixty-page ruling that revealed that he had been influenced by what he had heard from citizens' groups and individuals, as well as by his own investigations into the experience of busing. He had driven the route from a North Nashville, majority-black neighborhood out to the county's predominantly white eastern suburbs, where some of the neighborhood's students would be bused. It was a 20.6 mile route, and took forty-two minutes. He was concerned about the inaccessibility of the area for parents without cars, an "almost impossible barrier to liaison between parent and teacher."[100] Wiseman knew that experiences like this would be frequent for black students, and that some never attended school close to home. "No similar treatment of white children exists," he acknowledged.[101]

Judge Wiseman broadened his view of school desegregation from a statistical concern with resegregation in urban areas to a concern for the visible inequalities in Nashville's approach to busing. From this point of view, Wiseman saw the board's 1980 proposal as "a 'more of the same' type of remedy," and rejected it. He was concerned not only about the continued unequal burdens for black students, but, borrowing a phrase from Hugh Scott, its "rightness of whiteness" premise: the notion that desegregation helped black students learn by bringing them into contact with white students. This view, Wiseman believed, led school districts to focus on achieving particular levels of black enrollment in each majority-white school, rather than considering a desegregation measure that had black or white students in the majority. It defined segregation as a problem of black schools and black institutions, rather than one visible at white institutions and for white students as well.[102]

Wiseman described a "dramatic role reversal" in Nashville, as white school board officials called for more busing and black plaintiffs and interveners asked for less busing and some majority-black schools. He took seriously what he had heard about continued unequal travel and dislocation burdens, especially Hugh Scott's testimony about shifts between schools harming achievement. Most fundamentally, though, Wiseman worried about "The spectre [sic] that haunts all of the parties to this case, the Court, and the community," a "public school system populated by the poor and black, and a private school system serving the affluent and the white."[103] Unable to find a route to desegregation that would serve both sets of concerns, he chose to limit desegregation rather than risk angering white families with a more equitable plan.

Judge Wiseman's 1980 ruling called for a return to neighborhood schools at the elementary school level in kindergarten through fourth grade. If it was unpalatable for white families to be bused in, and too hard for black families always to be bused out, then Wiseman felt that the necessary result must be no busing at the elementary level. Extensive busing for desegregation remained in the middle and high school grades. Wiseman accepted as desegregated any school that was at least 15 percent minority, black or white. His was a strong statement for prioritizing the equitable treatment of students within busing over the achievement of "equitable" racial ratios that required each school to mimic the composition of the district overall. But he also criticized and disallowed blatant resegregation, as he predicted would occur under the interveners' plan, with its "unduly optimistic" plans for magnet programs to ensure desegregation, and he remained in favor of the comprehensive high school strategy that the interveners sought to undercut.[104]

Wiseman emphasized how previous school construction decisions connected to the unequal nature of busing in Nashville. He noted that the school board's commitment to comprehensive high schools led to overbuilding in suburban locations, thereby creating another excuse for closing city schools and another reason for urban students to spend less time close to home. In part to remedy this imbalance, Wiseman approved the construction of an inner-city comprehensive high school, to draw students from the historic zones of Pearl and Cohn High Schools, and to be called Pearl-Cohn. He also approved construction of a long-needed high school for the Goodlettsville and Madison areas, but one that would also draw from the growing black population in suburban northeast Nashville to yield a desegregated population. Wiseman ordered the closure of smaller traditional high schools that were largely white.[105] After these specific rulings, Wiseman turned the remaining planning over to the board, to outline a plan in advance of the opening of school for a year hence, in the fall of 1981.

Although he later referred to himself as "plowing new ground" in the *Kelley* case, he felt he was doing so with the support of precedent.[106] He saw the new plan he sanctioned as consistent with changing jurisprudence, where "the definition of a 'unitary' school system has expanded from *Brown* to *Milliken* from a mere destruction of barriers, to pupil assignment, to remediation and quality education." *Swann* mandated "no specific degree or racial mixing," Wiseman explained, nor was "'desegregation' defined as requiring every school to reflect the racial composition of the district as a whole." Racial ratios had moved, in Wiseman's view, from a necessary tool as of 1971 to a not completely worthy end in and of themselves.[107]

The school board, relieved by Judge Wiseman of the responsibility to confer with the plaintiffs and interveners as they prepared their plan, submitted a new version in January 1981. It had passed over the objections of the three black members of the board.[108] The plan followed Wiseman's 1980 tenets clearly: there would be no busing for the purpose of desegregation in grades K through 4, but promises of additional dollars for targeted educational programs for those schools. In grades 5 through 12, students would attend schools that had at least a fifteen-percent minority student presence, either white or black. The school board committed itself—though without the details of implementation—to reopen some central-city schools (as it would have to do to house elementary students close to home) and to seek to balance burdens in busing that remained, but Pearl would close as a high school, becoming a middle school instead.[109]

Attorneys Williams and Dinkins used the next few months to review and file objections to the plan, and to submit what appeared to Judge Wiseman to be a hastily drawn "conceptual" plan that contradicted many of their earlier arguments about the importance of continuity in elementary education. In an April 17, 1981, order approving the board's plan, Wiseman ended, for the moment, debate at the district court level, and MNPS began the administrative work of closing or reconfiguring schools and reassigning teachers to follow the newly sanctioned plan. Although Williams might have felt gratified that Wiseman had absorbed the arguments about disparate burden that had so long fallen on deaf judicial ears, he was not pleased with how Wiseman translated those concerns into practice. Rather than moderating desegregation as Williams had hoped, Wiseman had significantly rolled it back.

As a scholar who studied desegregation nationally, Vanderbilt professor Willis Hawley felt that while Judge Wiseman might in fact have taken a new route in desegregation, it was not the right one. Hawley felt that many school districts would be interested in the plan and try to replicate it, but that it would not pass constitutional muster. If it did, he felt it could bring the end of desegregation programs across the country.[110]

## The Defense of the White-Majority Racial Ratio

Avon Williams and partner Richard Dinkins waited until after the school board had taken Judge Wiseman's tenets and given them specific form before deciding to appeal. They filed late in the afternoon of Friday, May 15, 1981, just before the following Monday's deadline for appeal. Waiting for a decision on appeal left everyone connected to Nashville's public schools—black and white; parent, teacher, and child—unsure of where they would go in the coming September. It also created time for Williams and Dinkins to engage more directly with the NAACP Legal Defense and Education Fund (LDF). Although NAACP LDF attorneys were formally co-counsel on all stages of litigation in *Kelley*, with the breadth and depth of Avon Williams's experience in school desegregation cases, he and Dinkins handled district court–level advocacy largely on their own. When issues rose to the Sixth Circuit Court of Appeals—or beyond, to the Supreme Court—NAACP LDF attorneys became more directly involved.[111] Doing so meant navigating the inherent tensions between local advocates with their local knowledge of specific geographies (where the river curved, where the bridges were), and specific histories (of attachment to storied schools like Pearl), and the hard-won national standards that the LDF's strategy depended on.

In the summer of 1981, LDF attorney Bill Lann Lee and Williams discussed the case and their appellate strategy. From his office on Columbus Circle in New York, Lee worked on the appeal, drawing on the court transcripts from Judge Wiseman's courtroom. Williams and Lee agreed to challenge several aspects of Wiseman's order. They decided to contest Wiseman's decision to end busing for kindergarten through fourth grade, and to challenge the extreme disparate burdens at the middle school level, where the board proposed nearly exclusively one-way busing from city to suburb. Williams, as well as the local NAACP, was highly critical of these elements.[112]

Yet on the matter of the racial ratio, it became clear the extent to which Williams—with support from Hugh Scott—had moved in new directions in Judge Wiseman's courtroom, diverging from the LDF. In court, Scott and Williams argued for a less stringent application of the kind of racial ratios long guiding desegregation plans like *Kelley* and *Swann*. This was a direction the NAACP LDF could not support, as moving away from the so-called *Singleton* ratios that had guided desegregation in Nashville could reverberate nationally. To preserve the white-majority racial ratio, Lee argued against what Scott and Williams had suggested, and Wiseman had endorsed, for a white- or black-majority plan for desegregation. It took Lee pages of extensive footnotes to reckon with the record Williams and Scott had compiled, and then find ways to argue against it. He did so by casting Scott's testimony as that of an educator, not an attorney or desegregation expert. He ensured the point was clearly made: "To the extent Dr. Scott's testimony can be taken as advocating any 15 percent minimum objective *as a desegregation* measure, plaintiffs do not stand by it."[113] The LDF steered Williams back toward national standards after his own view of the local context had led him to diverge from these. Before the Sixth Circuit, Williams and Lee together defended the emphasis on racial ratios, even as Williams knew well that local interest in this approach—and his own—had faded tremendously.[114]

The Sixth Circuit agreed to stay implementation of Wiseman's plan pending their review. The stay came down on August 19, 1981, just two days before school was scheduled to open for the 1981–82 school year. The stay effectively turned the desegregation clock in Nashville back two years, to before hearings opened in Judge Wiseman's courtroom, returning the district to its desegregation plan as of 1979. Having reassigned more than a thousand teachers and closed several schools over the summer—while also moving furniture, teaching materials, and even portable classroom trailers from schools whose age cohorts or size had shifted—MNPS now had to reverse that work before school could open. To make time, MNPS delayed the opening of school for three weeks, offering often critical publications like the *Westview* the opportunity to run pictures of smiling children in classes at private schools, under the headline "Schools Open?" while other local papers ran more cheerful stories of local administrators applauding teachers' efforts to adjust quickly.[115] It was an extreme example of the "August shuffle" parents had bemoaned for years.[116]

The timing of Williams's and the LDF's appeal also clouded the board's first direct request to voters for a tax levy. Belying any earlier claims that resources devoted to busing would be better spent elsewhere within the schools, the Metro council took Judge Wiseman's ruling to reduce busing and close a few schools as an opportunity to cut the school district's budget. In response—and for the first time since consolidation—the school board decided to exercise the power granted in the Metro charter to initiate a property tax increase for school funds via voter referendum, rather than working through the council's taxing authority. The vote took place on September 2, 1981, with school still not open for the year. The measure went down to defeat by a five-to-one margin. Even before the stay, local papers expressed their view that the referendum was unlikely to pass; but the stay, and the reminder of remaining uncertainty in the district, worsened the odds and made it difficult for voters to separate their concerns about the state of desegregation in Nashville from their consideration of funding.[117]

The Sixth Circuit heard the plaintiff's appeal in the fall of 1981. It was an august three-judge panel—Judge Anthony M. Celebrezze had been President Kennedy's Secretary of Health, Education, and Welfare; Nathaniel Jones was a former NAACP chief counsel; and George Edwards had ruled earlier against the Nashville school board when it sought a way out of Judge Morton's 1971 busing order. In a two-to-one split, the court ruled on July 27, 1982, that Judge Wiseman had failed to properly interpret *Swann's* desegregation standards, and that tolerating schools that were 15 percent minority, black or white, "emasculated" the desegregation plan. Instead, Judges Jones and Edwards required the district to continue to "eliminate from the public schools all vestiges of state-imposed segregation," which could be done only through continued attention to racial ratios that used the district's demographics as their starting point. The Sixth Circuit maintained the *Singleton* ratios.[118]

Judge Celebrezze dissented in part, explaining that he supported Judge Wiseman's statistical definition of desegregation. Celebrezze noted the findings of fact upon which Wiseman's opinion rested—patterns of white flight and disparate burden chief among them—and explained that his colleagues had not challenged these findings. Celebrezze read *Swann* as Wiseman had, while going further than Wiseman to say that the court could consider plans in light of their effectiveness, meaning that plans could be shaped with the desire to prevent white flight. Celebrezze characterized Wiseman's effort in *Kelley* as a "sincere effort to bring a degree of finality to this longstanding issue."[119]

Judge Celebrezze's was the dissent, though. In reversing much of Judge Wiseman's 1980 order, the Sixth Circuit majority required that all schools in Nashville must have between 17 and 47 percent black students—eliminating the possibility of a school desegregated with a black majority and white minority, as Wiseman, Williams, and Scott had come to agree could be possible.[120] The circuit court also dismissed the plaintiffs' concern about the burden of busing, and in doing so undercut much of the rationale for Wiseman's turn toward neighborhood schools. Judges Edwards and Jones explained that "intentional effort" to allocate burdens unevenly would be unconstitutional, but that factors like "availability of schools" and "location" had to be considered in creating a "practical assignment system."[121] Despite the evidence of more than a dozen years of *Kelley* litigation, and legal emphasis on school construction since *Green*, the Sixth Circuit slipped into thinking of school facilities as fixed features standing outside of the making of segregation and the shaping of desegregation.

The transition from last appointed school board to first elected one took place while Nashville waited for the Court of Appeals to rule. In their first major action, the newly composed board voted to appeal the Sixth Circuit decision to the Supreme Court. Seeing in Nashville's case an opportunity to roll back busing, President Reagan's Justice Department filed an amicus brief with the court in support of the appeal. Yet the high court refused to hear the case, and thus in January 1983, *Kelley* returned to Judge Wiseman's courtroom. The school board began to work out the contours of its own plan, which it did largely in keeping with the guidelines established by the previous, appointed board.

Avon Williams gathered local leaders in his office to review the plan, and they listed familiar concerns in new language. Noting that the plan transported black students out of city neighborhoods for six of their first eight years in school, they found it particularly galling to see a new list of school closings in the same area. The roster "read like Dante's List of Lost Souls." Expressing frustration stemming from more than a decade of effort to rectify disparate burdens, the group spoke of desegregation's practice in Nashville as carrying "socio-psychological impact" that "begins to resurrect visions" akin to those effects of segregation on black children's psyches documented in Kenneth Clark's famous doll study that the Supreme Court drew upon in *Brown*.[122] Just before the board was scheduled to take a vote on their plan, board chair Kent Weeks let his colleagues know that he, board attorney William Willis, and Avon Williams had been engaged in intensive negotiations toward a new acceptable plan. The two attorneys' offices were just across a parking lot from one another in downtown Nashville, and camera crews kept watch, hoping to get a glimpse of the process.[123] Williams had indicated that nearly all of the board's plan would be acceptable, with a few modifications targeted at keeping or reopening schools in historically black communities. Ultimately, after further negotiation with Weeks and the board, the basic structure of the 1971 approach remained, but with symbolically significant adjustments to recognize black communities as sites for schooling. The central city lost both Pearl and Cohn, but gained a new comprehensive high school to be named Pearl-Cohn. A few black elementary schools reopened in the city core, serving students for one or two early grades; a few suburban schools closed instead; and the board planned a few academically selective magnets for central-city locations.[124]

For Avon Williams, who had argued for county-wide busing as early as 1971, busing's expansion represented something of a victory. After more than eight years of legal struggle and local activism, the urban neighborhoods around Pearl and Cohn High Schools would have a high school, but on the terms of the district's comprehensive plan rather than their own. The new school represented investment in an undeniably urban and historically black neighborhood, but without meeting Pearl's or Cohn's advocates' hopes for their community institutions. Pearl-Cohn opened in 1985, and over the next dozen years maintained a student population that was between a third and a quarter white, two-thirds to three-quarters black.[125] Not all of North Nashville's students attended the new local school, though, because the district continued to need North Nashville's students, as Hugh Scott had described it in Judge Wiseman's courtroom, as black paint to mix into the white base of the suburban comprehensive schools.[126] More than half of black teenagers in North Nashville rode buses to Hillwood High School, where they provided the desegregation quota for students from surrounding white suburbs.

## Conclusion

In the 1970s, busing's advocates hoped that statistical desegregation could be closely tied to equality of educational opportunity. In Nashville, busing often did produce significantly desegregated populations of students, more access to physical and curricular resources in schools, and social learning among students. Yet the experience of busing taught residents that robust educational equality did not flow from a single white-majority racial ratio alone. The racial ratio, endorsed by the Supreme Court in *Swann* and adopted and defended in *Kelley*, offered a thin vision of educational equality, one that could coincide with inequalities in the experiences of schooling—from micro-level interactions between students and peers to larger structures of tracking.

In the late 1970s and early 1980s, a diverse group of African American leaders in Nashville—each negotiating their own complex relationships with local and national agendas and their own histories with segregation and desegregation—tried to move the city toward a more robust vision of educational equality, one that valued statistical desegregation alongside concern that communities felt recognized and their students' experiences in school valued. Black community leaders, from school board members to ministers to parent advocates, struggled to reconcile for themselves how much statistical desegregation was worth: in closures of cherished institutions, in time and distance on the bus, in feelings of alienation at new schools in unfamiliar and sometimes inaccessible areas. Across nearly thousands of pages of court transcripts and dozens of hours of public hearings, desegregation appeared to be a matter of costs more than realized or potential benefits.

To the extent that the school board majority and school administrators addressed these questions, they did so while continuing to prioritize mitigating white resistance and withdrawal. They remained trapped within the white flight narrative. Working within this framework, the options they considered ranged from busing plans that continued to produce inequalities in the experience of schooling, to Judge Wiseman's proposal that chose, at the elementary level, no desegregation over unequal desegregation. White resistance determined which black communities could have schools; the primacy of the racial ratio made a place like Pearl an impossibility. There was no analogous veto of white institutions by black families.

The struggle over Pearl exemplified the struggle between thin and robust notions of educational equality. In familiar, if faulty, narratives of civil rights activism—particularly those that chart an integrationist rise before a separatist or nationalist decline—the rallying of local support around Pearl High School could appear to fit neatly into the latter.[127] And for some Nashvillians, particularly Leo Lillard, the characterization would be somewhat accurate. (It was accurate for white Bellevue exurban residents as well). The defense of Pearl was much broader, though, than the idea of separatism captures. When self-described "integrationists" like Barbara Mann argued for Pearl's persistence, they did so with both an appreciation for these institutions' historic importance within their communities and a desire for recognition and parity of treatment. These struggles owed less to major ideological shifts of the late 1960s and 1970s than to the challenges long faced by an African American minority in a metropolitan setting whose politics and economy were dominated by a mutually reinforcing web of white elected officials, business interests, and community institutions.

From 1983 to 1998, Nashville created statistical desegregation in its schools via busing, reaching all of the county's schools. Yet more busing came with less local support for it from black or white residents or local leaders. The new 1983 busing plan was both an expansion of desegregation, and its last gasp. After years of public debate that surfaced several substantial critiques of busing, the 1983 plan lacked a substantial response to these critiques. The middle path that Avon Williams sought on behalf of the plaintiffs—of integration with moderation, in Hugh Scott's words—did not fit in the dominant local narratives about desegregation.

# CHAPTER NINE

# The Long Road to the End of Desegregation

When Nashville schools opened in 1983 under a new court-approved plan, school administrators and civic leaders hoped for stability after five years of litigation and community debate. Their hopes were largely met; until 1998, Nashville schools worked within a plan that made their system one of the most statistically desegregated in the country. In the 1980s between 30 and 40 (of more than 130) schools annually exceeded the new court-specified ratio of 18 to 48 percent black enrollment, yet the district avoided the sharp racial isolation for both black and white students visible in so many metropolitan areas nationally. In most years, not a single district school operated without at least a 10 percent minority presence, black or white. Despite this relative success at statistical desegregation, the core questions debated in Judge Wiseman's courtroom in the late 1970s and 1980s remained unresolved: What did statistical desegregation accomplish? Was it enough? What did equitable desegregation look like? Yet again, the toughest sticking points in these debates turned on the spatial organization of schooling—which communities would get schools and why. Familiar questions about curriculum reappeared as well, attending less to vocational education and more to compensatory programs that promised additional resources could offset segregation's impact on students.

In the 1990s a confluence of local and national changes brought attention back to desegregation. A new superintendent, a chamber of commerce reengaged with education, and a new mayor together set a goal of "getting out from under" the *Kelley* court order. They saw their odds of doing so strengthened by decrees of "unitary status"—the legal term marking the end of previously "dual" or segregated systems—issuing from courtrooms around the country. The Nashville school board, with the encouragement of local elites, launched a six-year-long process that led ultimately to the board and representatives of the *Kelley* plaintiffs together seeking unitary status and the end of court-supervised desegregation in 1998. The district's new plan, certified by Nashville's federal district judge Thomas A. Wiseman in 1998, valued stability and close-to-home schooling most highly, and separated statistical desegregation from discussion of student learning. In practice, the new plan sharply increased racially isolated schools and undid much of the statistical desegregation busing created in Nashville over the previous decade. Desegregation proved to have—in policy terms, if not in the lives of individual students who had experienced it—a short half-life.[1]

## Busing's Last Decade

The official conversation about ending busing in Nashville did not begin until 1992, but in many ways the experience of the 1980s set the stage. If the 1970s had brought dramatic change in the social, curricular, and physical structure of Nashville's schools, then a five-year period of legal debate from 1978 to 1983 created prolonged uncertainty; the city rode out desegregation's next decade, enduring desegregation rather than embracing it or vociferously opposing it. The 1983 desegregation plan negotiated by Avon Williams and school board chair Kent Weeks kept much of the familiar structure of busing, expanded it throughout the county, and made a few modifications to better balance the burdens of desegregation. Now-Mayor Richard Fulton and others worried that the new plan would prompt more enrollment losses for the district, but on that measure as well as general public response, the 1980s saw less dramatic resistance. Unlike the major exodus of 1971, enrollment dipped slightly until the 1984–85 school year, reaching a low of 55,000 students, and then began a gradual climb that has continued since, although the proportion of white students continued to slide. A few communities—including those most visibly resistant to busing for desegregation a decade earlier—found ways to embrace busing to serve their own interests. Their stories remained the exception, however, amid local press coverage still emphasizing "racial conflict" in schools and marking central-city schools as troubled spaces. Nashville schools lagged surrounding rural and suburban counties in student achievement and high school completion, seemingly confirming locally what the new national discourse about educational crisis asserted generally—that, in the words of the presidential commission on education's *A Nation at Risk* report, American schools were engulfed in a "rising tide of mediocrity."[2]

The 1983 desegregation plan slated Antioch High School for closure because it was a small, noncomprehensive high school and because its student population was 94 percent white, outside of the court-specified racial ratio. Rather than making dramatic presentations to the school board—as had representatives from the Madison area, who brought a wreath of black flowers to a board meeting to mark the loss of their high school—representatives from Antioch instead chose to seize upon the court's definition of statistical desegregation. They requested and received permission from Judge Wiseman to use the three years before the school's planned closure to bring their school (and their community) up to the court-mandated 18 percent black minimum. To do so, they held meetings with neighborhood associations to encourage word-of-mouth recruitment, worked with the Metropolitan Development and Housing Authority (the renamed Nashville Housing Authority) to encourage scatter-site public housing locations and to host a fair housing luncheon in which they told area real estate agents of their interest in attracting black families. (Ironically given her profession's historic use of steering to preserve segregated white neighborhoods, one agent reminded her colleagues that they could pursue black residents, but that intentional steering by race was illegal). Antioch representatives also spoke with the Metropolitan Transit Authority to appeal for better bus service to make the area more accessible for families without cars.[3] By 1986, Antioch High School had increased its black student enrollment only by thirty students, to 9 percent of the total, but Wiseman extended the school's life. Whether due to intentional recruiting or population growth and diversification already under way, by 1991, Antioch High School passed the 18 percent standard. By the turn of the century, the area was one of the fastest growing and most diverse, in terms of race, national origin, and class, in the county.[4]

Antioch's story could at once reinforce and subvert dominant understandings of school segregation and desegregation. Seemingly fitting the de facto paradigm, Antioch illustrated the power of patterns of segregation in housing to shape segregation in schooling. But reversing that paradigm, it showed as well that incentives for desegregation in schooling could be powerful in encouraging desegregation in housing—that housing demographics could follow schooling, not only the reverse.[5] Neither, however, suggests that Antioch had somehow overcome all previous resistance to desegregation. Surely, public conversation about intentional residential desegregation was a far cry from the early-1950s school-sponsored "blackface minstrel" show, "complete with steamboat and wharf," that students performed at an Antioch elementary school, or from the flyers decrying busing as turning "your neighborhood schools into savage jungles" circulated at rallies attended by thousands in 1971, when the area was a home to particularly vocal anti-busing activism. The shift away from explicit racist expression to modest inclusion of black residents was at once significant and limited. As one Antioch resident asked in 1985, "If the problem is that Antioch does not have enough blacks, why didn't they do something about it earlier?" Recruiting black families into Antioch's community allowed white residents to retain their local school, and to encounter black students on their terms and turf instead of via busing to distant majority-black communities. As with many aspects of busing in practice, Antioch's efforts were at once laudable and far from fully egalitarian.[6]

Other white suburban parents weighed their resistance to sending their children to majority-black urban neighborhoods against the educational disruptions created by overcrowding in outlying majority-white communities. Families in the Edge-o-Lake neighborhood were frustrated that their outlying neighborhood had extensive overcrowding at the middle school level. They chose to suggest that their students be bused to central-city Cameron Middle School for all of their middle school years, preferring a stable four-year experience at Cameron, where space was sufficient, over their local overcrowded school.[7]

Some principals and teachers attempted to make newly county-wide busing a less alienating experience for students and families, and to bridge the geographic gap between neighborhood location and school site. Amqui Elementary, located on Davidson County's northeastern edge, served both local students—nearly all of whom were white—and black students who rode buses from suburban areas just north of the Cumberland River. A few days before school began, Amqui's principal and his faculty drove in a slow caravan through the distant neighborhood, stopping to introduce themselves to children playing outside and to their parents. Similarly, central-city Wharton Elementary faculty toured the four elementary schools— three suburban and one urban—from which the school drew its fifth and sixth graders.[8] Later, one school member initiated PTA meetings not only at her district's suburban schools, but also in the central-city neighborhoods from which students rode buses. Some schools held parent-teacher conference nights in central-city neighborhoods as well. As a geographer studying Nashville schools noted, these practices made school-family interactions more possible, but underlined the notion that "bused" families were fundamentally different from their neighborhood students, as "bused" students' families were visible for school officials only in their geographically and socially distant home communities.[9]

The 1980s brought multiple difficulties for Nashville's schools. Busing most frequently took the blame in public conversation, and opposition

9.1. Suburban Amqui Elementary School principal Arthur Irvin introduces himself
and gives a fourth-grade student his business card. Irvin led a caravan of the school
faculty through the student's distant neighborhood before school opened. *Banner,*
August 9, 1983. Courtesy of Nashville Public Library Special Collections.

to it helped explain the failure of tax increases for education that book-
ended the decade in 1981 and 1990.[10] Having designed the 1983 desegregation plan first to achieve court-specified racial ratios and then to function within the existing landscape of school facilities, MNPS administered
desegregation in ways that challenged not only families but peer and adult
relationships within schools. At Antioch High School, for example, by the
1990s students came to the school not only from a broad range of neighborhood environments, but from eight different paths through elementary
and middle schools. Children who lived in Antioch began their schooling at one of seven elementary schools, then followed one of twenty-two
different paths that ended at one of four different high schools, Antioch
High School being one of them. Other districts' approaches suggest that a
more cohesive approach was possible. Louisville, Kentucky, began busing

in 1975 by completely disassociating residence from school assignment, using the first letter of the student's last name instead. But after resistance to this approach, in the mid-1980s Louisville reorganized its desegregation plan to link geographically defined clusters of students to a smaller number of schools.[11]

Black people observing white anti-busing protesters usefully quipped, "It's not the bus. It's us." Surely they were right, but with busing implemented as it was in Nashville, at times it was "the bus" and "us." As Hubert Dixon III had noted about his experience, the jumble of school assignments and shifts across years posed difficulties for children's peer relationships; they likely challenged the development of long-term relationships with adults as well. The complexity of these plans prevented any coherent understanding of how particular locations in Nashville's landscape related to particular schools. This complexity affected many groups, and differently. Real estate agents, and the markets they helped shape, preferred tidy and visible links between school and home. For central-city families—more likely to be more mobile—complex busing schemes compounded educational disruption when moves of just a block or two in one direction or another could produce a change in school zone for students already shifting schools six or more times in their schooling.[12]

Busing's logistical challenges—experienced to different extents by parents differently positioned in the metropolis, and with different economic and social resources—were many. Yet these challenges did not, as many feared, undermine student achievement. Parents (as well as expert witnesses like Hugh Scott) had suggested that frequent changes between schools would lead to lower test scores. Vanderbilt scholar Richard Pride's research on test scores showed that despite the unpopularity of the shifts, they did not hurt student achievement. More generally, whatever busing's inconveniences and challenges, Nashville students' mean test scores appeared to have risen significantly over the 1970s and 1980s. This was the finding of an analysis done by superintendent Charles Frazier in 1992. Compared to the national average, Nashville's students on average had moved from the 40th percentile in 1971 to just at or above the national mean at the 50th percentile. Black students' mean scores rose most dramatically. The number of students scoring "below average" fell from around 70 percent (with some variation across subjects and grades) as of 1971 to roughly 25 percent by 1991. These gains helped close by half the still-large gaps between mean black and white student scores. Frazier's comparison should be read cautiously, as his report took only two points in time rather than tracing the intervening years; likely the tests involved had changed over the years as well. Although the general curve of student achievement, measured on standardized tests, both rose and saw small shrinkage of the gap between black and white students, the district's results were still far less than ideal. More than a quarter of its students failed to complete high school, and competency and achievement scores—even if rising—still lagged national averages and fell behind the school systems in adjoining counties.[13]

In the same years that test-measured student achievement seems to have climbed, support for vocational education fell markedly. From the late 1970s, when most Nashville high schoolers attended a comprehensive high school with both academic and extensive vocational offerings, vocational enrollments fell faster than high school enrollment. Falling enrollment reduced funding, which cut the number of courses a school could staff, which further threatened enrollment. Declining enrollment may have reflected student interest. It also reflected how, as Nashville administrator Lucille Nabors put it, students were "getting squeezed" by increasing state graduation requirements providing students less flexibility in course selection.[14]

More broadly, however, in the mid-1980s public voices on the left and the right criticized vocational education as ineffective and out of date—echoing long-established criticisms audible periodically throughout the twentieth century. The Democratic candidate to succeed Governor Lamar Alexander, Jane Eskind, described vocational education as failing to prepare students for the state's growth areas. A former state economic growth official spoke in even more stark terms in 1987, asserting that even though no one in the state knew what the $50 million in high school–level vocational funds accomplished, criticizing the program was like running "into a buzzsaw" from the state's pro-vocational education lobby.[15] Less than a decade after Nashville opened seven enlarged high schools defined as comprehensive by their new vocational facilities, the program lacked the promise it seemed to hold a decade earlier. Even if fewer Nashville students took vocational classes, whether useful or not, thousands still did—1,300 at Glencliff High School alone in 1989.[16]

The 1980s-era criticisms of vocational education raised fundamental questions, but came after the program made its mark on schools in Nashville. The vocational emphasis overall endorsed sorting students based on predictions of their future life course—an emphasis that, unless thoughtfully considered and monitored, was prone to reinforce racist tracking between vocational and academic courses or the "general" and "honors" tracks. Vocational education dollars also remade the physical landscape of schooling in Nashville. High schools became larger and more suburban in ways that endured even when vocational education waned. Scale had its own consequences. School discipline and safety, the frequent focus of public concern in the 1980s and 1990s, was also harder to achieve in larger schools. By the early 1990s some local observers made direct links between problems with discipline and the size of the district's high schools, which were more likely to feel impersonal and leave students disconnected—and possibly to contribute to the district's suspension rate, which far exceeded the state and area average (and which affected black students dispropor- tionately). Although bound by the district's established commitment to the comprehensive model, superintendent Charles Frazier shared in some of these concerns about the model.[17]

Rather than drawing attention to the policy choices—like frequent shifts between schools and incoherent pathways through district schools— that made the experience of busing challenging, local news coverage, par- ticularly the more conservative *Banner*, remained attached to "racial con- flict" as the prime story about Nashville's schools in the 1980s. A Hillwood High School pep rally turned into a sixty-student brawl, with one student injured with a knife. The *Banner* quoted a Hillwood teacher first: "This is a result of cross-town busing."[18]

Identifying the district's troubles as largely the result of the court order and its constraints became a convenient diversion, locating the source of difficulty in the federal courthouse and emphasizing the impossible over the possible. Just about everything that could go wrong could be blamed on busing, and busing itself was often blamed on an external, federal im- position. In fact, the experience of busing in Nashville depended just as much on local decisions as federal ones. As one citizen critic put it, the dis- trict both bent and hid behind the court order. Doing so limited its ability to imagine doing busing better.[19]

The district moved in a new direction in the 1980s in one respect. Nash- ville's 1983 desegregation plan created three new magnet schools, includ- ing one at the former Pearl High, with quota systems for desegregation and intentional use of central-city locations. Tennessee's Senator Lamar Alex- ander, like other Reagan-era Republicans, had been calling for increased parental choice in education. Avon Williams did support the use of a few magnet schools when their statistical desegregation was assured by a clear quota system. Each school reserved 66 percent of its spaces for white stu- dents and 33 percent for black students. Black students and white students entered separate admissions lotteries when demand exceeded supply.[20]

Even more than in the 1970s, Nashville's schools reached unprece- dented levels of statistical desegregation under the 1983 plan, outpacing most districts nationally. Yet in the 1980s and 1990s, the school district was far from embracing its success on this measure, instead becoming a place of "compliance and complaint," in the words of one former school board member.[21] Evidence of diminishing legal support for desegregation in other districts furthered the feeling that Nashville was in a holding pattern, awaiting desegregation's end rather than capitalizing on what achievements, even if imperfect, the district could claim.

## "Getting Out from Under"

In the early 1990s, local and national forces converged to create an opening for local elites to push for the end of court-supervised desegregation. Their efforts launched a five-year period of planning and debate, one at times frankly targeting "getting out from under the court order," and at other times placing desegregation within a broader conversation about "equity and excellence."

Metropolitan Nashville Public Schools head Charles Frazier retired in early 1992, after more than a decade in the position and a previous decade as a deputy to Elbert Brooks. In Frazier's successor, the board chose a candidate with no previous experience with Nashville schools, but prior work negotiating an end to court-ordered desegregation. Richard Benjamin came to Nashville from Ann Arbor, Michigan, in March 1992. Just a few months later, he called for the district to return to court to seek the end of the court order, to ask for a legal judgment that Nashville had moved beyond its history of a dual or segregated system and now had "unitary status." Benjamin was careful to assert that unitary status did not mean an end to desegregation. But just what defined desegregation, and how it would or would not be ensured in a post-court-ordered district remained unclear.[22]

Benjamin's remarks aligned well with the opinion of newly elected Mayor Phil Bredesen, who personified a new generation of Nashville leadership. Unlike Nashville's previous three mayors over twenty-eight years—Beverly Briley, Richard Fulton (elected as mayor after leaving Congress), and Bill Boner—Bredesen was not a Nashville native but a transplant. He built his wealth and claims to entrepreneurial expertise in the city's powerful private hospital management and health care sector. Bredesen identified as a moderate Democrat, and in his first State of the City address in 1992, he claimed at once to be committed to desegregation but to want Nashville to define its own route to "a truly integrated, truly fair school system" based on "our own commitment" rather than depending on a "federal judge somewhere to do this for us."[23] After those remarks, Brede-sen's public comments steered between direct calls to figure out "what we need to do to get out from under the court order and what the cost is" and general assertions that he still hoped schools could be "somewhat racially mixed."[24]

After many years of silence on desegregation, the powerful chamber of commerce emerged as a key voice pushing to end desegregation. Looking to generate more economic growth and keep up with regional champions like Charlotte and Atlanta, they hired an outside consultant on economic development strategy. Their report indicated that the Nashville area had the opportunity to compete for major corporate relocations if they "sub-stantially improve[d] the quality of . . . public schools."[25] Within local busi-ness thinking, the first step in doing so was the reduction or elimination of court-ordered desegregation. After two decades of disengagement with Nashville schools, as more and more of Nashville's elite became private school parents and board members, the chamber became an increasingly visible presence in local talk about education. They produced a highly pub-licized annual report on the school system. Although Benjamin suggested that the school system might make significant improvements even prior to a unitary status declaration, and board chair Edward Kindall reminded his colleagues that they were not wholly "under control of the federal courts," most local leaders implied a two stage process: first, unitary status; then, school improvement.[26]

The national legal climate also signaled that desegregation orders were coming to an end. With evidence from cities like Norfolk, Virginia, site of the first busing order to be lifted under a unitary status decree in 1986, and nearby Chattanooga, Tennessee, unitary declarations mounted. Cases from Oklahoma, Georgia, and Missouri made it clear that neither a return to statistically segregated schools nor continued segregation in some aspects of schooling would impede unitary status.[27] The school board could have proceeded directly to court, to petition for a judgment of unitary status for Nashville. But the potential for opposition from the plaintiffs—opposition that could lead to another phase of long-running hearings, debates, and possibly appeals—led the director, board, and attorneys to agree on a somewhat more inclusive process, in hopes that the district and the plain-tiffs could ultimately approach the court together to seek unitary status.[28]

Avon Williams had by this time become seriously ill, and Richard Din-kins took the lead as legal counsel for the *Kelley* plaintiffs. Dinkins ap-pointed six members to a newly formed Advisory Committee on Equity and Excellence. These delegates met, beginning in early 1993, with the other members of the twenty-one-person committee. The mayor appointed three, the school administration three, and each of the nine school board members chose one. The committee's conversations ranged broadly, covering everything from the suggestion that students wear uniforms to calls for keeping strict racial ratios at new magnet and neighborhood schools; from underrepresentation of black teachers in MNPS faculty to the possibility of zoning students to schools based on their parents' work addresses rather than residence. For some participants, the breadth of the conversation reflected valuable attention to aspects of "equity and excellence" beyond statistical desegregation; for others, the breadth of discussion simply dodged the real matter of whether or how statistical desegregation mattered for Nashville schools, whether it would continue, and through what mechanisms. The committee had in hand Charles Frazier's 1992 report indicating significant test score–measured achievement growth over Nashville's two decades of desegregation via busing but this information did not seem to figure in discussion of "rekindling" student achievement in the district.[29]

In December 1993, the citizens' commission submitted ninety-five recommendations and ten principles to the board. The committee's charge had mandated that they operate on consensus, which pushed the group toward the anodyne, but their report called for a "racially balanced student body, faculty and staff" in each school, for magnet schools to facilitate voluntary desegregation, and for monitoring mechanisms for both equity and excellence.[30] The report dodged questions over which the committee had split—including whether or not to recommend constructing or reopening long-shuttered elementary schools in central-city neighborhoods—that previewed the difficult road ahead to translate principles into practice while meeting public demands for less busing. But the committee also identified the core elements that did later shape Nashville's unitary status agreement: sending students to no more than three schools from kindergarten through twelfth grade and rationalizing student assignment by creating "feeder patterns" so that students would travel with a peer group from elementary to high school.

With the report of the Committee on Equity and Excellence in hand, the school board then confronted how to define a concrete plan for continued, or reduced, desegregation. Over the next two years, the board made little progress, circling around platitudes without defining what "valuing diversity" at the school level meant, or what mechanisms needed to be in place to define and ensure equity. The board also struggled to name desegregation's value amid strengthening emphasis on test score–measured student academic achievement. Kent Weeks, the white attorney and veteran school board member who had taken the lead in negotiating the 1983 desegregation plan across from Avon Williams, perceived a fundamentally different landscape a dozen years later. Weeks stated: "It's got nothing to do with color. . . . If kids achieve, what the hell is the difference?" Other white board members expressed similar sentiments in more measured tones, asserting that anticipated increases in academic achievement could substitute for desegregation.[31]

Like most Nashvillians, the board's two black members, Edward Kindall and Cornelius Ridley, hoped their communities' children could attend school closer to home. Both Nashville natives, Kindall and Ridley had deeply positive associations with black institutions in Nashville and had experienced urban renewal and its disruptions in their community. Despite their firm commitment to keeping or reopening schools in historically black neighborhoods, MNPS staff projections of what neighborhood-based school assignments would look like refocused Ridley's and Kindall's attention on desegregation as well. If the district used neighborhood zones, seventeen elementary schools (out of the district's fifty-seven) would exceed 90 percent white students, and another ten would have more than 90 percent black students—making more than half of the district's elementary schools highly racially isolated. Prompted by this stark information, Kindall and Ridley began to push for a more affirmative commitment to intentional desegregation from the board and argued against the possibility of large numbers of all-black schools, seeing in them both political vulnerability and lost learning opportunities.[32]

Both Kindall and Ridley graduated from segregated Nashville schools —a point that press coverage often included as if to dismiss their concerns about segregation by tying them to history rather than the present.[33] Ridley, a Pearl alum and former championship-winning basketball coach there and at Maplewood High School, was strongly committed to keeping Pearl-Cohn available to local North Nashville students, at times splitting with Kindall over the idea of converting the school to one or more magnet programs in hopes of facilitating voluntary desegregation.[34] Kindall and Ridley faced the challenge of not only arguing for desegregation measures as desegregation's legal levers weakened, but doing so on behalf of a community long central to black Nashvillians and long marginalized in white- and suburban-majority metropolitan politics.

If data about the extent of segregation under neighborhood school zoning crystallized the problem of resegregation, a different inquiry from Ridley helped clarify its potential academic consequences. Ridley, who had been most focused on retaining schools like Pearl-Cohn, asked the school district staff to compare student achievement via test scores at Pearl and at majority-white schools to which North Nashville students rode buses. The staff reported that black student scores at outer-suburban, majority-white Hillwood were the highest, above local Pearl-Cohn, but both were higher than at Hillsboro High School, an inner-ring suburban, predominantly white school.[35] Ridley, who had expected the data to show that black students were doing no better via busing, instead found he had expanded the debate and now had to consider how to pursue equal opportunity for those black students bused to and—as he put it—"hidden" within otherwise high-performing schools like Hillsboro.[36]

As Ridley's data request helped reveal, shifting the conversation to achievement did not mean a tidy end to questions of desegregation. Instead, more attention to achievement sharpened the focus on matters long submerged beneath continued talk of white flight and the discomforts of busing. Did statistical desegregation help Hillwood students achieve higher scores than Pearl-Cohn students? If so, what happened at Hillsboro to lessen or undermine any benefit from statistical desegregation? The board lacked empirically grounded answers to these questions, in keeping with public discourse on desegregation that turned to general assertions or instincts over evidence. Promises that a return to neighborhood elementary schools—particularly in urban black communities that had lacked them for more than two decades—would bring increased parent involvement and thereby an improvement in student achievement proved powerful.

That idea helped buttress the board's interest in neighborhood schools —which meant different things to suburbanites whose elementary schools at the earliest grades had long been in local neighborhoods, and to urban families whose schools had long been shuttered. The board ultimately opted for an only slightly modified version of the approach Judge Thomas Wiseman had ordered in 1981. They accepted much higher levels of racial (and class) concentration at many elementary schools.

A return to segregation came alongside more parental-choice provisions and the reassertion of ideas—echoes of 1960s compensatory education programs—that the curricular organization of schooling could offset segregation's consequences. Schools in the district's most concentrated poor and black neighborhoods became "enhanced option" schools. Families zoned to enhanced option schools had the option of that school or a more distant, and more diverse, school.[37] If they stayed in the local enhanced option school, they would have additional classroom resources, and class sizes reduced to fifteen to one. These enhancements would draw students from around the district, the board claimed. Yet the board did not provide transportation, and did not save spaces for out-of-zone students. Nor did the board reckon with the implications of special curricular approaches in enhanced option schools. As compensatory education programs had over decades, programs designed to provide special help conveyed messages of inherent difference that, in this case, worked against goals of desegregation. Richard Dinkins, representing the *Kelley* plaintiffs, initially opposed the enhanced options schools because he felt they would convey a "stigma" about their students and neighborhoods, but came to support the approach.[38]

The board's prior investment in large, comprehensive, and suburban high schools necessitated large geographic high school zones that produced relatively more diverse student populations than did neighborhood-zoned elementary schools. Although comprehensive high schools had this benefit, they were also the source of much concern, given the experience of the previous decades. The board and its advisory committee agreed now that smaller schools produced a "greater sense of community, less alienation, [and] the potential for fewer discipline problems." Yet existing school facilities kept large-scale the norm.[39]

After more than two decades in which many black urban Nashville families felt frustration over the experience of busing their youngest children away from home and the closure of local schools, while suburban families often complained about their more limited experience of busing in to city neighborhoods, Nashville lacked political will to work for statistically desegregated schools. Where the board did use noncontiguous zoning and produced more desegregated schools than the residential geography would have suggested, this was largely a lingering result of the decades of school closures in central city areas. Many black elementary students had to be bused to the western suburbs of Hillwood and Hillsboro because there were so few elementary-classroom seats in their home neighborhood. (After a wave of capital improvements that opened more city schools, the school board removed the last noncontiguous zones.) Nashville's inequitable approach to desegregation in the 1970s and 1980s created enemies not only in white Nashville but in black communities as well, either as opponents of desegregation or skeptics that the district could carry out desegregation fairly and equitably. Nashville's history, of remaking educational inequality in the era of desegregation via the spatial organization of schooling, lessened the chance that statistical desegregation could be considered as a component of equal educational opportunity in the 1990s and beyond.

One board member offered a persistent reminder about the constraints on thinking about desegregation in the early 1990s. Murray Philip, a resident of the northeastern suburbs of Nashville and a professional tile installer, ran for the board on an anti-busing platform and frequently affirmed what he saw as the unconstitutionality of any discussion of race in creating student assignment plans. There were others on the board who had deep skepticism about intentional desegregation, but Philip was the most exhaustingly vocal, objecting frequently to small aspects of the plan the board was gradually crafting while also lobbying the city council against it. Philip kept the specter of larger-scale legal involvement in sight, as he worked with representatives of the conservative Southeastern Legal Foundation, who stood ready to challenge any continued intentional desegregation in Nashville's plan.[40]

Magnet schools seemed to promise a way forward toward desegregation while avoiding the unpopularity and the legal uncertainties that came with compulsory assignment. Mayor Phil Bredesen, like other Tennessee politicians, endorsed the idea of magnets and called on the system to expand their number radically, suggesting five new magnets open per year; later he suggested that all assignment to public schools be choice-based. The board moved more slowly than Bredesen wanted, but did include 12 magnets located in "hard to desegregate" areas in its 1996 plan. Each would have a distinct curricular identity, but would use an admissions process that assured a student population that reflected the district's overall racial demographics. The plan also promised transportation to magnet schools—which had not been offered previously, and which had been a key factor in producing magnet school enrollments that, while racially diverse, served far fewer poor families than the district average.[41]

Having settled its approaches to zoning and voluntary desegregation, the board struggled over what was in many respects the most fundamental shift that a unitary status declaration from the court would bring: Would anyone, beyond the board itself, be paying attention to Nashville schools on measures of desegregation and equality? The board majority, claiming years of "good faith" compliance with court orders, argued that no monitoring provision was needed.[42] Yet its minority felt otherwise. The two sides compromised on an approach that was ultimately a victory for the majority. The board chose as its monitor a small community entity with little expertise in the field. Nashville exited desegregation with no effective monitor. Meanwhile, the well-resourced chamber of commerce initiated its own process for an annual evaluation of the district's successes and failures.

On July 23, 1996, the board passed the Commitment to the Future plan, rezoning all of Nashville's schools, outlining massive capital improvements necessitated by the plan, and promising additional educational programs such as those for the enhanced option schools. The next step—at least, according to the image of inclusivity created by the committee—was to take the board's plan back to the plaintiffs. But what if they objected, or found the plan unacceptable? There the clear mission of the previous years' work, and the leverage the board held in a period of diminishing judicial commitment to desegregation, came into view. Would the board proceed to court even if the plaintiffs objected to the plan? "Absolutely," board chair Kent Weeks replied. The motion to approach the court for unitary status passed by a vote of 7 to 2 in January 1997.[43]

And then there was the question of money. The Commitment to the Future expanded, as had the earlier committee discussions, into every area of schooling. It included many aspects that would increase operating expenses on an ongoing basis (although some were later cut)—adding art and music for all MNPS schools, providing transportation to magnet schools, and hiring more teachers to serve smaller classes in enhanced option schools. These additions added up to between $75 and $100 million annually, in addition to the anticipated $347 million in capital expenses to build and renovate schools. Mayor Bredesen, who was empowered to forward the full—or only a partial—version of the school board's requested budget to the council, wanted to "partition" the multipart plan, to get to the core of what he valued most: first, fund "what we need to do to get out from under the court order."[44]

By early 1998, the basic outline of the plan was settled and the capital expenditures had been winnowed to $206 million, largely through the mayor's insistence that the board plan for a modest 5 percent increase in student population after the return to unitary status, rather than the 20 percent the board (overoptimistically) projected. The majority of the expenditures targeted renovating or replacing long-closed city elementary schools. Nashville's business elite lined up firmly behind the plan. The Greater Nashville Association of Realtors became the first to endorse it, explaining their view that "once we get out from under the court order and once we start measuring our progress year by year . . . then we are going to have a world-class system." Vanderbilt's chancellor and the chamber of commerce followed just a few weeks behind, and the chamber encouraged its members to lobby city council members in favor of the plan.[45] They did, but the plan passed just by a hair—only one vote, on June 24, 1998.[46] There was little opposition to the ending of court supervision, but much opposition to the expenditure of funds even after cuts.

At the close of the twentieth century, Nashville gave up on desegregation, for reasons of both choice and compulsion. A challenging policy—made more so through the interplay of local and federal decisions about implementation—had fatigued both black and white families. As the 1994 president of the local NAACP saw it, "Desegregation hasn't been given the chance to work, and because it hasn't been given the chance to work, kids have suffered harder than they might have suffered in a segregated school."[47] Many who had looked to desegregation as a path to greater equality now saw a district that had too often taken statistical desegregation as a thin substitute for more robust educational equality.

Students like Hubert Dixon III looked back across decades to his own schooling and reflected that the disruptions and displacements of busing had been "worth it," in terms of both the social and intellectual quality of his schooling. The Nashville student in the next generation of his family, his niece Brittany, felt the same way, as did graduates of the district's high schools in the early twenty-first century. And aggregate test scores spanning the 1970s and 1980s appeared at least to suggest meaningful positive growth in student achievement for both black and white students in the busing years. Achieving statistical desegregation had been a complex and perpetual challenge for Nashville education officials, absorbing significant amounts of district resources and commitment on the part of staffers who felt they were struggling to serve their district well. And the process of extensive negotiation over years led to some unlikely friendships, as that between plaintiffs' counsel Richard Dinkins and superintendent Bill Wise. Yet Nashville's elected and civic leadership failed to articulate a positive argument for desegregation, just as they had failed to embrace desegregation as one part of a more robust educational equality.[48]

Voices like Dixon's, and of the thousands of students who followed him in Nashville schools, were never systematically gathered or appreciated in the process of debating the end of desegregation.[49] Their scattered accounts could not compete with the confidence of a new elite firm in their assertions that metropolitan growth could be tied to improved schools, and that the route to school improvement passed first through the end of court-ordered desegregation. A federal judiciary increasingly interested in ending rather than refining desegregation left advocates like Richard Dinkins little space in which to maneuver, aware that the school board was strongly positioned to pursue unitary status alone if they chose. The negotiated unitary status agreement felt like a way to ensure that the end of desegregation, visible on the horizon, could come with at least some recognition of the needs of Nashville's most vulnerable students.[50]

## A Boomtown with Schools for Poor Children of Color

Board members described Nashville's student assignment plan as a "desegregation plan" through their 1990s negotiations. After 1998, Nashville still had very few highly concentrated white schools (with more than 90 percent white students). Yet black students became much more likely to attend a highly concentrated black school (with more than 90 percent black students). As of 1995 in Nashville, there was only one school with that concentration of black students; by 2005, there were a dozen, and by the end of the decade, almost twenty. The same district that had less than 1 percent of its black students in a highly concentrated minority school as of 1991—when one-quarter of southern black students were in such schools—had more than 20 percent as of 2009. After decades of out-desegregating most American school systems, Nashville moved much closer to the segregated mean.

At the high school level, the district's eleven large comprehensive schools—and the big zones to serve them—remained relatively more statistically desegregated. None were highly concentrated (90 percent or more) black or white. As the history of busing in Nashville would predict, statisti-

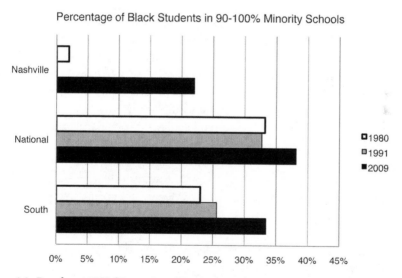

Percentage of Black Students in 90-100% Minority Schools

□ 1980
▨ 1991
■ 2009

9.2. Data from MNPS, "Twenty-Seven Year Analysis of Enrollment Patterns," file 1996, box 23, *Kelley*, and National Center for Education Statistics, Common Core of Data, with regional and national data from Genevieve Siegel-Hawley and Erica Frankenberg, "Southern Slippage: Growing School Segregation in the Most Desegregated Region of the Country," September 2012 (Los Angeles: Civil Rights Project). Chart prepared by Lauren Fox.

cal desegregation did not guarantee equality of opportunity. A researcher who spent fifteen months in a Nashville comprehensive high school in the early 2000s described it as demonstrating "racial inequality in academics" via continued tracking that "co-existed with limited racial equality in peer-group social status." That description captured much of what had changed, and not changed, in Nashville schools after more than four decades of de-segregation. Students built friendships in desegregated schools, experiencing a kind of social learning that mattered even if no one claimed it made a mark on test scores. But even as some students commented on the inequalities they saw regarding which students took which classes at their school, their understanding of this inequality remained limited. Just as their fore-bears (and contemporaries) relied on terms like "de facto segregation" in lieu of real interpretation of both state and private forces that fostered con-tinued segregation, the students defaulted to ideas of individual choice as the cause of racially identifiable tracks in their school. Students perceived academic tracking as the exclusive result of students' and parents' prefer-ences, and for those in higher-track classes, identified their position as the result of merit alone.[51]

The plan that won Nashville unitary status included mechanisms for voluntary desegregation that soon proved untenable, insufficient, or insufficiently supported. Only months after the 1998 court order, the school board ended magnet schools' race-conscious lottery system, following the advice of legal counsel that, if challenged in court, the system would be struck down as had similar plans in Boston.[52] The enlarged number of nonselective magnets in the district after 1998 became more highly con-centrated white or black. White parents left nonselective magnets in pref-erence for their zoned neighborhood schools, while black parents living nearby, and middle-class black parents from elsewhere in the district, saw magnets as better options for their children. For all families—but partic-ularly for poorer families—that the board never realized its earlier plans for full school bus transportation (only making public-bus vouchers avail-able) to magnet schools created a barrier to participation, and thus to desegregation.

"Getting out from under" the court order brought a variety of new kinds of energy into education in Nashville, none of which actually depended upon undoing busing or court supervision. All reflected a greater sense of ownership of and empowerment within Nashville's schools on the part of the business elite. The chamber of commerce stepped up its involvement not only in exhorting educational improvement, but trying to influence it. In the same year of the unitary status decree, the chamber established

SuccessPAC, a political action committee to collect and channel funds to chamber-supported school board candidates.[53] Mayor Phil Bredesen took the then-unusual step of advocating forcefully, and ultimately successfully, for the school district to adopt a particular curriculum. Valued by some conservative communities for its attention to the Western canon, the "Core Knowledge" curriculum grew out of E. D. Hirsch's 1988 best seller, *Cultural Literacy: What Every American Needs to Know.* The curriculum set out both specific topics (e.g., works of literature, historical figures) and the order in which they should be taught. For Bredesen and other of the curriculum's advocates, the program's uniformity was its greatest value. Parents in some school communities appeared newly interested in committing their resources to their now more neighborhood-identified public schools. In the affluent western suburbs around Julia Green Elementary, parents launched a private fund-raising effort to replace the school's four portable classrooms with a permanent addition. Their efforts raised immediate opposition from those who worried (rightly, as it turned out) that a return to neighborhood schools would deepen social and economic resource inequalities between different Nashville communities.[54]

Ending desegregation in Nashville meant different things for black communities differently positioned. Given the extent of black middle-class suburbanization over the 1980s and 1990s, students who lived around enhanced option schools like Napier resided in intensely class-segregated communities that continued to be isolated physically and economically from the growing city around them. By contrast, the now-suburban middle-class black population attended a mixture of statistically desegregated local public schools, schools with increasingly concentrated black student populations, or, increasingly, private schools.[55]

Post–unitary status Nashville offered its white students, and many of its middle-class black students, statistically desegregated schooling with both benefits and drawbacks. Many poorer black students, by contrast, attended the district's distinctly resegregated schools.[56]

The district's five enhanced option schools—ostensibly created to foster both resource-rich environments for high-poverty communities and to draw out-of-zone families to these environments—never came close to that latter goal. They served highly concentrated populations of black, almost exclusively poor, students. Their teachers acknowledged that they had more physical and financial resources and smaller class sizes, as had been promised in the plan. They also spent an additional twenty school days per year with their students (half as many as promised in the 1998 agreement). But teachers at enhanced option schools reported that "we have so much, and it still isn't enough." The challenges of concentrated poverty quickly out-matched the additional resources delivered under the new plan.[57] Despite the additional resources, Nashville's schools with the greatest levels of con-centrated poverty also proved the least likely to hire and retain the district's strongest teachers.[58]

Nashville schools looked dramatically different at the turn of the twenty-first century than they had two decades earlier not only because of the end of court-ordered desegregation. A biracial city long after many American metropolises became broadly diverse, Nashville experienced the beginnings of global immigration in the 1980s and early 1990s. Refugee resettlement programs brought first Vietnamese and then Iraqi Kurdish and Somali communities to town, in relatively small numbers. As these communities grew gradually, immigration from Mexico and other Central and South American nations began, and then grew dramatically. Latinos comprised less than a half a percentage point of the county population in 1990, but 4.5 percent by the end of the century and 9 percent in 2010. Given the relative youth of the community, Latino population growth transformed Nashville's schools, still described as 60 percent white and 40 percent black in public discourse into the late 1990s. Ten percent of Nashville's students were Latino by 2000, and 17 percent by 2010. Growth in immigrant communities pushed growth in Nashville school enrollment in the decade after unitary status, rather than the much hoped for and ul-timately unrealized return of white middle-class families to the district. By 2010, one-third of Nashville's public school students were white.[59]

Teachers living through the rapid diversification of their student popula-tions, as students came to their classrooms with multiple home languages and little English, turned to earlier experience of busing for desegregation as a framing device. They recalled the divisions in their schools (many of them in southeastern Nashville, like Antioch, or Hubert Dixon's alma ma-ter, Glencliff) as reminiscent of earlier years in which "neighborhood" stu-dents (almost always white, into the 1990s) met (black) "bused" students from distant urban neighborhoods in their schools. Patterns of in-school tracking by race that characterized the busing years in these teachers' mem-ories transformed into in-school tracking by language ability, between En-glish as a Second Language and other classes or even schools.[60]

Changes in the racial demography of the district were dramatic *after* the end of desegregation. Yet changes in the class demographics of MNPS may have been even more so. The proportion of poor students in the district's schools had risen steadily over the desegregation era, from 11 percent of students eligible for Title I programs in 1970, to 39.2 percent eligible for free or reduced-price school meals (admittedly a different measure) by 1993, and just under half by 1998. Poor students became much more intensely concentrated in Nashville's public schools as a whole *after* the end of court-ordered desegregation. In 2010, 72 percent of Nashville's students were eligible for free and reduced-price lunch.[61] This increase far outpaced the modest growth in the number of poor families in the county overall, which had risen from 10 percent to 13 percent in the same period.[62] The predictions by some school board leaders and local elites that ending desegregation would mean the return of white and middle-class students to Nashville's schools proved unfounded.

In its return to highly concentrated schools for black students and its new majority of poor students, Nashville's post–unitary status trajectory tracks the national pattern over the 1990s and 2000s. There was a widespread return to racially isolated schooling, even in those districts and regions, like the metropolitan South, where the most statistical desegregation had been achieved.[63] And Nashville also tracked the new southern norm in public school demographics, with most systems serving a majority of children from poor families beginning in 2010.[64]

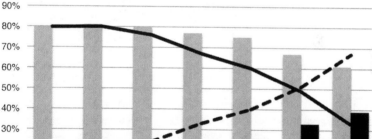

Metropolitan Nashville-Davidson County Population and School District Enrollment by Race, 1950-2010

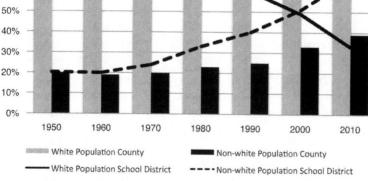

White Population County     Non-white Population County

White Population School District     Non-white Population School District

9.3. Data from US Census, 1950–2010; Tennessee Department of Education Annual Reports; "Twenty-Seven Year Analysis of Enrollment Patterns," file 1996, box 23, *Kelley*; and National Center for Education Statistics, Common Core of Data, accessed via www.nces.org. Chart prepared by Lauren Fox.

Subsequent rezonings in 2002 and 2008 deepened the trend toward resegregation set out in 1998. Changes in those years removed the last presumptions in favor of desegregation in Nashville's student assignment plan. Once newly built (or reopened) central-city elementary schools became available, North Nashville students for whom the default position had been traveling to the statistically desegregated schools in the western suburbs for elementary and high school now had to make an affirmative choice of a school in the suburbs or close to home. MNPS put real energy into informing each family of their options and securing an affirmative choice from them, but improving the implementation of parental choice was not the only motive in the 2008 rezoning. Amid a flurry of rumor and innuendo around the plan, which had been ventured and then stalled over eighteen months, the same mixture of politics and economics that had long sustained segregation and inequality in Nashville schooling continued. Representatives of suburban districts heard from their constituents that removing North Nashville students from their schools was a priority; educators and others returned to the familiar refrain that more middle-class and white families would return to those suburban schools if black city students no longer attended them.[65]

Private school attendance rates had increased steadily from the 1950s onward, so that few local business leaders—including those working via the chamber of commerce to advocate for school improvement—were Nashville public school parents.[66] When wealthier students remained in MNPS schools, they were concentrated in a few of its schools and in the system's selective magnets.[67] In desegregation's first decades, it had been possible to understand the core problem of inequality to be visible within Davidson County's borders. As more wealth moved across the county line, particularly to Williamson County to the south, inequality and segregation were at once visible within the district, and stark across the broader, multi-county metropolitan area.[68]

Although the trajectory of concern about desegregation seemed to be arcing consistently downward, a debate over the place of charter schools in the district contained signs of lingering commitment to the project. In 2012, wealthy parents in the Hillwood area supported a proposal for a new local charter school, initially without transportation for students in other parts of the district. At the cost of $3.4 million in state aid withheld by a pro-charter state commissioner of education, the Nashville Board of Education refused to support the proposal in part because of its potential to worsen segregation. However, the board continued to authorize charters likely to serve high concentrations of poor students of color.[69]

School board chair Kent Weeks and others spoke confidently over the 1990s that ending desegregation would mean improving achievement. This connection proved elusive. As of 2012, Nashville schools had come close to parity in the number of its black and white students graduating high school. Just over 80 percent of white MNPS students graduated within four years of beginning high school; 77.9 percent of black MNPS students did the same. For the district's growing Latino population, the figure was lower, at 71.6 percent. But even if black and white graduation rates seemed to be converging (if still at a lower rate than ideal), a stark gap remained in measures of what students were learning before being granted the diploma. As of 2012, more black high school students scored "below basic"—the lowest level—on state assessments in both Algebra I and English, while fewer achieved the "proficient" or "advanced" levels. Black students' scores trailed those of the district's economically disadvantaged students in aggregate, indicating that the experience of black students across economic levels remained distinct from that of their white peers.

By the early twenty-first century, Nashville had transformed itself into an economic boomtown. The previously modest regional banking and insurance center, with a smattering of industry, was now led by sectors that exemplified the new American economy. Its drivers came in entertainment—a music industry rooted in but growing beyond the traditional country genre—and health care (linked especially to private hospital management). Technical and support industries sprawled outward from this economic core, and the city enjoyed some popular cache with tourist guides and a NBC television series shining a spotlight there. In many respects the vision of the city's post–World War II chamber of commerce boosters had come to pass at last.

Many modes of opportunity for black Nashvillians unavailable several decades earlier had opened. Successful black bank executives gained

Table 9.1    Academic Achievement in Metropolitan Nashville Public Schools, 2012

| | Percentage of students "Below Basic" on state assessment, grades 9–12 | | | | Percentage of students "Proficient and Advanced" on state assessment, grades 9–12 | | | |
|---|---|---|---|---|---|---|---|---|
| | All students | Black students | White students | Economically disadvantaged | All students | Black students | White students | Economically disadvantaged |
| Algebra I | 16 | 26 | 13 | 22 | 55 | 38 | 62 | 45 |
| English | 11 | 18 | 8 | 17 | 61 | 40 | 68 | 46 |

*Source*: Tennessee Department of Education, Report Card, 2012, http://edu.reportcard.state.tn.us/pls/apex/f?p=2 00:20:1252881558938788::NO, accessed May 3, 2014. All figures shown are rounded to the nearest percentage point.

leadership in civic organizations, more black officials than ever sat in the Metro Council, and the city elected a black vice mayor. Yet from World War II to the end of the century, many of the core institutions of black life in Nashville had fallen on hard times. Pearl's closure was an important loss, but more symbolic than economic; weakened historically black colleges and universities—Fisk, Meharry, Tennessee State—meant diminished employment opportunities for black professionals. Nashville's boom often did not reach black workers, and especially black men. As of 2010, only 58.3 percent of Nashville's African American men of working age (between sixteen and sixty-four) were employed, placing the city among the forty worst in the nation on this measure. (For non-Hispanic whites, the figure was 72.9 percent). In the same decades in which the city boomed, the employment prospects of black men had fallen, down nearly ten percentage points from 1970. If the challenge of desegregation in Nashville had been refracted through multiple growth agendas, once growth arrived, it proved a poor guarantor of greater equality.[70] While Nashville's image boomed and some of its residents prospered extraordinarily, its public schools became institutions that served the poor.

### Conclusion

After nearly three decades of desegregation, Nashville leaders both black and white chose to accept the imperfect compromise that ended *Kelley* and their city's busing story. Despite immense investments of time and money over those decades, the core question of what statistical desegregation could offer students, and what else was needed to make robust equality, remained unanswered. Nashville's collective decisions about its schools too often remained guided at the end of desegregation as they had been throughout: by the hope for growth rather than the pursuit of equality. The district continued to pursue and value most the middle-class white suburbanites it wished to serve, while the district's actual students presented themselves each day, most needful of schools that sought equality and justice on their behalf.

# Conclusion

## Inequality Made and Remade

In the segregated and unequal contours of its schools in the 1940s, 1950s, and 1960s, Nashville shared much with many other American cities and metropolises. Black students, families, and their advocates there confronted a robust, multipart, and solidly constructed edifice of segregation and inequality.

Segregation's strength came in part from the legacies of prior decades of Jim Crow that marked the landscape in housing and wealth, and in the shape of educational structures and facilities. But segregation and inequality continued to be *made* well beyond World War II. Subsidized mortgages, ribbons of highways, favorable tax policy, new or promised school facilities, and a cultural endorsement of the suburbs as the right place for children encouraged suburbanization by white families in the 1950s and 1960s. Massive dislocations in North and South Nashville from highway construction and urban renewal helped push black families to make the same move when their resources, and cracks in the armor of the white suburb, allowed.

The meager progress toward desegregation visible in Nashville schools, as in most cities as of the late 1960s, reflected the impact not only of individual and collectively held racist judgment (although both surely existed). It bore witness to the weight of multiple and mutually reinforcing layers of state practice at work over the first two-thirds of the twentieth century. To an extent not previously acknowledged in works that treat schooling separately from basic structures of urban and suburban political economy, schools became central nodes in the making of the segregated metropolis.

Having made segregation and inequality in the first decades after World War II, Nashville accomplished something that very few American school districts did over the next three decades to the end of the century.

The district's schools brought large numbers of black and white students into schools together, across urban, suburban, and rural regions and class backgrounds. Doing so helped strike down some of the basic injustices and inequalities that attached to segregation, from disparate resource levels to curricular offerings.

Yet statistical desegregation did not assure—or in this case accompany—more robust equality in the experience of schooling, in the value that the district's policies and practices attached to its various students and communities. Inequality shifted form. The school district, federal courts, and local officials *remade* inequality by giving more weight to the felt needs and interests of local white students, families, and neighborhoods than to black students, families, and neighborhoods. Often official judgments in this regard were guided by the economic agendas of a growing, and growth-seeking, metropolis. At times in the name of growth, and at times out of political expediency, they allowed the achievement of statistical desegregation to stand as a thin substitute for something more substantial, and harder: robust equality of experience and opportunity within Nashville's schools.

Just as educational inequality shifted form from the era of segregation to the years of statistical desegregation, it did so again once federal court supervision of Nashville's schools ended. When legal pressure to desegregate subsided, Nashville's school officials removed nearly all the vestiges of their district's forty-one-year experience with desegregation. Despite elite and official promises to the contrary, ending desegregation did not yield the return of white students. In many respects, the city regressed to the national mean. Its schools became increasingly segregated, but in a particularly twenty-first-century form. Amid changing metropolitan demographics, with immigration from around the world producing a rapidly diversifying student population, fewer and fewer white students and middle-class students participated in public education in Nashville.

The full sweep of Nashville's desegregation story across four decades of court supervision, institutional resistance, and popular debate shows key if previously underappreciated factors in the story of desegregation. It points out the importance of policy choices in shaping desegregation, shifting the conversation from popular white resistance to a broad range of governmental actors and forms of state power. It documents the limits of metropolitan consolidation, which facilitated statistical desegregation but did not prevent lines of division within the jurisdiction that helped foster inequality. And it traces how black advocates for desegregation saw their visions of educational equality and their strategies for achieving it transformed by decades of desegregation in practice.

Recognizing the flaws, the inequalities, within one of desegregation's best-case scenarios—a metropolitan school district—is *not* to contribute to overly simple characterizations of desegregation as a failed project from a distant past. Instead, the complexities and challenges in Nashville's case can stand as useful reminders of how much has yet to be done, how much remains truly untried, in confronting segregation in schooling and beyond, as well as in linking desegregation to greater equality of educational opportunity. Surveying the scope of desegregation nationally, James Ryan (borrowing from G. K. Chesterton) commented that desegregation has not been found tried and wanting in the United States; it has not been tried. In Nashville, statistical desegregation was tried, and in many respects secured. But what was not tried was desegregation in the context of a robust commitment to equality of educational opportunity, with careful attention to the quality of students' experiences in schools and the continued effort toward desegregation alongside public recognition of and value for all of a metropolis's communities and children.[1]

The limits of historic attempts at desegregation may be of particular use at this moment. Skilled journalistic commentary is not only recognizing the massive inequality in American life, but rooting the story of inequality in deep historical analysis.[2] Similarly, retrospective looks at school segregation and inequality offer unflinching views of the rolling-back of what *Brown* accomplished.[3] Alongside increasingly sophisticated scholarly understanding of the ways in which segregation feeds inequality—from income and wealth disparities to violence and curtailed life expectancy—the time may be right to engage with desegregation as an important and necessary American project. In doing so, complex stories like Nashville's should be central, not to offer pat solutions or prohibitions, but instead to highlight the tensions that must be well and carefully negotiated, to ask probing questions about what it means to define equality in this twenty-first-century context.

Nashville matters, as well, for the ways in which its desegregation story reveals basic modes of educational inequality that stem from interactions between schooling and the political economy of the metropolis. These interactions help illustrate and explain the shifting nature of educational inequality in contexts with or without serious or sustained desegregation, and they demonstrate how schools have been forces in building the metropolitan landscape.

Appreciating these interactions between schooling and the metropolis helps move beyond one of the false dichotomies that appears in present-day discussion about schooling. One side argues that schools are *the* vehicle for remedying poverty and inequality, that the broader social and economic context of children's lives offer "no excuses" for schools not to bring all children to high levels of achievement.[4] The other calls for greater attention to social and economic contexts and their impact on childhood, arguing that schools alone cannot alter these contexts and their inequalities. This important point is, at times, taken to a caricaturing extreme—that context alone matters, that educational improvement will come from anywhere but the schools.[5] Nashville's story helps identify the problems with either extreme. Schools and cities construct one another; schools interact powerfully with the landscapes and economies in which they sit. Thus it is impossible to think of schools as isolated actors, and it is insufficient to frame schools as simply recipients of the social and economic forces that surround them.

## Historical Modes of Inequality, and History's Questions for the Present

Three modes of making and remaking inequality linked schooling to the political economy of the metropolis. The spatial organization of schooling, the curricular organization of schooling, and the public and legal narratives that characterized or claimed to explain segregation and inequality all became crucial loci for the making of educational inequality in Nashville, and then its remaking. These modes are by no means the only routes through which racism, inequality, and barriers to opportunity have, or do, flow into and through schooling. Yet the importance of each became visible in Nashville's case.

Each of these historic modes of making and remaking inequality also implies crucial questions for contemporary education practice and educational inequality in its present-day form. Neither Nashville nor any historical case offers pat prescriptions or cautions to be carted across the decades. However, Nashville's history does call attention to questions that might profitably be asked of our contemporary moment as well as of the past— questions that can help better identify persistent, if sometimes veiled, forces in the making of inequality.[6] It helps point out as well the troublesome limits of our present-day thinking about education and its possibilities.

The first mode of making and remaking inequality—the spatial organization of schooling, where schools sit in the metropolis, and which students attend which school—demonstrated the interaction of schooling with the pressures for metropolitan growth in Nashville. Seeing schools as generators of property value and attractive features of a growth metropolis helped construct and reinforce historic patterns of segregation. Schools marked the intersection of racialized ideas of space, community, and value, and planners and educators as well as real estate agents and individual home owners saw how segregation in schooling and housing reinforced one another.[7]

The suburban Hillwood area, for example, demonstrates the pattern well. There, in the 1950s and 1960s, planners, developers, and residents all defined the community as an upper-middle-class white enclave anchored by segregated white schools. Not only did individual families see their financial interests tied to the preservation of a segregated status quo, but the powerful and well-situated real estate sales and development industry profited from the inflated values that efforts to preserve segregation helped generate.[8] In the busing era, school location and student assignment choices that repeatedly favored suburban communities like Hillwood over city neighborhoods meant that Hillwood residents experienced busing with less travel time and more years in familiar local schools than did black students in central-city neighborhoods, many of whom rode buses to Hillwood. City neighborhoods saw their schools closed as Hillwood's remained open. Even as Hillwood residents bemoaned busing, they benefited from many decisions within its implementation shaped to meet their preferences first. After court-ordered desegregation ended in 1998, key actors in Hillwood sought again to make Hillwood's schools enclaves within the broader metropolitan district. Both local educators and real estate agents lobbied to revive school enrollment (among, they implied, local white residents) by ending one of the last remnants of desegregation in Nashville and returning those black students who rode buses to Hillwood to North Nashville–area schools.[9] In each of these phases, the spatial organization of schooling became central contested terrain, operating in direct connection to the pursuit of value and profit in land and housing.

If desegregation's pressures helped highlight the interactions between the spatial organization of schooling and metropolitan political economy, the changing twenty-first-century metropolis calls for continued attention to the spatial organization of schooling as well. In Nashville—as in Philadelphia, San Francisco, and New York, among others—some middle-class and wealthy residents today reject suburbs like Hillwood in favor of historic urban neighborhoods. To the extent that these newcomers decide to send their children to local public schools, they may create opportunities for increased desegregation by race and by class, potentially broadening the base of support for public schooling. Yet how these privileged arrivals will interact with local schools serving long-established and often poorer communities remains uncertain. They could seek to manipulate the spatial organization of schooling toward the creation of enclave schools, increasing their property values through segregation by class and/or skin color. The school system may enable them in doing so, choosing to prioritize their needs over those of the students long present in the area—possibly in the name of recruiting more middle-class families and the resources they bring into their schools.[10] The new metropolitan landscape of urban gentrification and suburban decay could auger only an inversion of previous patterns of spatial and economic privilege, often for white and wealthy communities, and neglect of communities of color and poor people.

Recent Nashville school policy debates bring these questions to the fore. In Nashville's 2008 rezoning, criticized by some for increasing the segregation experienced by North Nashville students, the district also chose to attach a racially diverse and increasingly gentrifying neighborhood close to downtown to a geographically neighboring but previously separately zoned North Nashville district. In so doing, it linked more white students and middle-class students to the area of most concentrated need in the school system; it also disrupted the opportunity created by the previous zoning to sell favored urban housing linked to favored suburban schooling.[11]

Additionally—and again, in Nashville as in many American cities—school choice programs are altering the spatial organization of schooling and student assignment. The district includes a growing number of charter schools, alongside discussions to increase choice within the district's schools as well. In 2014, Metropolitan Nashville Public Schools leaders proposed converting all the schools in East Nashville to schools of choice; charters occupy a large share of local education discourse. Choice plans may de-spatialize student assignment in ways that appear promising to advocates of equity long frustrated by restrictions on educational opportunity linked to residential segregation. It is yet unclear whether these approaches will further the segregation of the poor, or enable the making of enclaves for the rich, or whether they might—if intentionally managed in this direction—aid racial and class desegregation. The economic and political dynamics of property value and the power schools hold to make value and define community remains central to contemporary educational inequality, even when new interventions claim to radically alter historic linkages between schooling and residence.[12] What would it mean to shape the spatial organization of schooling toward the equitable distribution of educational resources and opportunity? And what kinds of popular democratic power would have to be marshaled toward this goal?

The curricular organization of schooling became a second mode of making and remaking educational inequality. In Nashville this pattern was especially visible around vocational education, attempting to link schooling to the local labor market. Multiple parties, at times coming together across otherwise sharp disagreements, hoped that schools could prepare students as workers and generate either new individual opportunity or collective economic growth. Yet this new focus reinforced rather than confronted the reality of a striated and discriminatory labor market. Crucially, vocational education introduced new opportunities to evade desegregation efforts—from student transfers to discriminatory tracking—and provided little basis on which to argue assertively for the humanistic educational value of desegregation. Encouraging schools to see students as future workers in a metropolitan landscape in which skin color demarcated labor market opportunity worked to justify segregation more than challenge it.

Today's labor and education discourses offer striking similarities to earlier eras. Sharp inequalities continue to characterize employment opportunity and income, and again, discussions of matching students to the labor market to reduce poverty and to leverage growth draw increasing support at a time when many other educational issues remain highly divisive. Powerful new advocates are lining up on the side of reinvigorated attention to vocational education.

In January 2014, in the speaking tour that followed his State of the Union address, President Barack Obama came to Nashville's McGavock High School to applaud the work under way there and to call for a renewed national emphasis on vocational education—now framed as "career and technical education." McGavock drew the president's attention because it houses five separate, smaller academies, each with a specific career focus. Others of Nashville's large comprehensive high schools are similarly subdivided. Some of the academies bear the names of the corporate partners who helped support them (and where their graduates may later seek employment): the CMT (Country Music Television) Academy of Digital Design and Communication, the Gaylord Entertainment Academy of Hospitality. The president applauded increases in graduation rates at these academies, and celebrated the story of students who were newly interested and engaged with workplace-focused programs and classes.[13]

Most likely, President Obama's staffers and planners did not know of the more than forty-year local history of vocational education that McGavock's academies called to mind. Nor did they know the specific stories of young people like Waverly Crenshaw, who found themselves initially shunted into vocational courses based on skin color and in spite of strong previous academic records, in the early 1970s McGavock. The 1970s-era embrace of vocational education lacked processes to ensure equality in the complex matter of matching schools to the labor market. What protections are needed within this effort in its new twenty-first-century form, under the label of "college and career readiness"?

This is importantly, but not exclusively, a matter of interrupting the historic linkages between racism (and sexism), employment discrimination, and vocational education. There is also the broader problem, of focusing schooling on worker preparation when workers face a steep climb to basic economic security. Current income inequality is sharper than it has been in nearly a century—with the wages of the lowest-paid 30 percent of workers falling in real terms since the 1970s, the median stagnating, and the top 10 percent skyrocketing. Meanwhile, in terms of the median wage, black workers have lost ground against white workers since 1979.[14] In the same mid- to late-twentieth-century decades in which black high school attainment rose significantly and made some progress in closing the gap with white educational attainment, white men remained more than twice as likely as black men nationally to make their way into the more dynamic and well-paid white-collar sector.[15] Economic growth since the mid-1970s has developed alongside increases in the proportion of Americans living in poverty.[16]

Schools seeking to produce workers may fit students some notches higher in the labor market than they might otherwise have found themselves, but these students still enter a market in which the lower tier includes work so ill paid and tenuous that even full-time employees can scarcely support themselves and their families. The exploitative shape of that labor market provokes educational questions: What kind of schooling can prepare students as future citizens able to seek and establish just boundaries on labor exploitation and wealth inequality? These are no less central educational problems than is the provision of skills and habits to suit students to work.[17]

Today's emphasis on vocational education echoes with the long American tradition of "educationalizing" poverty, displacing attention from structural interventions in the labor market to softer (and often less effective) educational strategies while fostering an idea of education as the key generator of growth and mobility. This pattern is even more troublesome as historic gaps between rich and poor open into even wider chasms of wealth, income, and opportunity.[18]

Segregation and desegregation, as with so many aspects of American life, have been sites of storytelling, of the making of popular as well as historical and legal narratives to explain what was happening and why. In

Nashville, as in national discourse, these narratives were at times powerful distortions and became a third mode of making and remaking inequality.

Before *Brown*, segregation had a visible and blunt explanation in the language of district policy and state law. Nashville's Buena Vista School, for example, was a "white" school because the school district labeled it as such and enforced this designation; the state constitution further prevented schooling black and white children together. But segregation and inequality, even as both persisted in interlocking fashion, took on increasingly vague or obscuring explanations over the postwar decades. In desegregation's first phase, Nashville educators and elites crafted a rhetoric of the city's "moderation" that veiled the depth of bureaucratic and official commitment to segregation. "Moderation" labeled Buena Vista "integrated" when it served a handful of black students alongside hundreds of white students.

By the late 1960s, most of Buena Vista's white students were gone, replaced by black students almost exclusively. Local and national legal advocates began to seek more assertive approaches to desegregation, and in the process faced the question of why Buena Vista now existed as a segregated school serving only black students. Available narratives did not address the multiple uses of government power that encouraged Buena Vista's transition from segregated white to black, reaching across federally encouraged white suburbanization via home finance and highway construction, to the promise of new school facilities in the suburbs, or to the barriers to these for black families and students. Legal, and later popular, narratives characterized Buena Vista's segregation—like that at both white suburban schools and other urban schools—as "de facto segregation." This label rendered the impact of decades of interlocking policies at the local, state, and federal levels as either inexorable or the product of aggregate individual action, making crucial and durable policy choices invisible. The narrative of "white flight" worked similarly. That term emphasized a powerful individual actor, typically the normative middle-class white family, and elided the multiple layers of often intertwining state action, in housing, education, taxation, and beyond, that helped such families to "flee." Even as scholars increasingly reject the "de facto" label and bring more nuance to the idea of white flight, these terms retain power in popular, and still some scholarly, discussions of cities and schooling.[19]

Via busing, Buena Vista became a statistically desegregated school over much of the 1970s, 1980s, and 1990s. With the end of busing for desegregation in 1998, Buena Vista reopened as an enhanced option school. It enjoyed a fresh renovation and housed extra programs and features that the school district imagined (and the court approved) as potentially attractive to white and/or middle-class families. But by the twenty-first century, Buena Vista was almost as statistically segregated by race (if for black children rather than white ones) and more segregated by class than it had been when Erroll Groves was one of the first black children to enter the school in 1957. As of 2012, Buena Vista served a population of 97 percent black children, and of its 434 students, 428 had family incomes low enough to qualify for free or reduced-price lunch.[20]

In court in the 1960s, 1970s, and 1980s, and in popular discourse today, Buena Vista's segregation appears as the product of "de facto segregation" and "white flight." Continued talk of individual choice over policy choices obscures the roots of historic and current segregation at Buena Vista, and limits the collective imagination about what possibilities might exist to respond to it.[21]

Recent litigation displays the ongoing trouble with how to narrate segregation and inequality. In its 2008 rezoning, MNPS set out new and more limited parameters within which North Nashville families could attend more statistically desegregated schools along the district's western edge rather than in the schools close to home with highly concentrated populations of black and poor students. A few local families sued the district over these changes and what they felt to be the increased inequalities of opportunity for their children. In evaluating the plaintiff's claims—and ultimately finding the district not responsible for civil rights violations—US District Court Judge Kevin Sharp captured well the paradoxes of contemporary desegregation litigation, especially when situated in longer historical context.

Judge Sharp recognized that the school district had acted in ways that increased racial concentration in already highly segregated North Nashville schools and that reduced desegregation in the western suburbs. Thus two of the three current elements for a claim of segregation—state action and segregative effect—were present. But the third—"segregative purpose," or intent—remained unmet. Policies that altered the lives of African American students and families disproportionately (carried forward in language of geography rather than skin color, for example) did not demonstrate sufficient intent.[22]

While the courts now hold high and stringent standards of intent for segregation's most proximate causes, they seem satisfied with a low and diluted understanding of segregation's historical roots. Judge Sharp noted the confines in which he worked, discussing early 1990s litigation such as *Freeman v. Pitts*, which, he wrote, set out the "legal (in)significance of segregated schools" that it deemed to be "created by private, individual decision." Elsewhere, contemporary segregation's historic causes appear "nearly inscrutable." Justice Antonin Scalia wrote in *Freeman* that the public and private actions that created segregation are multiple and intertwined and figuring out just what actions produced segregation would be "guesswork."[23]

These legal formulations of acausal or inscrutable segregation are like a magician's box: a place to put a difficult, complex history and make it seem to disappear. Yet, as rich historical scholarship over the past generation has shown—and as this book helps further—segregation's history is in fact quite knowable. Nonetheless, in much popular discourse and the law, decades of consequential, specific, documented governmental action to make segregation remain trapped in that magician's box. Legal standards require judges yet again to seek seemingly precise "intent," inside a very circumscribed time frame, for contemporary segregation. Together, narrow standards for intent alongside avoidance of historical causality render much contemporary school segregation legally without recourse. Judges in Nashville and beyond find themselves in a corner, unwilling to "[endorse] the historically poor performance of District schools or the racial and socioeconomic segregation of Nashville neighborhoods," but unable to fully investigate—much less act upon—these problems.[24]

As Nashville schools went from formal segregation to statistical desegregation, they demonstrated how deeply education is tied to, and helps construct, the political economy of metropolitan space. The interactions between schools and markets in land and labor help explain how inequality shifted form amid extensive statistical desegregation; narratives about segregation and inequality veiled these interactions and the policy choices that encouraged them. Although these interactions are by no means the only forms of inequality present in schools past or present, they demand attention for a complete understanding of educational inequality's roots and multiple forms.

## Education, Economy, and Democracy

Schools in Nashville—and in the United States more broadly—operate in multiple, complex, and influential interactions with metropolitan political economy. Yet recognizing these interactions does not mean taking them to be the sum total of schooling's purposes or its social meaning. The very text of the *Brown v. Board of Education* decision offers reminders of the breadth of US ambition for schooling. Among the crucial but less frequently quoted passages within Chief Justice Earl Warren's opinion in *Brown* sits one that reinforces the centrality of education to the function of American democracy: "Education is perhaps the most important function of state and local governments. . . . It is required in the performance of our most basic public responsibilities. . . . It is the very foundation of good citizenship."[25] These passages contain echoes of over two centuries of American thought about the basic purposes of public schooling in a democracy, in shaping citizens able to act on ideas of collective as well as individual good.

The stories of students who attended desegregating schools convey how they learned from interactions with one another and began to build the empathy, the skills of cooperation, and the desire for justice and cooperation crucial for (if often missing from) democratic practice. *Brown* referred to education's centrality to democracy as a core rationale for ensuring equality in schooling. And in practice, students like Hubert Dixon III helped make out of an imperfect desegregation plan an experience that held real, if not uncomplicated, promise for the making of a citizenry in a diverse democracy.

In Nashville's context, desegregation proceeded in ways much more explicitly responsive to concerns about schools and their capacity to produce economic value—via workers, via the housing market—than it did with education's democratic purposes in mind. In this regard, Nashville schools developed in ways consonant with the broader pattern in American educational discourse over the twentieth century, of a growing attention to schools' economic purposes and a shrinking regard for their democratic functions.[26] As Nashville demonstrates well, matching schooling to an unequal and discriminatory labor market and an unequal and discriminatory property market is a poor basis on which to construct equality in education.

*Brown*'s call for attention to education as preparation for citizenship is one reminder of the need to situate educational efforts not in the logic of the market, but in the logic of democracy. More robust and compelling views of this need are amply visible in the history of educational thought among black activists. From Frederick Douglass to Ella Baker, black leaders have theorized and advocated for education toward citizenship, toward freedom. They have done so amid deeply oppressive economic and political contexts, where matching education to the status quo in labor would mean the opposite of freedom. They also did so knowing the distorted nature of American democracy in their lifetimes, embracing citizenship without any naive or simplistic vision of democracy easily realized. They saw in education a chance to define meaningful freedom despite the constraints that existed all around them, and they reconstructed the idea of the citizen in this process.[27]

Their educational visions help point out the absences in Nashville's segregation and desegregation history and provoke another, crucial question for the present. Given how powerful economic agendas in education can be, what democratic forces might help set boundaries for these agendas? It is too simple to suggest that more attention to this question would have produced a different desegregation story in Nashville. But it is worth noting that desegregation, mandated by a Supreme Court that recognized schooling's crucial function in our democracy, was rarely shaped by or measured for its potential impact on the making of democratic citizens. In their own practices in schools, and their own reflections on the experience of desegregation, some Nashville students and teachers took this as their project. But neither their district, nor the national educational discourse of which it was a part, reinforced this point sufficiently.

Nashville proved able to marshal extensive state tools in the name of growth and profit. What could be accomplished if the same energy targeted robust citizenship? What if a metropolitan district approached desegregation as a necessary route to fairness, one quite modest in scale compared to the many interlocking layers of policy and action that had constructed segregation? There would be no guarantee of a thorough assault on all manners and consequences of racism. But doing otherwise meant statistical desegregation without educational equality, schools that experienced four decades of desegregation without recognizing what the benefits of schooling across divisions of skin color or class might be.

Segregation and educational inequality has shifted form. It appears today in ways different but no less vivid than when Hubert Dixon Jr. and his son Hubert Dixon III were students. In each of its phases, segregation and inequality have been supported and sustained by the interactions between schooling and capitalist markets in land and labor. These interactions have rarely been perceived, hidden instead in a fog of obscuring narratives. Clearing the fog to recognize the political economy of education is a first step. The next is to ask how a robust democracy might define and realize the schooling it needs.

# ORAL HISTORY AND INTERVIEW PARTICIPANTS

*All interviews conducted by the author, in Nashville, Tennessee, except where otherwise designated. Recordings in the author's possession.*

Cindy Acuff
Charles Allen
Nelson Andrews
Domenico Annese
Jeannette Armstrong
Victor Baggett
Paula Barkley
Rev. Bill Barnes
Andrew Benedict
Melvin Black
Dorothy Boyd
Dr. Elbert Brooks
Gena Carter
George Cate
Dan Covington
Mary Craighead
Waverly Crenshaw
Charles Davis
Hon. Richard Dinkins
Brittany Dixon
Hubert Dixon Jr.
Hubert Dixon III
Rev. V. H. (Sonnye) Dixon Jr.
Robert Eadler
Annette Eskind
Stephen Flatt
Charles Frazier
Milton Harris
Sen. Douglas Henry

Ola Hudson
Dr. Charles Kimbrough
Edward Kindall
Chester LaFever
Bill Lann Lee
Dwight Lewis
Kwame Leo Lillard
Dr. Bobby L. Lovett
Barbara Mann
Rev. Bruce Maxwell
Joseph May
Kathy Nevill
Dr. Robert Newbrough
Lyndell Norton
Semetta Coure Pulley
Dr. Sonya Ramsey
Phil Riner
John Seigenthaler
Eugene Speight
Rev. James Thomas
Michael Tribue
Bernard Werthan
Forrest Wilson
Dr. Aldorothy Wright
Five students at McGavock High
   School, May 2004
Three interviewees who chose to
   remain anonymous

NOTES

*Abbreviations used in the notes*

AWPI    Avon Williams Papers, Part I, Tennessee State University Special Collections

AWPII    Avon Williams Papers, Part II, Tennessee State University Special Collections

*Banner*    *Nashville Banner* newspaper

BBP    Beverly Briley Papers, MANDC

CM    Courthouse Move Collection, MANDC

CNBOE    City of Nashville Board of Education

COE    [Tennessee] Commissioner of Education Papers, RG 92, TSLA

DBP    Dick Battle Papers, MANDC

DMP    Dan May Papers, Tennessee Historical Society, TSLA

ETP    Eugene TeSelle Papers, VUSC

FFA    Ford Foundation Archives, Rockefeller Archives Center

FUBOHC    Fisk University Black Oral History Collection

GNAR    Greater Nashville Association of Realtors Collection, NPL

GP    Governors Papers, TSLA

GPCR    George Peabody College Records, VUA

HEQ    *History of Education Quarterly*

JEP    John Egerton Papers, VUSC

JUH    *Journal of Urban History*

JAH    *Journal of American History*

*Kelley* Records of Nashville school desegregation litigation, in *Kelley v. NCBOE, Kelley v. MNBOE,* and *Maxwell v. County Board,* NARA—Southeast, RG 21, Civil Actions 2094 and 2956

*Kelley v. NCBOE* *Robert W. Kelley et al. v. Nashville City Board of Education* (or *Board of Education of the City of Nashville*)

*Kelley v. MNBOE* *Robert W. Kelley et al. v. Metropolitan Nashville Board of Education* (or *Metropolitan County Board of Education* or *Metropolitan Board of Education*)

KMS Kelly Miller Smith Papers, VUSC

LDP Louise Davis Papers, Tennessee Historical Society, TSLA

LOC Library of Congress

MANDC Metropolitan Archives of Nashville and Davidson County

*Maxwell v. County Board* *Henry Maxwell et al. v. Davidson County Board of Education*

MCOH Metropolitan Consolidation Oral History, MANDC

MNBOE Metropolitan Nashville Board of Education

MTP Molly Todd Papers, VUSC

NARA National Archives and Records Administration

NCC Nashville Chamber of Commerce Papers, TSLA

NCES-CCD National Center for Education Statistics, Common Core of Data, accessed via www.nces.ed.org/ccd

NCROHP Civil Rights Oral History Project, NPL

NHAP Nashville Housing Authority Photographs, MANDC

NHGIS National Historical Geographic Information System, Minnesota Population Center, *National Historical Geographic Information System: Pre-Release Version 0.1,* University of Minnesota, 2004, www.nhgis.org

NMFP Nelson and Marion Fuson Papers, VUSC

NPL Nashville Public Library Special Collections

*NYT* *New York Times*

RHP Robert Horton Papers, MANDC

RHPA Robert Horton Papers, Addition, MANDC

SPF School Property Files, MANDC

*Tennessean* Nashville *Tennessean* newspaper

TNDOE Tennessee Department of Education

TSLA Tennessee State Library and Archives

USOE   United States Office of Education, HEW

VHP   Vivian Henderson Papers, Woodruff Library, Clark Atlanta University

VUA   Vanderbilt University Archives

VUSC   Vanderbilt University Special Collections

Note: All newspapers references, except where otherwise indicated, are from the *Banner* clippings files, Nashville Public Library Special Collections. When newspaper name and date are followed by (BOE), these clippings come from the Board of Education clippings files housed at MANDC.

INTRODUCTION

1.   Hubert Dixon Jr., interview, July 2004.
2.   Hubert Dixon III, interview, May 17, 2004. On early Nashville desegregation, see John Egerton, "Walking into History: The Beginning of School Desegregation in Nashville," *Southern Spaces*, May 4, 2009, www.southernspaces.org, accessed September 1, 2013; Sonya Yvette Ramsey, *Reading, Writing, and Segregation: A Century of Black Women Teachers in Nashville* (Urbana: University of Illinois Press, 2008), chapters 3 and 4; Benjamin Houston, *The Nashville Way: Racial Etiquette and the Struggle for Social Justice in a Southern City* (Athens: University of Georgia Press, 2012), chapter 2. *Robert W. Kelley v. Board of Education of the City of Nashville*, 159 F. Supp. 272 (1958); *Robert W. Kelley and Henry C. Maxwell, Jr., et al., v. Metropolitan County Board of Education of Nashville and Davidson County, Tennessee*, 317 F. Supp. 980 (1970); MNPS, "Twenty-Seven Year Analysis of Enrollment Patterns," *Kelley*, box 23, file 1996.
3.   *Schools for 1980*, 1964 (Nashville, TN: Metropolitan Planning Commission); Eugene Speight, interview, May 2004. Information on teacher demographics comes from district-level rather than school-level information. Voluntary teacher transfers had, by this date, created some very limited faculty desegregation. Ramsey, *Reading, Writing, and Segregation*, 102–4.
4.   Dixon III, interview. See chapter 6 for more specific description of Nashville's 1971 desegregation plan.
5.   Erika Frankenberg, Chungmei Lee, and Gary Orfield, "A Multiracial Society with Segregated Schools: Are We Losing the Dream?" (Cambridge, MA: Civil Rights Project, Harvard, 2003), figure 6; Gary Orfield and John T. Yun, "Resegregation in American Schools" (Cambridge, MA: Civil Rights Project, Harvard, 1999), table 22. Nashville enrollment statistics from MNPS, "Twenty-Seven Year Analysis."
6.   *Kelley v. MNBOE*, order, March 18, 1971, *Kelley*, box 6, file 1971 (1). Judge L. Clure Morton did not publish the 1971 busing order. Dixon III, interview. Erica Frankenberg and Chungmei Lee, "Race in American Public Schools: Rapidly Resegregating School Districts" (Cambridge, MA: Civil Rights Project, Harvard, 2002), 13.
7.   Amy Stuart Wells et al., *Both Sides Now: The Story of School Desegregation's Graduates* (Berkeley: University of California Press, 2008), chapter 3; Tracy E. K'Meyer, *From Brown to Meredith: The Long Struggle for School Desegregation in Louisville, Kentucky, 1954–2007* (Chapel Hill: University of North Carolina Press, 2013); Jack Dougherty, *More Than One Struggle: The Evolution of Black School Reform in Milwaukee* (Chapel Hill: University of North Carolina Press, 2004); US Commission on Civil Rights, "The Process of Change: The Story of School Desegregation in Syracuse, NY" (Washington, DC: Government Printing Office, 1968).

8.  Dixon III, interview; K'Meyer, *From Brown to Meredith*; Wells, *Both Sides Now*.

9.  Harvey Kantor and Barbara Brenzel, "Urban Education and the 'Truly Disadvantaged': The Historical Roots of the Contemporary Crisis, 1945–1990," in Michael Katz, ed., *The "Underclass Debate": Views from History* (Princeton, NJ: Princeton University Press, 1993), 366–40; Wells et al., *Both Sides Now*, 20. Nashville statistics from Charles Frazier to MNBOE, May 15, 1992, on file with May 15, 1992 agenda, MNBOE.

10. These represent general trends, but limitations in the data make for imperfect comparisons. I use Nashville SMSA data for 1960 (which includes Davidson, Sumner, and Wilson counties), but Davidson-only for 1990. The inclusion of more rural Sumner and Wilson is likely to depress attainment figures for both black and white students in these years somewhat. I use the figures for educational attainment for persons over 25, making the 1960s a fair measure of pre-*Brown* patterns, and the 1990 measure inclusive of students who had completed high school by the early 1980s. The 1960 figures here come from US Census, 1960, via NHGIS, and the 1990 American Community Survey, at www.factfinder.census.gov, accessed February 16, 2010. For national patterns, see John L. Rury and Shirley A. Hill, *The African American Struggle for Secondary Schooling, 1940–1980: Closing the Graduation Gap* (New York: Teachers College Press, 2012); Michael Katz, Mark Stern, and Jamie Fader, "The New African American Inequality," *Journal of American History* 92, no. 1 (June 2005): 75–108. On achievement data, see Richard A. Pride and David Woodward, *The Burden of Busing: The Politics of Desegregation in Nashville, Tennessee* (Knoxville: University of Tennessee Press, 1985), chapter 6.

11. For a visual summary of the achievement gap over time, see Greg J. Duncan and Richard J. Murnane, *Whither Opportunity? Rising Inequality, Schools, and Children's Life Chances* (New York: Russell Sage, 2012), figure 1.3.

12. Frankenberg, Lee, and Orfield, "A Multiracial Society," figure 6; Matthew D. Lassiter, *The Silent Majority: Suburban Politics in the Sunbelt South* (Princeton, NJ: Princeton University Press, 2005), table 12.1. On Nashville consolidation, see Don Doyle, *Nashville since the 1920s* (Knoxville: University of Tennessee Press, 1985); Brett W. Hawkins, *Nashville Metro: The Politics of City-County Consolidation* (Nashville: Vanderbilt University Press, 1966).

13. Frankenberg, Lee, and Orfield, "A Multiracial Society," figure 6; Orfield and Yun, "Resegregation," table 22; MNPS, "Twenty-Seven Year Analysis."

14. US Census, via NHGIS; Doyle, *Nashville*, chapter 7.

15. The leading proponent has been Myron Orfield, *Metropolitics: A Regional Agenda for Community and Stability* (Washington: Brookings, 1997).

16. US Census, 1940 to 2000, via NHGIS.

17. Robert Spinney, *World War II in Nashville* (Knoxville: University of Tennessee Press, 1996) and "Municipal Government in Nashville, 1938–1951: The Growth of the Public Sector," *Journal of Southern History* 61, no. 1 (February 1995): 77–112. For regional examples, see James C. Cobb, *The Selling of the South: The Southern Crusade for Industrial Development, 1956–1980* (Baton Rouge: Louisiana State University Press, 1982); Bruce Schulman, *From Cotton Belt to Sunbelt: Federal Policy, Economic Development, and the Transformation of the South, 1938–1980* (New York: Oxford University Press, 1991); N. D. B. Connolly, *A World More Concrete: Real Estate and the Remaking of Jim Crow South Florida* (Chicago: University of Chicago Press, 2014). On economic growth efforts, see Elizabeth Tandy Schermer, *Sunbelt Capitalism: Phoenix and the Transformation of American Politics* (Philadelphia: University of Pennsylvania Press, 2013). On

growth and revitalization efforts even amid decline, see Margaret Pugh O'Mara, *Cities of Knowledge: Cold War Science and the Search for the Next Silicon Valley* (Princeton, NJ: Princeton University Press, 2006) and Andrew Highsmith, *Demolition Means Progress: Race, Class and the End of the American Dream in Flint, Michigan* (Chicago: University of Chicago Press, 2015).

18. Josh Bivens, Elise Gould, Lawrence Mishel, and Heidi Shierholz, "Raising America's Pay" (Washington, DC: Economic Policy Institute, 2014); Colin Gordon, *Growing Apart: A Political History of American Inequality*, 2013. Retrieved from http://scalar .usc.edu/works/growing-apart-a-political-history-of-american-inequality/index, accessed May 15, 2014.

19. Lassiter, *Silent Majority*; Kevin Kruse, *White Flight: Atlanta and the Making of Modern Conservatism* (Princeton, NJ: Princeton University Press, 2006); Ronald P. Formisano, *Boston against Busing* (Chapel Hill: University of North Carolina Press, 1994); Jonathan Rieder, *Canarsie: The Jews and Italians of Brooklyn against Liberalism* (Cambridge, MA: Harvard University Press, 1985). See also Michael Klarman, "How *Brown* Changed America: The Backlash Thesis," *Journal of American History* 81, no. 1 (June 1994): 81–118. Brett Gadsden, *Between North and South: Delaware, Desegregation, and the Myth of American Sectionalism* (Philadelphia: University of Pennsylvania Press, 2012); R. Scott Baker, *Paradoxes of Desegregation: African American Struggles for Educational Equity in Charleston, South Carolina, 1926–1972* (Athens: University of Georgia Press, 2006); and Charles C. Bolton, *The Hardest Deal of All: The Battle over School Integration in Mississippi, 1870–1980* (Jackson: University Press of Mississippi, 2005) link resistance to policy choices in desegregation.

Key works focus on the experiences of African American students before and after desegregation: Vanessa Siddle Walker, *Their Highest Potential: An African American School Community in the Segregated South* (Chapel Hill: North Carolina, 1998); David S. Cecelski, *Along Freedom Road: Hyde County, North Carolina and the Fate of Black Schools in the South* (Chapel Hill: University of North Carolina Press, 1994); Dougherty, *More Than One Struggle*; Michael Fultz, "The Displacement of Black Educators Post-*Brown*: An Overview and Analysis," *HEQ* 44, no. 1 (2004): 11–45.

20. Derrick Bell, "*Brown* and the Interest-Convergence Dilemma," in Derrick Bell, ed., *Shades of Brown: New Perspectives on School Desegregation*, (New York: Teachers College Press, 1980), 90–106; Bell, *And We Are Not Saved: The Elusive Quest for Racial Justice* (New York: Basic Books, 1987). See also Jennifer Woodward, "How Busing Burdened Blacks: Critical Race Theory and Busing for Desegregation in Nashville–Davidson County." *Journal of Negro Education* 80, no. 1 (2011): 22–32 applies critical race theory to Nashville but similarly relies on interest convergence in place of causal analysis. On inequalities in the process of desegregation in the context of Chicago, see Dionne Danns, "Northern Desegregation: A Tale of Two Cities," *HEQ* 51, no. 1 (February 2011): 77–104.

21. See, for example, Lassiter, *Silent Majority*; Formisano, *Boston against Busing*. With the exception of Tracy K'Meyer's oral-history-focused *From Brown to Meredith*, Jacobs's *Getting around Brown*, and Joshua Dunn, *Complex Justice: The Case of* Missouri v. Jenkins (Chapel Hill: University of North Carolina Press, 2008), those studies that do extend into the 1970s and 1980s focus on cases with desegregation plans of much more limited reach. Sociological literature, particularly Wells et al., *Both Sides Now*, starts to fill this gap through the story of students' experiences.

22. Pride and Woodward, *Burden of Busing*; Sarah Garland, *Divided We Fail: How an African American Community Ended the Era of School Desegregation* (Boston: Beacon, 2013).

23. On histories of cities and histories of schools see Jack Dougherty, "Bridging the Gap between Urban, Suburban, and Educational History," in William J. Reese and John L. Rury, eds., *Rethinking the History of American Education* (New York: Palgrave MacMillan, 2007), 245–60. Influential recent urban histories, like Robert Self, *American Babylon: Race and the Making of Postwar Oakland* (Princeton, NJ: Princeton University Press, 2005), pushed the field to a new metropolitan framework but lacks attention to education. New work is narrowing the gap: Highsmith, *Demolition Means Progress*, and Emily Straus, *The Death of the Suburban Dream: Race and Schools in Compton, California* (Philadelphia: University of Pennsylvania Press, 2014). Lassiter, *Silent Majority*, Kevin Kruse, *White Flight*, and Becky Nicolaides, *My Blue Heaven: Life and Politics in the Working Class Suburbs of Los Angeles, 1920–1965* (Chicago: University of Chicago Press, 2002) see schools as key grounds for political transformation. Arnold Hirsch, "Second Thoughts on the Second Ghetto," *Journal of Urban History* 29, no. 3 (March 2003): 298–309, calls for attention to relationships between urban renewal and schooling. Amy Stuart Wells et al. call for understanding "a more complex and iterative relationship between schools and society," in "How Society Failed School Desegregation Policy: Looking Past the Schools to Understand Them," *Review of Research in Education* 28, no. 1: 47–99, 50.

24. Schermer, *Sunbelt Capitalism*, takes a similar view of "conservative" actors on the local economic growth scene.

25. The key works are: Michael Katz, *The Irony of Early School Reform* (Cambridge, MA: Harvard University Press, 1968); Samuel Bowles and Herbert Gintis, *Schooling in Capitalist America* (New York: Basic Books, 1978); Ira Katznelson and Margaret Weir, *Schooling for All: Class, Race, and the Decline of the Democratic Ideal* (New York: Basic Books, 1985). On business and moderation, see Karen Anderson, *Little Rock: Race and Resistance at Central High School* (Princeton, NJ: Princeton University Press, 2010); Steven Samuel Smith, *Boom for Whom: Education, Desegregation, and Development in Charlotte* (Albany: State University of New York Press, 2004); Elizabeth Jacoway and David R. Colburn, eds., *Southern Businessmen and Desegregation* (Baton Rouge: Louisiana State University Press, 1982).

26. See the articles in the March 2012 Special Section of the *JUH*. See also Andrew Highsmith and Ansley T. Erickson, "Segregation as Splitting and Segregation as Joining: Schools, Neighborhoods, and the Many Modes of Jim Crow," *American Journal of Education* 121, no. 4 (August 2015): 563–95; David G. Garcia and Tara J. Yosso, "'Strictly in the Capacity of Servant'": The Interconnection Between Residential and School Segregation in Oxnard, California, 1934–1954," *HEQ* 53, no. 1 (February 2013): 65–89.

27. I benefit from many perspectives on this idea, including Khalil Gibran Muhammad, *The Condemnation of Blackness: Race, Crime, and the Making of Modern Urban America* (Cambridge, MA: Harvard University Press, 2010); Charles Payne, "'The Whole United States Is Southern!' *Brown v. Board of Education* and the Mystification of Race," *JAH* 91, no. 1 (June 2004): 83–91; Peggy Cooper Davis, *Neglected Stories* (New York: Hill and Wang, 1997); Alice O'Connor, *Poverty Knowledge: Social Science, Social Policy, and the Poor in Twentieth-Century U.S. History* (Princeton, NJ: Princeton University Press, 2001). See also Clarissa Ryle Hayward, *How Americans Make Race: Stories, Institutions, Spaces* (New York: Cambridge University Press, 2013) and the discussion of story and narrative in critical race theory. See, for example, Richard Delgado, "Storytelling for Oppositionists and Others: A Plea for Narrative," *Michigan Law Review* 87, no. 8 (August 1989): 2411–41.

28. See chapter 5 on Williams's arguments in *Kelley*.
29. Matthew D. Lassiter, "De Jure/De Facto Segregation: The Long Shadow of a National Myth," in Matthew Lassiter and Joseph Crespino, eds., *The Myth of Southern Exceptionalism* (New York: Oxford University Press, 2009), 25–48; Gadsden, *Between North and South*.
30. James Anderson, *The Education of Blacks in the South, 1860–1935* (Chapel Hill: University of North Carolina Press, 1988), 1.
31. Amanda Seligman takes a critical view of the "white flight" paradigm in *Block by Block: Neighborhoods and Public Policy on Chicago's West Side* (Chicago: University of Chicago Press, 2005). See Self, *American Babylon*, as well. MNPS, "Twenty-Seven Year Analysis."
32. James Patterson, *Brown v. Board: A Civil Rights Milestone and Its Troubled Legacy* (New York: Oxford University Press, 2010); Jeannie Oakes, *Keeping Track: How Schools Structure Inequality*, 2nd ed. (New Haven, CT: Yale University Press, 2005); Kathryn Neckerman, *Schools Betrayed: Roots of Failure in Inner-City Education* (Chicago: University of Chicago Press, 2008); Wells et al., *Both Sides Now*.
33. See chapter 7.
34. Tennessee House Bill No. 1203, 1973.
35. Dixon III, interview; Dixon Jr., interview.
36. Dixon III, interview; Wells et al., *Both Sides Now*; TNDOE, *Annual Statistical Report*, 1980 and 1985.
37. Frazier to MNBOE, May 15, 1992.
38. U.S. Commission on Civil Rights, "Reviewing a Decade of School Desegregation, 1965–1975: Report of a National Survey of School Superintendents" (Washington, DC: The Commission, 1977); Patterson, *Brown v. Board of Education*, 172; George Vecsey, "Court Ordered Desegregation Arrives in Nashville," *NYT*, September 17, 1971, via ProQuest Historical Newspapers, accessed July 14, 2013.
39. Asa Hilliard, foreword to Vivian Gunn Morris and Curtis L. Morris, *The Price They Paid: Desegregation in an African American Community* (New York: Teachers College Press, 2002), xi.
40. For similar approaches to defining segregation, see john a. powell, "A New Theory of Integrated Education: True Integration," in Charles A. Boger and Gary Orfield, eds., *School Resegregation: Must the South Turn Back?* (Chapel Hill: University of North Carolina Press, 2005), 281–304; and Carl Nightingale, *Segregation: A Global History of Divided Cities* (Chicago: University of Chicago Press, 2012), passim.
41. The concept of equal educational opportunity remains useful even while acknowledging that at times it has operated as a rhetorical feint, a way to dodge seemingly harder questions of equality of outcomes. Without suggesting that opportunity is a sufficient substitution for robust outcomes, I use opportunity to underscore how much yet remains undone even toward this more modest of goals. For criticisms of the concept, see, for example, David Labaree, *Someone Has to Fail: The Zero-Sum Game of Public Schooling* (Cambridge, MA: Harvard University Press, 2010).
42. Adolph Reed Jr. and Merlin Chowkwanyun, "Race, Class, Crisis: The Discourse of Racial Disparity and its Analytical Discontents" *Socialist Register* 48 (2012): 149–75; Gloria Ladsen Billings, "Pushing Past the Achievement Gap: An Essay on the Language of Deficit," *Journal of Negro Education* 76, no. 3 (Summer 2007): 316–23. On statistical measurement, see Muhammad, *Condemnation*. See also Prudence Carter and Kevin Welner, eds., *Closing the Opportunity Gap: What America Must Do to Give Every Child an Even Chance* (New York: Oxford University Press, 2013).

CHAPTER ONE

1. Robert Spinney, "Municipal Government in Nashville, Tennessee, 1938–1951: World War II and the Growth of the Public Sector" *Journal of Southern History* 61, no. 1 (February 1995): 77–112, and *World War II in Nashville* (Knoxville: University of Tennessee Press, 1999); Benjamin Houston, *The Nashville Way: Racial Etiquette and the Struggle for Social Justice in a Southern City* (Athens: University of Georgia Press, 2012), chapter 3; Elizabeth Jacoway and David Colburn, eds., *Southern Businessmen and Desegregation* (Baton Rouge: Louisiana State University Press, 1982).

2. Bill Carey, *Fortunes, Fiddles and Fried Chicken: A Nashville Business History* (Franklin, TN: Hillsboro Press, 2000).

3. Tennessee Department of Employment Security, "The Labor Market in Nashville, Vol. VI, No. 5," June 1950.

4. Carey, *Fortunes, Fiddles*, 216.

5. Spinney, "Municipal Government."

6. Don Doyle, *Nashville since the 1920s* (Knoxville: University of Tennessee Press, 1985), 115–19.

7. Joseph May, interview, July 2007. See also Spinney, "Municipal Government," 106.

8. Yollette Trigg Jones, "The Black Community, Politics, and Race Relations in the 'Iris City': Nashville, Tennessee, 1870–1954" (PhD diss., Duke, 1985), 266–75, 313. Doyle, *Nashville*, 224–25.

9. Jones, "Iris City," 303–12; Spinney, *World War II in Nashville*, 67; Doyle, *Nashville*, 225–28. See also Theda Skocpol, Ariane Liazos, and Marshall Ganz, *What a Mighty Power We Can Be: African American Fraternal Groups and the Struggle for Racial Equality* (Princeton, NJ: Princeton University Press, 2006).

10. Doyle, *Nashville*, 228.

11. Note the absence of city planning in the works in Introduction, note 19.

12. Thomas Hanchett, *Sorting out the New South City: Race, Class and Urban Development in Charlotte, 1875–1975* (Chapel Hill: University of North Carolina Press, 1998), 168–70; Joseph Heathcott, "The Whole City Is Our Laboratory: Harland Bartholomew and the Production of Urban Knowledge," *Journal of Planning History* 4, no. 4 (November 2005): 322–55; Marc Weiss, *The Rise of the Community Builders* (New York: Columbia, 1987); Carl Nightingale, *Segregation: A Global History of Divided Cities* (Chicago: University of Chicago Press, 2012), passim.

13. W. E. B. DuBois, *The Philadelphia Negro: A Social Study* (1899; repr., Philadelphia: University of Pennsylvania Press, 1995); *The Pittsburgh Survey* (1909; repr., New York: Charitable Society of the City of New York).

14. Heathcott, "Whole City," 342.

15. On ways that states "make a society legible," see James Scott, *Seeing Like a State: How Certain Schemes to Improve the Human Condition Have Failed* (New Haven, CT: Yale University Press, 1998), 2–3; M. Christine Boyer, *Dreaming the Rational City* (Cambridge, MA: MIT Press, 1987).

16. Doyle, *Nashville*, 76–77; NCC, minutes of meeting of board of governors, October 21, 1953, NCC, reel 2, volume xiii, 66-67; biographical note on Irving Hand, Irving Hand Papers, Cornell University Division of Rare and Manuscript Collections, http://rmc.library.cornell.edu/EAD/htmldocs/RMM04855.html, accessed January 9, 2008. On planning practices and their impact on another southern city, see Hanchett, *Sorting Out*.

17. Walter C. Reckless, "The Initial Experience with Census Tracts in a Southern City," *Social Forces* 15, no. 1 (October 1936): 47–54.

18. Patrick J. Gilpin and Marybeth Gasman, *Charles S. Johnson: Leadership beyond the Veil in the Age of Jim Crow* (Albany: State University of New York Press, 2003), 114.

19. Reckless, "The Initial Experience," 47–48; Joel A. Smith, "A Method for the Classification of Areas on the Basis of Demographically Homogeneous Populations," *American Sociological Review* 19, no. 2 (April 1954): 201–7.

20. William H. Rohe and Lauren B. Gates, *Planning with Neighborhoods* (Chapel Hill: University of North Carolina Press, 1985), 23–28. On Clarence Perry and the neighborhood unit, see Howard Gillette, "The Evolution of Neighborhood Planning: From the Progressive Era to the 1949 Housing Act," *JUH*, 9 (August 1983), 421–44; Christopher Silver, "Neighborhood Planning in Historical Perspective," *Journal of the American Planning Association*, 51 (June 1985), 161–74; Larry Lloyd Lawhon, "The Neighborhood Unit: Physical Design or Physical Determinism?" *Journal of Planning History*, 8, (February 2009), 111–32; John D. Fairfield, *The Mysteries of the Great City: The Politics of Urban Design, 1877–1937* (Columbus: Ohio State University Press, 1993); Jason S. Brody, "Constructing Professional Knowledge: The Neighborhood Unit Concept in the Community Builder's Handbook," (PhD diss., University of Illinois, 2009); Tridib Banerjee and William C. Baer, *Beyond the Neighborhood Unit: Residential Environments and Public Policy* (New York: Plenum Press, 1984), 6–31; Peter Hall, *Cities of Tomorrow: An Intellectual History of Urban Planning and Design in the Twentieth Century*, 3rd ed. (Oxford, UK: Blackwell Publishers, 2002), 128–32; and Mel Scott, *American City Planning since 1890* (Berkeley: University of California Press, 1969), 475. See Steven Conn, *Americans against the City: Anti-Urbanism in the Twentieth Century* (New York: Oxford University Press, 2014), chapters. 3 and 4, on the planning milieu.

21. Irving Hand, "Planning of Residential, Commercial and Industrial Areas," in Mary McLean, ed., *Local Planning Administration*, 3rd ed., (Chicago: International City Manager's Association, 1959), 113.

22. James Dahir, quoted in Hand, "Planning," 111. The Cold War overtones resonate with Penny Von Eschen's argument in *Race against Empire: Black Americans and Anticolonialism, 1937–1957* (Ithaca, NY: Cornell University Press, 1997) and Samuel Zipp, *Manhattan Projects: The Rise and Fall of Urban Renewal* (New York: Oxford University Press, 2010).

23. Clarence A. Perry, "The Tangible Aspects of Community Organization," *Social Forces*, 8 (June 1930), 558–64, 562–63. See also "The Local Community as a Unit in the Planning of Urban Residential Areas," in Ernest Burgess, ed., *The Urban Community: Selected Papers from the Proceedings of the American Sociological Association, 1925* (New York: Greenwood Press, 1968; c1926), 238–412, quotation on 238.

24. Hand, "Planning," 110.

25. Ibid., 107–10.

26. Ibid., 122.

27. Reginald Isaacs, "The 'Neighborhood Unit' Is an Instrument for Segregation," *Journal of Housing* 5 (August 1948): 215–18, quotation on 215; James Dahir, "Neighborhood Planning Is a 'Three-in-One' Job," *Journal of Housing* 5 (October 1949): 270–72, quotation on 272; Letters to the Editors, *Journal of Housing* 5 (September 1949).

28. Ibid., 115; Scott, *American City Planning*, 475.

29. Hand, "Planning," 112.

30. See David Freund, *Colored Property: State Policy and White Racial Politics in Suburban America* (Chicago: University of Chicago Press, 2007).

31. "Planning Highlights, 1957–1960," 1960 (Nashville: Nashville City Planning Commission and Davidson County Planning Commission), 28.

32. Cheri Alice Roberts, "The Effects of Federal School Desegregation Orders on School Plant Planning with Emphasis on the Nashville, Tennessee Experience" (master's thesis, University of Tennessee, 1973); correspondence in SPF, file Cole School.

33. CNBOE, minutes, 1951, MNBOE, vol. 1951–1954, 31, 80, 87, 126, 196, 227, 277, 280–81, 288; *Schools for 1980*, 1964 (Nashville: Metropolitan Planning Commission). McKissack, see Andrew Wiese, *Places of Their Own: African American Suburbanization in the Twentieth Century* (Chicago: University of Chicago Press, 2004), 139, 68–70.

34. See Consolidated Developers to J.E. Moss, December 13, 1957, and Moss to Board, December 16, 1957, in SPF, file Caldwell; Charlotte Park brochure, SPF, file Charlotte Park.

35. Albert Wm. Johnson and Frank L. Turner to Allen Dobson, March 27, 1959, SPF, file Hillwood.

36. W. Raymond Denney to J. E. Moss, November 30, 1962, SPF, file Hillwood.

37. J. E. Moss to W. Raymond Denney, December 3, 1962, in SPF, file Hillwood.

38. Spinney, *World War II*, xii.

39. Doyle, *Nashville*, 217.

40. "Petition for Writ of Certiorari," *NASAEAA&A Grand Lodge of the Knights of Pythias, et al. v. Nashville Housing Authority et al.*, CM, box Capitol Hill Redevelopment Project, Nashville Housing Authority, 4.

41. Doyle, *Nashville*, 126; Spinney, *World War II*, 64.

42. Quoted in Spinney, *World War II*, 64.

43. Spinney, "Municipal Government," 102–3; Spinney, *World War II*, 64, 110–14; "Mayor Commends Move for Removing Capitol Slums," *Tennessean*, April 25, 1949; editorial, "Erasing the Blight," *Tennessean*, April 25, 1949.

44. Doyle, *Nashville*, 121. Nick Boone and Gerald Gimre comments at Louise Davis, Notes for Capitol Hill Development Article, in LDP, box 13, file 8.

45. See images at Doyle, *Nashville*, figures 42 and 43; John Acuff comments in Davis, Notes for Capitol Hill Development Article, 20; Spinney, *World War II*, xiii.

46. "Modern Dreamers Made It Come True," undated clipping c. 1957, GNAR (reprocessed November 2014), box 3, file 14, scrapbook 1; Ed Hughes, "Nashville Cleans up Slum, Increases Yield on Taxes," *Atlanta Journal*, October 1, 1957, GNAR, III-C, clippings.

47. Louise Davis, Draft Article on Capitol Hill, c. 1963, in LDP, box 13, file 18, 9.

48. Architect Edwin Keeble, quoted in Betsy Rowlett, "Blighted Capitol Area Called 'Outrageous Slum,'" *Tennessean*, April 24, 1949.

49. Imogene Wright Bolin, "Planning in Metropolitan Nashville and Davidson County, Tennessee: Before and after Consolidation" (master's thesis, University of Tennessee, 1968), 268.

50. Domenico Annese, interview, second session, November 17, 2006, Pleasantville, NY.

51. See Arnold R. Hirsch, *Making the Second Ghetto: Race and Housing in Chicago, 1940–1960* (Chicago: University of Chicago Press, 1998), 268–75; Andrew R. Highsmith, "Demolition Means Progress: Urban Renewal, Local Politics, and State-Sanctioned Ghetto Formation in Flint, Michigan," and Irene V. Holliman, "From Crackertown to Model City? Urban Renewal and Community Building in Atlanta, 1963–1966," *Journal of Urban History* 35, no. 3 (March 2009): 348–68 and 369–86; Nathan Connolly, *A World More Concrete: Real Estate and the Remaking of Jim Crow South Florida* (Chicago: University of Chicago Press, 2014).

52. Doyle, *Nashville*, 125, Spinney, *World War II*, 64.

53. NHA, "The Redevelopment Plan for the Capitol Hill Redevelopment Project, UR Tenn 2-1," March 1952, in Capitol Hill Redevelopment Project, NHA, CM, Introduction; Annese, interview, first session September 28, 2006, Pleasantville, NY.

54. "Modern Dreamers."

55. NHA, "Redevelopment Plan," Introduction.

56. Columbia Oral History Research Office, "The Reminiscences of Gilmore David Clarke," 1960, 267.

57. NHA, "Redevelopment Plan," 8; "Modern Dreamers."

58. Emanual Crawford and Ronald Ennis, memo to Citizen's Advisory Committee, September 24, 1969, MTP (unprocessed), box 23, file Housing—Citizen's Advisory Committee on Housing and Urban Development—Business, General, 1967, 69, 70, 6.

59. Ibid., 20.

60. Excerpt of City Council minutes, April 29, 1952, in CM, box Capitol Hill Redevelopment Project, Nashville Housing Authority.

61. Hughes, "Nashville Cleans Up Slum"; ". . . And They Said It Couldn't Be Done," *Tennessean*, December 8, 1957, and "This to This," undated clipping, c. 1957, GNAR (reprocessed November 2014), box 3, file 9.

62. "Modern Dreamers."

63. "Aerial View of Progress," *Tennessean*, December 2, 1957; "Petition for Writ of Certiorari," 4. For similar cases, see Jon C. Teaford, *The Rough Road to Renaissance: Urban Revitalization in America, 1940–1985* (Baltimore: Johns Hopkins University Press, 1990) and Holliman, "From Crackertown."

64. *Alfred Starr et al. v. Nashville Housing Authority*, 145 F. Supp. 498 (1956), 503; "Demurrer and Answer of H. Sanders Anglea Et Al," *Pythias v. NHA*, June 2, 1952, CM, Capitol Hill Redevelopment/Nashville Housing Authority, 3–4; "Petition for Writ of Certiorari," 4.

65. NCC, minutes, Meeting of Executive Committee, April 20, 1951, NCC, reel 2, vol. XII, 203.

66. F. C. Sowell, "A Citizen's Responsibility," 1952, MANDC, Chamber of Commerce Printed Material, file 1950–59, 8.

67. E. C. Tompkins, "C. of C. Leader Urges Federal Spending Curb," *Banner*, May 20, 1949; Davis, draft of article on Capitol Hill, 7.

68. "Modern Dreamers"; "Blight Areas Cost City Most, West Says," *Tennessean*, October 5, 1956.

69. Spinney, *World War II*; James C. Cobb, *The Selling of the South: The Southern Crusade for Industrial Development, 1956–1980* (Baton Rouge: Louisiana State University Press, 1982); Bruce J. Schulman, *From Cotton Belt to Sunbelt: Federal Policy, Economic Development, and the Transformation of the South, 1938–1980* (New York: Oxford University Press, 1991).

70. Hughes, "Nashville Cleans up Slum"; Tom Normand, "Complaints Hit Model Cities Work," *Banner*, January 8, 1969; Jack Eisen, " . . . In Action," *Mortgage Banker*, June 1962, GNAR (reprocessed November 2014), box 3, file 16, scrapbook 1; NCC, minutes of Board of Governors meeting, August 23, 1963, NCC, reel 2, vol. XVI, 5; NCC, minutes of meeting of Executive Committee, February 19, 1957, NCC, reel 2, vol. XIV, 97.

71. On university growth and urban renewal, see Margaret Pugh O'Mara, *Cities of Knowledge: Cold War Science and the Search for the Next Silicon Valley* (Princeton, NJ: Princeton University Press, 2006).

72. Rev. Bill Barnes, *To Love a City: Congregation's Long Love Affair with Nashville's Inner City* (Nashville: O.N.E., n.d. [c. 2007]), 61; Annese, interview, first and second sessions. Inman Otey recounted an Edgehill version of this zoning/urban renewal profit scheme at "Edgehill Urban Renewal Meeting," 4; Jeremy Hill, "Country in the Suburbs? The Grand Ole Opry and Suburban Nashville" (paper given at the 2008 meeting of the American Studies Association, Albuquerque, NM).

73. Annese, interview, first session.

74. NCC, minutes of Board of Governors meeting, November 18, 1965, NCC, reel 2, vol. XVI, 5. On elite relationships, see Diane Pecknold, *The Selling Sound: The Rise of the Country Music Industry* (Durham, NC: Duke University Press, 2007).

75. Hill, "Country in the Suburbs?"; NCC, minutes of Board of Governors meeting, May 22, 1969, NCC, reel 2, vol. XVI, 4.

76. Dick Battle, "Nashville's Urban Renewal Caravan Visits Baltimore," *Banner*, August 7, 1956; Eugene Dietz, "Jan. 1 Target Date for Blight Study," *Tennessean*, September 16, 1956.

77. Dick Battle, "Urban Renewal Tour Inspires Leaders," *Banner*, August 10, 1956.

78. Dietz, "Jan. 1 Target Date"; "Modern Dreamers."

79. Eugene Dietz, "Home Owner Ratio Factor in Renewal," *Tennessean*, September 25, 1956; rough draft of "The Purposes of the Project," undated, c. 1960, RHPA, box 6, file 40, 1.

80. "Annual Report," 1959 (Nashville: NHA) MTP (unprocessed), box 23, file NHA Annual Reports 1958, 1966–68, 5. Inspector quotes are from Bill Carey, "A City Swept Clean: How Urban Renewal, for Better and for Worse, Created the City We Know Today," *Nashville Scene*, December 5, 2008.

81. Dick Battle, "E. Nashville Area Picked for Urban Renewal Planning," *Banner*, June 27, 1956.

82. "No Hurry-Up Job," *Tennessean*, September 23, 1956.

83. NCC, minutes of meeting of Board of Governors, July 24, 1956, 48; Dick Battle, "Urban Renewal Simple to Explain," *Banner*, October 19, 1956.

84. Battle, "E. Nashville Area Picked"; "Annual Report," 3–4; unidentified clipping, November 6, 1957, GNAR, series III-C, box 1, file 1960s.

85. "Table of Public Housing Tenant Statistics by Race: 1964 and 1969," February 11, 1970, *Kelley*, box 7, Plaintiff's Exhibit 1B.

86. Hand, "Planning," 122.

87. Project boundary map at Battle, "E. Nashville Area Picked."

88. NHAP, box 3, files 1 and 14.

89. This section borrows from Ansley T. Erickson, "Building Inequality: The Spatial Organization of Schooling in Nashville, Tennessee, after *Brown*," *JUH* 38, no. 2 (March 2012): 241–70.

90. *Plessy v. Ferguson*, 163 U.S. 537 (1896). The opinion uses the term "equal but separate," from the Louisiana statute, but "separate but equal" is used colloquially. The school board argued that desegregation orders had nothing to do with their decisions regarding Meigs and another expanded high school at "Opposition to Motion for Further Relief," *Kelley v. MNBOE*, October 1, 1968, *Kelley*, box 2, file 1968, 5. On equalization efforts before *Brown*, see Mark Tushnet, *The NAACP's Legal Strategy against Segregated Education* (Chapel Hill: University of North Carolina Press, 1987); Charles C. Bolton, "Mississippi's School Equalization Program, 1945–1954," *Journal of Southern History* 66, no. 4 (November 2000): 781–814.

91. In the planning phase, both Meigs and Warner were formally segregated institu-

tions. In the 1960s, Meigs remained all-black, while Warner served significant numbers of black and white students. Joseph R. Garrett, "Pupil Enrollment," 1970, *Kelley*, box 11, file 4.

92. "Project Seen in Ugly Stage," *Tennessean*, May 21, 1961.

93. NHA, Annual Report, 1968.

94. "Table of Public Housing Tenant Statistics."

95. "Ministers Form Housing Push," *Tennessean*, March 24, 1961.

96. Ibid.; "Annual Report."

97. Frank Ritter, "Renewal Plan Called Model," *Tennessean*, March 25, 1964.

98. NHAP, box 1, file 19.

99. "Table of Public Housing Tenant Statistics;" Dick Battle, "NHA Obeys HUD Order, Drops 'Free Choice' Tenancy," *Banner*, September 26, 1968.

100. Editorial, "County Plan for Housing Foresight at Its Best," *Tennessean*, October 21, 1957.

101. Canzada Hawkins, interview, July 2004.

102. Carl Abbott, *The New Urban America: Growth and Politics in Sunbelt Cities* (Chapel Hill: University of North Carolina Press, 1981), 54–57.

103. Daniel Grant, "Urban and Suburban Nashville: A Case Study in Metropolitanism," *Journal of Politics* 17, no. 1 (February 1955): 82–99, 97; Bertil L. Hanson, *A Report on Politics in Nashville* (Cambridge, MA: Joint Center for Urban Studies, 1960), I-11; *Baker v. Carr*, 369 U.S. 186 (1962).

104. US Census, 1960, via NHGIS.

105. Robert Spinney explains this Byzantine structure well in "Municipal Government," 93–100.

106. Grant, "Urban and Suburban Nashville," 94.

107. Ibid., 87. On septic tanks, see Adam Rome, *The Bulldozer in the Countryside: Suburban Sprawl and the Rise of American Environmentalism* (Cambridge: Cambridge University Press, 2001), chapter 3.

108. Grant, "Urban and Suburban Nashville," 84; US Census via NHGIS; Parks, "Grasping at the Coattails," 155–56.

109. NCC, minutes, meeting of Executive Committee, February 13, 1951, 203.

110. Robert James Parks, "Grasping at the Coattails of Progress: City Planning in Nashville, Tennessee, 1932–1962" (master's thesis, University of Tennessee, 1971), 155–56; Doyle, *Nashville*, 197.

111. On the growth-focused metropolis, see John Logan and Harvey Molotch, *Urban Fortunes: The Political Economy of Place* (Berkeley: University of California Press, 1987); Mark Purcell, "Metropolitan Political Reorganization as a Politics of Urban Growth: The Case of San Fernando Valley Secession," *Political Geography* 20, no. 5 (June 2001): 613–33.

112. Victor Johnson, interview with Carole Bucy, c. 1995, MCOH, Tape A.

113. C. Beverly Briley, interview with Paul Clement, 1980, MANDC, Century III Oral History; Biographical brochure, RHP, box 3, file 15.

114. Doyle, *Nashville*, 180–81.

115. Briley recounted his taking this leadership position in Briley, interview.

116. C. Beverly Briley, "Keynote Address, Urban County Congress, National Association of County Officials," March 15, 1959, DBP, box 20, file 2, 6.

117. Ibid., 9.

118. Ibid., 8.

119. Briley, "Keynote," 15–16.

120. Grant, "Urban and Suburban Nashville," 91; Brett W. Hawkins, *Nashville Metro: The Politics of City-County Consolidation* (Nashville: Vanderbilt University Press, 1966); on school overcrowding, see TNDOE, Annual Statistical Report, 1960. On the national shortage of schools in the 1950s suburbs, see James L. Sundquist, *Politics and Policy: The Eisenhower, Kennedy, and Johnson Years* (Washington, DC: Brookings Institution, 1968).

121. NCC, minutes, meeting of Executive Committee, April 20, 1951.

122. Doyle, *Nashville*, chapter 7; Houston, *Nashville Way*, 134–37.

123. Doyle, *Nashville*, 202.

124. Houston, *Nashville Way*, 134–37. Unfortunately, Looby's papers do not detail his thinking, and the records of the charter commission do not survive.

125. Quoted in Houston, *Nashville Way*, 137.

126. Ibid., 37.

127. Houston, *Nashville Way*, 134–37.

128. Doyle, *Nashville*, 202–3; Hawkins, *Nashville Metro*, 148.

129. Dick Battle, "Annex Suit Taken under Advisement," *Banner*, May 26, 1961; Doyle, *Nashville*, 204–5.

130. Doyle, *Nashville*, 205–6; Hawkins, *Nashville Metro*, 133–36.

131. Doyle, *Nashville*, 209–10.

132. Ibid., 204–6.

133. "'Scare' Tactics Laid to Jacobs," *Tennessean*, June 9, 1962; Houston, *Nashville Way*, 136.

134. Doyle, *Nashville*, 205–7; Hawkins, *Nashville Metro*, 76; Code of the Metropolitan Government of Nashville–Davidson County, part 1, article 11, chapter 5.

135. George Barrett, interview with Ben Houston, June 2003, http://ufdc.ufl.edu/UF00093255/00001, accessed December 9, 2013.

136. Houston, *Nashville Way*, 136.

137. "Civic-Minded Quartet Asks Charter," *Banner*, June 16, 1961.

138. Houston, *Nashville Way*, 134–38.

139. Johnson, interview, Tape A; "Aladdinews," August 4, 1961, Smithsonian Institution, Lemelson Center, Aladdin, box 71, file 4.

140. George Cate, interview, July 2007; Doyle, *Nashville*, 209–12.

141. Doyle, *Nashville*, 209–11.

142. Ibid., 212.

143. Ibid., 214.

144. Briley, interview.

145. The Code of the Metropolitan Government of Nashville–Davidson County, part 1, article 11, chapter 5.

146. MPC, *Schools for 1980* (Nashville: MPC, 1964).

CHAPTER TWO

1. John Egerton, "Walking into History: The Beginning of School Desegregation in Nashville," *Southern Spaces*, May 4, 2009, www.southernspaces.org, accessed September 1, 2013. Street quoted in John Egerton, Terrie Lawrence, and Rachel Lawson, *A Child Shall Lead Them* (Magellan Press Films, 2008).

2. Quoted in "Looby Raps Segregated Education," NPLDC, November 2, 1950, http://digital.library.nashville.org/cdm/singleitem/collection/nr/id/2352/rec/1, accessed January 15, 2014.

3. On Little Rock, see Karen Anderson, *Race and Resistance at Central High School*

(Princeton, NJ: Princeton University Press, 2009); Elizabeth Jacoway, *Turn Away They Son: Little Rock and the Crisis That Shocked the Nation* (New York: Free Press, 2007); Tony Freyer, *Little Rock on Trial: Cooper v. Aaron and School Desegregation* (Lawrence: University Press of Kansas, 2007); and Ben F. Johnson, III. "After 1957: Resisting Desegregation in Little Rock." *Arkansas Historical Quarterly* LXVI (Summer 2007): 258–83. On Prince Edward County, see Matthew Lassiter and Andrew B. Lewis, *The Moderate's Dilemma: Massive Resistance to School Desegregation in Virginia* (Charlottesville: University of Virginia, 1998), and Christopher Bonastia, *Southern Stalemate: Five Years without Public Education in Prince Edward County, VA* (Chicago: University of Chicago Press, 2012). Benjamin Houston critiques the image of moderation in *The Nashville Way: Racial Etiquette and the Struggle for Social Justice in a Southern City* (Athens: University of Georgia Press, 2012), passim.

4.  CNBOE, minutes, 1951, MNBOE, vol. 1951–1954, 410.

5.  Mark Tushnet, *The NAACP's Strategy against Segregated Education* (Chapel Hill: University of North Carolina Press, 1987); Jack Dougherty, *More Than One Struggle: The Evolution of Black School Reform in Milwaukee* (Chapel Hill: University of North Carolina Press, 2004); Numan Bartley, *The Rise of Massive Resistance: Race and Politics in the South During the 1950s* (Baton Rouge: Louisiana State University Press, 1969); Charles C. Bolton, "Mississippi's School Equalization Program, 1945–1954: A Last Gasp to try to Maintain a Segregated Educational System," *Journal of Southern History* 66, no. 4 (November 2000): 781–814. See also Myron Oglesby-Pitts, *To Teach Like Mary: Getting It Right at First* (Pittsburgh: RoseDog, 2010).

6.  Quoted in Sonya Ramsey, *Reading, Writing, and Segregation: A Century of Black Women Teachers in Nashville* (Urbana: University of Illinois Press, 2008), 72.

7.  Ibid., 30, 294.

8.  Ibid., 31; CNBOE, minutes, 196.

9.  CNBOE, minutes, 410.

10. CNBOE, minutes, May 13, 1954, MNBOE.

11. CNBOE, minutes, MNBOE, vol. 1951–1954, 41–42, 227, 294. Photos documenting poor conditions in SPF, file Central High School.

12. CNBOE, minutes, 294–95; Robert Spinney, *World War II in Nashville* (Knoxville: University of Tennessee Press, 1996) 7.

13. CNBOE, minutes, 60.

14. Ibid., 25–26, 30, 179. For another example, see "Board 'Hands Down' Murphy School to Colored Students," *Nashville Globe and Independent*, January 1, 1957.

15. On transferring white schools to black students, see Kevin Kruse, *White Flight: Atlanta and the Making of Modern Conservatism* (Princeton, NJ: Princeton University Press, 2006), 164–69; Kevin Fox Gotham, *Race, Real Estate, and Uneven Development: The Kansas City Experience, 1900–2000* (Albany: State University of New York Press, 2002), 93–100.

16. "Southside Group Seeks New School for Negroes," *Tennessean*, March 6, 1952; Yolette Trigg-Jones, "The Black Community, Politics, and Race Relations in the 'Iris City': Nashville, Tennessee, 1870–1954" (PhD diss., Duke, 1985); 333–37.

17. CNBOE, minutes, 31, 197; Ramsey, *Reading, Writing*, 28–32.

18. TNDOE, *Annual Statistical Report*, 1960.

19. Ibid.; Davidson County Schools, *Annual Statistical Report*, July 7, 1954, TNDOE, RG 273, roll 7, box 8, file 32.

20. CNBOE, minutes, 30.

21. Davidson County Schools, *Annual Statistical Report*.

22. Ramsey, *Reading, Writing*; Michael Fultz, "The Displacement of Black Educators Post-*Brown*: An Overview and Analysis," *HEQ* 44, no. 1 (March 2004): 11–45; Adam Fairclough, *A Class of Their Own: Black Teachers in the Segregated South* (Cambridge, MA: Belknap Press, 2007).

23. Ramsey, *Reading, Writing*, 47–55.

24. Transcript of proceedings, *Maxwell v. County Board*, October 24–27, 1960, *Kelley*, box 2, Transcripts 10/24–27/60, 206.

25. This is a point not unique to Nashville, but common across remembrances of segregated black schools. See Vanessa Siddle Walker, *Their Highest Potential: An African American School Community in the Segregated South* (Chapel Hill: University of North Carolina Press, 1996); Vivian Gunn Morris and Curtis L. Morris, *The Price They Paid: Desegregation in an African American Community* (New York: Teachers College Press, 2002); David S. Cecelski, *Along Freedom Road: Hyde County, North Carolina and the Fate of Black Schools in the South* (Chapel Hill: University of North Carolina Press, 1994). See also Barbara Shircliffe, *Best of That World: Historically Black High Schools and the Crisis of Desegregation in a Southern Metropolis* (Cresskill, NJ: Hampton, 2006); Oglesby-Pitts, *To Teach Like Mary*.

26. Perry Wallace, interview, August 4, 2005, NCROHP; Donzell Johnson, interview, May 20, 2003 NCROHP; Mary Frances Berry, interview, September 5, 2003, NCROHP (used with permission).

27. Gena Carter, interview, November 13, 2012, Providence, RI.

28. Berry, interview (used with permission).

29. "Ruling Makes No Changes Immediately," *Banner*, May 17, 1954.

30. Quoted in Hugh Davis Graham, "Desegregation in Nashville: The Dynamics of Compliance," *Tennessee Historical Quarterly* 25, no. 1 (Summer 1966): 135–54, 140, 42. See also Hugh Davis Graham, *Crisis in Print: Desegregation and the Press in Tennessee* (Nashville: Vanderbilt, 1967).

31. Trigg-Jones, "The Black Community"; Robert Spinney, *World War II in Nashville* (Knoxville: University of Tennessee Press, 1999), 66–67.

32. CNBOE, minutes, June 10, 1954, 127–28.

33. Ramsey, *Reading, Writing*, 91–93, 112–14.

34. On equalization elsewhere, see Tushnet, *The NAACP's Strategy*. James Patterson, *Brown v. Board of Education: A Civil Rights Milestone and Its Troubled Legacy* (New York: Oxford University Press, 2001); editorial, "Need Is the New School Test," *Tennessean*, July 2, 1955.

35. "Southside Group Seeks New School"; Jones, "Iris City," 333; CNBOE, minutes, 224.

36. CNBOE, minutes, 213; Ramsey, *Reading, Writing*, 78. On the Lorches, see Jacoway, *Turn Away Thy Son*, 5–6.

37. CNBOE, minutes, 133.

38. CNBOE, minutes, 213.

39. "Answer of Mrs. O. W. Benson, et al [Defendants]," *Kelley v. CNBOE*, November 16, 1955, *Kelley*, box 1, file 1955, 7–8; transcript of proceedings, *Kelley v. CNBOE*, April 14, 1958, *Kelley*, box 1, file 1958 (1), 183–84.

40. This report is on file at the MPC Library.

41. On Sims, see Daniel Sharfstein, "*Brown*, Massive Resistance, and the Lawyer's View: Cecil Sims, Nashville Moderate," (unpublished paper in author's possession).

42. Cecil Sims, "The Segregation Decisions: A Lawyer's View," November 10, 1955, reprinted in Fred. A. Bailey, "Forum: Memphis, the Peabody, and the SHA: A Fifty-Year Commemoration—the Southern Historical Association and the Quest for Racial

Justice, 1954–1963," *Journal of Southern History* 71, no. 4 (November 2005): 833–52; Charles G. Neese, letter to Frank Clement, November 1, 1954, GP 47—Clement I & II, box 38, file 14.

43. Matthew Lassiter, "De Jure/De Facto Segregation: The Long Shadow of a National Myth," in, eds., *The Myth of Southern Exceptionalism*, Matthew D. Lassiter and Joseph Crespino (New York: Oxford University Press, 2009), 25–48.

44. Memoirs of Avon N. Williams, NPLSC; Will Sarvis, "Leaders in the Court and Community: Z. Alexander Looby, Avon N. Williams Jr., and the Legal Fight for Civil Rights in Tennessee, 1940–1970," *Journal of African American History* 88, no. 1 (Winter 2003): 42–58; Bill Carey, *Fortunes, Fiddles and Fried Chicken: A Nashville Business History* (Franklin, TN: Hillsboro Press, 2002).

45. Richard Dinkins, interview, third session, August 20, 2013, by telephone.

46. "Complaint," *Kelley v. CNBOE*, September 23, 1955, *Kelley*, box 1, file 1955, 5; "Answer of Mrs. O. W. Benson et al.," 2.

47. "Complaint"; "Supplemental Answer to Amended Complaint," *Kelley v. CNBOE*, November 13, 1956, *Kelley*, box 1, file 1956, exhibit D.

48. Graham, "Desegregation," 149–54.

49. Transcript of the testimony of William H. Oliver, *Kelley v. CNBOE*, January 28, 1958, *Kelley*, box 1, file 1958 (1), 4; transcript of proceedings, 97; Artie Pate, "An Investigation of the Desegregation Process in the Metropolitan Nashville–Davidson County Public School System, 1954–1969" (EdD diss., George Peabody College, 1981), 60.

50. Fultz, "Displacement."

51. Transcript of proceedings, 97. John Egerton estimated that there were eight such schools. Egerton, "Walking into History." Hugh Davis Graham reports that "Negroes with some justice claimed that the board could and did racially segregate the school districts by employing as zoning criteria certain specific qualities, such as low scores on reading and aptitude tests, which were in effect correlates of race," but I have not encountered evidence to support this view. Graham, "Desegregation," 144–45.

52. Pate, "An Investigation," 78; transcript of proceedings, 199–200.

53. Hubert Dixon Jr., interview, July 2004.

54. On Little Rock, see Freyer, *Little Rock on Trial*, and Johnson, "After 1957." Lani Guinier, "From Racial Liberalism to Racial Literacy: *Brown v. Board of Education* and the Interest-Divergence Dilemma," *Journal of American History* 91, no. 1 (June 2004): 92–118.

55. Albert Cason, "Ford to Build Plant Here if Site Open," *Tennessean*, July 14, 1955; William Keel, "Schools a Factor in Ford Decision," *Tennessean*, July 15, 1955.

56. Keel, "Schools a Factor."

57. Julie Hollabaugh, "Building Reflects Aladdin Progress," *Tennessean*, November 17, 1960.

58. Transcript of the testimony of William H. Oliver, 6–8.

59. MNPS, "Pupil Enrollment," 1970, *Kelley*, box 11, file 4; Egerton, "Walking into History," appendices.

60. Graham, "Desegregation," 144.

61. "Answers to Interrogatories," *Kelley v. MNBOE*, November 26, 1969, *Kelley*, box 5, 1970 (2), No. 40. See also Graham, "Desegregation," 144.

62. Transcript of the testimony of William H. Oliver, 7–8. Egerton, "Walking into History," is the most careful and recent accounting.

63. Louis Peltason, *Fifty-Eight Lonely Men: Southern Judges and School Desegregation* (New York: Harcourt, Brace & World, 1961), 156.

64. Graham, "Desegregation," 147–48.

65. "Memorandum Brief for Defendants," *Kelley v. CNBOE*, November 11, 1956, *Kelley*, box 1, file 1956, 11–12.

66. Graham, "Desegregation," 141–43, 150–51.

67. "Supplemental Answer and Counter-Claim," *Kelley v. CNBOE*, July 6, 1957, *Kelley*, box 1, file 1957 (1); "Plaintiff's Memorandum Brief in Opposition," *Kelley v. CNBOE*, September 6, 1957, *Kelley*, box 1, file 1957 (1).

68. Graham, "Desegregation," 150.

69. Ibid., 151.

70. "Brief for Defendants in Support of Plan," *Kelley v. CNBOE*, April 28, 1958, *Kelley*, box 1, file 1958 (1), 15. Freyer, *Little Rock*, makes this point about weak leadership in Little Rock.

71. Patterson, *Brown v. Board*, 101–2; Houston, *Nashville Way*, 66–67.

72. "Petition for Injunction," *Kelley v. CNBOE*, September 12, 1957, *Kelley*, box 3, file 1957 (1).

73. Tennessee White Citizens Council flyers, exhibits to the Affidavit of W. H. Oliver, *Kelley*, box 1, file 1957(1).

74. Pate, "An Investigation," 64.

75. Graham, "Desegregation in Nashville," 151.

76. Statement of James R. Gilliam, *Kelley v. CNBOE*, September 12, 1957, *Kelley*, box 3, file 1957 (1).

77. Pate, "An Investigation," 64; Houston, *Nashville Way*, 47–64.

78. Quoted in Pate, "An Investigation," 33, 122, 127.

79. Transcript of proceedings, *Maxwell v. County Board*, 191; Affidavit of W. H. Oliver, *Kelley v. CNBOE*, September 1957, *Kelley*, box 1, file 1957; Houston, *Nashville Way*, 70–71.

80. "City School Zones Redrawn for First Grade," *Banner*, July 31, 1957, MANDC, clippings, file Schools, Metro, VF 26.

81. Transcript of proceedings, 120–24.

82. Ibid., 381–82; Ramsey, *Reading, Writing*, 86.

83. Ramsey, *Reading, Writing*, 86; Anna Holden, *A First Step toward School Integration* (New York: Congress on Racial Equality, 1958).

84. Transcript of the testimony of William H. Oliver, 7–8.

85. Ibid., 16–17.

86. Holden, *A First Step*, 3–4.

87. Transcript of the testimony of William H. Oliver, 13.

88. Affidavit of Miss Mary Brent, *Kelley v. CNBOE*, September 12, 1957, *Kelley*, box 3, file 1957 (1).

89. Ibid.

90. Affidavit of Stella Mae Grooms, *Kelley v. CNBOE*, September 12, 1957, *Kelley*, box 3, file 1957 (1).

91. Graham, "Desegregation," 151.

92. Transcript of the testimony of William H. Oliver, 28; affidavit of W. H. Oliver.

93. Quoted in Pate, "An Investigation," 67. The *Banner* editorialized on the side of the Tennessee Federation for Constitutional Government's 1956 attempt to reject desegregation on the basis that the 14th Amendment was invalid. Graham, "Desegregation," 143.

94. Pate, "An Investigation," 75.
95. Egerton, Lawson, and Lawrence, *A Child Shall Lead Them*.
96. Ibid.; "Face the Nation Transcript," September 15, 1957, GP 47—Clement I & II, box 259, file 8, 7.
97. Pate, "An Investigation," 69.
98. "Report of Nashville Board of Education," December 6, 1957, *Kelley*, box 1, file 1957 (2), 2.
99. Ramsey, *Reading, Writing*, 93; Graham, "Desegregation," 153; transcript of proceedings, *Maxwell v. County Board*, 39–41. For the 1963–64 figures, see Pate, "An Investigation," 70.
100. Pate, "An Investigation," 74.
101. Holden, *First Steps*, 13–14.
102. Egerton, Lawrence, and Lawson, *A Child Shall Lead Them*.
103. Quoted in Ramsey, *Reading, Writing*, 87.
104. Eugene Weinstein, "A Report on School Desegregation in Nashville and Davidson County," April 1963, in MTP (unprocessed), box 26, file Race Relations—Nashville Community Relations Council, 4.
105. Pate, "An Investigation," 70.
106. V. W. Henderson and Mrs. C. W. Hayes to Thurgood Marshall, August 4, 1961, and V. W. Henderson to Thurgood Marshall, October 19 1960, VHP, box 30, file 7; N. H. Williams Jr., A. Z. Kelley, and V. W. Henderson to All Local Ministers, August 10, 1960, VHP, box 30, file 9.
107. Avon Williams, "'Negro Problem' a Community Problem," April 24, 1961, VHP, box 30, file 16, 1.
108. Ibid.
109. Ibid., 2.
110. Ibid., 3.
111. Weinstein, "A Report," 5.
112. Quoted in Pate, "An Investigation," 11–12.
113. Henry H. Hill, "Changing Options in American Education," quoted in transcript of proceedings, *Kelley v. CNBOE*, April 14, 1958, *Kelley*, box 1, file 1958 (1), 131–33.
114. "Petition for a Writ of Certiorari to the US Court of Appeals for the Sixth Circuit, Draft, 1959," *Kelley v. CNBOE*, in LOC, NAACP, box V:2282, file *Kelly* [sic] *v. Board of Education*, 1956, no. 7, 13.
115. For historical versions of this debate, see David Tyack, *The One Best System: A History of American Urban Education* (Cambridge, MA: Harvard, 1974); Kliebard, *The Struggle for the American Curriculum*, chapters 4–5; Larry Cuban, *How Teachers Taught: Constancy and Change in American Classrooms, 1890–1990* (New York: Teachers College Press, 1993); Jeannie Oakes, *Keeping Track: How Schools Structure Inequality*, 2nd ed. (New Haven, CT: Yale University Press, 2005).
116. Brent quoted in transcript of proceedings, 84. Sims quoted in Houston, *Nashville Way*, 58.
117. Houston, *Nashville Way*, chapter 1; David Halberstam, *The Children* (New York: Random House, 1998).
118. Transcript of proceedings, 128–33.
119. Ibid., 132–34.
120. Ibid., 16–17.
121. Ibid., 21.
122. Ibid., 81.

123. Transcript of proceedings, *Maxwell v. County Board*, October 24–27, 1960, *Kelley*, box 2, file Transcripts 10/24–27/60, 49, 78.

124. Transcript of proceedings, 155.

125. Ibid., 105–7.

126. Ibid., 178, 196.

127. Ibid., 65, 343–46.

128. Ibid., 101, 173.

129. Ibid., 95, 268–74.

130. Ibid., 420.

131. On standardized tests and scores, see Nicholas Lemann, *The Big Test* (New York: Farrar, Straus, & Giroux, 1999); Carlos Kevin Blanton, "From Intellectual Deficiency to Cultural Deficiency: Mexican Americans, Testing, and Public School Policy in the American Southwest, 1920–1940," *Pacific Historical Review* 72, no. 1 (February 2003): 39–62; Judith Raftery, "Missing the Mark: Intelligence Testing in Los Angeles Public Schools, 1922–1932," in John L. Rury, ed., *Urban Education in the United States* (New York: Palgrave MacMillan, 2005), 159–78.

132. Pate, "An Investigation," 83. TNDOE, annual report, 1962.

CHAPTER THREE

1. For examples of other contexts in which ideas of difference and curriculum interacted, see Carlos Kevin Blanton, "From Intellectual Deficiency to Cultural Deficiency: Mexican Americans, Testing, and Public School Policy in the American Southwest, 1920–1940," *Pacific Historical Review* 72, no. 1 (February 2003): 39–62; David Gamson, "From Progressivism to Federalism: The Pursuit of Equal Educational Opportunity, 1915–1965," in Carl F. Kaestle and Alyssa Lodewick, eds., *To Educate a Nation: Federal and National Strategies of School Reform* (Lawrence: University Press of Kansas, 2007), 177–201.

2. Martha Minow, *Making All the Difference: Inclusion, Exclusion, and American Law* (Ithaca, NY: Cornell University Press, 1990), 19–23. Thanks to Harvey Kantor for suggesting this text.

3. Ibid., 53–56.

4. Quoted in Herbert Kliebard, *The Struggle for the American Curriculum, 1899–1958* (New York: RoutledgeFalmer, 2004), 12.

5. James Anderson, *Education of Blacks in the South, 1865–1935* (Chapel Hill: University of North Carolina Press, 1988), chapter 2; Michael Rudolph West, *The Education of Booker T. Washington* (New York: Columbia, 2006).

6. Norton Grubb and Marvin Lazerson, *The Education Gospel* (Cambridge, MA: Harvard University Press, 2006).

7. Katherine Neckerman, *Schools Betrayed: The Roots of Failure in Inner City Education* (Chicago: University of Chicago Press, 2008), chapter 5. There is a dearth of work exploring vocational education in the post–World War II years.

8. Benjamin E. Carmichael, "Recent Trends in Selected Enrichment Services" (PhD diss., George Peabody College for Teachers, 1954), 154–57; J.B. Calhoun, Memo to G.E. Freeman, April 10, 1956, COE, reel 109 (108 on box), box 374, file 5, frame 002393.

9. Ibid., 5; Vivian W. Henderson, "Negro Participation in Apprenticeship Training Programs in Tennessee," 1963, VHP, box 42, file 15, 5; Tennessee Council on Human Relations, Survey of Opportunities for Vocational and Technical Training in Tennessee, January 1964, VHP, box 34, file 8, 3.

10. On the limitations of vocational education for black students, see James Anderson, "The Historical Development of Black Vocational Education," in Harvey Kantor and David Tyack, eds., *Work, Youth, and Schooling: Historical Perspectives on Vocationalism in American Schooling* (Stanford, CA: Stanford University Press, 1982), 180–222.

11. Robert Spinney, *World War II in Nashville: The Transformation of the Home Front* (Knoxville: University of Tennessee Press, 1998), 56–58. See Ira Katznelson, *When Affirmative Action Was White: The Untold History of Racial Inequality in Twentieth Century America* (New York: Norton, 2008).

12. Don Doyle, *Nashville since the 1920s* (Knoxville: University of Tennessee Press, 1985), 230–34; Vivian T. Henderson, "Employment Opportunity for Nashville Negroes," September 1960, NMFP, box 1, file 24.

13. Nashville City Schools, "Annual Reports, 1949–1954," 56.

14. "Estimates of T& I Program," 1948, MANDC, Unprocessed Education Collection, box Voc Ed, 46–47. These two schools seem to follow the regional pattern. See James W. Whitlock and Billy J. Williams, *Jobs and Training for Southern Youth* (Nashville: Peabody College, 1963), 24.

15. Carmichael, "Recent Trends," 199.

16. Henderson, "Employment Opportunity," 8.

17. Ibid.

18. "Vocational Training in Schools Advocated," *Tennessean*, February 11, 1955; DCBOE, "Minutes," February 3, 1955, MNBOE, vol. July 1953–January 1957, 207; Henderson, "Employment Opportunity," 8, Benjamin Slaughter, "Tailoring: 4500 Hour Course of Study," n.d., c. 1947, MANDC, Unprocessed Education Collection, box Voc Ed, 46–47. Evidence on course offerings also comes from the annual collections of photographs of vocational and "co-op" students at Pearl included in the Pearl High School Alumni Room, Martin Luther King Magnet School. State Department of Education, "Directory of Trade and Industrial Education Personnel," June 1960, COE, reel 129 (128 on box), box 375, file 2.

19. Transcript of proceedings, *Kelley v. CNBOE*, April 14, 1958, *Kelley*, box 1, file 1958 (1), 193–95.

20. Henderson, "Employment Opportunity," 8.

21. Anderson, *Education of Blacks*, chapter 6.

22. Cooperative Training Program display photographs, Pearl High School Alumni Room; ibid., 3.

23. A. Z. Kelley, memo to all local ministers, August 10, 1960, VHP, box 30, file 9; Mrs. C. M. Hayes et al., memo to Vocational Committee and Instruction Committee, Nashville City School Board, February 22, 1962, VHP, box 30, file 8; John Britton, "Best City in the South for Negroes: Many Cry 'Tokenism,' but Nashville Has the Most 'Tokens,' *Jet*, December 5, 1963, 14–21.

24. David Halberstam, *The Children* (New York: Vintage, 1999), 187.

25. Mahlon Griffith, "Employment Progress in Nashville," 1961, VHP, box 30, file 14, 2; V. W. Henderson, Untitled Notes, c. 1962, VHP, box 30, file 10.

26. Nashville NAACP, "Summary of Some of the Cases and Complaints Involving Employment of Negroes in Federal Agencies and in Business Firms Doing Business with the United States Government," n.d., [1961], VHP, box 30, file 14, 1.

27. Henderson, "Employment Opportunity," 3.

28. Henderson, "Negro Participation," 5.

29. Henderson, "Employment Opportunity," 2.

30. Herman H. Long and Vivian W. Henderson, "Negro Employment in Tennessee State Government," December 14, 1962, GP 49—Clement III, box 537, file 17, 3.

31. Ibid., 5.

32. Ibid., 8–9.

33. Long and Henderson, "Negro Employment," 12; V. W. Henderson, memo to Phillip Camponeschi (Ms. Draft), n.d., VHP, box 150, file 1, 5–6.

34. Ibid., 7.

35. Vivian W. Henderson, "Economic Opportunity and Negro Education," reprint from the American Teachers Association Bulletin, March 1962, VHP, box 28, file 5, 6.

36. Ibid., "Guidance Clinic with High School and Junior High School Teachers—Draft Agenda, 1963," VHP, box 28, file 5.

37. Department of Personnel, State of Tennessee, Application and Statement of Qualifications, June 1962, VHP, box 28, file 3.

38. Henderson, "Economic Opportunity," emphasis in original; Anderson, "Historical Development." For another view of mixed support for and concern over vocational education, see Lisa Levenstein, *A Movement without Marches: African-American Women and the Politics of Poverty in Postwar Philadelphia* (Chapel Hill: University of North Carolina Press, 2009), chapter 4.

39. V. W. Henderson, untitled manuscript, 1961, VHP, box 28, file 4.

40. V. W. Henderson and Mrs. C. W. Hayes, letter to Conference of Southern Governors, September 23, 1961, VHP, box 30, file 7.

41. Henderson, "Economic Opportunity," 3.

42. Amos Jones, interview, October 13, 1972, FUBOHC.

43. Julie Roy Jeffrey, *Education for Children of the Poor: A Study of the Origins and Implementation of the Elementary and Secondary Education Act of 1965* (Columbus: Ohio State University Press, 1978); Richard F. Elmore and Milbrey W. McLaughlin, "Steady Work: Policy, Practice, and the Reform of American Education," 1988 (Washington, DC: National Institute of Education).

44. Cornell Report quoted in "Highlights of the School Survey Report," *The Link*, November 1963, MANDC, Education, box Education Council—Bogen, 1.

45. See Pate, "An Investigation of the Desegregation Process," 86.

46. James Coleman et al., *Equality of Educational Opportunity* (Washington, DC: HEW, 1966). See Jeffrey, *Education for Children of the Poor*; Hugh Davis Graham, *The Uncertain Triumph: Federal Education Policy in the Kennedy and Johnson Years* (Chapel Hill: University of North Carolina Press, 1984); Patrick McGuinn and Frederick Hess, "Freedom from Ignorance? The Great Society and the Evolution of the Elementary and Secondary Education Act of 1965," in Sidney M. Milkis and Jerome M. Mileur, eds., *The Great Society and the High Tide of Liberalism* (Amherst: Massachusetts, 2005).

47. Alice O'Connor, *Poverty Knowledge: Social Science, Social Policy, and the Poor in Twentieth-Century US History* (Chicago: University of Chicago Press, 2001), 16–17. See also the special issue on compensatory education, *Teachers College Record* 114, no. 6 (2012).

48. Harold A. Stinson, "Proposal, Nashville Education Improvement Project," February 15, 1965, FFA, 006400238, reel 5491, frame 0713.

49. Docket excerpt, Board of Trustees meeting, April 2–3, 1964, FFA, 006400238, reel 5491, frame 0668. See Harvey Kantor and Robert Lowe, "Class, Race, and the Emergence of Federal Education Policy: From the New Deal to the Great Society," *Educational Researcher* 24, no. 3 (April 1995): 4–11 and 21.

50. The participating schools are listed at Stinson, "Proposal," frame 0711. There is

some confusion in the Ford records about exactly which schools were involved in the project, but the preference for focusing on South Nashville schools, with some exceptions, is clear. For a view of Ford's work in another context, see John P. Spencer, *In the Crossfire: Marcus Foster and the Troubled History of American School Reform* (Philadelphia: University of Pennsylvania Press, 2012), chapter 2.

51. Stinson, "Proposal," frame 0772; Francis Parkman and Pat Rice, "Nashville Education Improvement Project," August 18, 1972, FFA, 006400238, reel 5491, frame 1223.

52. Stinson, "Proposal," frame 0765–1769.

53. Docket excerpt, Board of Trustees meeting, FFA, 006400238, reel 5491, frame 0669; Ralph Bohrson, memo to Edward J. Meade Jr., December 12, 1965, FFA 006400238, reel 5491, 1-2.

54. Bohrson, memo to Meade, 4.

55. "Tentative Proposal, Nashville Educational Improvement Project," November 11, 1964, GPCR, box 2118, file Nashville Educational Improvement Project.

56. "Model Cities Program—Educational Phase," April 21, 1967, UPP, box 2, file Misc. Memos Rough Draft; MNBOE, board agenda, October 11, 1966, MNBOE, Sec 3F. On conflations of disability and disadvantage, see Adam R. Nelson, *The Elusive Ideal: Equal Educational Opportunity and the Federal Role in Boston's Public Schools, 1950–1985* (Chicago: University of Chicago Press, 2005), chapter 5.

57. Stinson, "Proposal," frame 0779–80.

58. Parkman and Rice, "Nashville Education Improvement Project," frame 1236.

59. "Model Cities Program—Educational Phase."

60. Kantor and Lowe, "Class, Race, and the Emergence of Federal Education Policy."

61. Parkman and Rice, "Nashville Education Improvement Project," frame 1223; Felix C. Robb, letter to Robert Lynch, March 22, 1966, FFA, 006400238, reel 5491, frame 1371; Ben F. Cameron, memo to Frank Bowles, February 1, 1964, FFA, 006400238, reel 5491, frame 1402. The Educational Improvement Project was a pilot for the larger Comprehensive (or Great Cities) School Improvement Program, which spent $31 million over ten years in twenty-five cities (Brenda Newman, memo to file, August 18, 1972, FFA, 006400238, reel 5491, frame 1226).

62. "Model Cities Program—Educational Phase."

63. On local expenditures of Title I funds, see Nelson, *The Elusive Ideal*; McLaughlin, "Steady Work," as well as Graham, *Uncertain Triumph*; McGuinn and Hess, "Freedom from Ignorance?"

64. MNBOE, Minutes, October 11, 1966; transcript of proceedings, *Kelley v. MNBOE*, February 3, 1970, *Kelley*, file 3, box 6, 1616, 1618.

65. *Kelley v. MNBOE*, "[Defendants'] Answers to Interrogatories," *Kelley v. MNBOE*, November 26, 1969, *Kelley*, box 5, file 1970 (2), no. 38. *Kelley*; MNPS, "A Program of Compensatory Efforts for the Educationally and Culturally Deprived of Metropolitan Nashville-Davidson County," December 1965, MANDC, BOE, box 1, file 12. A product of early 1960s social science, the "poverty line" was a fluid construction, especially so in its first decade. See O'Connor, *Poverty Knowledge*, 183–84. The very low poverty line at use in these statistics (a family income level of $2,000) makes absolute judgments difficult, but the relative comparisons remain useful.

66. Kantor, "Education, Social Reform;" Ira Katznelson, "Was the Great Society A Lost Opportunity?" Steven Fraser and Gary Gerstle, eds., *The Rise and Fall of the New Deal Order*, (Princeton, NJ: Princeton University Press, 1989), 185–211.

67. Quoted in Lurad Rhinehart England, "The Development of Public Vocational Edu-

cation in Tennessee" (PhD diss., George Peabody College for Teachers, 1952), 15–16, 336-38, 368. Excluding home economics would have yielded an even lower percentage.

68. NCC, minutes, meeting of Board of Governors, June 12, 1951, NCC, reel 2, vol. XII, 222 and minutes, meeting of Board of Governors, August 23, 1955, NCC, reel 2, vol. XIII, 215; "Middle Tennessee: Land of Industrial and Agricultural Opportunity," c. 1952, GNAR, series II-C, box 1, file 1960s; NCC, minutes of meeting of Board of Governors, October 21, 1953, NCC, reel 2, volume XIII , 66–67; Teachers of the Nashville Public Schools, "Democracy's Hope: A Manual for Teaching Democracy in the Secondary Grades," 1952, TSLA, RG 273 – Department of Education, roll 2, box 1, file 33, 52–53. See Kim Phillips-Fein, *Invisible Hands: The Making of the Conservative Movement from the New Deal to Reagan* (New York: Norton, 2009), chapters 3–4, and Elizabeth Fones-Wolff, *Selling Free Enterprise: The Business Assault on Labor, 1945-1960* (Urbana: University of Illinois Press, 1995).

69. Teachers of the Nashville Public Schools, "Democracy's Hope," 42.

70. NCC, minutes, meeting of Board of Governors, April 29, 1959, NCC, reel 2, vol. XV, 78.

71. NCC, minutes, meeting of Board of Governors, June 12, 1951, NCC, reel 2, vol. XII, 225.

72. NCC, minutes, meeting of Board of Governors, January 31, 1957, NCC, reel 2, vol. XIV, 96.

73. Dick Battle, "City Hall: Local Industries Highlight Need of Vocational Courses," *Banner*, February 15, 1957; "City, County Push Plan for Trade School," *Banner*, March 15, 1957; NCC, minutes, meeting of Board of Governors, June 12, 1951, 225.

74. "Tennessee Governor's Conference on Education Beyond the High School," May 21, 1958, COE, roll 104, box 311, file 3, frame 2508-11.

75. "City, County Push Plan"; *Nashville Metropolitan Area Skill Survey 1957* (Nashville, TN: Tennessee Department of Employment Security). For the national discussion, see, for example, Garth L. Mangum, ed., *The Manpower Revolution: its Policy Consequences* (Garden City: Anchor, 1966).

76. Tennessee Municipal League, "A Recommended Program of Tennessee Economic Development," c. October 1957, GP 47—Clement I & II, box 151n, file 9, 2.

77. Cobb, *Selling*, 161–63. Cobb identifies increased interest in skill beginning in the late-1950s, which corresponds with Nashville's story here.

78. Battle, "City Hall: Local Industries."

79. "City, County Push Plan."

80. "Opening Campaign Address of Buford Ellington for Governor of Tennessee," 1958, COE, reel 105, box 312, file 5, frame 0738, 7.

81. Graduation rates are both notoriously inexact and difficult to trace historically. I take the eighth-grade enrollment of Nashville City Schools for the 1949–1950 school year, compare it to the twelfth-grade enrollment for 1954–55, when those eighth graders would have become seniors, and compare this to the number of diplomas issued that year. The results show, roughly, 40 percent of white eighth graders graduating on time, as compared with 37 percent of their black peers ("Annual Statistical Report," 1955 (Nashville, TN: State Department of Education); Nashville City Schools, "Annual Reports, 1949-1954," 1954, in Education, MANDC). This view does not, however, take account of students moving in to or out of the district between eighth and twelfth grades, nor does it consider students who left school

*before* eighth grade. For national trends, see Michael Katz, Mark Stern, and Jamie Fader, "The New African American Inequality," *Journal of American History* 92, no. 1 (June 2005): 75–108, figure 5.

82. Cobb, *Selling*, 161. Cobb also argues that secondary-level education mattered less than junior colleges or technical schools. Nashville's story demonstrates this to be true, for the 1960s, but secondary schools take on a heightened role in the 1970s.

83. Wallace Westfeldt, "Urgent Need Seen for Technical School," *Tennessean*, February 14, 1958.

84. NCC, minutes, meeting of Board of Governors, February 22, 1955, NCC, reel 2, Volume XIII, 181–3; Henderson, "Employment Opportunity," 5.

85. "Nashville Metropolitan Area Skill Survey," 8, 38–39.

86. Ibid. See also Owen, "Follow-up Study," 9–10; England, "Development of Public Vocational Education," 305.

87. For a kindred interpretation, see Sandra Stein, *The Culture of Education Policy* (New York: Teachers College Press, 2004).

88. Brenda Cox, memo to Ralph Bohrson, May 16, 1967, FFA, 006400238, reel 5491, frame 1374–75.

89. Sam McPherson, "Industrial Training Plan Necessary, Harris Says," *Banner*, December 12, 1964.

90. Aide memoir of lunch conversation with Pat Wilson, c. February 28, 1962, GPCR, box 2120, file David K. Wilson.

91. NCC, "Nashville—Capitol City with Industrial Labor Force."

92. "Support for Vocational-Technical Education," *American Education*, July 1970, 31 details the pattern from 1965 to 1969.

93. John Rury provides a survey in "Growth in African American High School Enrollment, 1950–1970: An Underappreciated Legacy of the *Brown* Era," *Washburn Law Journal* 53 (2013–14): 479–507. Claudia Goldin, "America's Graduation from High School: The Evolution and Spread of Secondary Schooling in the Twentieth Century," *Journal of Economic History* 58, no. 2 (June 1998): 347.

94. Rury, "Growth in African American High School Enrollment," tables 1 and 3. Nashville likely had higher average rates than the more rural state's.

95. Westfeldt, "Urgent Need." On the national trend, see Sherman Dorn, *Creating the Dropout* (Westport, CT: Praeger, 1996).

96. Eugene Dietz, "Dropout Rate Higher Here," *Tennessean*, December 8, 1963.

97. Ibid.

98. For example, see Second Middle Tennessee Conference on School Dropouts, November 14, 1963, in MTP (unprocessed), box 22; Eugene Dietz, "Concern up for Dropouts," *Tennessean*, September 1, 1963, in MANDC clippings, file Schools, Metro 1963-4, Dropouts.

99. Nashville Council of PTAs, Survey of Drop-Outs, 1963, in MTP (unprocessed), box 22.

100. Dr. Virginia Dobbs and Mr. Joseph Garrett memo to John H. Harris re: School Dropouts, May [n.d.], 1965, on file with board agenda, MNBOE, MNPS.

101. Clara May Benedict, "A Study of Vocational Curriculum Models Related to Employment Opportunities, Employers Reactions, and the Present Program at Cohn High School" (Sp.Ed. thesis, George Peabody College for Teachers, 1966), 26.

102. Ibid., 32.

103. Ibid., 32–33.

104. Ibid., 32; Whitlock and Williams, *Jobs and Training*, 9–10.
105. Quill Cope, letter to Thomas A. Johnson, May 23, 1957, COE, reel 110 (111 on register), box 325, file 9.
106. Conference on Education beyond the High School, "Report of Group 16," COE, reel 102, box 307, file 1; "Nashville Metropolitan Area Skill Survey," 41.
107. See James Bryan Conant, *The American High School Today* (New York: McGraw-Hill, 1959); articles by John L. Rury and Floyd M. Hammack in Floyd M. Hammack, ed., *The Comprehensive High School Today* (New York: Teachers College Press, 2004). See also David Angus and Jeffrey Mirel, *Failed Promise of the American High School* (New York: Teachers College Press, 1999); William G. Wraga, *Democracy's High School: The Comprehensive High School and Educational Reform in the United States* (Lanham, MD: University Press of America, 1994).
108. John H. Harris, "The Senior High School in Metropolitan Nashville Davidson County," June 28, 1966, DBP, box 20, file 18, 1.
109. See pages 34–35.
110. Conant, *American High School*.
111. See pages 53, 56.
112. Harris, "The Senior High School," 3.
113. Ibid., 4–5.
114. Ibid., 34.
115. Ibid., 11.
116. Ibid., 15.
117. Vocational teacher, interview, July 10, 2007; MNBOE, minutes, November 28, 1967, MNBOE.
118. MNBOE, minutes, June 13, 1967, MNBOE.
119. Kay Morris, "McGavock High to House Four Little Schools in One," *Banner*, June 28, 1968; MNBOE, agenda, November 14, 1967, MNBOE. Edwin Mitchell, letter to C.R. Dorrier, August 16, 1970, DMP, box 1, file 11.
120. MNBOE, minutes, June 13, 1967, MNBOE.
121. Kathleen Harned, "A History of McGavock High School: The Creation of the Comprehensive Concept in Nashville, Tennessee" (EdD diss., Tennessee State University, 1998), 9–10; MNPS, "Capital Schools in Metropolitan Nashville—Davidson County, Tennessee," COE, reel 132, box 385, file 5.

CHAPTER FOUR

1. *Atlanta Daily World*, March 21, 1961, via Proquest Historical Newspapers; Benjamin Houston, *The Nashville Way: Racial Etiquette and the Struggle for Social Justice in a Southern City* (Athens: University of Georgia Press, 2012); David Halberstam, *The Children* (New York: Vintage, 1998).
2. John Egerton, "Walking into History: The Beginning of School Desegregation in Nashville," *Southern Spaces*, http://southernspaces.org/2009/walking-history -beginning-school-desegregation-nashville, accessed January 15, 2014.
3. Beverly Briley, "The Metropolitan Government of Nashville-Davidson County, Tennessee: A Case Study," September 7, 1967, RHP, box 1, file 8, 7.
4. See Joseph Heathcott and Maire Agnes Murphy, "Corridors of Flight, Zones of Renewal: Industry, Planning and Policy in the Making of Metropolitan St. Louis, 1940–1980," *JUH* 31, no. 2 (January 2005): 151–89.
5. "Urban Renewal Covers 25 Pct. Of Old Nashville," *Banner*, July 25, 1969. "Nashville

Stands at Modernization Forefront," undated clipping, c. 1962, GNAR, series I-D, box 1.

6. *Schools for 1980*, 1964 (Nashville, TN: Metropolitan Planning Commission).

7. See Kenneth Jackson, *Crabgrass Frontier: The Suburbanization of the United States* (New York: Oxford University Press, 1985); Thomas J. Sugrue, *The Origins of the Urban Crisis: Race and Inequality in Postwar Detroit* (Princeton, NJ: Princeton University Press, 1998); Arnold R. Hirsch, *Making the Second Ghetto: Race and Housing in Chicago, 1940–1960* (Chicago: University of Chicago Press, 1998); Robert Self, *American Babylon: Race and the Making of Postwar Oakland* (Princeton, NJ: Princeton University Press, 2005). This chapter draws heavily on Ansley T. Erickson, "Building Inequality: The Spatial Organization of Schooling in Nashville, Tennessee, after *Brown*," *JUH* 38, no. 2 (March 2012): 240–71.

8. *Schools for 1980*, 4–6; James Taylor, *School Sites: Selection, Development, and Utilization* (Washington, DC: US Dept of Health, Education, and Welfare, 1958), 29–30, 34–35. For earlier versions of similar size standards, see Russell A. Holy, *The Relationship of City Planning to School Plant Planning* (New York: Teachers College, 1935). See also Noreen McDonald, "School Siting," *Journal of the American Planning Association*, Vol 76, No. 2, (March 2010); Steven Conn, *Americans against the City: Anti-Urbanism in the Twentieth Century* (New York: Oxford University Press, 2014).

9. Taylor, *School Sites*, 29–30, 34–35.

10. James L. Sundquist, *Politics and Policy: The Eisenhower, Kennedy, and Johnson Years* (Washington, DC: Brookings, 1968), chapter 5.

11. David Freund, *Colored Property: State Policy and White Racial Politics in Suburban America* (Chicago: University of Chicago Press, 2007).

12. This is a central point in the articles, including my own, in a special issue on housing and schools: *JUH* 38, no. 2 (March 2012).

13. MNBOE, agenda, January 25, 1966, MNBOE; Bill Carey, *Fortunes, Fiddles and Fried Chicken: A Nashville Business History* (Franklin, TN: Hillsboro Press, 2000), 59, 203–4.

14. MNBOE, minutes, August 13, 1968, MNBOE; MNBOE, minutes, January 14, 1969, MNBOE; MNBOE, agenda, September 28, 1971, MNBOE. On developers donating land to the school system to facilitate the building of new schools in suburban areas of Charlotte-Mecklenburg County, NC, see Steven Samuel Smith, *Boom for Whom: Education, Desegregation and Development in Charlotte* (Albany: State University of New York Press, 2004), 97.

15. See chapter 1.

16. For advertisements touting H. G. Hill, West Meade, and Hillwood schools, see, for example, section D, May 4, 1964, May 4, 1968, May 5, 1968, January 12, 1969, May 4, 1969, January 11, 1970, and May 3, 1970.

17. On links between schools and housing markets, see Kevin Fox Gotham, *Race, Real Estate, and Uneven Development: The Kansas City Experience, 1900–2000* (Albany: State University of New York Press, 2002); Kevin Kruse, *White Flight: Atlanta and the Making of Modern Conservatism* (Princeton, NJ: Princeton University Press, 2006), 165–68; Jack Dougherty, "Shopping for Schools," *JUH* 38, no. 2 (March 2012): 205–24.

18. *Schools for 1980*, 17. This number includes both city and county schools before consolidation. It varies somewhat with school openings and closings over the decade.

19. Domenico Annese, interview, first session, September 28, 2006.

20. Ibid.

21. Joe C. Williams, "Services the Planner May Provide the Educator," August 22, 1963, in RHP, box 4, file 7, 7.

22. Williams, "Services the Planner May Provide," 5–6.

23. Ibid., 5–6.

24. Ibid.; Davidson County Planning Commission, "Staff Memorandum on Planning Unit Analysis and the City of Nashville," August 1961, RHPA, box 3, file 28, 21; *Schools for 1980*, 101. Williams might have been discussing John Early Elementary, overcrowded as of 1961 and 1964.

25. MNPS, "Building and School Improvement Study (BASIS) Draft: Facilities Survey," *Kelley*, box 7, Plaintiff's Exhibits 2 of 2, 28–29.

26. Quotations at *Schools for 1980*, 4; "Board of Education Policy for Site Selection and School Building Construction," Appendix B to Plan, August 19, 1970, *Kelley*, box 6, file 1970 (2), 2.

27. "Board of Education Policy for Site Selection," 2; "Defendants' Proposed Findings of Fact and Conclusions of Law, and Post-Trial Brief," *Kelley v. MNBOE*, March 16, 1970, *Kelley*, box 5, file 1970 (2), no. 339, for example. On the historical development of the idea of de facto, see Matthew Lassiter, "De Jure/De Facto Segregation: The Long Shadow of a National Myth," in Matthew D. Lassiter and Joseph Crespino, eds., *The Myth of Southern Exceptionalism* (New York: Oxford University Press, 2009), 25–48.

28. *Schools for 1980*, 11–13.

29. On interpretive frames in government, see James Scott, *Seeing Like a State: How Certain Schemes to Improve the Human Condition Have Failed* (New Haven, CT: Yale University Press, 1998).

30. *Schools for 1980*, 8.

31. Ibid., 7–8.

32. MNBOE, minutes, January 9, 1968, MNBOE, for use of ASAs in 1968; Cecil R. Herrell, Memo to R. Don O'Donniley, May 21, 1979, AWPII, unprocessed.

33. *Schools for 1980*, 4.

34. Ibid., 7–8.

35. Ibid., 10.

36. Irving Hand, "Planning of Residential, Commercial and Industrial Areas," in Mary McLean, ed. *Local Planning Administration*, 3rd ed. ed. Mary McLean (Chicago: International City Manager's Association, 1959), 117, 119.

37. *Schools for 1980*; John W. Egerton, "Analysis of Data from Interrogatories Submitted to Metropolitan School System," February 3, 1970, *Kelley*, box 11, file 4 (1 of 2); Gerald Gimre, "Urban Renewal: The Nashville Story," undated clipping from *Tennessee Town and City*, c. 1962, DBP, box 1, file 5, 26.

38. MNBOE, minutes, November 28, 1967, MNBOE; MNBOE, agenda, September 13, 1966, MNBOE.

39. John H. Harris, "The Senior High School in Metropolitan Nashville Davidson County," 1966, DBP, box 20, file 18, 8–9.

40. "Two Rivers Mansion," http://www.nashville.org/parks/historic/two_rivers.asp, accessed March 26, 2010.

41. L. T. Alexander to Mr. Detchon, August 3, 1966, SPF, file McGavock.

42. MNBOE, minutes, June 13, 1967, MNBOE; Harned, "A History of McGavock," 13.

43. *Schools for 1980*, 345–50; MNPS, "Building and School Improvement Study (BASIS)," 1971, *Kelley*, box 7. See also Metropolitan Planning Commission, "Amendment I to Schools for 1980," December 20, 1967, filed with *Schools for 1980* report, MPC Library. Quotations from *Schools for 1980*, 107, 10–11.

44. "Opposition to Motion for Further Relief," *Kelley v. MNBOE*, October 1, 1968, box 2, file 1968, *Kelley*, 8–10; Harris, "The Senior High School," 65; MNBOE, "Long Range School Facility Plans," on file with board agenda, July 9, 1974, MNBOE, MNPS." The board did discuss needing to revise the report in light of desegregation mandates, but the adjustments it made were minor, regarding a few individual schools, rather than its core principals. MPC, "Amendments to *Schools for 1980*," on file with the report, MPC Library.

45. MNPS, "BASIS," 131–33, 59–60.

46. *Kelley v. MNBOE*, "Opposition to Motion for Further Relief, October 1, 1968, in *Kelley*, box 2, file 1968, 8–10; Board of Education Policy for Site Selection, 1.

47. Quoted in Wendell E. Pritchett, "Which Urban Crisis? Regionalism, Race and Urban Policy, 1960–1974," *JUH* 34, no. 2 (January 2008): 274.

48. Unsigned memo to the Metropolitan Commission on Human Relations, Sub-Committee on Housing, December 5, 1966, box VI: F121, file 7, NAACP. For another example of attempts to improve rather than end urban renewal, see Jennifer Hock, "Bulldozers, Busing, and Boycotts: Urban Renewal and the Integrationist Project," *JUH* 39, no. 3 (2013): 433–53.

49. "Table of Public Housing Tenant Statistics by Race: 1964 and 1969," February 11, 1970, in *Kelley*, Plaintiff's Exhibit 18, 1970; Dick Battle, "NHA Obeys HUD Order, Drops 'Free Choice' Tenancy," *Banner*, September 26, 1968.

50. Ola Hudson's family moved from Edgehill to the area around Murphy school in 1951. Ola Hudson, interview, NCROHP, May 21, 2004. Mark S. Israel et al. to Beverly Briley, c. September 1966, LOC, NAACP, box VI: F121, file Tennessee—Nashville Edgehill Urban Renewal Project 1965-67, Section IV; NHA, "The Redevelopment Plan for the for the Capitol Hill Redevelopment Project, UR Tenn 2-1," March 1952, CM, Capitol Hill Redevelopment Project, Nashville Housing Authority, 17–18.

51. "Edgehill Study Area Preliminary Estimates," May 15, 1961, RHPA, box 1, file 50.

52. Elsewhere, NHA reported 2,117. NHA, "Comments by the Nashville Housing Authority on Resolution of August 29, 1966," c. September 1966, LOC, NAACP, box VI: F121, file Tennessee—Nashville Edgehill Urban Renewal Project 1965-67, section V, 1; NCC, "Capitol City Planning for the Future," undated clipping, 1962, RHP, box 4, file 18, 2; NCC, minutes, Board of Governors meeting, February 24, 1966, NCC, reel 2, vol. XVI, 3; Rev. Bill Barnes, *To Love a City* (Nashville: ONE, n.d).

53. Don Stringer, "But the People Come First," *Banner*, August 24, 1961; "Defendants' Proposed Findings," no. 103; Land acquisition map, MTP, unprocessed; Kay Morris, "Urban Renewal Plans Face Reduction," *Banner*, March 24, 1964.

54. "Nashville Stands;" Gimre, "Urban Renewal," 26; CNBOE, minutes, 1951, 281.

55. MPC, "Capital Improvements Budget and Program," November 1969, *Kelley*, box 11, file 6, A-26.
   My reading of the 1954 Housing Act suggests that this use was in fact outside the boundaries of the legislation, which prohibited expenditure of federal funds on "public buildings" and defined these to be outside the scope of urban renewal projects. Nonetheless, Nashville seems to have managed this kind of financing repeatedly in the 1960s, for schools in the Edgehill and East Nashville project areas. United States Senate Committee on Banking and Currency, "Summary of Provisions of the Housing Act of 1954," (Washington, DC: GPO, 1954), 22–23; Committee on Banking and Currency, "Section-by-Section Summary of the Provisions of S 1922, the Housing Act of 1961, as Amended by the Senate," (Washington, DC: GPO, 1961), 9; Tennessee State Advisory Committee to the US Commission

on Civil Rights, "Housing and Urban Renewal in the Nashville-Davidson County Metropolitan Area," February 1967, in RHP, box 1, 3–4; Gimre, "Urban Renewal;" Committee on Banking and Currency, "Summary of Provisions of the Housing Act of 1954," 22–23. On local and federal funding, Charles Allen, interview, May 25, 2007, Newport News, VA.

56. *Kelley v. MNBOE*, "Defendants' Proposed Findings," no. 113.

57. "Nashville Civil Rights and Community Groups Protest Edgehill Urban Renewal," in Tennessee Council on Human Relations newsletter, September 1966, NMFP, box 1, file 8.

58. Rob Elder, "Housing Progress? Yes, but Does It Help the People Who Live There?" and "For Sale Signs Greet Negro Neighbors," *Tennessean*, undated, c. 1968, in ETP (unprocessed), box 5, file Information on Nashville. On "serial displacement," see Mindy Fullilove, *Root Shock: How Tearing Up City Neighborhoods Hurts America, and What We Can Do about It* (New York: One World/Ballantine, 2004).

59. NAACP, "Relocation Data, Edgehill Urban Renewal Area."

60. Mansfield Douglas et al., "Resolution," September 11, 1966, LOC, NAACP, box VI: F121, file Tennessee—Nashville Edgehill Urban Renewal Project 1965–67, Section III.

61. Tennessee State Advisory Committee, "Housing and Urban Renewal," 16.

62. "Edgehill Unit Raps Housing," *Tennessean*, November 16, 1966.

63. Tennessee State Advisory Committee, "Housing and Urban Renewal," 3–4.

64. Battle, "NHA Obeys HUD Order."

65. Tennessee State Advisory Committee, "Housing and Urban Renewal," 12.

66. Keel Hunt, "Edgehill Project Ghetto Held Possible," *Tennessean*, September 14, 1967.

67. Tennessee State Advisory Committee, "Housing and Urban Renewal," ii.

68. Ibid., 7–8.

69. Rob Elder, "Weaver to Hear Housing Charge," *Tennessean*, November 16, 1967; Martha Ragland, letter to Robert C. Weaver, December 22, 1967, NMFP, box 1, file 8.

70. Edward H. Baxter, letter to Gerald Gimre, July 14, 1967, LOC, NAACP, box VI: F121, file Tennessee—Nashville Edgehill Urban Renewal Project 1965–67, section VIII; "Group Eyes Court Fight to Halt Edgehill Housing," *Tennessean*, January 19, 1968.

71. On the highway planning process, see Houston, *Nashville Way*, 204–9; Raymond A. Mohl, "Citizen Activism and Freeway Revolts in Memphis and Nashville: The Road to Litigation," *JUH* 40, no. 5 (September 2014): 870–93; *Nashville I-40 Steering Committee v. Ellington*, 387 F.2d 179 (6th Cir. 1967), *cert. denied*, 390 U.S. 92 (1968).

72. Vivian W. Henderson, memorandum to Nashville Branch NAACP re: Housing among Negroes in Nashville, February 28, 1962, VHP, box 30, file 8; Edward Kindall, interview, October, 2006.

73. Domenico Annese, interview, second session, November 17, 2006. See also Edward T. Kindall and Beverly Kindall, *A Walk Down Historic Jefferson Street*, self-published, 2012.

74. Mohl, "Citizen Activism and Freeway Revolts," 884–85.

75. Edwin Mitchell Oral History, February 18, 1972, FUBOHC.

76. Quoted in Houston, *Nashville Way*, 209.

77. Kenneth Jost, "W. Nashville Group Hears Urban Renewal Debate," *Tennessean*, September 15, 1970.

78. Jack E. White Jr., "Nashville's Model Cities Program: An Unborn Partnership," 1971

(Nashville: Race Relations Information Center); R. Don O'Donniley, "A Case Study of Metropolitan Nashville and Davidson County, Tennessee's Application for a Model Cities Grant: The Decision-Making Process in Selecting a Model Cities Neighborhood," (master's thesis, University of Tennessee, 1969); Richard Creswell, et al., "Nashville Model Cities: A Case Study," *Vanderbilt Law Review* 25 (1972): 727–844.

79. Jacque Srouji, "Model Cities Plan to Utilize Local Skills," *Banner*, September 31, 1967.

80. See the articles by Dick Battle in Nashville Public Library Special Collections, *Banner* clippings file "Model Cities, 1967–69;" William Greenburg, "Bus Tour Spotlights Area Slums," *Tennessean*, February 10, 1967. On bus tours, see Joseph Heathcott, "The City Quietly Remade: National Programs and Local Agendas in the Movement to Clear the Slums, 1942–1952," *JUH* 34, no. 2 (January 2008): 221–42.

81. Norman Braden, interview, July 23, 2004, NCROHP; Michael Tribue, interview, May 20, 2004.

82. Cindy Acuff, interview, July 22, 2004; Braden, interview.

83. MNPS, Offices of Assistant Superintendent for Instruction and Area Superintendent, "Memo to Mary Pellow and Eugene TeSelle," May 7, 1973. AWPII, unprocessed; transcript of proceedings, *Kelley v. MNBOE*, March 3, 1980, *Kelley*, box 19, vol. 7, 6367–77.

84. Transcript of proceedings, *Kelley vs. MNBOE*, October 2, 1968, *Kelley*, box 3, file 10/2 & 10/3 1968 Transcripts, vol. I, 37, and, for another example of out-of-zone attendance, 61–67.

85. *Goss v. Board of Education of Knoxville*, 373 U.S. 683 (1963).

86. MNBOE, "School Attendance Areas," [in Answer to Interrogatory #40, February 1970], *Kelley*, box 5, file 1970 (2).

87. "Motion for further relief and to add parties as additional and/or intervening plaintiffs," *Kelley v. MNBOE*, September 16, 1968, *Kelley*, box 2, file 1968, 8, 11. School board members offered a different representation of the same enrollment data. They counted all children attending a school with one child not of their race as in integrated schools, and thus claimed 32.14 percent "mixed" schools in 1964–65 to 75.35 percent in 1969–70. Transcript of proceedings, *Kelley v. MNBOE*, February 3–17, 1970, *Kelley*, box 6, transcripts file 3, 1231, 1228–38. See also Joseph R. Garrett, "Pupil Enrollment," 1970, *Kelley*, box 11, file 4.

88. Transcript of proceedings, *Kelley v. MNBOE*, February 3–6, 1970, *Kelley*, box 6, file 1971 (3) and transcripts file 1, 301.

89. Transcript of proceedings, 765–67.

90. Rob Elder, "Negro Home Hunters Find Problems," *Tennessean*, c. 1967, undated clipping, ETP (unprocessed), box 5, file Information on Nashville.

91. Transcript of proceedings, *Kelley v. MNBOE*, 761–69.

92. Rob Elder, "Integration an Uphill Struggle," *Tennessean*, c. 1967, undated clipping, ETP (unprocessed), box 5, file Information on Nashville. See Gotham, *Race, Real Estate, and Uneven Development*; Beryl Satter, *Family Properties: Race, Real Estate, and the Exploitation of Black America* (New York: Metropolitan Books, 2009); Hirsch, *Making the Second Ghetto*; Sugrue, *Origins of the Urban Crisis*; Amanda I. Seligman, *Block by Block: Neighborhoods and Public Policy on Chicago's West Side* (Chicago: University of Chicago Press, 2005).

93. I surveyed the classifieds in the *Tennessean* (which was published cooperatively with the *Banner* and shared classified ads) for the first Sunday in May from 1955 through 1975.

94. Elder, "Integration an Uphill Struggle."

95. Transcript of proceedings, 1383–84.

96. Sonya Ramsey, *Reading, Writing, and Segregation: A Century of Black Women Teachers in Nashville* (Urbana: University of Illinois Press, 2008), chapter 3; Eugene Speight, interview, May 14, 2004; Myron Oglesby-Pitts, *To Teach Like Mary: Getting It Right at First* (Pittsburg: RoseDog Books, 2010); Ola Hudson, interview.

97. Frank Ritter, "School Walls Falling Apart at John Early," *Tennessean*, February 17, 1965, and related clippings in MANDC clippings, file Schools, Metro—Clippings, VF 26.

98. Gena Carter, interview, November 13, 2012, Providence, RI; Charles Davis, interview, June 3, 2004; Waverly Crenshaw, interview, February 2004; Semetta Coure Pulley, interview, May 8, 2004.

99. Amos Jones interview, FUBOHC October 13, 1972.

100. Acuff, interview.

101. Garrett, "Pupil Enrollment."

102. Don Doyle, *Nashville since the 1920s* (Knoxville: University of Tennessee Press, 1985), 217. Doyle cites administrator Robert Horton on the city's far out-pacing its similarly sized peers in urban renewal projects and receiving a much larger proportion of federal funds on a per-capita basis.

103. Louise Davis, Notes on David K. Wilson, LDP, box 40, file 5; John Seigenthaler, interview, March 12, 2013; Edwin Mitchell, "The Negro Looks at Nashville: Forward or Backward," Emory Manuscript, Archives, and Rare Book Library, Robert Churchwell Papers, box 1, File Correspondence, 1943–1979; "Leaders Told Program's Backward, Not Forward," *Tennessean*, October 12, 1967.

CHAPTER FIVE

1. Quotation from "Motion for Further Relief and to Add Parties as Additional/Intervening Plaintiffs," *Kelley v. MNBOE*, September 16, 1968, *Kelley*, box 2, file 1968.

2. *Goss v. Board of Education of Knoxville*, 373 U.S. 683 (1963); "Motion for Further Relief"; *Green vs. County School Board of New Kent County, Va.* 391 U.S. 430 (1968).

3. Documents related to the fight are collected in *Kelley*, box 3, file 1968 (3) and file documents dated 1968. See also James T. Laney, memo to Nashville Community Relations Council, October 30, 1968, NMFP, box 2, file 15, VUSC. Quotation from order, *Kelley v. MNBOE*, December 9, 1968, *Kelley*, box 2, file 1968.

4. *Alexander v. Holmes County Board of Education*, 396 U.S. 19 (1969).

5. "Opposition to Motion for Immediate Relief," *Kelley v. MNBOE*, November 17, 1969, *Kelley*, box 3, file 1969.

6. "William E. Miller, U.S. Judge, 68, Dies," *NYT*, April 13, 1976, via ProQuest Historical Newspapers, accessed July 10, 2013.

7. *Kelley v. MNBOE*, 317 F. Supp. 980 (1970).

8. Matthew Lassiter, "De Jure/De Facto Segregation: The Long Shadow of a National Myth," in Matthew D. Lassiter and Joseph Crespino, eds., *The Myth of Southern Exceptionalism* (New York: Oxford University Press, 2009), 25–48. Distinctions between public and private discrimination originated in the *Civil Rights Cases*, 109 U.S. 3 (1883).

9. *Swann v. Charlotte-Mecklenburg Board of Education*, 306 F. Supp. 1299 (1969).

10. Transcript of proceedings, *Kelley v. MNBOE*, February 2–17, 1970, *Kelley*, box 6, file transcripts file 3, 692–99.

11. See figure 4.3, p. 131.

12. Transcript of proceedings, 1058, 1130–33.

13. Ibid., 1042, 127, 140.
14. This process is described in more detail in chapter 3.
15. Transcript of proceedings, 1153–55, 645.
16. Transcript of proceedings, 1357–74.
17. Transcript of proceedings, 301; Joseph Garrett, "Pupil Enrollment," 1970, *Kelley*, box 11, file 4.
18. *Kelley v. MNBOE*, 317 F. Supp. 980 (1970). Miller mischaracterized the zone lines as drawn before *Brown* when they were readjusted a few years after *Brown*. See chapter 2.
19. Ibid.
20. *Kelley v. MNBOE*, 317 F. Supp. 980 (1970).
21. Canzada Hawkins, interview, July 2004.
22. *Kelley v. MNBOE*, 317 F. Supp. 980 (1970).
23. Ibid.
24. Ibid.
25. Frank Sutherland, "School Officials Work to Open under a New Integration Plan," *Tennessean*, August 23, 1970; *Kelley v. MNBOE*, 317 F. Supp. 980 (1970).
26. *Deal v. Cincinnati*, 369 F. 2nd 55 (1966); Jack Dougherty, "Conflicting Questions: Why Historians and Policymakers Miscommunicate on Urban Education," in Kenneth Wong and Robert Rothman, eds., *Clio At the Table: The Uses of History to Reform and Improve Educational Policy* (New York: Peter Lang, 2008), 251–62.
27. *Kelley v. MNBOE*, 317 F. Supp. 980 (1970).
28. Elbert Brooks, interview, June 30, 2007.
29. Minutes, MNBOE, July 28, 1970, MNBOE.
30. Ibid.
31. Transcripts of proceedings, *Kelley v. MNBOE*, March 8, 1971, *Kelley*, box 8, transcripts file 1, 39–40; Frank Sutherland, "Tough Decision Faced by School Board," *Tennessean*, August 16, 1970.
32. Nashville City Schools, "Annual Reports, 1949–1954," 1954, MANDC, Education; "A Comprehensive Survey of Social Welfare in Metropolitan Nashville and Davidson County," 1968 (Nashville, TN: Council of Community Services) RHPA, box 7.
33. Dan May, untitled statement, 1970 or 71, DMP, box 10, file 27.
34. Transcript of proceedings, 47–48.
35. Robert Churchwell, "Board Puts off School Zoning," *Banner*, August 15, 1970.
36. Bradford S. Brown to Henry H. Hill, Chairman of Advisory Committee on Pupil Integration and Zoning, August 13, 1970, MNBOE Agendas, volume 1970-71, 1–3.
37. Pat Welch, "Board Submits Plan in Time," *Tennessean*, August 20, 1970.
38. Transcript of proceedings, 67–68. Brooks's comments were reinforced by Carlyle Beasley, head of transportation for MNPS (transcript of proceedings, 369).
39. Citizens Advisory Steering Committee, memo to Board of Education Re: School Zoning and Pupil Integration, 1970, MNBOE Agendas, vol. 1970-71, MNPS, 2–3.
40. Robert Churchwell, "School Report Assures 'Neighborhood' Concept," *Banner*, August 13, 1970; Churchwell, "Board Puts off School Zoning"; Frank Sutherland, "24 Schools Involved in Zone Change Plan," *Tennessean*, August 13, 1970.
41. "Plan," *Kelley v. MNBOE*, August 19, 1970, *Kelley*, box 6, file 1970 (3).
42. Frances Meeker, "Only 19 Schools Meet Guidelines," *Banner*, August 21, 1970; Edwin Mitchell, letter to C. R. Dorrier, August 16, 1970, DMP, box 1, file 11; "Plan Submitted in Response to the Court's Memorandum of August 27, 1979," *Kelley v. MNBOE*, February 22, 1980, *Kelley*, box 12, file 1980 (1), Section III.

43. Transcript of proceedings, *Kelley v. MNBOE*, February 3–6, 1970, *Kelley*, box 6, file transcripts file 3, *1258*; "Answer of Plaintiffs to Petition Filed by Defendants on or about May 31, 1973," *Kelley v. MNBOE*, June 19, 1973, *Kelley*, box 9, file 1973 (1); Bill Lann Lee, interview, February 26, 2013 by telephone. MNPS said vacant seats were for compensatory programs (transcript of proceedings, 1191). On private versus public in housing, see David M. P. Freund, *Colored Property: State Policy and White Racial Politics in Suburban America* (Chicago: University of Chicago Press, 2007), chapter 1.

44. "Comprehensive Study of the Secondary School Plan to Include Junior and Senior High School" [Appendix C to "Plan"], August 19, 1970, *Kelley*, box 6, file 1970 (3), 1; Churchwell, "Board Puts off School Zoning"; "Board of Education Policy for Site Selection and School Building Construction" [Appendix B to "Plan"], August 19, 1970, *Kelley*, box 6, file 1970 (2), 3.

45. "Objections of Plaintiffs to School Zoning and Pupil Integration Phases of Defendants' School Desegregation Plan Filed 19 August 1970," *Kelley v. MNBOE*, December 29, 1970, *Kelley*, box 3, file 1970 (1)a, 4.

46. Citizens Advisory Steering Committee, memo to Board of Education Re: Staff Integration, August 7, 1970, MNBOE Agendas, vol. 1970–71, MNPS, 49; Advisory Committee on Staff Integration, memo to Members of the Steering Committee Re: Proposed Procedures for Staff Integration, August 7, 1970, MNBOE Agendas, vol. 1970–71; Churchwell, "Board Puts off School Zoning," *Banner*, August 15, 1970; transcript of proceedings, 108–11.

47. "Objections of Plaintiffs to School Zoning," 3.

48. Several historical accounts have documented this pattern. See Adam Fairclough, *A Class of Their Own: Black Teachers in the Segregated South* (Cambridge, MA: Belknap, 2007) and Michael Fultz, "The Displacement of Black Educators Post-*Brown*: An Overview and Analysis," *History of Education Quarterly* 44, no. 1 (March 2004). On Nashville, see Sonya Yvette Ramsey, *Reading, Writing, and Segregation: A Century of Black Women Teachers in Nashville* (Urbana: University of Illinois Press, 2008), indicating less outright firing of teachers than in other contexts (112).

49. Andrew Schlesinger, "Unitary System Still in Works, Brooks Says," *Tennessean*, August 29, 1970.

50. Order, *Kelley v. MNBOE*, August 25, 1970, *Kelley*, box 3, file 1970.

51. "Education on the Move," *Banner*, August 24, 1970.

52. "Brief in Support of Motion to Amend Findings and to Make Additional Findings and Motion to Alter or Amend Judgment," *Kelley v. MNBOE*, July 26, 1971, *Kelley*, box 6, file 1971 (2), 2.

53. "Objections of Plaintiffs to Desegregation Plan Filed by the Division of Equal Opportunity," *Kelley v. MNBOE*, July 7, 1971, *Kelley*, box 6, file 1971 (2), 3.

54. Pat Welch, "Eakin Parents Ask Right to Intervene in School Case," *Tennessean*, August 8, 1970; "Complaint by Intervening Plaintiff," *Kelley v. MNBOE*, August 24, 1970, box 3, file 1970 (1).

55. Eugene TeSelle, untitled filing to the court, *Kelley v. MNBOE*, 1971, n.d., *Kelley*, box 6, file 1971 (2).

56. John Egerton, "The Slow-burn Early Years of School Integration," *Tennessean*, January 14, 1996 (BOE).

57. *Swann v. Charlotte-Mecklenburg Board of Education*, 402 U.S. 1 (1971).

58. This representation derives from several sources: "Plan;" US Office of Education [USOE], "Desegregation Plan: Metropolitan Nashville and Davidson County

School System," June 1, 1971, *Kelley*, box 7, file 6/1/1971 desegregation, 32; Richard A. Pride and David Woodward, *The Burden of Busing: The Politics of Desegregation in Nashville, Tennessee* (Knoxville: University of Tennessee Press, 1985), 74–82; and maps and zone descriptions published in the *Banner* and *Tennessean*, August 7, 1971. It is consistent with descriptions of the busing scheme as experienced by former Nashville students in interviews in February through July 2004. Pride and Woodward recognize that "because of the logistical complexity of busing, each school was practically a unique case involving some type of alteration in the general plan" (Richard A. Pride and David Woodward, *The Burden of Busing: The Politics of Desegregation in Nashville, Tennessee* [Knoxville: University of Tennessee Press, 1985], 76). The greatest variation appears to have occurred in racially diverse neighborhoods close to the city center, and in cases where schools' grade structures varied.

59. Similar patterns occurred in other districts. See Barbara Shircliffe, *Best of That World: Historically Black High Schools and the Crisis of Desegregation in a Southern Metropolis* (Cresskill, NJ: Hampton, 2006); Jeffery A. Raffel, *The Politics of School Desegregation: The Metropolitan Remedy in Delaware* (Philadelphia: Temple University Press, 1980). The Second Circuit denied a challenge from the Congress of Racial Equality to a Norwalk, Connecticut, desegregation plan specifically on the basis of unequal burdens and school closures, holding that such discrepancies did not violate the equal protection clause (in *Norwalk CORE v. Norwalk Bd. of Education*, 298 F. Supp. 213 [1969], affirmed at the Second Circuit March 10, 1970, discussed in "Equal Protection of the Laws," *Harvard Law Review* 83, no. 6 [April 1970]: 1434–40).

60. Memorandum opinion, *Kelley v. MNBOE*, May 20, 1980, *Kelley*, box 12, file 1980 (3), 28–30. School opening and closing times are listed in memorandum to order issued August 17, 1972, *Kelley v. MNBOE*, August 17, 1972, *Kelley*, box 8, file 1972 (1), 540.

61. Nashville was not the only school system to have such an inequitable busing scheme. Charlotte, North Carolina's first busing plan required black students to travel for ten of their twelve years of schooling; in the process of developing the plan, the board had considered closing all historically black schools. The plan ultimately approved by Judge McMillan included the requirement that no historically black schools be closed or underutilized, a provision missing in Nashville. See Davison Douglas, *Reading, Writing and Race: The Desegregation of the Charlotte Schools* (Chapel Hill: University of North Carolina Press, 1995), 216–17. Wilmington, Delaware's plan closed all central-city, majority-black schools. In Judge McMillan's 1969 opinion in *Swann*, he stated that "dozens" of school districts had adopted this approach to desegregation. 306 F. Supp. 1291 (1969).

62. On the critical interpretation of graphical representations of data, see Edward Tufte, *Visual Display of Quantitative Information*, 2nd ed. (Cheshire, CT: Graphics Press, 2001) and *The Cognitive Style of Power Point*, 2nd ed. (Cheshire, CT: Graphics Press, 2006).

63. Nashville City and Davidson County Planning Commission, "Estimated Distribution of Population of Davidson County, Tennessee 1950–1958" (Nashville, 1959).

64. MPC, "Projected Distribution of Residential Population in Nashville-Davidson County to 1985," 1969 (Nashville, TN: MPC), Maps 4, 5 and 8; MNPS, "BASIS," 4, 15. The 1969 population projection maps for 1970–75 and 1975–80 did identify small central-city areas with population growth, but the 1980–85 map showed a return to population loss there, thus reinforcing the perception that the overall trajectory was that of decline. The 1969 projection report did include absolute population figures for each planning unit, but presented these only in long tables much more difficult to visualize.

65. "Defendants' Proposed Findings of Fact and Conclusions of Law, and Post-Trial Brief," *Kelley v. MNBOE*, March 16, 1970, *Kelley*, box 5, file 1970 (2), no. 213.

66. 1960 and 1970 US Census, via NHGIS.

67. "Inner City Blight—Analysis, Proposals," 1973 (Nashville: MPC), 9–13; 1960 and 1970 US Census, via NHGIS.

68. Ibid., 9.

69. "Inner-City Blight," 9–11.

70. MNPS, "Building and School Improvement Study (BASIS) Draft: Facilities Survey," *Kelley*, box 7, plaintiff's exhibit 2 of 2, 93–94, 97.

71. 1960 and 1970 US Census, via NHGIS. I use children ages five to fourteen to measure school-age population.

72. See, for example, articles by Dick Battle in the *Banner*: "Council to Get Fast Model City Follow-up," November 20, 1967; "Ireland Street Project Area's Model Problem," December 4, 1967; Benjamin Houston, *The Nashville Way: Racial Etiquette and the Struggle for Social Justice in a Southern City* (Athens: University of Georgia Press, 2012), chapter 5.

73. Quoted in "Objections to Interrogatories," *Kelley v. MNBOE*, November 21, 1969, *Kelley*, box 3, file 1969, 1.

74. Order, 2; order, *Kelley v. MNBOE*, March 18, 1971, *Kelley*, box 6, file 1971 (1).

75. Frances Meeker, "Pupil Locater [sic] Maps Sought in Federal Suit," *Banner*, August 24, 1970.

76. "Memorandum in Support of Defendants' Objections to Interrogatories," *Kelley v. MNBOE*, December 4, 1969, *Kelley*, box 3, file 1969, 1–2.

77. "Objections to Interrogatories," exhibit 1; Welch, "Eakin Parents"; Meeker, "Pupil Locater"; Avon N. Williams, letter to Guy W. Cooper, March 17, 1971, *Kelley*, box 6, file 1971 (2).

78. Order, *Kelley v. MNBOE*, August 25, 1970, *Kelley*, box 3, file 1970 (1); *Kelley v. MNBOE*, 436 F.2d 856 (1970).

79. Pupil locator map filed in oversized storage with *Kelley*.

80. MNBOE, minutes, Aug. 14, 1970, MNBOE; transcript of proceedings, 575, 591–96, 609.

81. "Education Parks: Appraisals of Plans to Improve Educational Quality and Desegregate the Schools," 1967 (Washington, DC: U.S. Commission on Civil Rights), Clearinghouse Publication No. 9. Thanks to Matt Lassiter for suggesting this source.

82. Richard Dinkins, interview first session, July 2004; Dorren Klausnitzer, "Wise Brings Deseg Experience," *Tennessean*, January 29, 1997.

83. In fact, one location on Briley Parkway—the recently selected home of the new Grand Ole Opry—was chosen because it was widely understood to be suburban space. Jeremy Hill, "Country in the Suburbs? The Grand Ole Opry and Suburban Nashville" (paper given at the 2008 meeting of the American Studies Association, Albuquerque, NM).

84. *Kelley v. MNBOE*, 317 F. Supp. 980 (1970).

85. "Objections of Plaintiffs."

86. Garrett, "Pupil Enrollment."

87. Ibid.

88. Concerned Citizens for Integrated Schools, "Summary and Interpretation of a Proposal for Integration of Public Schools," *Kelley*, box 6, file 1971 (2), 1.

89. Concerned Citizens for Integrated Schools, "Summary and Interpretation of a Proposal," 7.

90. HEW's use of the BASIS report is described at USOE, "Desegregation Plan," 30–31.

On criteria, see MNPS, "Building and School Improvement Study (BASIS)," 1971, *Kelley*, box 13, file trial exhibits #25-34G, 266.

91. MNPS, "BASIS," chapter 1.

92. USOE, "Desegregation Plan," 30, explains closures, and changes in status and closures are listed in "Fifteen Year Analysis." Descriptions of Clemons and Pearl are at MNPS, "BASIS," 131–33, 159–60. On the Howard School closing, see USOE, "Desegregation Plan," 30, and MNPS, "BASIS," 147.

93. USOE, "Desegregation Plan," 32; petition, November 1979, KMSP, box 69, file 2. Other locales proposed total closure of black schools, including Hillsborough County, Florida, and Hyde County, North Carolina, where such a plan was implemented and sparked school boycotts by black families (Barbara Shircliffe, *Best of that World: Historically Black High Schools and the Crisis of Desegregation in a Southern Metropolis* [Cresskill, NJ: Hampton Press, 2006], 126, and Cecelski, *Along Freedom Road*).

94. Avon Williams, press release, April 4, 1985, box 5, file Correspondence April 1985, AWPI.

95. MNBOE, minutes, September 28, 1971, MNBOE.

CHAPTER SIX

1. Elbert Brooks to E. C. Stimbert, August 25, 1971, COE, reel 103, box 308a, file 9; George Vecsey, "Court-Ordered Busing Arrives in Nashville," *NYT*, September 17, 1971; "Nashville Told to Step Up Busing," *NYT*, July 4, 1971. Enrollment figures from MNPS, "Twenty-Seven Year Analysis of Enrollment Patterns," *Kelley*, box 23, file 1996.

2. This interpretation of resistance builds appreciatively from Brett Gadsden's insight that opposition to busing became a constructive force in its shaping desegregation. See Brett Gadsden, in *Between North and South: Delaware, Desegregation, and the Myth of American Sectionalism* (Philadelphia: University of Pennsylvania Press, 2012), chapter 5; Annette Eskind, interview, July 5, 2007.

3. On interactions between desegregation, compensatory education, bilingual education, and testing, see Adam Nelson, *The Elusive Ideal: Equal Educational Opportunity and The Federal Role in Boston's Public Schools, 1950–1985* (Chicago: University of Chicago Press, 2005); R. Scott Baker, *Paradoxes of Desegregation: African American Struggles for Educational Equity in Charleston, South Carolina, 1926–1972* (Columbia: University of South Carolina Press, 2006). On "family values," see Robert Self, *All in the Family* (New York: Hill and Wang, 2012). On pro-growth uses of state power and its implications for conservatism, see Elizabeth Tandy Schermer, *Sunbelt Capitalism: Phoenix and the Transformation of American Politics* (Philadelphia: University of Pennsylvania Press, 2013). While I agree with Gareth Davies that federal education policy grew in the 1970s, I also see a shift in the ideological underpinnings of this involvement: *See Government Grow: Education Politics from Johnson to Reagan* (Lawrence: University Press of Kansas, 2007).

4. James T. Wooten, "Busing for Desegregation to Affect 350,000 Pupils in the South," *NYT*, August 15, 1971, via Proquest Historical Newspapers, accessed June 26, 2013.

5. On the Hattie Cotton bombing and the narrative of moderation, see chapter 2.

6. Jim O'Hara, "Unitary School Appeal Try Vowed," *Tennessean*, August 15, 1970; Matthew D. Lassiter, *The Silent Majority: Suburban Politics in the Sunbelt South* (Princeton, NJ: Princeton University Press, 2005); Kevin Kruse, *White Flight: Atlanta and the Making of Modern Conservatism* (Princeton, NJ: Princeton University Press, 2006).

7. "Parents Plan Meeting with School Board," *Banner*, August 24, 1970; MNBOE, min-

utes, August 25, 1970, MNBOE. On Jenkins, Wayne Whitt, "Jenkins Switches with the Pitches," *Tennessean*, May 2, 1971.

8. Frances Meeker, "Crowd of 400 Protests, Judge Halts Hearing," *Banner*, March 12, 1971; "School Hearings Resume, but Doors Locked," *Banner*, March 16, 1971; "500 Opponents of School Busing Barred from Nashville Hearing," *Washington Post*, March 17, 1971.

9. Beverly Briley to Mr. and Mrs. Alvin Pentecost, September 20, 1971, BBP, box 7, file 69.

10. Meeker, "School Hearings Resume."

11. Ibid.

12. Nonpartisan elections functioned without a party primary, and thus new candidates could rise to prominence without building party support. See Lester M. Salomon and Gary L. Wamsley, "The Politics of Urban Land Policy: Zoning and Urban Development in Nashville," in James F. Blumstein and Benjamin Walter, eds., *Growing Metropolis: Aspects of Development in Nashville* (Nashville, TN: Vanderbilt University Press, 1975), 151–90, 155.

13. Tom Normand, "Young Democrats Hear 6 Mayoral Candidates," *Banner*, July 30, 1971.

14. Wayne Whitt, "Mayor Briley Re-Elected," *Tennessean*, August 27, 1971.

15. On home owner rights and conservatism, see Lassiter, *Silent Majority*, and Kruse, *White Flight*.

16. Constituent letter to Beverly Briley, September 20, 1971,BBP, box 7, file 69.

17. Officer Russ Hackett, "Notes on Concerned Parents Association, Inc. Rally," BBP, box 8, file 80, BBP.

18. "Jenkins Says His Poll Gives Him 32% of Vote," *Tennessean*, July 30, 1971.

19. Sanders Anglea to Beverly Briley, phone message, n.d. [August-September 1971], BBP, box 6, file 64.

20. Beverly Briley to MNBOE, August 25, 1971, BBP, box 6, file 62.

21. Dick Battle, reporter's notes, March 13, 1971, DBP, box 27, Notebook 3/5/71–3/31/71. These notes are difficult to read; I am relying only on legible sections.

22. C. Beverly Briley, interview with Paul Clement, 1980, MANDC, Century III Oral History.

23. Beverly Briley, news release, September 13, 1971, BBP, box 8, file 76; "Four Mayor Candidates Oppose Busing Increases," *Banner*, June 2, 1971; "Briley Raps Integration 30-Day Rule," *Banner*, August 13, 1970. In Briley's replies to constituent letters, he dates his opposition to 1958, with no explanation. The references to 1958 are in Briley's standard reply to multiple constituent letters, BBO, box 7, file 69.

24. Briley to John Gannon, October 8, 1971, BBP, box 6, file 64.

25. Wayne Whitt, "Briley vs. Jenkins: Old Pro vs. a Fresh Face," *Tennessean*, August 22, 1971.

26. "Saving Four Senior Highs Jenkins' Aim," *Tennessean*, August 20, 1971. Jenkins inaccurately represented black community concerns elsewhere. See "Road's Route Would Hurt Blacks, Jenkins," *Tennessean*, August 20, 1971; Tom Flake, "Jenkins Contradicted on Parkway Expansion, *Banner*, August 23, 1971.

27. On DCIPC's attempts, see Edwin Mitchell, interview, FUBOHC February 18, 1972, and Dan May to Ira Mendell, August 30, 1971, DMP, box 6, file 8.

28. Whitt, "Mayor Briley Re-Elected."

29. "Rally at Fairgrounds Speedway," *Banner*, September 8, 1971.

30. "Victims of Forced Busing Awake!" BBP, box 8, file 76; Frank Sutherland and Tom Gillem, "Pickets Up at Schools, Rolls Down," *Tennessean*, September 14, 1971.

31. Hubert Dixon III, interview, May 17, 2004.

32. Frank Sutherland and Tom Gillem, "Bus Options to Be Aired Today," *Tennessean*, September 22, 1971; "Jenkins Ends Bus Picketing, Cites New Group," *Banner*, September 24, 1971.

33. W. Lipscomb Davis to Members of the Nashville Chamber of Commerce, June 21, 1971, and NCC, "A Statement of Policy and a Plea for a Calm Community," BBP, box 8, file 76; paid advertisement, *Banner*, June 22, 1971 (emphasis in the original). Other statements strike the same tone. See an unsigned statement, likely from Dan May, BBP, box 7, file 74.

34. For another example of business-minded calls for moderation in desegregation, see Karen Anderson, *Little Rock: Race and Resistance at Central High School* (Princeton, NJ: Princeton University Press, 2010). On the business response to busing in Charlotte, see Stephen Samuel Smith, *Boom for Whom: Education, Desegregation, and Development in Charlotte* (Albany: State University of New York Press, 2004).

35. Rev. Bill Barnes, *To Love A City: A Congregation's Long Love Affair with Nashville's Inner City* (Nashville: O.N.E., n.d. [c. 2007]), 102–6; Kitty Smith, Memo to Board of Education, October 10, 1971, MNBOE Agendas, MNPS.

36. "United Parents for Quality Education," August 16, 1971, and "United Parents for Quality Education in Metropolitan Nashville," n.d. [1971], BBP, box 7, file 80.

37. Hubert Dixon Jr., interview, July 2004.

38. Rosentene Purnell to Beverly Briley, October 22, 1971, BBP, box 6, file 64; Social and Political Action Committee to Elliott Richardson, October 16, 1971, attached to Beverley Briley to Kelley Miller Smith, November 2, 1971, BBP, box 7, file 1969; Amos Jones, interview, FUBOHP, October 13, 1972.

39. Multiple anecdotes suggest continued use of restrictive covenants, colloquially if not formally. A 1967 advertisement for a home in the most exclusive of Nashville's neighborhoods described the area as a "choice restricted area good for a long time" (classified section, *Tennessean*, January 8, 1967). *Dr. Sammie Lucas, et ux., v. Clifford Earl Hooper et al.*, 381 F. Supp. 1222 (1974). See Andrew Wiese, *Places of Their Own: African American Suburbanization in the Twentieth Century* (Chicago: University of Chicago Press, 2004) and Becky Nicolaides, *My Blue Heaven: Life and Politics in the Working-Class Suburbs of Los Angeles, 1920–1965* (Chicago: University of Chicago Press, 2002); Amanda Seligman, *Block by Block: Neighborhoods and Public Policy on Chicago's West Side* (Chicago: University of Chicago Press, 2005); Kevin Kruse, *White Flight*; Sugrue, *Origins of the Urban Crisis*. For Nashville examples, see Alfred C. Galloway's testimony, transcript of proceedings, *Kelley v. MNBOE*, February 3, 1970, box 7, 761–69; real estate agent, interview, 2004.

40. Roger Richardson, "Busing in Nashville: Welcome Aboard, If You Can Squeeze In!" *Etc.* [yearbook], 1976, on file at McGavock High School.

41. Among others, see phone messages from R.B. Owens to Briley, n.d. [1971], and Bro. Miles to Briley, August 17, 1972, BBP, box 8, file 77. Inaugural Watauga membership list attached to L.S. to Alexander Heard, May 9, 1970, Vanderbilt University Archives, RG300, box 368, file Mary Jane Werthan.

42. Brooks to Stimbert; affidavit of Dr. Elbert Brooks, cited in *Kelley v. MNBOE*, 463 F.2d. 732 (1972). The 1971 desegregation plan increased the number of students transported by 44 percent, but given withdrawals from the system the actual increase was somewhat smaller.

43. Elbert C. Brooks, letter to E. C. Stimbert, August 25, 1971, COE, roll 103, box 308a, file 9; "Report to the Court," *Kelley v. MNBOE,* October 19, 1971, *Kelley,* box 6, file 1971 (3), 3; Richard A. Pride and David Woodward, *The Burden of Busing: The Politics of Desegregation in Nashville, Tennessee* (Knoxville: University of Tennessee Press, 1985), 99.

44. Dean Kotlowski emphasizes Nixon's mores supportive choices. See "With All Deliberate Delay: Kennedy, Johnson and School Desegregation," *Journal of Policy History* 17, no. 2 (2005): 155–92 and *Nixon's Civil Rights: Politics, Principle, and Policy* (Cambridge, MA: Harvard University Press, 2001).

45. Aldorothy Wright, interview, October 5, 2006; Mrs. Robert Dickerson to Beverly Briley, September 14, 1971, BBP, box 7, file 68. Public statements by Beverly Briley are in BBP, box 7, file 69. School opening and closing times are listed in memorandum to order issued August 17, 1972, *Kelley v. MNBOE,* August 17, 1972, *Kelley,* box 8, file 1972 (1), 540.

46. Memorandum, *Kelley v. MNBOE,* August 25, 1972, *Kelley,* box 8, file 1972(2), 3–5 and memorandum to order issued August 17, 1972, 3–4.

47. Letters to C. Beverly Briley, August 1972, BBP, box 8, file 76.

48. "Tennessee Race May Turn on Busing," *NYT,* September 10, 1972, via ProQuest Historical Newspapers, accessed March 14, 2010; John Egerton, "The Slow-Burn Early Years of Nashville School Integration," *Tennessean,* January 14, 1996 (BOE).

49. Affidavit of C. Beverly Briley, *Kelley v. MNBOE,* August 22, 1972, *Kelley,* box 8, file 1972 (1), 1–2. Mayor Briley's relationship with Judge Morton may also have been colored by the judge's frank criticism of Briley's administration of its Model Cities program, which he referred to as a "good model of what not to do," as there was "no real evidence of citizen participation in the program." Briley had expressed much opposition to any citizen participation (Tom Ingram, "Morton Hits Model Cities Participation," *Tennessean,* July 29, 1972); "Nashville's Model Cities Program: An Unborn Partnership," 1971 (Nashville, TN: Race Relations Information Center), 9.

50. Louis Peltason, *58 Lonely Men* (Urbana: University of Illinois Press, 1961).

51. Memorandum, *Kelley v. MNBOE,* August 25, 1972, *Kelley,* box 8, file 1972(2), 3–5.

52. "L. Clure Morton, 82, Ex-Judge Who Aided Nashville Integration," *NYT,* April 19, 1998, via ProQuest Historical Newspapers, accessed March 14, 2010.

53. Egerton, "The Slow-Burn Early Years."

54. "Judge Frank Gray, Jr." http://www.tnmd.uscourts.gov/gray_frank_jr, accessed March 21, 2010.

55. *Kelley v. MNBOE,* 372 F. Supp. 540 (1973), note 12.

56. Ibid., quote on 62–63.

57. Pat Welch, "HEW Like Alabama School Board?" *Tennessean,* January 5, 1972.

58. Ken Clawson, "Sens. Baker and Brock Fight Busing Order," *Washington Post,* September 23, 1971, via ProQuest Historical Newspapers. Baker quote in Subcommittee on Constitutional Rights, Committee on the Judiciary, US Senate, "Busing of Schoolchildren," http://congressional.proquest.com.ezproxy.cul.columbia.edu/congressional/result/congressional/pqpdocumentview?accountid=10226&pgId=4c953b7f-3097-4987-8a1d-d9120bddda02, accessed December 21, 2012. Representative Richard Fulton's mailings and public statements are in BBP, box 8, file 78. For an example of Nixon's public rhetoric, see "Address to the Nation on Equal Educational Opportunities and School Busing," March 16, 1972, *The Public Papers of the Presidents of the United States,* http://name.umdl.umich.edu/4731812.1972.001, accessed January 2, 2013.

59. Pride and Woodward, *Burden of Busing,* 104.

60. Memorandum, 5; Pride and Woodward, on hotlines; James Wooton, "School Chiefs in South Perplexed on Busing," *NYT*, September 7, 1971, accessed via ProQuest Historical Newspapers.

61. On the importance of resistance in defining desegregation policies, see Gadsden, *Between North and South*, chapter 5.

62. "Memorandum to Hon. L. Clure Morton from the Defendants," *Kelley v. MNBOE*, July 17, 1972, *Kelley*, box 9, file 1972, 1.

63. On private schooling and desegregation, see Joseph Crespino, *In Search of Another Country: Mississippi and the Conservative Counterrevolution* (Princeton: Princeton University Press, 2007).

64. Ray Osborne to Bill Wise, October 27, 1971, SPF, file Cole School.

65. Eugene TeSelle, "To the Study Subcommittee," July 18, 1973, AWPII, unprocessed.

66. Transcript of proceedings, *Kelley v. MNBOE*, June 26, 1979, *Kelley*, box 18, file Transcripts of Trial 6/26/79, 170–73; Percy Priest CAC presentation, January 10, 1978, AWPII, unprocessed; Lakeview CAC, statement, *Kelley*, box 27, part 3; Ray Campbell, "NAACP Wants School Additions Shut," *Banner*, June 21, 1979.

67. Transcript of proceedings, *Kelley v. MNBOE*, February 3–6, 1970, 462, *Kelley*, box 6; "Answer of Plaintiffs to Petition Filed by Defendants on or about May 31, 1973," *Kelley v. MNBOE*, June 19, 1973, *Kelley*, box 9, file 1973 (1); Bill Lann Lee, interview, February 26, 2013, by telephone.

68. George Cate, interview, June 27, 2007.

69. Goodlettsville-Madison High School zone described in "Long Range Plan, 1975," *Kelley v. MNBOE*, *Kelley*, box 13, exhibit 10, 1979; "Petition for Contempt"; Lillian D. Edens, letter to Avon Williams, February 22, 1980, AWPII, unprocessed.

70. MNPS, "Report to Citizens' Advisory Committee," January 21, 1975, *Kelley*, box 12, file 1975.

71. MNPS, "Report to Citizens' Advisory Committee," 12.

72. "[Plaintiff's] Petition for Contempt," 2.

73. Lassiter, *Silent Majority*; Davison Douglas, *Reading, Writing and Race: The Desegregation of the Charlotte Schools* (Chapel Hill: University of North Carolina Press, 1995).

74. Judge Thomas A. Wiseman listed the motions that Gray had not responded to in *Kelley v. MNBOE*, 429 F. Supp. 167 (1980). Earlier letters to the court requesting counsel went unaddressed as well.

75. Richard Fulton, "A Special Report: School Busing," Fall 1971, BBP, box 8, file 79; *Congressional Record*, Proceedings and Debates of the 92nd Congress, September 21, 1971, HR 10779, https://bulk.resource.org/gao.gov/92–318/00006C8C_36451.pdf, accessed August 13, 2013.

76. I thus concur with Jeannie Oakes's view of vocational education as a reinforcement of existing political, economic, and social hierarchies rather than an intentional project of elite conspiracy (Oakes, *Keeping Track: How Schools Structure Inequality*, 2nd ed. [New Haven, CT: Yale University Press, 2005]).

77. Richard Dinkins, interview, third session, August 20, 2013; Senator Douglas Henry, interview, July, 2007, notes in author's possession.

78. Buford Ellington, "Combined Quotes on Vocational Education," 1969, GP 50 Ellington II, box 85, file 1, 1.

79. Legislative Council Committee, "Study on Social Problems, Vol. 3: Extent of Poverty and Social Welfare," 1973 (Nashville, TN: State of Tennessee), 60.

80. "Industrial Expansion," 1960, GNAR, series I-A, box 4, file Board Minutes 1960–61, 1.

81. William Carter, letter to Frank Clement, August 8, 1963, GP 49 Clement III, box 503, file 17; R.B. Marshall, letter to W. R. Smith, GP 48 Ellington I, box 15, file 2.

82. Don Gillard, "Tenn. Promoters Greeted, Cussed," c. 1960, GP 48 Ellington I, box 36, file 3; "Detroit Team Trip," October 17, 1962, GP 48 Ellington I, box 15, file 3.

83. Buford Ellington, "Tennessee Communities Share in Benefits from Industrial Operations," May 2, 1967, GP Buford Ellington, box 23, file 1, 5; Dan W. Calgy to Frank Clements, November 20, 1963, GP 49 Clement III, box 506, file 1, 2.

84. Ellington, "Combined Quotes on Vocational Education," 1.

85. John Mihalic to Charles Dunn, October 10, 1967, COE, reel 129 (128 on box), box 376, file 1, frame 00836; W. A. Seeley to Joe Morgan, January 12, 1961, COE, reel 129 (128 on box), box 375, file 2, frame 00100; Ken Morrell, "$6.7 Million Being Spent in Vocational Training Setup," *Banner*, November 29, 1961; SH Roberts, "Remarks for Seminar on State Planning and Economic Development, US Dept of Commerce," February 23, 1968, GP 50—Ellington II, box 49, file 5, 2.

86. Legislative Council Committee, "Study on Vocational Educational Programs in Grades 7–12," (Nashville: State of Tennessee, 1973), 14–15, 24–25.

87. George O. Wilson to Joe Morgan, August 17, 1960, COE, reel 129 (128 on box), box 375, file 2.

88. E. C. Stimbert, memo to Gov. Winfield Dunn Re: Proposed Industrial Training Office Implementation, February 25, 1972, GP 51 Dunn, box 69, file 4; "State to Unveil Industry Training on Wheels Unit," *Tennessean*, May 30, 1974. James Cobb discussed similar programs in South Carolina and other states in *The Selling of the South: The Southern Crusade for Industrial Development, 1936–1980* (Baton Rouge: Louisiana State University Press, 1982), 167. John Egerton interview with Ben Hirst, "Notes for Tennessee: Seizing Opportunity," JEP, box 41, file 17.

89. Conversion from Samuel H. Williamson, "Six Ways to Compute the Relative Value of a U.S. Dollar Amount, 1774 to Present," MeasuringWorth, http://www .measuringworth.com/uscompare/, accessed April 6, 2015.

Legislative Council Committee, notes, undated, 1973, in TSLA, RG 60 Committee Reports, box 67, 88th General Assembly Legislative Materials Education Committee; Benjamin E. Carmichael, "Commissioner's Report: Summary of Major Programs under Development by the State Department of Education," 1975 (Nashville, TN: Tennessee Department of Education), 8; "Dropout Rate Cited: Vocational Training Push Set," *Knoxville News-Sentinel*, February 22, 1973; Robert Churchwell, "Metro Educational Proposal Submitted," *Banner*, December 28, 1973.

90. Tennessee Legislature, "House Bill No. 1203," Legislative Journals and Acts (Nashville: 1973), 1061–64.

91. Henry, interview; on the vocational education lobby, see also James Sundquist, *Politics and Policy: The Eisenhower, Kennedy, and Johnson Years* (Washington, DC: Brookings Institution, 1968). For context on the era's interest in "human capital," see Alice O'Connor, *Poverty Knowledge: Social Science, Social Policy, and the Poor in Twentieth-Century US History* (Chicago: University of Chicago Press, 2001), 141–42; Ira Katznelson, "Was the Great Society a Missed Opportunity?," in *The Rise and Fall of the New Deal Order*, Steve and Gary Gerstle Fraser, eds., (Princeton, NJ: Princeton University Press, 1989); Judith Stein, *Running Steel, Running America: Race, Economic Policy, and the Decline of Liberalism* (Chapel Hill: University of North Carolina Press, 1998), chapter 3.

92. *House Joint Resolution No. 190*, 87th General Session, 1971 Session, 1576–77.

93. Legislative Council Committee, "Study on Vocational Education," 6.

94. Ibid., 8, 20, 31.
95. Ibid., 9.
96. Ibid., iv, 6–7, 33–34.
97. Marland's push for career education illustrates what Norton Grubb and Marvin Lazerson call "vocationalism," the embrace of career preparation throughout American schools, beyond the vocational curriculum. See *American Education and Vocationalism: A Documentary History* (New York: Teachers College Press, 1974) and *The Education Gospel* (Cambridge, MA: Harvard University Press, 2006).
98. James Rhodes, *Alternative to a Decadent Society* (Indianapolis, IN: Howard W. Sams & Co., 1969), 23–31.
99. Jefferson Cowie, "Nixon's Class Struggle: Romancing the New Right Worker, 1969–1973," *Labor History* 43, no. 3 (August 2002): 257–83, 281.
100. Legislative Council Committee, "Study on Vocational Educational Programs," 1, 11–12.
101. Council of Community Services, "A Comprehensive Survey of Social Welfare in Metropolitan Nashville and Davidson County," 1968 (Nashville, TN: Council of Community Services) in RHPA, box 7, 73.
102. Cornwell, *Biographical Directory of the Tennessee General Assembly, Vol. VI, 1971–1991*, 276–77.
103. *House Joint Resolution No. 65*, 87th General Session, 1971 Session, 1431–33.
104. Tennessee Public Acts, 88th General Assembly, 1973 Session, 1061–64.
105. Winfield Dunn, untitled statement on HB 1204, GP 51 Dunn, box 182, file 2; Leonard K. Bradley, memo to Governor Dunn, July 2, 1974, GP 51 Dunn, box 130, file 4.
106. Pride and Woodward, *Burden of Busing*, 65.
107. Memorandum Opinion, *Kelley v. MNBOE*, June 28, 1971, *Kelley*, box 6, file 1971 (2).

CHAPTER SEVEN

1. Enrollment figures from MNPS, "Twenty-Seven Year Analysis of Enrollment Patterns," *Kelley*, box 23, file 1996.
2. Hubert Dixon III, interview, May 17, 2004.
3. Roslyn Arlin Mickelson, "Subverting *Swann*: First- and Second-Generation Segregation in the Charlotte-Mecklenburg Schools," *American Educational Research Journal* 38, no. 2 (Summer 2001): 215–52.
4. Richard A. Pride and David Woodward, *The Burden of Busing: The Politics of Desegregation in Nashville, Tennessee* (Knoxville: University of Tennessee Press, 1985), 107–25.
5. Charles Frazier to MNBOE, May 15, 1992, on file with agenda, May 15, 1992, MNBOE.
6. See Mickelson, "Subverting *Swann*," 218–23; Amy Stuart Wells et al., *Both Sides Now: The Stories of School Desegregation's Graduates* (Berkeley: University of California Press, 2009).
7. Wells et al., *Both Sides Now*; John Egerton, *Education and Desegregation in Eight Schools* (Evanston, IL: Center for Equal Education, 1977), 72–81, quotation on 81.
8. Wells et al., *Both Sides Now*.
9. Stephen Flatt, interview, June 2, 2004; Dixon III, interview.
10. Area III Budget Advisory Committee, "Report of the Sub-Committee on Study," n.d. [c. May 1973], AWPII, unprocessed; Wells et al., *Both Sides Now*, chapter 3.
11. Flatt, interview; Cindy Acuff, interview, July 22, 2004; Waverly Crenshaw, interview, February 2004; Charles Davis, interview, June 3, 2004.

12. Sonya Ramsey, interview, March 6, 2013, by telephone. Similar observations in Constance Ridley Smith, "The Advantages and Disadvantages of the Desegregation Experience in Metropolitan Nashville Davidson County Public Schools, 1961–1976," (PhD diss., Northern Caribbean University, 2015). On gender and the extracurriculum, see Mary Barr, *Friends Disappear: The Battle for Racial Equality in Evanston* (Chicago: University of Chicago Press, 2014).

13. Wells et al., *Both Sides Now*, 184–93.

14. Flatt, interview; Rev. Amos Jones interview, October 13, 1972, FUBOHC.

15. Flatt, interview; Jones, interview; Milton Harris, interview, May 14, 2004; Davis, interview.

16. Pride and Woodward, *Burden of Busing*, 152.

17. Davis, interview; Crenshaw, interview; letter to Judge Thomas Wiseman, May 25, 1980, *Kelley*, box 16, collected exhibit 263, vol. 2; Semetta Coure Pulley, interview, May 8, 2004. I identify letters to Judge Wiseman by date rather than name; individual names are not important to this analysis.

18. Griffith quote in Saundra Ivey, "Integration 'Learning' Process Still Going on Here," *Tennessean*, May 25, 1979.

19. Sonya Ramsey, *Reading, Writing, and Segregation: A Century of Black Women Teachers in Nashville* (Urbana: University of Illinois Press, 2008), 105–23.

20. Mary Craighead, interview, March 24, 2004.

21. Ramsey, *Reading, Writing, and Segregation*, 112, 116, 118, 127.

22. Ramsey, *Reading, Writing, and Segregation*, 110; Robert Churchwell, "Schools Seen Overcoming Desegregation Problems," *Banner*, September 21, 1973. On students' perceptions of teacher support for, or resistance to, desegregation, see Smith, "Advantages and Disadvantages."

23. Davis, interview; Dixon III, interview.

24. *Etc.* (yearbook), 1975, MANDC; Kathleen Harned, "A History of McGavock High School: The Creation of the Comprehensive Concept in Nashville, Tennessee" (EdD diss., Tennessee State University, 1998), 9–10, 14, 46–47; Chester LaFever, interview, April 2004; Eugene Speight, interview, May 2004.

25. Acuff, interview.

26. Pulley, interview; Rob McGee, interview, May 14, 2007.

27. Susan Thomas, "Glencliff Official Feels Talks, Meets Will Hike Attendance," *Tennessean*, November 13, 1978; "Glencliff Works Out a Crisis," *Tennessean*, November 18, 1978; Dwight Lewis, "Officials Report Glencliff Tension Eased," *Tennessean*, November 22, 1978; Bob Heeth, "Glencliff Attendance Returning," *Banner*, November 14, 1978.

28. Letter to Judge Wiseman, March 16, 1980, *Kelley*, box 16, collected exhibit 263, vol. 2.

29. Pride and Woodward, *Burden of Busing*, 145–48.

30. Egerton, *Education and Desegregation*, 72–81; Saundra Ivey, "Faculty Desegregation a Time of Adjustment," *Tennessean*, May 23, 1979; Wells et al., *Both Sides Now*, 130–37.

31. Egerton, *Education and Desegregation*, 72–81.

32. The series ran in the *Tennessean* from May 13 to May 27, 1979.

33. Saundra Ivey, "Racial Slurs Can Trigger Violence, Misunderstanding," *Tennessean*, May 24, 1979; "Student Petition Protests Photographs," *Tennessean*, May 25, 1979; "Hillsboro Program Praised, Defended," *Tennessean*, May 26, 1979. *Tennessean* editor John Seigenthaler recalled the difficult editorial considerations involved in

choosing to print these photographs that portrayed students negatively (Siegenthaler, interview, March 12, 2013).

34. Hubert Dixon Jr., interview, July 2004.

35. Egerton, *Education and Desegregation*, 79.

36. G. Bruce Hartmann, "An Economic Analysis of Black Nashville" (PhD diss., State University of New York, Albany, 1974), 42; Rev. Bill Barnes, interview, June 29, 2007; Kathy Nevill, interview, April 15, 2004.

37. On the impact of black suburban movement on desegregation, see Jack Dougherty, *More Than One Struggle: The Evolution of Black School Reform in Milwaukee* (Chapel Hill: University of North Carolina Press, 2004). See R. Scott Baker, *Paradoxes of Desegregation: African American Struggles for Educational Equity in Charleston, South Carolina, 1926–1972* (Columbia: University of South Carolina Press, 2006); Steven Samuel Smith, *Boom for Whom: Education, Desegregation, and Development* (Albany: State University of New York Press, 2004); and Ben F. Johnson III, "After 1957: Resisting Integration in Little Rock." *Arkansas Historical Quarterly* LXVI (2007): 258–83, for other examples of important class divisions in desegregation.

38. Pride and Woodward, *Burden of Busing*, 77, illustrates these zones.

39. Dixon, interview; Flatt; interview; Crenshaw, interview; Aldorothy Wright, interview, October 2006; Charles Kimbrough, interview, August 2007.

40. Jeannie Oakes, *Keeping Track: How Schools Structure Inequality*, 2nd ed. (New Haven, CT: Yale University Press, 2005); James Anderson, "The Historical Development of Black Vocational Education," in Harvey Kantor and David Tyack, eds., *Work, Youth, and Schooling: Historical Perspectives on Vocationalism in American Schooling*, (Stanford, CA: Stanford University Press, 1982), 190–91; Crenshaw, interview.

41. Egerton, *Education and Desegregation*, 78.

42. MNPS, "Capitol Schools in Metropolitan Nashville-Davidson County, Tennessee," 1971, COE, reel 132 (131 on box), box 385, file 5.

43. Mickelson, "Subverting *Swann*."

44. Leonard Alberstadt et al., "Statement to the MNBOE and Advisory Committee," November 6, 1979, in KMSP, box 69, file 7, VUSC, 1–2. North High School, a historically segregated white school that had become all black by 1971, had even more dramatic levels of white boycott. MNPS, "Twenty-Seven Year Analysis."

45. Letter to Mayor Briley, September 20, 1971, BBP, file 69, box 7.

46. "Many Pearl Transfer Requests Denied," *Tennessean*, October 19, 1979.

47. Charles Frazier, interview, July 2007.

48. Wells et al., *Both Sides Now*, 72–75, 94–99, 115–25.

49. MNPS, "Twenty-Seven Year Analysis."

50. Letter to Judge Thomas Wiseman, October 11, 1979, *Kelley*, box 15, collected exhibit 263; Acuff, interview. *Kelley*, box 9, contains copies of student requests for and administrative reports on transfers. For compilations of the data, see Carolyn B. Tucker to Avon Williams, June 29, 1979, AWPII, unprocessed.

51. Pride and Woodward, *Burden of Busing*, 186–87; *Kelley v. MNBOE*, 479 F. Supp. 120 (1979).

52. Harvey Kantor, "Education, Social Reform, and the State: ESEA and Federal Education Policy in the 1960s," *American Journal of Education* 100, no. 1 (November 1991): 47–83; David F. Labaree, "The Winning Ways of a Losing Strategy: Educationalizing Social Problems in the United States," *Educational Theory* 54, no. 4 (November 2008): 447–60.

53. "Enrollments in Vocational Education Programs," submitted to the Dept. of Health, Education, and Welfare, for the 1971 school year, GP-Dunn, box 69, file 3; "Vocational and Technical Education," September 23–25, 1965, COE, reel 114 (115 on register), box 338, file 6.

54. Harvey Kantor and David B. Tyack, introduction to *Work, Youth, and Schooling: Historical Perspectives on Vocationalism in American Education* (Stanford, CA: Stanford University Press, 1982). A late-1960s shift in recordkeeping confounds a more detailed examination of enrollment within state records. The 1968 Vocational Education Act prioritized reaching "disadvantaged" students, who could be poor *or* from a racial minority, and the state aggregated both groups under "disadvantaged."

55. TNDOE, *Annual Statistical Report*, 1969; TNDOE, *Annual Status Report on Female and Male Students in Vocational Education*, 1982. On gendered stereotypes about work, see Alice Kessler-Harris, *Out to Work: A History of Wage-Earning Women in the United States* (New York: Oxford University Press, 1982). On gender divisions in vocational education, see John Rury, *Education and Women's Work: Female Schooling and the Division of Labor in Urban America, 1870–1930* (Albany: State University of New York Press, 1991); Harvey Kantor, *Learning to Earn: School, Work, and Vocational Reform in California, 1880–1930* (Madison: University of Wisconsin Press, 1988); Geraldine Joncich Clifford, "'Marry, Stitch, Die, or Do Worse': Educating Women for Work," in Kantor and Tyack, eds., *Work, Youth and Schooling*, 223–68.

56. Clara May Benedict, "A Study of Vocational Curriculum Models Related to Employment Opportunities, Employers Reactions, and the Present Program at Cohn High School" (Sp.Ed. thesis, George Peabody College for Teachers, 1966), 31–32.

57. James W. Whitlock and Billy J. Williams, *Jobs and Training for Southern Youth* (Nashville: Peabody College, 1963), 9–10.

58. Michael B. Katz, Mark Stern, and Jamie J. Fader, "The New African American Inequality," *JAH* 92, no. 1 (June 2005): 75–108.

59. "Some of the Outstanding Accomplishments of Frank Clement during His Term as Governor," 1965, GP-Clement III, box 529, file 27. On the importance of public sector employment for African Americans, see Michael Brown et al., *Whitewashing Race: The Myth of a Color-Blind Society* (Berkeley: University of California Press, 2003), 19. The local expansion is consistent with the national pattern, where black women went from 5.4 percent of the clerical workforce in 1950 to 21.4 percent in 1970 and 33.1 percent in 1980 (Delores P. Aldridge, "Black Women and the New World Order," in Irene Browne, ed., *Latinas and African American Women at Work: Race, Gender, and Economic Inequality*, [New York: Russell Sage, 1999], 357–79).

60. On the increase in black women's clerical employment in the 1950s, 60s, and beyond, see: Bette Woody, *Black Women in the Workplace: Impacts of Structural Change in the Economy* (Westport, CT: Greenwood, 1992); Venus Green, *Race on the Line: Gender, Labor, and Technology in the Bell System, 1880–1980* (Durham, NC: Duke University Press, 2001). Evidence for post-secondary placement was even stronger, with Tennessee reporting more than 95 percent of the more than 1,200 students trained in office occupations at that level having found full-time jobs in their field or related fields. "Follow-up of Enrollees in Preparatory Vocational Education Programs," submitted to the Department of Health, Education, and Welfare by the Tennessee Department of Education, January 1969, GP-Ellington II, box 15, file 3. Bernard Werthan, interview, August 2007; "Table 5: Total and Black Employment by Occupation, 1978," AWPII, unprocessed.

61. On the national pattern, see Woody, *Black Women in the Workplace: Impacts of Struc-*

*tural Change in the Economy,* 66; Jane Berger, "When Hard Work Doesn't Pay: Gender and the Origins of the Urban Crisis, Baltimore, 1945–1985" (PhD diss., Ohio State University, 2007); Phil Riner, interview, July 2007. On the dispersion of manufacturing, see Thomas J. Sugrue, *The Origins of the Urban Crisis* (Princeton, NJ: Princeton University Press, 1998); John Valhaly Jr., "The Location of Service and Office Activities in Nashville-Davidson County, 1970," *Land Economics* 52, no. 4 (November 1976): 479–92, esp. 486–91.

62. Benedict, "A Study," 31–32.

63. John Egerton, "Unemployment in Nashville (1975)—Research and Background Materials—Interviews," [n.d.] JEP, box 21, file 1. Milton Harris recalled masonry as one area of municipal employment for which boys could be trained at schools like McGavock (Harris, interview).

64. I reviewed McGavock High School yearbooks from 1971 to 1988. Yearbooks, and photographs, are an imperfect basis for interpretation of racial designations, but given the volume of images available there and the dearth of statistical information elsewhere, they must be taken into account (McGavock yearbooks on file at MANDC and at McGavock High School).

65. "Disadvantaged" is not a proxy for "African American" in Tennessee, with its large poor white population. Enrollment figures from "Enrollments in Vocational Education Programs."

66. Melvin Black, interview, June 28, 2007.

67. Anderson, "Historical Development."

68. Egerton, "Unemployment in Nashville."

69. Ibid.

70. Frazier, interview; Riner, interview; Sen. Douglas Henry, interview, July 2007.

71. On vocational education's outcomes, see Grubb and Lazerson, *American Education and Vocationalism: A Documentary History,* 47–48. On clerical education for women, see Clifford, "Marry, Stitch, Die, or Do Worse" and Herbert Kliebard, *Schooled to Work: Vocationalism and the American Curriculum, 1876–1946* (New York: Routledge Falmer, 2004), 213–16. Glenn R. Bettis and Carroll Hyder, "A Study to Develop and Implement a One and Five-Year Student and Employer Based Follow-up Study of Secondary Vocational Education Programs." (Johnson City, TN: East Tennessee State University, 1978) offered preliminary evaluation data.

72. By the late 1970s and early 1980s, there were several white flight–focused critiques of busing. The most influential were James Coleman et al., *Trends in School Segregation* (Washington, DC: Urban Institute, 1975) and David Armor, *White Flight, Demographic Transition, and the Future of School Segregation* (Santa Monica: Rand, 1978). For another local case where concerns about white flight drove policy making, see Dionne Danns, "Northern Desegregation: A Tale of Two Cities," *HEQ* 51, no. 1 (February 2011): 77–104.

73. Pride and Woodward, *Burden of Busing,* 85–90.

74. Ibid., 94.

75. Ibid., 132–36.

76. Ibid., 105.

77. Ibid., 137–39.

78. Ibid, 126–31; Forrest Wilson, interview, July 19, 2007.

79. N. Gregory Mankiw and David N. Weil, "The Baby Boom, the Baby Bust, and the Housing Market," *Regional Science and Urban Economics* 19 (1989): 235–58, 237–38.

80. Ibid., 237–38.

81. "Percy Priest CAC Presentation to Metropolitan School Board," January 10, 1978, and Duncan and Beaufait to L. C. Biggs, April 5, 1978, AWPII, unprocessed; Citizen's Advisory Committee, District III, "Statement on Recommended Rezoning Plan Policy Guidelines," KMSP, box 69, file 7.

82. "Estimated Number of Public School Students (G1–12) per 100 Household Population, 1977," in [no author given—likely MPC] "Service Area Alternatives for an Inner City High School," n.d, c. 1979, in KMSP, box 69, file 5, following page 9.

83. "Social Types in Nashville-Davidson County, TN," 1976 (Nashville, TN: Metropolitan Planning Commission).

84. Ibid., 17.

85. Ibid., 1, 5, 14–25. Black boys and black girls ages five to seventeen in census tracks with over 50 percent black residents in 1970 numbered 14,618 (US Census, via NHGIS).

86. One local observer saw the Metropolitan Planning Commission to be interested in making "a long-range plan with racial and socio-economic balance," as of the mid-1970s, in contrast to the school district's staff willing to "acquiesce in segregationist policy" (Eugene TeSelle, "To the Study Subcommittee," July 18, 1973, AWPII, unprocessed).

87. Transcript of proceedings, *Kelley v. MNBOE*, February 3–17, 1970, *Kelley*, box 6, file 3, 1028–140, quotations on 1032, 1119; High school zones planning map, AWPII, unprocessed.

88. Eugene TeSelle, "To the Study Subcommittee."

CHAPTER EIGHT

1. Erica Frankenberg and Chungmei Lee, "Race in American Public Schools: Rapidly Resegregating School Districts" (Cambridge, MA: Civil Rights Project, Harvard University, 2002), 13.

2. Derrick Bell, "*Brown* and the Interest-Convergence Dilemma," in Derrick Bell, ed., *Shades of Brown: New Perspectives on School Desegregation* (New York: Teachers College Press, 1980), 90–106. See also "Serving Two Masters: Integration Ideals and Client Interests in School Desegregation Litigation," *Yale Law Journal* 85, no. 4 (March 1976): 470–516.

3. On Ocean Hill-Brownsville, see Jerold Podair, *The Strike That Changed New York* (New Haven, CT: Yale University Press, 2004); Wendell Pritchett, *Brownsville, Brooklyn: Blacks, Jews, and the Changing Face of the Ghetto* (Chicago: University of Chicago Press, 2002); Daniel Perlstein, *Justice, Justice: School Politics and the Eclipse of Liberalism* (New York: Peter Lang, 2004). Dionne Danns, *Desegrating Chicago's Public Schools* (New York: Palgrave MacMillan, 2014).

4. Jack Dougherty, *More Than One Struggle: The Evolution of Black School Reform in Milwaukee* (Chapel Hill: University of North Carolina Press, 2004).

5. Tomiko Brown-Nagin, *Courage to Dissent: Atlanta and the Long History of the Civil Rights Movement* (New York: Oxford University Press, 2011).

6. James Ryan, *Five Miles Away, A World Apart: One City, Two Schools, and the Story of Educational Opportunity in Modern America* (New York: Oxford University Press, 2010).

7. Edwin Mitchell, interview, February 18, 1972, FUBOHC; Kwame Leo Lillard, interview, November 15, 2012.

8. Bill Lann Lee, interview, February 26, 2013 by telephone.

9. MNBOE, minutes, April 11, 1978, MNBOE.

10. Kelly Miller Smith, "Black Ministers Condemn School Plan as 'Racist'," December 1976, KMSP, box 68, file 4, 1.

11. Social Action Committee Interdenominational Ministers Fellowship [hereafter, SAC-IMF] to Board of Education of Metropolitan Nashville, January 11, 1977, KMSP, box 68, file 7, 3.

12. Irving Hand, "Planning of Residential, Commercial and Industrial Areas," in Mary McLean, ed., Local Planning Administration, 3rd ed. (Chicago: International City Managers' Association, 1959), 107–110; ibid., 1.

13. Saundra Ivey, "School Closing Plans Draw Fire," Tennessean, November 23, 1977.

14. SAC-IMF to Board of Education, 1; Newton Holiday to Judge Thomas Wiseman, April 24, 1980, Kelley, collected exhibit 263, box 16.

15. For examples, see MNBOE, minutes, January 10 and 24, 1978, MNBOE.

16. Charles Watts to Dr. Brooks and Administrative Staff, January 5, 1977, KMSP, box 68, file 6. Craig Kridel generously shared his research on Pearl's history.

17. Transcript of proceedings, Kelley v. MNBOE, May 1, 1980, Kelley, box 20, 18.

18. MNBOE, minutes, February 14, 1978, MNBOE.

19. SAC-IMF to Board of Education, 3.

20. Louise S. Smith, "Up the Health Career Ladder," 1977, KMSP, box 68, file 6, 2–3.

21. Cecil R. Herrell, memo to R. Don O'Donniley, June 18, 1979, KMSP, box 69, file 6, table 2.

22. Morton recused himself in memorandum, Kelley v. MNBOE, August 25, 1972, Kelley, box 8, file 1972 (2); Thomas A. Wiseman Jr. and Frank Gray Jr., "Biographical Directory of Federal Judges," www.fjc.gov/history/home.nsf/page/judges.html, accessed April 25, 2015.

23. Kelley v. MNBOE, 479 F. Supp. 120 (1979), 6–7.

24. Kelley et al. v. Metropolitan County Board, 479 F. Supp. 120 (1979), 6.

25. On this discourse in anti-busing activism in Charlotte, see Matthew Lassiter, Silent Majority: Suburban Politics in the Sunbelt South (Princeton, NJ: Princeton University Press, 2006), chapter 6.

26. Letter to Judge Wiseman, November 16, 1979, collected exhibit 263. (I identify letters by date rather than name as names are not important for my analysis here. I identify by name individuals involved in Kelley beyond letter writing.)

27. Letter to Judge Wiseman, February 4, 1980, collected exhibit 263.

28. On the centrality of notions of family, see Robert Self, All in the Family: The Realignment of American Democracy since the 1960s (New York: Hill and Wang, 2012) and Natalia Mehlman Petrzela, Classroom Wars: Sex, Language, and the Creation of Modern Political Culture (New York: Oxford University Press, 2015).

29. Letters to Judge Wiseman, February 4, 1980, collected exhibit 263.

30. Letter to Judge Wiseman, May 26, 1980, collected exhibit 263.

31. Letter to Judge Wiseman, August 17, 1979, collected exhibit 263, and transcript of proceedings, Kelley v. MNBOE, June 26, 1979, Kelley, box 18, 43–52.

32. See p. 220–22.

33. Wells et al., Both Sides Now, 217.

34. Charles Frazier, interview with author, July 17, 2007, notes in author's possession.

35. Lassiter, introduction; Gerald Grant, Hope and Despair in the American City: Why There Are No Bad Schools in Raleigh (Cambridge, MA: Harvard University Press, 2009).

36. Avon Williams to Hugh Scott, May 10, 1983, AWPII, unprocessed.

37. "DC Gets First Black Superintendent," *Jet*, September 17, 1970, 25.
38. Transcript of proceedings, *Kelley v. MNBOE*, March 3, 1980, *Kelley*, box 19, 41.
39. Ibid., 198.
40. Ibid., 106.
41. Ibid., 139.
42. Ibid., 189–93.
43. Ibid., 16–20; Frank Gibson, "Waverly-Belmont to Close," *Tennessean*, June 13, 1973.
44. Transcript of proceedings, *Kelley v. MNBOE*, July 5, 1979, *Kelley*, box 20, 66.
45. Ibid., 54.
46. Ibid., 57, 60.
47. Ibid., 61.
48. On the falsity of the dividing line between integrationism and separatism in education, see Russell Rickford, "Integration, Black Nationalism, and Radical Democratic Transformation in African American Philosophies of Education, 1965–1974," in Manning Marable and Elizabeth Kai Hinton, eds., *The New Black History: Revisiting the Second Reconstruction* (New York: Palgrave MacMillan, 2011), 287–317.
49. MNPS, "Fifteen-Year Analysis of Enrollment Patterns," 1984, *Kelley*, box 21; Nat Crippens and Bob Roney, "Consultant's Report: Metro Nashville Schools on Proposed Changes in Court Ordered Desegregation Plan," n.d., c. 1977, on file with board agendas, April–May 1977, MNBOE, 5.
50. Annette Eskind, interview, July 5, 2007.
51. League of Women Voters, Board Agenda, April 12, 1977, MNBOE, MNPS.
52. Crippens and Roney, "Consultant's Report," 2–3.
53. "Memorandum Regarding Plaintiff's Charges of Disparate Burden," *Kelley v. MNBOE*, May 1, 1980, *Kelley*, box 12, file 1980 (2), 12.
54. Pride and Woodward examine the views of each school board member in *Burden of Busing*, chapters 9 and 10.
55. "Memorandum Regarding Plaintiff's Charges," 2.
56. The number of black children on buses doubled, while the number of white students increased by one-third ("Nashville Told to Step Up Busing," *NYT*, July 4, 1971).
57. Transcript of proceedings, June 26, 1979, 86. See also Richard Duncan and Fred Beaufait, "Percy Priest CAC Presentation to Metropolitan School Board," January 10, 1978, and Duncan and Beaufait to L.C. Biggs, April 5, 1978, AWPII, unprocessed.
58. Transcript of proceedings, *Kelley v. MNBOE*, March 3, 1980, *Kelley*, box 19, 3153.
59. "Memorandum Regarding Plaintiff's Charges," 1.
60. N. A Crippens to Judge Thomas Wiseman, Feb 29, 1980, *Kelley*, box 12, file 1980 (1).
61. "Memorandum Describing Plan Proposed by Defendant Board of Education," *Kelley v. MNBOE*, May 1, 1980, *Kelley*, box 12, file 1980 (2), 4–5.
62. Ibid., 1.
63. N. A. Crippens, "A Pearl/Cohn or Cohn/Pearl Proposal," 1980, *Kelley*, box 12, file 1980 (1).
64. Students in these city neighborhoods attended (optional) kindergarten at one school, grades 1–2 in another school either close to home or in a different neighborhood within the thirty-minute travel limit, grades 3–4 in a suburban school, and grades 5–6 in a city neighborhood. "Plan Submitted in Response to the Court's Memorandum of August 27, 1979," *Kelley v. MNBOE*, February 22, 1980, *Kelley*, box 12, file 1980 (1),13–14, 17.
65. "Memorandum Describing Plan," 4–5.

66. Barbara Mann, Isaiah T. Creswell, and DeLois Wilkinson, "An Analysis of the Metropolitan Nashville-Davidson County School Board Desegregation Plan by Black School Board Members," February 29, 1980, *Kelley*, box 12, file 1980 (1), 1–2.
67. James Haney to Isaiah T. Creswell, January 14, 1980, KMSP, box 69, file 1.
68. DeLois Wilkinson, interview, October 31, 2002, NCROHP.
69. Transcript of proceedings, 3086–87.
70. Ibid., 3118.
71. Ibid.
72. Ibid., 3275.
73. Ibid., 3112.
74. Letters to Judge Thomas Wiseman, collected exhibit 263.
75. Kwame Leo Lillard, interview, first session, October 2012, notes in author's possession.
76. Letter to Judge Thomas Wiseman, May 25, 1980, collected exhibit 263.
77. Juan Williams, *Eyes on the Prize: America's Civil Rights Years, 1954–1965* (New York: Penguin, 1988), 121.
78. Kwame Leo Lillard, interview, second session, November 29, 2012, by telephone.
79. Higgins quoted in Memorandum Opinion, *Kelley v. MNBOE*, May 20, 1980, *Kelley*, box 12, file 1980 (3). Helen Pate Bain to Judge Thomas Wiseman, February 1, 1980, *Kelley*, box 15, collected exhibit 263, vol. 2.
80. Elbert Brooks, interview, June 30, 2007.
81. Doug Underwood, "My View," *Westview*, February 14, 1980.
82. Doug Underwood, "My View," *Westview*, April 3, 1980.
83. Gloria D. Wells, letter to the editor, *Westview*, January 31, 1980; "Movement Started for the City of Bellevue," *Westview*, January 31, 1980.
84. Transcript of proceedings, 6105, 6113; *Atlanta Daily World*, January 8, 1978; "2,000 Gather at BHS Gym for School Board Meeting," *Westview*, January 10, 1980.
85. Transcript of proceedings, 6113.
86. "Area Census Statement," *Westview*, January 31, 1980, 5; Lillard, interview.
87. "Support Short for Save Our Schools," *Westview*, April 3, 1980.
88. "Petition to Intervene," *Kelley v. MNBOE*, February 28, 1980, *Kelley*, box 12, file 1980 (1), 1. One of the petition signatories was Councilman Vernon Winfrey, whose daughter Oprah is a Pearl alumna.
89. "Intervenors' 'Equity' Plan," *Kelley v. MNBOE*, February 29, 1980, *Kelley*, box 12, file 1980 (1), 1.
90. Lillard, interview.
91. Enrollment statistics are from MNPS, "Fifteen-Year Analysis of Enrollment Patterns," 1984, *Kelley*, box 21.
92. "Intervenor's Plan: Full Details," *Kelley v. MNBOE*, April 14, 1980, *Kelley*, box 12, file 1980 (3), 3.
93. "Bellevue, Pearl, Cohn Join to Promote Cluster Plan," *Westview*, January 24, 1980.
94. "Intervenors' 'Equity' Plan."
95. Richard Jackson to Avon Williams, February 6, 1980. AWPII, unprocessed; Lillard, interview.
96. Transcript of proceedings, May 1, 1980, 42.
97. Mary Moody Wade to members of the Metropolitan Council, September 23, 1971, BBP, box 6, file 63.
98. "School Board Bill Fails, Try Again," *Westview*, May 8, 1980; "Petition 'Over the Top," *Westview*, August 14, 1980; George Cate, interview, June 27, 2007.

99. Charles Frazier, interview; Pride and Woodward, *Burden of Busing*, 272; "Petition Asking Elected Schoolboard," *Banner*, August 15, 1980.
100. *Kelley v. MNBOE*, 492 F. Supp. 167 (1980), 46.
101. Ibid.
102. Ibid; transcript of proceedings, July 5, 1979, 120.
103. Ibid., 50, 70–71.
104. *Kelley v. MNBOE*, 492 F. Supp. 167 (1980).
105. Ibid.
106. Quoted in Don Doyle, *Nashville since the 1920s* (Knoxville: University of Tennessee Press, 1985), 269.
107. *Kelley v. MNBOE*, 492 F. Supp. 167 (1980).
108. Pride and Woodward, *Burden of Busing*, 258.
109. Ibid., 259.
110. Ibid., 262.
111. Bill Lann Lee, interview; Dinkins, interview, third session, August 18, 2013, by telephone.
112. Ibid., 257.
113. *Kelley*, Brief for Plaintiffs-Appellants, October 30, 1981. AWPII, unprocessed; Dinkins, interview.
114. Ibid.
115. "Schools Open?" *Westview*, September 3, 1981.
116. Letter to Judge Thomas Wiseman, July 27, 1979, collected exhibit 263.
117. Lisa Sanders and Jim Lindgren, "Schools Cope with Readjustments," *The Goodletts-ville Gazette*, September 2, 1981.
118. *Kelley v. MNBOE*, 687 F. 2d 814 (1982).
119. Ibid.
120. Ibid.
121. Ibid., 30.
122. Nashville NAACP, "Statement to the School Board," March 15, 1983, AWPII, unprocessed.
123. Dinkins, interview.
124. Pride, *Burden of Busing* 258, 273–77.
125. Enrollment figures from NCES-CCD, "Public Elementary/Secondary School Universe Survey," http://nces.ed.gov/ccd/, accessed March 15, 2010.
126. Transcript of proceedings, 31.
127. This oversimplified narrative has been amply criticized, largely because it distorts the range of ideologies and strategies at work throughout the extensive black freedom struggle. Within history of education, see Jack Dougherty, *More Than One Struggle*; Rickford, "Integration, Black Nationalism, and Radical Democratic Transformation." For a statement of the problem, see Jacqueline Dowd Hall, "The Long Civil Rights Movement and the Political Uses of the Past," *Journal of American History* 91, no. 4 (March 2005): 1233–63; and Nikhil Pal Singh, introduction to *Black Is a Country: Race and the Unfinished Struggle for Democracy* (Cambridge, MA: Harvard University Press, 2005).

CHAPTER NINE

1. Order of final judgment, *Kelley v. MNBOE*, n.d., c. September 26, 1998, *Kelley*, box 24, file *Kelley v. Metro Board of Ed*.
2. National Commission on Excellence in Education, *A Nation at Risk: The Imperative*

*for Educational Reform: A Report to the Nation and the Secretary of Education* (Washington, DC: GPO, 1983); MNPS, "Twenty-Seven Year Analysis of Enrollment Patterns," *Kelley*, box 23, file 1996; Jim O'Hara, "Test Results Place Metro 98th of 131," *Tennessean*, September 9, 1983 (BOE).

3. Dana Pride, "Neighbors Create Own Deseg Plan," *Banner*, August 18, 1997 (BOE); Renee Vaughn, "Antioch Aim: Harmonious Integration," *Tennessean*, June 17, 1985 (BOE).

4. Pride, "Neighbors Create Own Deseg Plan."

5. For more recent evidence across districts, see Genevieve Siegel-Hawley, "City Lines, County Lines, Color Lines: An Analysis of School and Housing Segregation in Four Southern Metropolitan Areas, 1990–2010," *Teachers College Record* 115: no. 6 (2013): 1–45.

6. "Antioch School to Present Minstrel," *Tennessean*, May 17, 1951; Vaughn, "Antioch Aim"; Nashville Spiritual Council, Inc. flyer, BBP, box 8, file 76.

7. Lakeview CAC statement, November 27, 1979, *Kelley*, box 27, file Collective Exhibit 70.

8. Roni Rabin, "Amqui Educators Hope Visit Quiets Fears of New Students," *Banner*, August 9, 1983 (BOE); Elise Frederick, "Teachers Go on Students' Bus Rides," *Banner*, September 9, 1983 (BOE).

9. Kathy Nevill, interview, April 15, 2004; Jamie Winders, *Nashville in the New Millennium* (New York: Russell Sage, 2013), 78–102.

10. Dorren Klausnitzer, "Benjamin: Don't Blame Oilers," *Tennessean*, April 16, 1996 (BOE).

11. Tracy E. K'Meyer, *From Brown to Meredith: The Long Struggle for School Desegregation in Louisville, Kentucky, 1954–2007* (Chapel Hill: University of North Carolina Press, 2013), 110–18.

12. Thomas J. Sugrue, *Sweet Land of Liberty: The Forgotten Struggle for Civil Rights in the North* (New York: Random House, 2009) attributes the comment to Julian Bond (483). Hubert Dixon III, interview, May 17, 2004.

13. Charles Frazier to MNBOE, May 15, 1992, on file with May 15, 1992 agenda, MNBOE; Dorren Klausnitzer, "Too Many in High School Skipping Out on Education," *Tennessean*, February 24, 1996 (BOE).

14. Roni Rabin, "Falling Vocational Enrollment Costly for Schools," *Banner*, May 21, 1984.

15. James C. Cotham III, "Opinion: High School Vocational Programs Costly and Ineffective," *Banner*, September 3, 1987 (BOE).

16. Paul Oldham, "1300 Glencliff Students Take Vocational Courses," *Tennessean*, March 22, 1989.

17. *Report of the Advisory Committee on Equity and Excellence*, December 16, 1993, 5, included within MNBOE, "A Commitment to the Future," *Kelley*, box 24, file *Kelley v. MNBOE*, doc. no. 19 and attachments; Charles Frazier, interview, July 17, 2007, notes in author's possession. Elbert Brooks, interview with the author, June 30, 2007, Nashville, Tennessee.

18. "Hillwood Pep Rally Erupts in Fight, 1 Stabbed," *Banner*, November 4, 1983 (BOE).

19. MNBOE, minutes, August 28, 1997, excerpted in *Report of the Advisory Committee*; statement of Percy Priest CAC, *Kelley*, box 27, file Collective Exhibit 70; "Stability, Not Change, for Schools Director," *Tennessean*, January 17, 1997 (BOE).

20. Lamar Alexander, "Why Not Let Parents Choose the Public School Their Child Attends?" March 5, 1985. AWPI, box 6, file Correspondence 1985; Catherine Hancock "Hume-Fogg as Magnet Hasn't Attracted Many," *Banner*, May 31, 1983 (BOE).

21. Kathy Neville, interview, April 15, 2004.

22. Glenda Alexander, "Dismantling Court-Ordered Desegregation: A Case Study of the Decision-Making Process in Nashville, Tennessee" (PhD diss., Vanderbilt University, 2001), 114; MNBOE, minutes, September 29, 1992, in MNBOE, "A Commitment"; Dana Pride, "Focus on Children, Attorneys Tell Panel," *Banner*, March 23, 1993 (BOE).

23. John Egerton, "Metro Schools Poised to Move into Bigger League," *Tennessean*, July 31, 1996 (BOE).

24. Jeff Wilkinson, "Commitment to the Future Is a Tough Sell to Skeptical Politicians," *Banner*, October 8, 1996 (BOE); Gail Kerr, "The Mayor and the Metro School Plan," *Tennessean*, October 27, 1996 (BOE).

25. Dennis Bottorf, "Publishing Magnate Knows Importance of Business Partnerships with Schools," *Banner*, May 3, 1995 (BOE).

26. MNBOE, minutes, August 28, 1997, in MNBOE, "A Commitment."

27. *Board of Education of Oklahoma City v. Dowell*, 498 U.S. 237 (1991); *Freeman v. Pitts*, 503 U.S. 467 (1992); *Missouri v. Jenkins*, 515 U.S. 1139 (1995).

28. MNBOE, minutes, November 24, 1992, in MNBOE, "A Commitment."

29. Dana Pride, "More Inner City Schools, Black Teachers Sought," *Banner*, October 5, 1993 (BOE) and "Metro Schools Desegregation Panel Remains Stalled," *Banner*, December 7, 1993 (BOE); Reagan Walker, "Equity, Excellence Committee Reviews All Facets of Education," *Tennessean*, August 15, 1993 (BOE); "Memorandum in Support of Joint Motion for Approval of Settlement, for Unitary Status, for Dissolution of All Injunctions, and for Dismissal of Case," *Kelley v. MNBOE*, September 25, 1998, *Kelley*, box 24, file *Kelley v. MNBOE*.

30. Dorren Klausnitzer, "Deseg Report Splits Panel on Specifics," *Tennessean*, November 14, 1993 (BOE).

31. Dorren Klausnitzer, "Group Closer to Desegregation Plan," *Tennessean*, March 26, 1995 (BOE); Dorren Klausnitzer, "The Schools Plan: Should Color Matter?" *Tennessean*, March 26, 1995 (BOE).

32. Dana Pride, "Board Requests Deseg Changes," *Banner*, December 7, 1994 (BOE).

33. See, for example, Klausnitzer, "Group Closer."

34. Dana Pride, "Plan Unfolds, Making Pearl-Cohn an Open Magnet," *Banner*, February 14, 1996 (BOE).

35. Dorren Klausnitzer, "Black Students and Test Scores: A Tale of Three Schools," *Tennessean*, April 28, 1996 (BOE).

36. Dorren Klausnitzer, "Probation list called too short," *Tennessean*, June 15, 1996 (BOE).

37. MNBOE, "Commitment."

38. Dorren Klausnitzer, "Board Invites Plaintiff Input," *Tennessean*, October 20, 1996 (BOE); Dana Pride, "Board Members Boggled by Deseg Plan Concerns," *Banner*, October 21, 1996 (BOE).

39. MNBOE, "A Commitment," 40–42.

40. MNBOE, minutes, June 9, 1998, in MNBOE, "A Commitment."

41. Ellen Goldring and Claire Smrekar, "Technical Summary Report: Nashville," in Corrine M. Yu and William L. Taylor, eds., *Difficult Choices: Do Magnet Schools Serve Children in Need?* (Washington, DC: Citizen's Commission on Civil Rights, 1997), 89–113, 92.

42. "[Defendants'] Motion in Support of Join Motion," 2.

43. Klausnitzer, "Board invites"; Dorren Klausnitzer, "Board Vote May Hasten End of Busing," *Tennessean*, January 19, 1997 (BOE).

44. Wilkinson, "Commitment to the Future."

45. Paul Donsky, "Chamber Endorses Plan for New Schools, Tax Hike," *Tennessean*, May 20, 1998 (BOE).
46. Paul Donsky, "Council Backs Deseg Plan," *Tennessean*, June 24, 1998 (BOE). Phil Bredesen and Jay West to June Lambert, March 25, 1998, Kelley, box 24, file *Kelley v. MNBOE*, doc. 13–15 and attachments.
47. Carrie Ferguson and Dorren Klausnitzer, "Why Is Busing No Longer the Only Way?" *Tennessean*, December 4, 1995 (BOE).
48. Dixon III, interview; Brittany Dixon, interview, June 8, 2004; interviews with five McGavock High School students, May 2004; transcript of proceedings, *Kelley v. MNBOE*, June 26, 1979, Kelley, box 18, file transcripts of trial 6/26/79, 341; obituary, Dr. Bill M. Wise, *Tennessean*, July 7, 2011; Richard Dinkins, interview, first and second sessions, June 2004 and March 12, 2013.
49. Amy Stuart Wells et al., *Both Sides Now: The Stories of School Desegregation's Graduates* (Berkeley: University of California Press, 2009), 217.
50. Charles Frazier, interview, July 17, 2007, notes in author's possession.
51. Holly Maluk Plastaras, "Cross-Race Friendships and Segregated Peer Groups among Teens: An Educational Anthropology Study" (PhD diss., Emory University, 2005), 23, 203–9, quotation on 203.
52. Paul Donsky, "Race-Based Lottery Ends for Magnets," *Tennessean*, December 15, 1998 (BOE).
53. Paul Donsky, "Vote May Reshape School Board," *Tennessean*, May 18, 1998 (BOE).
54. Ibid.; Liz Murray Garrigan, "Political Notes," *Nashville Scene*, April 17, 1997; Dwight Lewis, "Why Did Generous White Parents Wait until Now to Act?" *Tennessean*, October 15, 1998 (BOE).
55. NCES-CCD.
56. Siegel-Hawley and Frankenberg, "Southern Slippage"
57. Claire Smrekar and Ellen B. Goldring, "Neighborhood Schools in the Aftermath of Court-Ended Busing: Educators' Perspectives on How Context and Composition Matter," in Smrekar and Goldring, eds., *From the Courtroom to the Classroom: The Shifting Landscape of School Desegregation* (Cambridge, MA: Harvard Education Press, 2009), 157–90.
58. Jamie Sarrio, "Teacher Inequalities Still Haunt Nashville Schools," *Tennessean*, October 18, 2009.
59. Dorren Klausnitzer, "Desegregating Schools: Enhanced v. Regular," *Tennessean*, October 19, 1996 (BOE); NCES-CCD.
60. Winders, *Nashville in the New Millennium*, 78–102.
61. Tennessee State Department of Education, School Report Cards, https://www.tn.gov/education/reportcard/, accessed May 3, 2014.
62. US Census, 1990, 2000, and 2010, via Social Explorer, www.socialexplorer.org, accessed August 15, 2012.
63. John Charles Boger and Gary Orfield, *School Resegregation: Must the South Turn Back?* (Chapel Hill: University of North Carolina Press, 2005), 1–25; Sean Reardon et al., "*Brown* Fades: The End of Court-Ordered School Desegregation and the Resegregation of American Public Schools," *Journal of Policy Analysis and Management* 31, no. 4 (Fall 2012): 876–904.
64. Shaila Dewan, "Southern Schools Mark Two Majorities," *NYT*, January 6, 2010.
65. *Spurlock v. Fox*, 2012 US District Lexis 104790 (July 27, 2012); Jeff Woods, "Separate. Equal?" *Nashville Scene*, August 28, 2008; Pedro Garcia, "Refusal to Resegregate," February 5, 2008, copy in author's possession.

66. NCES-CCD; *Tennessean*, May 11, 2008.
67. NCES CCD.
68. Household Income, US Census, 1970, 1980, 1990, and 2000, prepared by Social Explorer, www.socialexplorer.org, accessed July 12, 2013.
69. Stephanie Banchero, "Segregation Fear Sinks Charter School," *Wall Street Journal*, June 27, 2012, via www.wsj.com, accessed April 22, 2015; Joey Garrison, "School Board Rejects Great Hearts," *Nashville City Paper*, June 26, 2012.
70. Mark V. Levin, "Race and Male Employment in the Wake of the Great Recession," http://www4.uwm.edu/ced/publications/black-employment_2012.pdf, accessed May 9, 2014; Jonathan Meador, "Nashville, Memphis among Worst U.S. Cities to Be Black, Male and Unemployed," *Nashville Scene*, July 17, 2012.

CONCLUSION

1. James Ryan, "Understanding *Brown v. Board of Education*," http://www.huffingtonpost.com/james-e-ryan/understanding-brown-v-board_b_5344523.html, accessed May 22, 2014.
2. The leading example is Ta-Nehisi Coates, "The Case for Reparations," *The Atlantic*, June 2014.
3. See, for example, the prize-winning work of Nikole Hannah-Jones, "Segregation Now," http://www.propublica.org/article/segregation-now-the-resegregation-of-americas-schools/#intro, accessed May 2, 2015.
4. Stephen Thernstrom and Abigail Thernstrom, *No Excuses: Closing the Racial Gap in Learning* (New York: Simon and Schuster, 2004).
5. For a nuanced view of this position, see Prudence Carter and Kevin Welner, introduction to *Closing the Opportunity Gap: What America Must Do to Give Every Child an Even Chance* (New York: Oxford University Press, 2013). Diane Ravitch, *Reign of Error: The Hoax of the Privatization Movement and the Danger to America's Schools* (New York: Vintage, 2014).
6. See Jonathan Zimmerman on this view of thinking about the present and the past, in Susan E. Lederer et al., "Interchange, History in the Professional Schools," *JAH* 92, no. 2 (September 2005): 553–76.
7. On the "racial theory of property value," see Carl Nightingale, *Segregation: A Global History of Divided Cities* (Chicago: University of Chicago Press, 2012).
8. On enclave schools, see Jeffrey R. Henig, Richard C. Hula, Marion Orr, and Desiree Pedesclaux, *The Color of School Reform: Race, Politics, and the Challenge of Urban Education* (Princeton, NJ: Princeton University Press, 1999).
9. *Spurlock v. Fox*, July 27, 2012, LEXIS 104970.
10. Maia Bloomfield Cucchiara, *Marketing Cities, Marketing Schools: Who Wins and Who Loses When Schools Become Urban Amenities* (Chicago: University of Chicago Press, 2013).
11. *Spurlock v. Fox*.
12. Jack Dougherty, "Shopping for Schools: How Public Education and Private Housing Shaped Suburban Connecticut," *JUH* 38, no. 2 (March 2012): 205–24; Amy Stuart Wells, Douglas Ready, et al., "Divided We Fail: The Story of Separate and Unequal Suburban Schools 60 Years after *Brown v. Board of Education*," 2014 (New York: Teachers College), 13–17.
13. Duane W. Gang, "Obama Pushes Education in Nashville," *Tennessean*, January 30, 2014; "The Academies of Nashville, 2013–2014," http://www.mnps.org/AssetFactory.aspx?did=83859, accessed May 9, 2014.

14. For an excellent summary, see Colin Gordon, *Growing Apart: A Political History of American Inequality*, http://scalar.usc.edu/works/growing-apart-a-political-history-of -american-inequality/index, accessed May 9, 2014.

15. Michael B. Katz, Mark Stern, and Jamie J. Fader, "The New African American Inequality," *JAH* 92, no. 1 (June 2005): 75–108; John L. Rury and Shirley A. Hill, *The African American Struggle for Secondary Schooling, 1940–1980: Closing the Graduation Gap* (New York: Teachers College Press, 2011).

16. Gordon, *Growing Apart*; Claudia Goldin and Lawrence F. Katz, *The Race between Education and Technology* (Cambridge, MA: Belknap Press, 2010) documents slowed economic mobility since the 1970s but attributes this to slowed educational attainment.

17. This section borrows from ideas developed in Ansley T. Erickson, "Slavery and American Colleges: Historical Entanglements that Matter for Understanding Inequality Today," *Teachers College Record*, May 30, 2014, via www.tcrecord.org.

18. Harvey Kantor, "Education, Social Reform, and the State: ESEA and Federal Education Policy in the 1960s," *American Journal of Education* 100, no. 1 (November 1991): 47–83; David F. Labaree, "The Winning Ways of a Losing Strategy: Educationalizing Social Problems in the United States," *Educational Theory* 54, no. 4: 447–60.

19. Ansley T. Erickson, "The Rhetoric of Choice: Segregation, Desegregation, and Charter Schools," *Dissent* (Fall 2011): 41–46.

20. John Egerton, "Walking into History: The Beginning of School Desegregation in Nashville," *Southern Spaces*, May 4, 2009, www.southernspaces.org/2009/walking -history-beginning-school-desegregation-nashville, accessed May 9, 2014; MNPS, "Twenty-Seven Year Analysis of Enrollment Patterns," *Kelley*, box 23, file 1996; TNDOE, Report Card 2012, http://edu.reportcard.state.tn.us/pls/apex/f?p=200:1: 2847253873645618::NO, accessed May 15, 2014.

21. Erickson, "Rhetoric of Choice."

22. *Spurlock v. Fox.*

23. Ibid.

24. Ibid.

25. *Brown v. Board of Education*, 347 U.S. 483 (1954).

26. Jal Mehta, *The Allure of Order: High Hopes, Dashed Expectations, and the Troubled Quest to Remake American Schooling* (New York: Oxford University Press, 2013).

27. See, among other excellent works, Barbara Ransby, *Ella Baker and the Black Freedom Movement: A Radical Democratic Vision* (Chapel Hill: University of North Carolina Press, 2005); Charles M. Payne and Carol Sills Strickland, *Teach Freedom: Education for Liberation in the African-American Tradition* (New York: Teachers College Press, 2008); Hilary Moss, *Schooling Citizens: The Struggle for African American Education in Antebellum America* (Chicago: University of Chicago Press, 2009).

# INDEX

Page numbers followed by *f* indicate figures and maps; those followed by *t* indicate a table.

Made in the USA
Lexington, KY
04 September 2019